How Britain *Really* Works

How Britain *Really* Works

Understanding the Ideas and Institutions of a Nation

STIG ABELL

JOHN MURRAY

First published in Great Britain in 2018 by John Murray (Publishers)
An Hachette UK Company

1

© Stig Media Limited 2018

A CIP catalogue record for this title is available from the British Library

Hardback ISBN 978-1-47365-839-4
Trade paperback ISBN 978-1-47365-841-7
Ebook ISBN 978-1-47365-840-0

Typeset in Bembo MT 11.5/14 pt by Palimpsest Book Production Limited,
Falkirk, Stirlingshire

Printed and bound by Clays Ltd, St Ives plc

John Murray policy is to use papers that are natural,
renewable and recyclable products and made from wood grown in
sustainable forests. The logging and manufacturing processes are expected to
conform to the environmental regulations of the country of origin.

John Murray (Publishers)
Carmelite House
50 Victoria Embankment
London EC4Y ODZ

www.johnmurray.co.uk

For Nadine,
although I never call you by that name

Contents

Acknowledgements

I always thought this page would be a happy one to write, denoting that the process of writing all the other pages was nearly over. And I was totally correct; this is the nicest bit of the whole process.

The idea for this book – indeed for writing any book – came as a result of the brilliant editor Mark Richards visiting me one summer day, after he had read an online piece I had written about football. Despite being annoyingly younger than me, he has been a calm and wise figure throughout the subsequent process, and a very fine editor for a first book. His colleague Joe Zigmond tackled the early drafts with vigour, intelligence and occasionally commendable restraint. And Morag Lyall was then a wondrously diligent copy-editor. Without them all, it would have been basically all rambling footnotes.

The book has only reached publication at all because I had the fortune of knowing Cathryn Summerhayes, literary agent extraordinaire. I am so grateful to her that I can forgive her incomprehensible objection to my male Ugg boots. Rosie Gailer from John Murray has been amazing in the publicity department.

I have spoken to countless people in writing this, but special mentions must go for their assistance to Justin Walford, Mark Hartley, Paul Cowley, Ray Tallis, Toby Lichtig, Chris Freeman, Stephen Watson, Nick Hine, Sam Coates, Paddy Ashdown and Xand Van Tulleken. Some people have had the dubious pleasure of reading early drafts, and were then able to offer invaluable improvements: Suzanne Wright, Jenny Kleeman, James Sanders, Jeanette Sanders, Victoria Smith, David Shriver, Ruth Scurr, Robert Douglas-Fairhurst and Steve Kennedy. I am grateful to them all.

I have been lucky enough always to work at places filled with intelligent people, conversations with whom have helped me understand what is going on in the country. Special thanks must go to all the production team at LBC (and the various producers of my show there: Lewis Vickers, Cat Farnsworth, Sam Lovell, Chris Hemmings and the amazing Julia Moore). I hope the cake was some compensation. At Sky News, I get – almost every week – to talk about how Britain really works, and my thinking has been shaped by the best two Annas in broadcasting (Botting and Jones), and my regular companions on screen Carole Malone and Jenny Kleeman. My colleagues at the *Sun* and now the *TLS*, and *Front Row* on Radio 4, could not have been more supportive of me. And holding my professional life together for the last five years has been my assistant El Stokes, without whom I would never be in the right place or right frame of mind to do anything.

P. G. Wodehouse once dedicated a book to his daughter, 'without whom it would have been written much sooner'. My two children, Nelly and Teddy (with Phoebe on the way), are the main motivation for me writing at all, and have never once (okay, very rarely) been anything other than a joy. My parents, as you will see in the book, started me out reading and writing, and their hard work and determination have been a constant inspiration to me.

But the final word of gratitude must go to my incomparable wife and best friend, Nadine, whom I met fourteen years ago, and who has made every single moment of my life better ever since.

And this our life, exempt from public haunt,
Finds tongues in trees, books in the running brooks,
Sermons in stones, and good in everything.
I would not change it.

William Shakespeare, *As You Like It*, Act II, Scene 1

All right, I can see the broken eggs. Now where's this omelette of yours?

Attributed to Panaït Istrati (1884–1935)

Introduction

For 'tis your thoughts that now must deck our kings,
Carry them here and there; jumping o'er times,
Turning the accomplishment of many years
Into an hour-glass: for the which supply,
Admit me Chorus to this history;
Who prologue-like your humble patience pray,
Gently to hear, kindly to judge, our play.

William Shakespeare, *Henry V*, Prologue

I come from Loughborough. Somebody had to.* It is in the middle of the Midlands, the centre of the country; a provincial town of unremarkable aspect, hollowed-out industry, a university known for sporting prowess, and not much else. My home was near a council estate (where my dad grew up), but sufficiently far up the hill from it for a sense of progress to be observed. We had wide streets to ride bikes on, grassy fields near playgrounds where we could kick a football about or – in later teenage years – pass furtive joints, attempt inept couplings.

We had nearby poverty, but also a prevalent sense, to my naive awareness at least, of a town that was coping, holding itself together

---

* Welcome to the footnotes, a disorganised jumble of relevant facts and information, in structural homage to the disorganised jumble of Britain, the subject of this book. Don't worry, there won't be too many per page (the rest are discreetly positioned at the back). This opening line mimics the first words in Bill Bryson's *The Lost Continent* (1989), one of the great travel books that I have read and read again.

in its own unexceptionalism. It has often been a political bellwether*
for the country. Loughborough voted Tory in the early years of my
life (symbolising the Middle England of Thatcher), before defecting
to Tony Blair in my teens. It has subsequently returned to the
Conservatives. Like most provincial parts of the UK, it voted to
leave the EU (by around 8 per cent). After I had left, it got its first
Starbucks, its first Nando's, its first sex shop. The middle of the
middle, of the muddle. A symbol of the subject of this book.

I am the last of the pre-internet generation. I got my first mobile
phone in my twenties, my first email address when I went to university.† Of course, like you, I am now saturated by information,
overwhelmed by it, my life controlled by technology, a world of bright
screens in the dark, of tweets and thirty-second videos, of data and
detail hurtled at my head just faster than my capacity to absorb it. It
was not ever thus. When I was growing up, a search for a fact meant
my dad, with furrowed brow, looking for a book in the house somewhere. A belief, sometimes mistaken, in authority. Don't worry, this
is not going to become a Luddite dirge about modernity (although
it may come close at certain points): there is now more knowledge
accessed more easily by more people than ever before, and that is a
good thing. We are living in a new age of the autodidact: expertise
is within our grasp more readily than at any time in human history.
This book could not have been written, for example, without all the
government materials now available only a click away.

But I still feel lucky enough to have had the opportunity to fall in
love with books, in a way that – despite their and my efforts – my
children will never have. Books were a finite resource for me: there
was a limited number of them, and no Kindles or implausibly cheap
paperbacks zoomed in by Amazon to replace them. One of my

---

* You'll often find folk spelling this 'bellweather', on the basis it is a metaphor
to do with prevailing climatic conditions. Not true: a 'wether' is a castrated ram
who leads a flock of sheep; farmers put a bell on it, so they can tell in which
direction the flock is going.
† I also was one of the few non-drug-dealers to have a pager, in case anybody
wanted to get in touch with me. The thrill of a romantic assignation arranged via
pager is very similar, I imagine, to that occasioned by the rustle of scented paper
in illicit correspondence of the Victorian period.

favourites was something called *The Reader's Encyclopaedia*, edited by a man called William Rose Benet. It was essentially an abbreviated guide to the most important aspects of world literature from the beginning of human memory to 1965 (when my edition was published). A joyously subjective, ramshackle selection of information.

If I had thought about it, I would have thrilled at the use of the definite article (*The* Reader) and the placement of that apostrophe; it was an encyclopaedia for just one reader: me. Everything about the book bespoke hard-earned knowledge. The first entry is about Jeppe Aakjaer, who – as I think we all recall – was a Danish poet and novelist at the turn of the twentieth century. He is followed by the biblical Aaron, Shakespeare's Aaron and Aaru ('in Egyptian mythology, the fields of Aaru are the abode of the blessed dead and of the gods').

I have the book still before me, its spine cracked, its pages sepia-toned, displaying the scars of effortful use. My dad gave it to me when I graduated with a degree in English literature because I had used it so much as a child, thrilled (as I still am) by the exotic range of authorised learning at my fingertips. I mention this as it has provided the inspiration for the book you have before you now.

Because although information about Britain is everywhere, it is also sometimes hard to find, to interpret and to absorb. There are plenty of books about different parts of it (and I will recommend some of them along the way), but not an obvious place that has centralised and collated information useful to anyone who wants to think about what sort of country Britain has really become. We are now all growing up in a maelstrom of detail without the opportunity to pause to understand it. I want this book, if possible, to provide that pause. To be the reader's encyclopaedia of Britain for one reader: for you, for me.

The idea came when I realised that, while I am party to as much news as anybody, there were lots of stories I recognised but did not entirely understand, heard all too briefly but lacked the time to comprehend fully. Our national conversation is full of events, individuals and ideas that we often take no trouble to explore properly: bond markets; the Suez Crisis; the Malayan Emergency; the rise in prison numbers; inflation; fluctuating immigration figures; the Profumo affair; PISA scores; the Beveridge Report; PFI; legal aid;

National Service; the Windrush generation; the post-war consensus; Rivers of Blood; devolution; the Irish question; Black Wednesday; the changing class system; OFSTED; social care; the case of Baha Mousa; the Maastricht Treaty; hypothecated taxes; the gender pay gap; the banking crisis; Universal Basic Income; National governments; the Munich Agreement; low inflation; deficit and debt; EFTA; OECD; AV; the SDP; and so on, and on. I knew of many of these things, but not much about them. And yet they seemed important; I wanted to have them explained as clearly as possible.

Now I am no Disraeli,[1] whom we'll meet shortly and who said, 'Whenever I want to read a book, I write one', but I was attracted to the idea of finding a way of answering many of the nagging questions that exist when it comes to Britain. This is my attempt to do that.

Why should you listen to me at all? It is a perfectly reasonable question,* especially amid these postmodern times in which – as we shall see – notions of any form of authority have been understandably undermined. 'People in this country have had enough of experts,' said Michael Gove (who will pop up in Chapter 4, on our education system) in 2016, and there was a germ of a point beneath his cynical populism. The great banking crash of 2008, set to stultify our economy for decades, constituted – as we confront in Chapter 1 – a colossal failure of expertise, of hubris for the few that swiftly, and lastingly, became nemesis for the many. Any survey of decision-making in Britain over the last few centuries easily avoids being a celebration of the triumph of the especially competent.

This book is not written from the perspective of an expert, then, but continually from the perspective of someone in search of the basis for any expertise: knowledge. My qualification is perhaps no more or less than my persistent curiosity. I am not a trained journalist (and I'll explain a bit more about my career in Chapter 7), but I have spent many years around the twin businesses of politics and media: both machines based around using information in the pursuit of power. I have run a press regulator; I have advised companies seeking to avoid terminal crisis, as a public relations consultant; I was the managing

* Though, if you are reading this, thank you for taking a punt on the book anyway.

4

editor of the *Sun*, the largest tabloid newspaper in the country; I hosted a phone-in show on LBC, Britain's main talk radio network, for three years; I now edit the *Times Literary Supplement*, a journal that joyfully devotes itself to discovering the answers to esoteric questions. I have had a muddle of a working life, but that perhaps befits someone now attempting to analyse the muddle of this country.

So is there a presiding theory, a philosophy that binds the nation together? I am tempted to quote the screenwriter William Goldman, who was asked about how Hollywood really works: 'Nobody knows anything . . . not one person in the entire motion picture field knows for a certainty what's going to work. Every time out it's a guess and, if you're lucky, an educated one.'

Britain is a bit like this: nobody in charge really knows anything; they are simply moving from crisis to crisis, punctuated by occasionally transitory success, before being buffeted by circumstance once more. In turn, our structures and institutions have developed in haphazard fashion, a series of accretions and amputations, bits woven together and then pulled apart, new grafts on old scars. It is an organic mess, of sorts. Indeed, when we consider this country, we are like Charles Darwin[2] again:

> It is interesting to contemplate a tangled bank, clothed with many plants of many kinds, with birds singing on the bushes, with various insects flitting about, and with worms crawling through the damp earth, and to reflect that these elaborately constructed forms, so different from each other, and dependent upon each other in so complex a manner, have all been produced by laws acting around us.

If anything, this book will seek to define the laws that have acted upon our own tangled bank of Britain: the laws of economics, justice, equality, collaboration and aggression. But I am less optimistic than Darwin, who largely believed that things got better according to a plan ordained by God. There is simply no omniscient, benevolent guide in real life.* The story of modern Britain is one of

---

* Here is a handy motto from the American author Thomas Pynchon, in his bewildering novel *Gravity's Rainbow* (1973): 'Decisions are never really made – at best they manage to emerge, from a chaos of peeves, whims, hallucinations and all-round assholery.'

progress in parts, but also stasis and stagnation in others, nostalgia and retrospection elsewhere. I am part of a generation who may not be better off than its parents, and will bequeath a troubled country to its own children, who may be presented with greater challenges still.

We have, in this United Kingdom, an economy that will produce no real wage-growth for more than a decade, has millions working but in poverty, a health service buckling under increased demand, an ever expanding prison population, an unequal education system that fails working-class white boys, a justice system that over-prosecutes black people. This is presided over by a political process that is only concerned with the contingencies of a short-term electoral cycle, and is becoming increasingly polarised between extremes of left and right, between nationalism and multiculturalism, globalisation and isolation.

In 2017, amid the cloacal murk of political social media, a term of mild abuse grew up: 'the centrist Dad'. It represented fun poked by those on the left (the Corbyn crowd, understandably ebullient at the electoral success of their movement) at those in the middle of their party, the Blairites, the 'moderates' whom they had left behind. Now I have nothing to do with internal Labour Party angst, hold no particular candle for Blair, and have no tribal allegiance whatsoever. But I thought to myself: I'm from the middle, I'm a father; what's wrong with being a 'centrist Dad'? And this book, if not a clarion call for centrism, at least stems from a fundamental belief that we need to understand both sides of any argument, that we can recognise the benefits of different perspectives, and that we should understand where points of dispute meet. We are in the middle of a mess, a muddle, and the centre might be the best position from which to understand that.

In that spirit, each chapter will cover a different aspect of British life: the economy; politics; healthcare; education; the military; law and order; media, old and new; and our shared sense of national identity. Hopefully, each will be an explainer, a chance to consider the individual issues that affect our every day. But there is a connection between all the sections, too. This is not – or tries not to be – a book of abstractions; it is a book about the consequences of decisions in the real world. John Ruskin★ said this back in 1860: 'Among the delusions which at different periods have afflicted mankind, perhaps the greatest – certainly the least creditable – is modern economics based on the idea that an advantageous code of action may be determined irrespectively of the influence of social affection.'

We should, in other words, examine the mess that comes from the policy. Ruskin is a bit of an inspiration for me, actually; a man endlessly gripped by the need to explain, to find out more. And this book is – I suppose – gothic in a way he would have recognised: full of excrescences and moving parts, preserving the marks of its working methods. I have tried to answer questions that occur to me, to include rather than remove, to add details that interest me, in the hope that this will provide a coherent enough picture to interest you.

At the end of the book, instead of giving a bibliography in the manner of an academic work, I thought I would suggest some good fiction to read, which very broadly touches upon the areas I have covered in the preceding pages. We all, in the end, enjoy a good list. The novels I recommend do not provide a definitive guide to the country, of course (indeed some of them come from other countries, but touch on universal issues). They are not all serious, and many are unlikely to give you any facts to cling on to. They skew heavily towards my own reading preferences, inevitably: the Victorian greats; the modernists; and – above all – P. G. Wodehouse, the writer who has given me more pleasure than any other, who still acts for me as a bulwark against mental unrest. Taken together, though, they will, I hope, give you – as they have me – something else: joy, fascination, despair, distraction, grounds for thought.

★ A great polymath, writer, painter, thinker and reformer; a significant and brilliant man. And yet it would surely be wrong of me not to share this story: he never consummated his marriage to Effie Gray on the grounds – it is conjectured – that he was so surprised and appalled by the fact that she had pubic hair. His knowledge of anatomy had hitherto come only from smooth Greek statues. She told her father that Ruskin 'had imagined women were quite different to what he saw I was'; Ruskin wrote: 'her person was not formed to excite passion. On the contrary, there were certain circumstances in her person which completely checked it.' Make up your own mind.

One of the authors whose books thankfully appeared in my Loughborough home was the genially brilliant travel writer, Bill Bryson, an American who has repeatedly tried to understand Britain, and thus something of a presiding spirit for me as I write. He might act, if only for a moment, as a counterbalance to my sense of gloom about this country. This is from *Notes from A Small Island* (1995):

> Here is a country that fought and won a noble war, dismantled a mighty empire in a generally benign and enlightened way, created a far-seeing welfare state – in short, did nearly everything right – and then spent the rest of the century looking on itself as a chronic failure. The fact is this is still the best place in the world for most things – to post a letter, go for a walk, watch television, buy a book, venture out for a drink, go to a museum, get lost, seek help, or stand on a hillside and take in a view.

If this is still the case, as we shall see, it is more by luck than design. And it also refers to a very different country to the Britain of today. Since Bryson was amiably musing in 1995, his thoughts focusing on the distinctly analogue experience of being alive, the following (digital) developments have taken place to alter the world fundamentally, and our experience of our nation within it: broadband; Wi-Fi; blogs; Bitcoin; email; Google; Amazon; Uber; Facebook; Twitter; Wikipedia; eBay; Spotify; WhatsApp; YouTube; Snapchat; Kindle; iPods, then iPhones, then iPads. I am probably missing quite a lot there, too.

Technology affects our sense of identity: how we see ourselves, and how we see our relations with others. We now can become more tribal with more people, share ideas democratically or segregate ourselves defensively; unshackle our lives from the demands of the workplace or chain ourselves immovably to our professional existence. Our children are developing differently as individuals, never home alone or free from peer pressure; always being guided towards the limitless stores of distraction and danger that are available friction-free to them.

It is not a coincidence that this surge in connectivity is disrupting industries (the media – as we shall see in Chapter 7 – being an excellent, but not an isolated, example of this). It is not a coincidence that our collective mental health is changing, and for the worse. There is something approaching a pandemic of mental break-down in Britain at the moment, small-scale tragedies that, taken together, represent large-scale policy and resourcing problems. It is easier than ever to do many of the basic things in life, but we are becoming unhealthier at the same time as we do them (or have them done for us). Prolonged existence is, perhaps, not an unmiti-gated boon. We live to endure an epidemic of fatness, chronic ailments, loneliness and anxiety. Britain has to accommodate us as we do so.

Taken all in all, then, this felt like a reasonable time to consider the state of the nation. Our country feels like a gigantic experiment, conducted on the fly, with no control, and no clear sense of where we are going amid the chaos. But it is also a product of its past, and its past decisions on how to educate us, care for us, imprison us, fight for us, divide and unite us. Over the next few hundred pages (and couple of hundred footnotes), I will try to establish how Britain really works, how we got to where we are, or at least give you the information to help you make such a judgement. And if you hate it, you can always tell me on Twitter, and make both of our lives a misery for a fraction of a moment.

I

Economics

The curious task of economics is to demonstrate to men how
little they really know about what they imagine they can design

Friedrich Hayek (1899–1992)

Look around you now. We don't get the chance to think about
this much, but the complexity of our surroundings is staggering.
You might be sitting on a sofa in your living room, touching
material produced in one country, processed and stitched in another,
reassembled in yet another, before being delivered to you in return
for a promise about your own capacity to pay that is almost entirely
notional.

Often when I go on a train or in a car, I look out of the window
and experience a momentary flicker of vertigo. So many lives
glimpsed in a micro-second, never to be considered again. In my
mind, I half-see the vectors of everybody's movements like lines on
an imagined map in my head, busily criss-crossing, ant-like and
heedless. Walking on roads built by a team of the never-met, passing
shops stocked with goods that have been made, ordered, packed,
processed, stacked and displayed to be consumed at a predictable
rate by who-knows-who.

Sip a coffee: who grew it, processed it, stuck it in a curiously
semi-recyclable cup? Put it on the table: who made the table, who
felled the tree, who designed the blade that cut it, who mined
the metal that made the alloy that made the blade? Modern life is
an Escher-like series of interconnected structures, dizzyingly and
uninventably complex. And getting more complex every day.

Sherlock Holmes got it half right when he experienced his own moment of vertigo in *A Case of Identity*, drawling at the indomitable Watson:

> We would not dare to conceive the things which are really mere commonplaces of existence. If we could fly out of that window hand in hand, hover over this great city, gently remove the roofs, and peep in at the queer things which are going on, the strange coincidences, the plannings, the cross-purposes, the wonderful chains of events, working through generations, and leading to the most outré results, it would make all fiction with its conventionalities and foreseen conclusions most stale and unprofitable.

The commonplaces of existence are really the subject of this chapter: how the country functions at its economic heart. It is a story of both linear predictability (of 'plannings' and 'foreseen conclusions'), but also of continued and continuing 'cross-purposes'. The economic history and future of Britain is – like all economics really – full of queer things and disputed conclusions. As Alfred Marshall★ put it: 'The laws of economics are to be compared with the laws of the tides, rather than with the simple and exact law of gravitation. For the actions of men are so various and uncertain, that the best statement of tendencies, which we can make in a science of human conduct, must be inexact and faulty.'

In other words, it is no surprise that you and I don't really understand economics, because neither do economists. But we can point to tendencies, certainly, and we can try to make sure we understand the times when those tendencies change, and the historical backdrop against which that has happened.

So: back to our moments of vertigo. How the hell did it happen that I am clutching a Starbucks cup, sitting in a black chair made of plastic, metal and some sort of wipe-clean fibre, wearing cheaply produced jeans and a T-shirt, peering through superbly engineered

---

★ Marshall was a Victorian economist, who wrote the *Principles of Economics* (1890), and – despite being originally a mathematician – argued that economics should not become too dominated by maths. That argument has, sadly, not entirely succeeded. Rock-star economist Thomas Piketty argued recently that economists are still 'all too often preoccupied with petty mathematical problems of interest only to themselves'.

spectacles at my empty office, in a building (constructed to set requirements, approved as safe, cleaned and maintained by unseen heroines, toiling unthanked late at night) in a city of several million people? The French economist Frédéric Bastiat[1] asked the question, slightly more eloquently: 'What, then, is the ingenious and secret power that governs the astonishing regularity of movements so complicated, a regularity in which everybody has implicit faith, although life and happiness are at stake?'

The answer is the economy; more especially the free-market, liberal, capitalist economy. Here Britain is not an island, entire of itself, but a part of a much bigger and more complex ecosystem, reliant upon the behaviour of nations and institutions outside its control. It is all part of a vastly imperfect system that manages – against all odds – to achieve regularity of movements in our lives. As we will also see, this cuts both ways: regularity is another word for immobility, for imprisoning people in circumstances from which they cannot escape. And the free market, actually, is not entirely free, and never has been. And liberal (or neo-liberal) economics is often not that liberal. But we will get to that.

Over the course of this chapter, we will work out the ups and downs of modern capitalism, its crises, and the threat that it is returning to some of the follies of Victorian times, of the period when Sherlock Holmes might have stalked the streets of London, uncaring of the poverty that passed him by.

Some basic questions to begin with, and then a quick trip through the history of (British) capitalism.

What is the economy?

It is anything to do with spending money, or managing wealth that has been created. It is the system through which we make all our transactions that, in brutalist terms, comprise our daily existence. We spend money by consuming goods and services produced by others. Production occurs thanks to a combination of labour (people working) and capital (machines, materials). We obtain money by earning it, borrowing it, inheriting it or it being transferred to us by the government (for example through the welfare state). We hand over money in the form of taxes on income and capital, goods and services (VAT), and business.★

The government is responsible for overseeing the economy, without intervening too much in the free market. What counts as 'too much' is one of the things this chapter might help you work out. The government takes income from taxation, plus whatever borrowing[2] it needs, to pay for the services we all use: health, defence, transport links, education and so on. It spends more than £750 billion every year on this. It is the largest employer in the country by a colossal extent.[3] At one extreme, we could have no governmental support, and we would live in a monochrome dystopia of self-reliance; at the other it could control every aspect of our existence, and we would live in a communist dictatorship. Politics is, effectively, the attempt to pick a spot between the two and defend it.[4] We'll talk about that some more in Chapter 2.

What is money?

Money is a simply a system of credit; a shared delusion of exchange.[5] It is not real. Indeed, it is less real than it once was. At one point, in the eighteenth century, people like the philosopher John Locke[6] believed that money was largely based on its intrinsic value; that is to say the most important thing about money was coinage and the precious metal inside it. The value of money was connected to the amount of good stuff it contained, which could then be altered.[7]

While the literal value of the coinage was indeed once important (and monarchs 'debased' it by reducing the amount of precious metal

★ We hand over money to three authorities: the central government (by income tax, VAT, corporation tax etc.); devolved governments; and local governments (via council tax and business rates). We pay more than £600 billion a year in tax overall. The government excuses more than £150 billion as tax relief in various ways: no capital gains tax on the main home; relief on pension income; Gift Aid for charities; VAT reductions; and so on.

in it, and so made it stretch further), it masked the larger principle that coinage's main role was to act as tokens of credit and debt in the pursuit of trade. Today, 97 per cent of all money has no physical existence, and none of it has any connection to precious metals. If everybody wanted to turn their assets and savings into cool hard cash, they simply could not.

But don't worry, money has always operated as a system of credit. The Romans, for example, did lots of big property deals. They didn't dig around for thousands of coins to pay for them; they used notional transfers of credit. '*Nomina facit, negotium conficit*': 'secure the bond, seal the deal', as the poet Horace said. Medieval Britain wasn't simply a land filled with sturdy lock-boxes and hard-earned shillings. The accounting system of the court and elsewhere was done using tally sticks, little bits of kindling covered in marks and notches, each representing financial transactions.

If you ever get the chance to visit the Houses of Parliament, and you find yourself wandering through a crumbling, Neo-Gothic building, filled with rodents and MPs, you are somewhere built on the smouldering remnants of an older structure destroyed by tally sticks. The story goes that the practical Victorians – all utilitarian and self-involved – saw the storage of Britain's economic history as a needless chore, so they burned it. Charles Dickens takes the tale on: 'The stove, over gorged with these preposterous sticks, set fire to the panelling; the panelling set fire to the House of Lords; the House of Lords set fire to the House of Commons; the two houses were reduced to ash.'

We all think of coins as the most important part of the historical economy because, in the name of housekeeping, some barbaric Victorians destroyed the 'preposterous sticks' that were our other tokens of exchange. Coins last better than sticks and pieces of paper. They can be dug up by denim-clad enthusiasts with wild hair and metal detectors. The thing to remember is that money is more than currency; it simply is a system of signs that we have – over the years – come to agree on as a means of expressing a store of value. When people mention the basic incompatibility of people, and our singular failure to get on, the invention of money – albeit in its various currencies – is a pretty unanswerable counter-example of our commonality.

Indeed, the value of the currency is something that can be traded in the world's exchanges; and it can go up and down (which is what traders are betting on).[8] We all know that one of the consequences of the news about Brexit (of which, alas, more later) was that the pound 'crashed'.* This is because traders were concerned that the British economy might suffer, and did not want to be lumbered with British money, so they sold pound-denominated investments, driving prices down. When the pound is worth less, it is good for exports,† because foreign buyers need less of their own currency to buy the same quantity of UK goods, and so UK exporters can reduce their prices or increase their margins.‡ It is bad for imports, because UK buyers need more of their own currency to buy the same amount of goods. This extra cost is likely to be passed on to the consumer in the form of price rises, leading to what is called inflation (see below).

So we have a workable sense of what the economy is, and a simplistic version of how money works. Now to look at how the two came to create modern Britain.

---

* Thanks to Brexit, the pound was classed within the ten worst performing currencies of 2016, worse than the Argentine peso, but better than the Sierra Leonean 'Leone'. Take that, Third World!

† A low pound is also good for companies that make their living in other currencies. Remember that currency exchange is a zero-sum game: if the pound goes down, the dollar goes up. The top 100 companies are collected in the FTSE 100, and their performance monitored. Generally, they are companies who do much of their business in dollars outside Britain, so their value rises when the pound falls. If anyone tells you that 'the FTSE at an all-time high' is a sign of British economic health, kick them in the shins.

‡ Worth remembering that the UK imports more than it exports. We have a negative balance of trade of around 3–5 per cent.

A brief history of (British) capitalism

Capitalism is, simply, the organisation of the economy in pursuit of profit or, as Karl Marx[9] put it (rather more pejoratively), 'solely the restless stirring for gain. The absolute desire for enrichment . . . passionate hunt for value'. It contrasts with, say, feudalism (organisation in pursuit of hierarchical service) or communism (in pursuit of political equality). While the problems attached to it are many, it is one of the most successful ideas ever conceived by human beings. Capitalism has improved the modern world, and measurably so. In 1800 the world's economy was like Bangladesh: the average human being consumed $3 per day; today we consume more like $100 worth of goods and services, more than we need.

Thanks to capitalism, indeed, the world is a literally brighter place. Take this statistic:[10] in 9000 BC it took 50 hours of human labour to achieve 1,000 lumen hours of lighting; in 1800 it took 5 hours; in 1900; it took 0.22 hours; in 1992 it took 0.00012 hours. The power of the market, thanks to the jumpstart of the Industrial Revolution, is responsible for increasing shared wealth and thus well-being across the world.

There is no agreed date for the Industrial Revolution, but it took place over the course of the eighteenth century. Interestingly, there is no consensus about why Britain at that period was able to host such an epoch-altering movement, although it is likely to be a lucky combination of a number of factors all occurring simultaneously: innovation; legislative support; the rule of law; improvements in transport links; the Protestant work ethic; a society largely compliant in terms of accepting hierarchy; the sturdy wealth, linked to land, of an investor class.★

Innovation was certainly critical: inventions such as the flying shuttle (1733), the spinning Jenny[11] (1764), Watt's[12] condenser necessary for

★ W. C. Sellars and R. J. Yeatman, in their imperious pseudo-history *1066 And All That* (1930), also came up with this reason, which has a core truth within it: 'the discovery (made by all the rich men in England at once) that women and children could work for 25 hours a day in factories without many of them dying or becoming excessively deformed'.

a steam engine (1769) or Arkwright's[13] for a water frame (1769) meant that there was a new capacity for automation that fundamentally altered mankind's ability to produce goods. The country moved from a farming-dominated economy to a manufacturing-dominated economy for the first time. We are only just moving on from that.

The most famous example of how manufacturing could change comes in Adam Smith's[14] era-defining book called *An Inquiry into the Nature and Cause of the Wealth of Nations* (1766). He used the example of pin-making to explain how division of labour (improved industrial organisation) could massively increase production: on his own, a worker could produce 20 pins per day; on a production line of specialised workers, ten people could produce 4,800 per day. In 1832 Charles Babbage[15] established that a factory could produce 8,000 pins per day per worker. By 1980, Clifford Pratten – a productivity expert – calculated that current technology could enable the production of 800,000 pins per day.

As the Victorian period advanced, further improvements were introduced to maintain this economic revolution, to place productivity and trade at the core of the nation: development of central banking; labour laws; growth of industrial insurance; introduction of the old age pension and income tax. Take the Limited Liability Company (LLC), which sounds boring but is critical to our understanding of the modern economy. Although such entities were invented in the sixteenth century, they were given legal force in 1854. Before that, shareholders of a company were directly liable for all losses themselves. They were, therefore, risk-averse, as any failure would result in personal penury. With an LLC, shareholders were minimally liable (the cost of failure would not need to be bankrolled by them) and able to take more risks than ever before.

Marx called this development 'capitalist production in its highest development'; *The Economist* argued that the inventor of the idea 'might earn a place of honour with Watt, Stephenson[16] and other pioneers of the Industrial Revolution'. But you are probably already seeing the potential problem: this is the beginning of the divorce of finance and corporate life from reality. Companies can begin to play not with their own, but – in the words of Adam Smith – 'other people's money'.* As we shall see, this leads to all sorts of problems down the road.

In any event, the nineteenth century represented the consolidation and expansion of the industrial gains of the eighteenth century. Britain first, and then America, became colossally dominant in the worlds of manufacture and trade. In 1860 Britain owned 20 per cent of the world's manufacturing output, 46 per cent of the world's trade in manufactured goods, with just 2.5 per cent of the world's population.†

This was achieved at the cost of massive inequality and poverty: there were parts of Manchester where life expectancy was a haunting seventeen years (30 per cent lower than 800 years before). Wealth was concentrated in the hands of a few people, who held it in the form of land and government bonds (debt sold to them by the government). In many respects, little has changed: 'land' has become urban property rather than farming; 'bonds' are just now more widely spread (and more complex) investments. The few and the many, as Jeremy Corbyn might say, remain far apart. We shall explore later whether a new Victorian era is indeed upon us.

The principle behind the expansion of the economy was one of selfishness, of each person striving to make money for their families and – in so doing – growing the economy for all. This was best characterised by Adam Smith when he said that 'It is not from the benevolence of the butcher, the brewer, or the baker that we expect our dinner, but from their regard to their own interest.'

What follows is the idea that, left to its own devices, such behaviour will allow the economy to regulate itself. Adam Smith summarises this once more: 'By pursuing his own interests, the individual frequently promotes that of the society more effectually than when he really intends to promote it.'

Smith's metaphor of the 'invisible hand' directing affairs was

---

* We recall Margaret Thatcher's famous remark: 'The problem with socialism is that you eventually run out of other people's money.' In the end, both capitalism and socialism rely on someone, somewhere to foot the bill.
† Compare modern China: 15 per cent of output, 14 per cent of trade, 19 per cent of population.

suggestive of something palpable but not present, a force that registered enough to propel industry and the markets forward. The
problem is – and one should remember this when especially Tory
governments argue against market interference or 'state meddling'
– there has never been and will never be a truly free market.*
Government is always doing something: whether regulating competitiveness (as it does periodically and futilely with, say, the energy
market); controlling immigration and so the labour supply; providing
tax breaks to certain industries, imposing punitive taxes to affect our
consumption habits on others; creating partnerships between private
and public companies.

British and American growth in the eighteenth and nineteenth
centuries was, indeed, predominantly constructed through a mechanism of government support and interference. The American
politician Alexander Hamilton[17] made the argument a long time ago
that the state needed to nurse 'industries in their infancy': this meant
protectionist tariffs on foreign goods (making local goods better
value) and government support on crucial industries. Donald Trump
is a child of Hamilton, in that sense.

By 1860, such a protectionist approach meant that the British
economy was strong enough to open up trade with other countries
more freely, and other countries (primarily America and Germany)
benefited. By the First World War, Britain was no longer the leading
industrial nation in the world. Since then, it has dwindled even
further. Britain suffered greatly, as did the rest of the developed
world, during the Great Depression of the 1930s, which spread out
from the stock market crash of 1929 in America (the grandfather of
all banking crises).

The poverty endured by Britain was to spark the beginnings of
plans for the increased welfare state that we recognise today. Listen
to the words of journalist J. B. Priestley, whose *English Journey* (1936)
can sound occasionally like a post-apocalyptic fiction:

---

* This idea is strongly articulated by rock-star economist Ha Joon-Chang, who
says that 'few countries have become rich through free-trade, free-market policies,
and few ever will.' His brilliant book *23 Things They Don't Tell You About Capitalism*
(2010) is very useful, especially for someone who started out with more than 23
Things He Didn't Know About Capitalism to Begin With.

Wherever we went there were men hanging about, not scores of them but hundreds and thousands of them. The whole town looked as if it had entered a perpetual penniless bleak Sabbath. The men wore the drawn masks of prisoners of war. A stranger from a distant civilisation . . . would have arrived at once at the conclusion that Jarrow had deeply offended some celestial emperor of the island and was now being punished. He would never believe us if we told him that in theory this town was as good as any other and that its inhabitants were not criminals but citizens with votes.

Then global conflict intervened once more. The glory years for capitalism in the Western world and – tellingly – further afield, followed the end of the Second World War. Conflict provided an economic shock to the system that was positive: a supercharge of industrial development for military purposes that led to technological improvements for businesses. Thanks to the Marshall Plan (known formally as the European Recovery Program), the US provided more than $13 billion of economic stimulus to a continent that was on its knees after the war.

From 1945 to 1973 the modern capitalist world was truly forged, and most truly successful. In 1944 the Bretton Woods Agreement[18] created the International Monetary Fund (which lends money to countries with cash problems) and the World Bank (which lends money to countries for infrastructure projects). Globalisation and governmental support were the order of the day: the European Economic Community★ was founded; the General Agreement on Trade and Tariffs was introduced, making business cheaper and more proximate across the globe. There was widespread global growth: per capita income in Western Europe grew annually at 4.1 per cent; 'miracle economies' of the Far East (Korea and Singapore, for example) did even better.

★ This evolved into the European Union, from which Britain decided to exit in 2016 (see the next chapter for the full carnage). At the beginning, the EEC embodied the notion of governmental co-operation in the pursuit of capitalism. An alternative motivation was set out in *Yes Minister*, by the suavely cynical civil servant Humphrey Appleby in conversation with the naive minister Jim Hacker: 'The Germans went in to cleanse themselves of genocide and apply for readmission to the human race.'

Around this time, the economist Simon Kuznets plotted a curve that became famous for showing how inequality had increased during the initial period of industrialisation, but declined afterwards in this Golden Age. He was right: post-war Britain truly developed the welfare state in the aftermath of the war; it invented the NHS as we know it now (as we shall discuss in Chapter 3). What Kuznets couldn't know is that his downward curve did not last, and trouble was brewing.

In 1973 the cost of oil rose by 400 per cent, which drove prices for most goods higher. This led to inflation, in fact inflation's smirking cousin 'stagflation', because although prices were rising (thanks to the oil, which meant that costs of increased production and distribution of goods were passed on to the consumer), the economy was stagnating, and consumers were suffering the old double whammy as a result.

What is inflation?

Inflation is the process by which goods and services become more expensive. It has been claimed to be a modern invention, oddly. Between 1800 and 1913 inflation was between -0.2 per cent and +0.25 per cent. This is probably because currency was tied to something concrete: its value was linked to the value of precious metal. Britain left the gold standard in 1931 (the US did so in 1971), which meant that the amount of currency in circulation did not need to have a relationship to the amount of gold in storage. More money could be printed, and this meant its value could decline and prices could go up.

Governments do not mind a reasonable level of inflation, generally, because they tend to owe a lot of money, and, if the value of money declines, so the level of debt decreases. Indeed, governments fear deflation: if goods decline in value, people stop spending, as they know the price will be better in six months. The economy shrinks as a result. Consumers do mind inflation because things they buy are pricier, and very often their earnings do not increase in proportion: the effect of it on livelihoods and savings can be pernicious indeed.

However, economists, even now, do not agree how good or bad it is for the state as a whole. The IMF concluded that any inflation under 8 per cent had no impact on the growth of the economy. But the fetishisation of low and stable inflation was one cause of the banking crisis in 2008: the Bank of England and economists were so reassured by low inflation that they ignored signs that a problem was looming; if inflation was low, how could there be a crash? Well it was, and there was.

What is the Bank of England?

A necessary question, especially as we approach the modern times of British capitalism. The brilliant financial and literary journalist John Lanchester[19] has dubbed it 'a cross between Hogwarts, the Death Star and the office of Ebenezer Scrooge'. It was created (in 1694) in the aftermath of the Glorious Revolution, because the new Dutch King and Queen of England[20] needed cash and could not be trusted not to debase the currency as a way of getting it. The BoE became the institution responsible for monetary policy, independent from government. Basically, the Bank is responsible for setting interest rates (how much it costs to borrow money;* and how much saved money grows) and the amount of money in circulation (which affects inflation). That is monetary policy. The government is responsible for fiscal policy: how much it thinks it can get away with screwing you with taxes. The central bank is probably the most important thing in Britain you don't really think about as much as you should. Adam Smith said that 'the stability of the Bank of England is equal to that of the British government.' In 1844, as part of the Victorian supercharging of capitalism mentioned above, it became the Lender of Last Resort, the super-bank capable of bailing out and supporting other banks. Do you think it ever needed to? You are goddamn right it did.

---

* Interest rates affect inflation: the easier it is to borrow, the more people spend, the more prices rise. So high interest rates can be used to lower inflation, which is something the Bank of England sees as an important mechanism to control.

Back to the seventies, then, where inflation was high and the presiding orthodoxy of capitalist growth was wobbling. Interest rates were raised in order to convince people to stop spending and so reduce inflation; these high interest rates attracted foreign investors, which meant that the pound became more valuable. This, in turn, meant it cost more of other currencies to buy British produce, and so exports suffered. The economy went into recession.*

The government sought to find other ways to limit inflation too, one of which was to reduce salaries in the public sector. The trade unions would not wear this, and a series of wide-ranging strikes – which in many ways came to symbolise the decade – started. In late 1973 action by coal miners led to an energy crisis (compounded by high oil prices), compelling the Conservative government to enforce an order by which commercial premises could only use electricity for three consecutive days a week. TV stations had to shut down at 10.30 p.m. every night. For those of us born in the 1980s, the dystopian mess of the 1970s feels like an almost unimaginable vision. It is the very opposite of today's hyperconnected, twenty-four-hour world of shiny modernity; it was a time of graft and limitation, disconnection and frustration. Left-wing people will tell you that never has Britain been more equal. And that is probably right: but it was equality of failure in many respects. The Prime Minister Edward Heath called an election in February 1974, with the infamous question–cum–slogan: 'Who governs Britain?'. The answer was, typically: nobody. There was a hung Parliament (with Labour having the most seats; and the Tories the most votes). Neither side's approach to the looming catastrophe was trusted. An election a few months later gave Labour a small majority, and the responsibility for handling the industrial crisis fell to them.

On 22 January 1979 there was the biggest national strike in more than fifty years, involving lorry drivers, ambulance drivers, train drivers, gravediggers, waste collectors. This was the centre of the infamous 'winter of discontent',[21] which cost Labour power,[22] and brought to British politics a new way of economic thinking.

* Technically defined as two consecutive quarters when a country's GDP falls. Otherwise, it is just a slump or a downturn.

This new orthodoxy rose in both the US and the UK, personified by the politicians who would come to represent the 1980s: Margaret Thatcher[23] and Ronald Reagan.[24] They believed that the problem with post-war society was that it was too dependent on the state, and that the true philosophy of capitalism had lost its way. The answer was to stimulate spending by cutting taxes;* to restrict the power of the unions; to reduce the welfare state and other governmental support systems; and to deregulate the markets so that individuals and companies were freed up to pursue their individual greed.† The free market would become free once more. Adam Smith's non-benevolent butchers and bakers were converted – by this approach – to bankers and brokers.

Easy to see some flaws in this, in retrospect. Butchers and bakers produce real, tangible essentials of life: increased competition can – in theory – drive quality and reduce price. The markets shift around increasingly unreal tokens of exchange, of little obvious societal benefit to anybody: bankers and brokers truly do not care about you even a little bit. Plus this Thatcherite-Reaganite approach has a contradictory aspect: it stimulates the economy by making the rich richer (more liable to spend), but reduces welfare support and so makes the poor poorer (less liable to spend). This is called – in theory – 'trickle-down economics', a neo-liberal staple. One consequence is that it is liable to broaden inequality for obvious reasons. Set against that, the tax cuts also benefit those of low-to-middle incomes, which is ultimately why Thatcher was so popular over so many areas of the country.

Another extension of the free-market philosophy arrived in the 1990s: the Private Finance Initiative (PFI). By this process (pursued by governments ever since; rebranded as PF2 under David Cameron),

---

* In 1974 the top rate of earned income tax was 83 per cent, and tax on investment income was 98 per cent. Figures hard to imagine now. Margaret Thatcher brought them immediately down to 60 per cent in 1979 and 40 per cent in 1988. She cut the basic rate of income tax over her tenure from 33 per cent to 25 per cent.

† Remember Gordon Gekko in the film *Wall Street*? Probably not, if you are under thirty, in which case many thanks for reading an old-fashioned book printed on dead trees.

development of public sector infrastructure has been entrusted to private companies, who take responsibility for both construction and operation.

This should allow the efficiencies of the free market to lower prices by increased competition, so providing greater value for money. However, there is now an outlandish £200 billion of government money invested in more than 700 PFI schemes, which provide long, guaranteed contracts to suppliers lasting up to thirty years. This money is, technically and misleadingly, 'off the books' of the state, existing solely within the operational finances of the contractor. Often the contracts contain payments linked to inflation, which means their cost expands out of proportion with economic growth. In 2011 the National Audit Office said that PFI 'has the effect of increasing the cost of finance for public investments relative to what would be available to the government if it borrowed on its own account'. In 2018 the NAO was unable to see any clear evidence of economic benefits of the scheme (or even a coherent way of measuring whether they exist). We shall see more of this issue in Chapter 3, when we look at PFI in the health service.

As will be familiar to students of the banking crisis, the government is – with PFI – practically responsible for all the risk, despite the operation being ostensibly private. The problem is that – if a company providing a key service, like a hospital, fails – the government is on the hook for the infrastructure and will have to find a way to keep the contract going. Meanwhile, the private sector in all other circumstances gets to reap the benefit alone.

So, as our story reaches the period of modern capitalism, it is worth reflecting on how much has changed in the last thirty years. Two areas stand out: globalisation; and the industrial landscape.

When did Britain stop making things?

In 1970 Britain still made things: manufacturing employed 35 per cent of all people. Now it is probably less than 10 per cent. We have gone from the 20th largest manufacturing economy in the world to the 116th. Our trade surplus (how much we buy of things versus how much we sell of things) has gone from around +5 per cent to around -3 per cent. Manufacturing output as a share of GDP* was 37 per cent in 1950; it is now 13 per cent. While the crippling strikes of the 1970s made things much worse, the level has fallen especially quickly since 1990.[†] This means the workforce requirements and possibilities for the country have changed hugely over the last 200 years, increasing pace in modern times.[25]

Parts of the country built around manufacturing (which, in Britain, is largely outside the cities, and especially the south-east) have seen their source of employment obliterated. Britain used to be the 'workshop of the world'; now that has shifted to other countries, especially China. Which brings us to . . .

What does globalisation look like?

Globalisation comes from the increased connectedness of countries across the world, especially by trade.[‡] It was a deliberate policy by the end of the nineteenth century of both Britain and America to accept free trade in order to find new markets; this process was hastened by the arrival of global institutions like the IMF and World

---

* I am glad you asked: 'What is GDP?' The Gross Domestic Product is the monetary value of everything the country produces, minus the cost of production. As with almost everything in economics it is based on a lot of estimation: because each product is made of other products, and you don't want to count the value twice; and the cost of production is basically guesswork. GDP is currently growing by just over 2.5 per cent.

[†] Productivity has collapsed too. This is measured by the amount of GDP divided by the number of hours worked. GDP itself measures output, but it can obviously be increased simply by having more people in the country (hence the macroeconomic value of immigration). Productivity is how much value is being created per hour. In 2000 the annual increase in productivity was around 26 per cent; in 2016 it was 2.3 per cent. The last time we saw growth that low was during the Napoleonic Wars. Some people, I am being serious, blame our dwindling attention spans on mobile phones.

[‡] Ironically, this tends to concentrate wealth in giant global corporations: 30–50 per cent of all global trade is within firms. The 200 largest corporations produce 10 per cent of the world's economic output.

Bank, which sought to promote free-market ideals to others. In the pre-war era, globalisation was in the form of colonialism, connection based on enforced submission and exploitation, the envelopment by European countries of others into their empires. In 1913 nearly half of domestic capital and three-quarters of industrial capital of Asia and Africa was owned by Europeans. Britain's wealth was increased by getting cheap raw materials and labour, without troubling too much about the human cost.

Countless other statistics exist to show how the West's position of dominance has since been eaten away over the years, with the centre of global gravity shifting ever eastwards. In 1900 75 per cent of goods and services were produced in the US and Europe; in 2010 that was down to 50 per cent; in 2050 it will be 25 per cent. However, it is worth considering, if only for our own humility, that for large chunks of history (prior to the medieval period) the East – especially China – was a far more developed place, economically and culturally.[26] In 1500 one European city (Paris) could make it into the global top ten in terms of size. By 1800, it had been joined by London and Naples. By 1900, there was only one non-European city (Tokyo) in the top ten. Now, there are no European cities, and just two (São Paulo and Mexico City) with any sort of European antecedence at all. We have seen over the last 500 years, the rise and fall of the West.★

We have also seen the rise and fall of British industry over the same time. Some of this is due to technology: automation makes manufacturing more efficient; more can be produced more cheaply with fewer people. Industry, therefore, diminishes in importance as part of the overall economy. Some of it is due to the increased competitiveness of other countries, who are willing to compromise on working conditions for their employees and on the quality of their raw materials.† Some of it is due to our own national failures. The Industrial Revolution – as we have seen – was a triumph for

★ A counter-argument to this: the transference of people from rural to urban areas is not necessarily a true sign of prosperity. The fact that the West does not contain vast cities may not itself be a bad thing.
† Cough, China!

the three 'I's: investment, innovation and invention.[27] Britain today is terribly constructed to drive that sort of economic growth. In the seventies, our investment ratio[28] was 20 per cent; it is now 15 per cent. This is, and it is seldom discussed, the lowest in the Western world. Spending on research and development is well beneath the global average. We do not innovate or develop much anymore; it is as if our creative impetus has dissipated over the last century, like a former athlete whose muscles have softened and sagged, and whose former glory is scarcely visible beneath the surface.

Indeed, one definition of globalisation is the transfer of wealth and power from the poorest in rich countries to the richest in poor countries. Whole areas of the country become 'hollowed out': the reason for their existence (like, say, ceramics for villages in Nottinghamshire) disappear; no other industry replaces them. As we shall see elsewhere, the consequences of this imbalance in the political arena are huge.

In any event, after the 1980s many of the conditions of the modern British economy were in place: idealisation of the free market; globalised trading and production; deregulation of the banking industry; the decline of manufacturing and the rise of the service industry. This economy is, as we all now know, a precarious thing. Before 1975 there had been virtually no banking crises for decades; since then anywhere between 5 and 35 per cent of countries have been in crisis at any one time.[29] Since 2008, twenty-five countries have had debilitating crises. Which, finally, begs a big question . . .

How does the financial world work; and how does it connect to the real world?

The story of modern capitalism is the story of the separation of finance from reality. For a very long time, banks supplied loans to people or businesses they knew a great deal about, with the basic expectation that the loan would be returned with appropriate interest. There was a separation between banks that gave loans and banks that directed investments.* For a long time, the price of stocks and shares† were simply functions of the value of a company, whose main priority was to invest for the future and to provide returns (or dividends) to long-term shareholders. In the 1960s the average period of someone holding a share was five years; in 2007 it was a little over six months. Investment had lost its original meaning, and became simply a mechanism to shift assets around until they made money.

As the financial markets were deregulated in the 1980s, so followed the introduction of different products and markets. When we think of high finance, we think of stocks and shares, but in fact the bond market is far more important. This involves the trading of debt: you buy a bond from a company or government; it owes you the money and must return it at a given date plus interest. Simple enough. Except for the fact that the bonds can be combined with other bonds and endlessly traded so the original transaction involving two entities is exploded into fragments, and the trades are gambles on whether the value of the bond will increase or decrease over time.[30] Nobody cares about the merits of the original deal, or the original date of repayment. Something tangible has been made intangible, which is fine until somebody wants to call it in. As we shall see, the financial markets work just as long as nobody questions their reality, at which point: poof! They explode, and we all pay.

This leads us to the derivative markets, which are actually a kind of metaphor for the unreality of high finance. A derivative is a deal that *derives* its value from the performance of an entity,‡ but is disconnected

---

* This was a matter of US law: the Glass–Steagall Act of 1932 made it illegal to be both a retail and an investment bank. The law was repealed in 1999 after heavy lobbying from the financial sector. Thankfully, there was no epoch-altering financial bust involving those banks less than a decade later.

† As we shall see, the financial sector never uses a simple phrase when it can get away with even minor obfuscation. Stocks and shares are the same thing.

‡ They include futures (the orange juice example below) and forwards (very similar); swaps (when two sides agree to exchange assets); and options (the right for the owner to buy or sell an asset at a specific price in the future). A good example of a swap is given in *The Big Short* by Michael Lewis: the credit default swap. Basically, a guy convinced traders to trade to him insurance on dodgy mortgage deals: he bet on the fact that the deals would default; the swap was his money for insurance, in return he would collect if the mortgage indeed defaulted.

from that entity. This is an example of a 'future': I might decide to pick a product like frozen orange juice* ahead of the harvest of oranges. I bet that the value of orange juice will be a certain amount and agree to pay a certain price for it at a certain date; the owner of the asset gets the money early (ahead of the harvest, so reducing his risk) and if the eventual price ends up lower than my prediction I have lost, higher than my prediction I have won. Clear? Kind of? What is confusing is that the derivative can be bought and sold an infinite number of times between now and the harvest date, and so becomes worth far more than the original product, *and ultimately has no connection to it.* Same number of oranges in the world; their value multiplied by an incomprehensible number. A trillion dollars in derivatives are traded every day in London alone – the equivalent of half the UK economy, without altering the number of tangible assets in existence. How can that be real? It cannot.

It gets worse. Let's return to the idea of the derivative trading of multiple bonds, or debt. At one point, in the 1990s, the idea grew that instead of single loans being traded, they could be packaged together into a variety of financial products, which could themselves be endlessly traded. This led to the rise of Asset Based Securities (ABS): each one representing the pooling of thousands of loans (for homes, cars, business etc.) into one big bond. Or Residential Mortgage Backed Security (RMBS): the same thing, just for mortgages. This wasn't complicated enough, so it was taken one step further: Collateralised Debt Obligations (CDO) were combinations of multiple ABSs, each combining different levels of risk. The idea was that the good risk (i.e. the loans to people who might actually be able to repay) would act as life-rafts for the bad risk (the 'sub-prime'[†] loans that are essentially junk).

This process is called securitisation, because it gives people a false sense of security.[31] Amazingly, everybody in authority thought – if they thought at all, which they didn't; and if they understood it at all, which they didn't – that this increased complexity was a good

---

* And yes I am using this because it features in the Eddie Murphy film *Trading Places*.

[†] See where this is going?

thing. The IMF thought it made 'the financial system more resilient': high risk underwritten by low risk meant that the system simply could not fail. It did fail. It also simply created a 'shadow' banking system where deals were done with no relation to the original value of the asset. In 2007 the shadow banking system was worth 9.5 trillion euros. In the US it was much more. In Britain, one bank (RBS) had a balance sheet larger than the entire UK economy.

This is all balls-achingly clear with hindsight, of course. But it is not unreasonable for people to assume that those at the top of their profession could have shown a bit of foresight, or indeed just 'sight' at the time. But they could not fully understand themselves what they had created. A large CDO, according to the Bank of England, contains enough data to fill a billion pages. And – without wishing to be uncharitable – these finance folk are not particularly big readers. The real thinkers were looking elsewhere: at inflation and interest rates. There was 'intellectual apartheid' in the financial system, in the words of economist Felix Martin; criminal, culpable negligence, in the opinion of many.

So what actually happened in the banking crisis?

Some questions are so epochal, even someone divorced from the real world feels compelled to ask them. In November 2008 the Queen opened an extension to the London School of Economics and inquired – terribly politely, one assumes – why nobody predicted the crash. The answer came from the British Academy a year later: 'In summary, the failure . . . while it had many causes, was principally a failure of the collective imagination of many bright people, both in this country and internationally, to understand the risks to the system as a whole.'

Intellectual apartheid; complexity; consumer hubris; fragmentation: a failure of experts.* Yes, we all have to take a bit of responsibility

---

* Historically, economists have always offered a nice line in mock humility. J. K. Galbraith had the best lines: 'the only function of economic forecasting is to make astrology look respectable'; 'economics is extremely useful as a source of employment for economists'. As it turns out, there was nothing mock about this humility at all.

here. Many people in this period borrowed money for vastly over-priced houses, or cars, or ran up credit card bills for shiny goods they did not need. As a society, we all devalued the need to balance the books. Banks were operating in the context of an age of catastrophic profligacy that had manifestations everywhere. What triggered the crash was the recognition (gradual and then sudden) that the assets being traded were worthless, and the collective pretence that all was well could not be sustained. In America by 2007 banks had become addicted to 'sub-prime'[32] mortgages; those loans had been packaged up with other loans, and, instead of the good propping up the bad, the bad infected the good. Once it was recognised that the loans in the real world could never be repaid, the market around them collapsed. Two big banks (Bear Sterns and Lehmann Brothers) were bankrupted, because their assets no longer had enough real-world value to support them.

In Britain, the bank Northern Rock had a similar problem: a large book of mortgage lending to people who could never pay, propped up by short-term bonds elsewhere. When the international markets wobbled, investors started to look at the value of the bank's assets, and got worried. They pulled their money. Confidence collapsed.

Remember: banks are used to problems of liquidity (cash supply); they are endlessly moving around loans and investments. The term used is 'maturity gap': some of your debts might be called in, while other sources of income are longer maturing. At last resort, the Bank of England can step in and provide liquidity support in those instances, and all is generally well. This was much, much worse: it was not a cash-flow problem; the problem was that the underlying assets weren't worth anything like as much as everyone had believed. So the Bank of England couldn't just provide a loan to tide the bank over until payday. There was no payday in sight. The govern-ment had to step in and assume the burden of the (worthless) assets. Northern Rock was nationalised, and other banks followed.

For a period, this became the new normal. The UK spent 8.8 per cent of its GDP – more than £150 billion – recapitalising the banks. That's more than it spends on the NHS in a year. Think about that next time you are stuck in a crowded waiting room, bleeding quietly into your shoes.

At one level, the banking crisis represented the failure of free-market capitalism. Because all these bankers, when they were winning, kept the cash for themselves; when they were losing, they were propped up by the rest of us. Intervention was necessary to keep the market afloat; and intervention was necessary elsewhere too. Lessons had been learned from the Great Depression in the 1930s, and the philosophy of the economist John Maynard Keynes[33] was employed: spend during a recession, to stop the economy from shrinking further. The government spent about £31 billion stimulating the economy: reducing VAT, starting big capital projects. Together, the government and the Bank of England made sure that more money was introduced into the economy,* interest rates were kept low to keep people spending. Capitalism needed support, and it got it.

And after this salutary rescue, this humbling of the mighty, it is right to record that nothing much has changed. The markets are still as unreal as ever;[34] still endlessly cycling through trades of gigantic sums of other people's money; still as central to the British economy as ever.

Where are we now?

But we now live in a country still shaped by the aftermath of the financial crisis. The principle of spending to prevent recession was replaced by one of cutting to reduce our resultant debt. The cuts took place; but the debt has still grown. From 2010 onwards, the government has been pursuing an 'austerity' agenda, in an attempt to balance our books. John Lanchester has called 'austerity' an 'attempt

---

* This is called quantitative easing. Essentially, the Bank buys government bonds, which raises their prices, which enables those selling them (banks, companies, pension funds) to buy more assets (like shares). This in turn encourages companies to spend and invest more, and banks to lend more. Eventually, in theory, more money is introduced into the system as a whole.

to make something moral-sounding and value-based out of specific reductions in government spending which cause specific losses to specific people'.

Let's pause to establish what it means for a government to be in debt (TL; DR:* not much). You will hear the terms 'debt' and 'deficit' often used interchangeably on television and radio, but the difference is simple: deficit is how much the government needs to borrow each year to balance its books; debt is the accumulation of each year of deficit. The debt has increased since 2008 due to two main factors: the government spent lots of money bailing out the banks; because the economy went into recession, it took in much less money from tax receipts, as people earned and spent less. Each year, the government tries to reduce the deficit or even actually take in more than it borrows; and largely it fails (it has only succeeded thirteen times since the Second World War). Back in 2015, the then Chancellor George Osborne predicted a surplus by 2020, but Brexit has put the kibosh on that,[35] and the date has been pushed back to 2025.

Debt is best measured as a percentage of GDP, because then we can see how it compares to what we are really worth as a country. In times of war, countries will borrow just about anything, because the alternative might be annihilation. In 1815, when Britain had been fighting Napoleon for twenty years (sometimes alone), the debt was 200 per cent of GDP. It spiked again in 1919 and 1945 for obvious reasons. It was as low as 29 per cent in 2002, before rising again under Tony Blair, as he borrowed money for public projects (raising it to 37 per cent). Post-crash it has spiked once more and is now running at around 80 per cent.

Does this matter? Well, the answer is probably that it does not. Remember we are still in the unreal world of high finance. Nobody seems to expect a government to clear all the debt from its bonds,[36] or thereby actually reduce the debt to zero (which, given its size, would be impossible). And the effect of a high level of debt for an economy like Britain's is not clear. Like everything else, it impacts on

---

* A needless experimentation on my part with youthspeak. It stands for: Top Line; Don't Read. I do still want you to read, obviously. You know I didn't know what ICYMI meant for ages; I had actually missed it.

confidence: will investors lend money to a country over its head in debt? The answer is yes, but not as favourably as to economies with more balanced books. As with households, a lot of debt leaves you vulnerable to catastrophe, as your resources are weakened in the event you suddenly need money for something; and you have to pay the interest on all the borrowing.* But some people (Jeremy Corbyn and Donald Trump, for example) would argue that, at a time of low interest rates, when borrowing is cheap, it is a good idea for governments to borrow more, not less. Debt is an opportunity, not a burden.[37]

All we need to know for our purposes is that (from 2008 until at least after the election of 2017) the government has wanted, if possible, to reduce its public spending, and so the annual deficit. This is, as Lanchester suggests, partially for ideological reasons. In the end, we are still in the neo-liberal world of state reduction, and the cutting of welfare; we still, despite lots of knocks, believe in the benefits of capitalism.

What does austerity look like?

It is a programme of reduction in public spending, across everything except the NHS (which is ring-fenced because of the affection in which it is held by the public) and foreign aid (which is ring-fenced to the perpetual bemusement of a great many people)† to the tune

---

* That was, in 2017, around £43 billion, or 3 per cent of GDP. The Shadow Chancellor, John McDonnell, could not, in November 2017, answer how much it cost to pay the interest on the debt, and now you can.
† It is a UN recommendation that a country spends 0.7 per cent of its GDP on foreign aid. From what I can see, this is an entirely arbitrary number, and one followed by very few countries other than the UK (which recently enshrined it in law). On the plus side, it acts as a visible sign of our commitment as a generous and humane nation. On the downside, it becomes a target that has to be hit, and therefore is spent on whatever project occurs within the correct accountancy period, rather than whatever worthwhile project needs our help the most. Hence cash going to an Ethiopian version of the Spice Girls or to a project to preserve Madagascan fish (giving the *Sun*, when I was there, the pretty funny headline 'Funding Nemo'). Spending money on footling foreign projects, while British people use food banks, is not a good look.

of around £12 billion in the years following 2015. This has included reducing the number of people liable to receive welfare from the state, and to cut the amount that those remaining do receive: in the areas of income support, housing support, disability support, and so on. The proposed figure to be cut from welfare funding has been designated as £9 billion (much of which was agreed, even up to the 2017 election, by both main parties). The theory of cutting something like unemployment support – widely believed, but not entirely substantiated – is that reducing welfare will incentivise people to work. The argument against this is that it might discriminate against people who are unable (either physically, mentally or socially) to do so, condemning them to penury and poverty. It also struggles to answer the point that a large number of people on welfare are already working, just in jobs that do not pay them a sustainable living.

Many of these policies have met with criticism, it must be said. Take tax credits. These are basically a subsidy from the government for those on low incomes; an income supplement. This is a bizarre idea, if you pause to consider it: the state is trying to make good the unwillingness of a private employer to pay a sufficient wage. In 2015 the government tried to reduce the cost of this system of state aid by £6 billion by 2020, by raising the threshold at which point people could benefit from tax support. This would have cost low-paid workers on average around £1,300 a year. There was a revolt (including by the House of Lords) and the proposal was shelved.

The 'bedroom tax' was another part of the austerity programme, but one that survived the revolt. It is actually known as the 'under-occupancy penalty',[38] and has some reason behind it: people on housing benefit should not live in properties with extra bedrooms, when poor people, not on benefit, could never afford the same. So housing benefit is reduced for every spare room, saving £500 million a year. The problems with it are considerable though: it discriminates against disabled people, who need extra rooms for carers; it drives people from their homes and communities with no guarantee of smaller properties available;[39] it means that if an occupant dies, then the resultant spare room will immediately become a burden.

In the end, views on austerity are conditioned by worldview: do you believe the state should be as small as possible, and people should be as self-reliant as possible; or do you believe that the state should be a benevolent entity, doing whatever is possible to give support to the most needy? This debate – as old as humanity – has been given added pungency by the banking crisis: why can you give £150 billion to negligent wealthy bankers to cover their mistakes, but not support someone with a disability? The latter is a hard question to answer indeed. Or rather easy to answer but hard to stomach: we live in a society where banking needs to be sustainable; we live in a society where a disabled person's plight affects only that person.

Is this a new Victorian era?

We know that the post-war belief in ever-reducing inequality* was something of an illusion, but it is worth reflecting on how bad the situation now is in Britain. As ever with economics, nobody agrees very much. Thomas Piketty believes that the prevailing course of capitalism is a return to the Victorian model of rich few, manifold poor. Certainly, wealth is concentrated in the assets – primarily houses – of the wealthy. By 1945, private capital had reduced to three times private income; it is now nearer six times. Private capital tends to be locked into individual wealth, it does not trickle down to the rest of the economy. In Piketty's view 'inherited wealth will make a comeback': as in Victorian times, social mobility will suffer.

Certainly, after the banking crisis of 2008, people's capacity to earn has been damaged. The Institute for Fiscal Studies (IFS) has said that workers will not see their wages, in real terms, recover to their 2008 level until 2021; they call the intervening period 'the lost decade'.[40] On average, people will be poorer than they were a decade before. If inflation does increase as a result of Brexit, they may be a lot poorer. We know that, although the mean wage has increased

---

* Income inequality is measured by economists using something called the Gini co-efficient, varying between zero (when everybody earns the same) and one (when one person has everything). In the UK, it has been hovering around 0.3 since the financial crash.

in our economy, the median wage has remained stubbornly stuck:[41] this means that the overall pot is increasing, but the benefits are skewing to the top half. Since 1977 the richest fifth of households have seen the greatest percentage increase; the poorest fifth have seen the lowest. The poorest fifth have 8 per cent of the national income; the richest have 40 per cent. And, backing up Piketty, wealth (assets, savings and investments) is even more unequal than income: the poorest 50 per cent have around 9 per cent of the wealth; the richest 10 per cent have 45 per cent.[42] In his view, this prevents the benefits of a society being shared: 'the past devours the future'.

Even those who argue that inequality is not getting worse (relative to previous decades)[43] must accept that its starting position is pretty bad. And we have seen the political consequences: a prevailing mood against the wealthiest, which is both cultural and geographical.* One response has also been to suggest that globalisation is to blame, in the sense of its effect of increasing immigration into this country. Globalisation is, certainly, to blame in some senses: as we have seen, Britain used to be a massively dominant manufacturing country on the scale of China; now much of our wealth comes from a dodgy financial sector that nearly bankrupted us.[44] But the economics of immigration is an important issue in modern Britain.

Are immigrants ruining the economy and stealing our jobs?

Normal caveat applies here,† but it is unlikely that immigration is the bogeyman to the UK economy. Since 1997 we have had net migration into the UK of more than 100,000, and for the last couple of years before Brexit it was more than 300,000. And, despite the amount of time we all spend discussing it,‡ we are still not clear on the net impact on the economy. In 2000 the Home Office found

---

* See Brexit, UKIP, etc.
† No economists can agree on ANYTHING.
‡ Nearly equalled by the amount of time we talk about not being allowed to talk about it due to 'political correctness'.

that immigrants contributed £31.2 billion to the economy, and used benefits and state services worth £28.8 billion, a net positive economic effect of almost £2.5 billion. The same period, judged by MigrationWatch,* found a net negative effect of £1 billion. The reason for the discrepancy is that there is no agreed metric for the impact on public services (and how that might affect economic growth); no agreement how much of shared costs (like defence) to attribute to migrants; and no agreement about gauging lifetime contributions or not. More recent figures from University College London estimated that between 1995 and 2011 immigrants from the EU created a positive fiscal impact of over £4 billion, and from outside the EU a negative impact of £118 billion. In the same period, the impact of British nationals was a negative cost of £591 billion (because basically, as citizens, we are all a burden on each other).

There is some agreement that recent migrants contribute more than older migrants, and that EU migrants contribute more than non-EU migrants (the latter something you would not have heard much in the Brexit debate). At the very least, it is clear that immigration has had no devastating impact on the economy. Jonathan Wadsworth, of the London School of Economics, would go further: 'Immigration is at worst neutral and, at best, another economic benefit.' The latter argument is shared by the Office of Budget Responsibility (OBR),[45] which has judged that – if net migration is reduced by 80,000 a year – the government would have to borrow an extra £16 billion over five years to make up the difference in income.

All this makes sense if you consider it rationally, rather than patriotically. Migrants to the UK tend to be young,[46] and here to work:[47] those sort of people tend to use public services less and pay more in income tax. The other part of the equation often missed is that an increase in people in the country creates an increase in demand for paid goods and services: every time a Bulgarian buys a

---

* The cynic in me is unsurprised that an institution entirely and noisily devoted to articulating the problems of the current level of immigration would find problems with the current level of immigration.

coffee in Britain, he is increasing our GDP; when enough Bulgarians buy coffees, there will be a demand for a new coffee shop, which will employ people[48] and so positively impact on the economy.*

It is also not the case that, on a national scale, immigrants take jobs from British people, or significantly reduce wages overall.[49] However, it is likely that lower income workers are likely to be more affected than higher: immigrant labour is more destabilising in the lower end of the market. In the areas of highest migration, though, there was no increase in the fall of jobs of UK-born workers. This is not to say that anyone who feels that competition from immigrants has deprived them of a job, or undercut their rates, is lying or a racist.[†] There will be communities where an influx of immigrants has unsettled the established economy. But probably not many, and not enough to skew the overall picture.

Here is another statistic, which begs another question. Unemployment is currently at less than 5 per cent; around 75 per cent of people in the country are employed, the highest figure since records began. There is no widespread indigenous unemployment, again intuitively showing that there has been no massive job loss due to immigration. But the follow-up question is vital: if so many people are employed, why are so many people poor?

Why is low unemployment not better for us?

Keynes once said: 'Look after unemployment and the budget will look after itself.' It is perhaps not recognised sufficiently that this, once self-evident, truth no longer holds true for the British economy. A sobering thought for you: over half the people living in relative poverty work for a living. In the last decade, the number of people in working-poor households has increased by 2 million. These citizens get up in the morning, try to earn a wage, and cannot get by

---

* This rebuts something called 'the lump of labour fallacy' which is the belief that there is a finite amount of jobs in a country. In fact, and it is kind of obvious, an increased population needs an increase in services, which have to be provided by paid employees.
† Some will be lying racists, of course, but you get them everywhere.

without the stigma and the hardship of serious poverty. There is an economic model called the 'Phillips Curve', demonstrating the notion that decreased unemployment should increase inflation, because wage-earners will spend more and drive prices up. This hasn't happened quite as much as it should have, because many people in employment do not earn enough to spend. Overall, more than 13 million people in the UK live below the poverty line.

While the government, in 2016, introduced the National Living Wage (at £7.20 per hour, rising hopefully to £9 per hour by 2020), and so gave a pay rise to 1.3 million people, it has not solved the problem. First, it only applies to over-twenty-fives, so does not help those starting out in the employment market. Second, it is not necessarily going to provide enough for a truly comfortable life.[50] It is also a good example of free-market failure: one of the principles of free-market capitalism is that the market sets the prices; people are paid what they deserve. This policy represents the sort of interventionism that is normally derided by capitalists.

It is likely that, in the government's quest to reduce unemployment, it has lost sight of the purpose of employment in the first place: a dignified and pleasant existence. Our 'employment' statistics count people in part-time work, or failed self-employment, people for whom work is not guaranteed every day. Currently, over a quarter of all employment is part-time (up from a tenth in the last twenty years); and nearly 3.5 million people are searching for more hours of work than they currently get (that number was under 2.5 million in 2002). Around 900,000 Britons were on zero-hours contracts in 2017, which means their income was dependent on the economic performance, needs or whims of their employer. In an act of self-deluding euphemism, this is often characterised as the 'gig economy', which makes it sound all-empowering and fun, like being in a band. On the one hand, it may be liberating: to earn extra money by renting out a flat on Airbnb or being a part-time Uber driver. On the other hand, there is a risk that the under-employed will effectively become the servants of the actually employed. The Chartered Institute of Personnel and Development estimated that 1.3 million are working in the gig economy, 58 per cent of whom are using it to top up their normal income.

When the government instructed former Labour strategist Matthew Taylor in 2016 to investigate the changing nature of employment, he produced a report that urged the aim of creating 'good work for all'. It is, charitably, a worthy intention that seems unlikely to succeed.[51]

Contrast the elderly here. The proportion of pensioners living in relative poverty has fallen from 50 per cent in the 1990s to about 15 per cent today. Why? Because they are removed from the turbulent waters of the modern economy. Their pensions have been triple-locked, which mean they rise with prices, average earnings or by 2.5 per cent, whichever is higher. Wages for the employed have stagnated in this time: inflation has been outstripping earnings by a considerable amount. Old people are more likely to own assets, especially houses, that have appreciated dramatically.* House prices in London have risen by around 50 per cent in the last seven years, which is lovely if you bought a house on the cheap in 1973 (you bastards). If you didn't, you are likely to rent, and in London tenants now must pay a third of their disposable income just to live in someone else's property. And rents are increasing disproportionately in comparison to earnings, with potentially disastrous consequences. In 2017 a report by the charity Shelter projected that up to a million people could be homeless by 2020, as a result of not being able to afford to pay rent. As it stands, homelessness has increased every year between 2012 and 2017. In 2016 the number of homeless children in Britain was an astonishing 120,000. It is a national crisis, tragedy and badge of shame.

The housing crisis in the UK is – among other things – a simple function of supply and demand:† the population has increased (largely

---

* If you think about it, the value of property is a curious way to measure the health of the economy, but we do it all the time. If my house grows by 10 per cent in value, I am not appreciably richer; I can't benefit the economy by spending more. All it means is that, if I move house, I will have to spend more buying my new property. High house prices only benefit the downsizing elderly (and their kids), or those who leave London for the countryside (the urban rich).
† 'Teach a parrot the terms supply and demand and you have an economist,' said Victorian thinker Thomas Carlyle. We will meet him again later; he was not a very nice man.

due to immigration) in the last decades, but the number of houses for that population has not kept pace. And, as the people who own homes (the middle-aged and elderly who entered their prime purchasing period at a time when houses were affordable) are living longer, the bank of available housing is not being renewed quickly enough either. Essentially, there needed to be around 300,000 houses built every year for the last several years to provide sufficient supply. In the last forty years, that figure has never been reached; indeed, in recent times, half of that figure has not been reached.* In 2001 the UK population was 59 million in a country of 21.2 million homes; in 2016 it was 65 million with 23.7 million homes. Whenever people discuss problems in housing in this country, it boils down to this: not enough are being built.

And this is another example of market failure. Whereas local authorities used to be responsible for building sufficient houses (and they did not, as those who have lived on council estates may testify, always do this well), since the 1980s this has been deferred more to the private sector, including housing associations working for profit. They have not filled the gap.† The only answer to the problem of not enough houses is to build more houses. It is so simple even a politician should understand that‡.

Instead, recent governments have sought to assist the other side of the equation: through 'Help to Buy' schemes, they want to subsidise the mortgage process by guaranteeing cheap loans. But that does not assist the supply problem of not enough houses, it merely helps to ensure that inflated prices of the assets can better be met. Because, as we know, what happens when supply does not meet

---

* In 2016 there were around 115,000 houses built (23 per cent by public authorities). In 1968 the record was 436,000 (40 per cent by public authorities).

† Except for people who buy property for the purpose of renting it out for profit. So a lot of new housing merely exists to take money from renters to benefit people who own houses already.

‡ At the moment, developers can hoard land and then sell it to the government at a price reflective of what it would be worth if it had planning permission (in this way £20,000 of agricultural land can sell for £2 million). Labour has the bright idea of compelling them to sell it at cost, which could lead to a reduction in the cost of building council houses of a handy £10 billion.

demand: prices go up. And that is what gives us our unaffordable housing market. There was a marvellous letter to a newspaper recently that illustrates how the situation has changed: 'In 1965 I was a fireman earning £1,000 a year and I bought a house for £3,500 with a mortgage of three times my salary. Today that very ordinary property is valued at £650,000, so a buyer would need a £50,000 deposit and an income of £200,000 a year. This shows how utterly impossible the situation is for young people.'

Thank you, John Searle of Grantham for teaching me how to be so succinct! The problem he explains is particularly acute in London and the south-east, where demand is always rising. If public sector workers (firefighters police, teachers, nurses) cannot afford to own property in an entire city, why should they stick around to be punished by grasping landlords? London is a city of rich people being supported (cared for, taught, saved, protected) by poor people who can no longer afford to live there. This is economic apartheid in the clearest terms.

So, in this country, there is economic inequality in age, inequality in jobs, and inequality in geography. When we look at the 'recovery' from the 2008 crash, we are really seeing that life in parts of London wobbled but then carried on as normal: house prices kept rising for longer than expected; the financial sector is still in business. Outside London, the picture is vastly different. If we[52] look at GDP per head, only two regions of Britain have surpassed the levels of 2007; almost every other part of the country is still poorer ten years on. Britain is being hollowed out before our eyes, but because the capital city can still boast unaffordable housing and because the state did not allow the banks to drown in their own toxic vomit, we can pretend that it is not.

So what about Brexit and the economy?

This book is not magical, and it cannot plausibly reflect the economic outcome of so much uncertainty, which will continue until long after the negotiation between the United Kingdom[53] and the EU has been concluded.

What is at stake is the ability of Britain to be a successful trading country in the future. Within the EU, the UK was part of the single market and customs union, a bloc of states that traded with the world en masse. The condition of membership of this bloc was the free movement of people, capital, services and goods. As you know, it was the first of these that was so unpalatable to many British people. Membership of the single market is incompatible with any restriction on European immigration.

Outside the union, the UK will not only have to negotiate trading terms with the EU, but it must seek to do the same with every other major country in the world. It may be able to do so successfully; it may not. One metaphor for the issue of Brexit is this: you live in a house that is habitable, even comfortable, but with problems (including intrusive neighbours); you could move house, certainly, but you would have to move without looking around the new place, having a survey performed, or really exam-ining the pros and cons; it is possible that you could end up somewhere nicer, more private and roomy, at a more comfortable mortgage; it is also possible that you could end up in an apartment facing a wall, which smells of urine and defeat. Risk-takers, or those who don't find the current house that pleasant, believed we should try the move and get something better. People currently comfortable or cautious did not agree.

The effects of Brexit on the economy might include the danger of the free trade of the single market being replaced by a less favour-able trade agreement with tariffs imposed.[54] This, coupled with any wobbles in the pound, could mean that goods and services we import become more pricey, creating inflation. Restrictions on the UK's ability to provide financial services to the rest of Europe could lead to that industry – a major plank of our economy – shifting elsewhere. On the one hand, goodbye to evil bankers; on the other hand, goodbye to a chunk of GDP. A reduction in immigration could lead to a reduced tax intake from healthy young people, which would have to be replaced elsewhere.

There is potential upside, of course. A country unshackled by the common decision-making of twenty-seven countries could be more nimble and successful at making its way in the world. We could do better, just as we could do worse. The true indictment inherent in the Brexit vote is that many people felt that the latter was actually untrue: in modern capitalist Britain, they might as well gamble as they had already descended to the bottom.

So has capitalism failed us; and can it be fixed?

Yes, and no. First, it is worth remembering the words of economist Joseph Schumpeter that 'pessimistic views about a thing always seem to the public mind to be more profound than optimistic ones'. Doom-mongers are generally sexier than bright-eyed gushers, but should not be trusted more. And, taking the long view, the British economy – indeed all Western economies – has been a fantastic success story. Generally, as history progresses, things – to quote a famous political anthem – can only get better.[55]

We see this in all sorts of measurable ways, like increased lifespan, or decrease in death from starvation. An American economist, Richard Fogel, has argued that 'physical poverty' (being short of life-sustaining things) has been replaced by 'spiritual poverty' (being short of material desires). He pointed out that in 1875 the average US family spent 74 per cent of its income on food, clothing and shelter; in 1995, it spent 13 per cent.

This argument can certainly be taken too far. We know in the UK that rents can consume a high proportion of income; we know that the usage of food banks has risen in the last decade;[56] we know that a majority of people feel that their children may be worse off than themselves. The question is, therefore, how much further intervention is necessary to improve the lot of such a large number of our citizens.

First, we must dispense with the notion that state intervention is something to be avoided. That line has been historically crossed and re-crossed, and obliterated by the financial crisis. In previous years, right-wing economists would have told you about something called 'moral hazard', which is the idea that if you support people who either act improperly or have failed by market standards, you are rewarding incompetence or waste. The theory is that you therefore create the danger that nobody will try to behave properly or succeed on their own merits, because they know that a safety net will always exist to preserve them. When the banking crisis hit, of course, moral hazard was ignored and the banks were bailed out.

Moral hazard theory is behind objections to a large welfare state, and can clearly be taken too far. In 1845 *The Economist* magazine was up in arms at the notion that the state should provide support for those starving to death in the Irish famine. 'Charity,' it said, 'is the national error of Englishmen.' About a million people died in that famine.

So, if the state should be active, what could it do to redistribute wealth? The first would be to examine the tax system, and a couple of interesting ideas exist. Thomas Piketty believes in a 'progressive annual tax on capital', by which people holding large-yielding assets (property, bonds etc.) would have to pay a small percentage of their value every year. The wealth would not remain static in a small number of hands; a proportion would have to be liquidated and shared. There are a couple of problems with this, however. First, from a practical point of view, it would only work if it could be globally applied, as rich people employ smart people to hide their assets if they can. Second, our neo-liberal friends would argue that such a tax would be punishing the wealthy, and so checking aspiration. This is a flip-side version of the moral hazard argument: if you penalise people for behaving well (in capitalist terms), then they will stop doing so, income-generation will be lost, and we will all become poorer.[57]

The Oxford economist* Paul Collier has offered a further development to counter this line of thinking: 'In future, taxation needs to make distinctions based less on how much money has been made, and more on how it has been made.' Context is king: if someone has earned their money from gainful employment, they should be taxed high, but not prohibitively so; if they have earned their money from stockpiling assets, they should be taxed very highly indeed. So, the barons of the asset economy – whose money

---

* Writing in the *Times Literary Supplement*, the paper I edit. Pick up your copy today!

is locked in property or bonds, serving no public good – should have to cough up. To Collier, this would be concentrated in the metropolis: 'London is a vast reserve of unexploited potential: it is the new oil.' Titans of industry, or even those working in services who have done well for themselves, would be protected. The moral arguments of the left and the right can be satisfied; the national arguments about north-south divides would be addressed, because the wealth of the latter will be put to use to address the poverty of the former.

Once we have accepted that Adam Smith's 'free hand' needs some guidance, we can look elsewhere. We have seen that the growth of modern capitalism has shifted the motives of companies from innovation and consolidation to short-term 'shareholder value maximisation'. In Germany* large corporations have two-tier structures: a management board and a supervisor board (half of whom are workers, who have to approve decisions). Theresa May flirted with the idea of enforcing this structure, and then got distracted by Brexit. But our new interventionist capitalism could return to it.

Unequal salaries can also be considered in this context. Jeremy Corbyn offered up, in January 2017, the idea of a 'maximum earnings limit' of, say, £1 million.[58] As with lots of ideas by Jeremy Corbyn at that period (before his resurrection as an electoral force in the spring of 2017), the blithering execution was suspect, but the motivation was not. Many people with stagnant wages are rightly appalled at CEOs who earn 300 or 400 times the amount they do (and whose salaries have risen 80 per cent in the last decade). Perhaps if a worker-led supervisory board had to approve the CEO package, such abuse would be reduced.

The public sector could attempt more large infrastructure projects (very much including housing), funded by government, in order to keep the economy stimulated. This is against the philosophy of austerity, and instead approaches the currently low interest rates as an opportunity to increase borrowing for the purposes of building.

---

* Not coincidentally still a major manufacturing country, with a comparatively small financial sector.

In 2010 this would have felt politically unlikely, as one of the messages from the Conservatives in the election was that Labour public spending had got out of control. But the left–right split on borrowing seems to have shifted a bit. Donald Trump swept to power[59] on the back of a policy of a $1 trillion infrastructure programme. When both major political parties in Britain were in search of leaders in 2016, borrowing to invest was a policy that oddly came from both sides of the political spectrum.[60] It still remains on the table as a viable option.

Under Jeremy Corbyn, too, the spectre of nationalisation has arisen once more: a desire for the state to control industry for the benefit of the taxpayer. This does not have an entirely happy history, as we have seen. There is, however, something of a persistent clamour for it in the rail sector, which has seen appalling performance in its current privatised state: prices rising with inflation, not wage increases (a staggering 30 per cent between 2010 and 2018); passengers losing 3.6 million hours a year due to delays. Whether or not you feel government-run services would function better is, perhaps, a question of politics. As it stands, there is a sense that – in our railway system – the private contracting between the government and rail providers means, ultimately, that profit is ensured for a few companies, and loss is underwritten by the rest of us.

In all these debates (and we could have one about the energy market too), it is simply no use for free marketeers to argue about interference. There is a belief that somehow the freedom of markets is connected to personal freedom, that interfering with it is tantamount to accepting economic slavery from the state.[61] As we have seen, this is not historically true: the two high points of capitalism (the Victorian period for the British and American nations; the post-war period for the wider world) were powered by state intervention of one sort or another. It was the interventionist economics of Keynes that prevented the banking crisis from becoming the second Great Depression. The status quo of free-market thinking cannot sustain itself: bolder, more meddlesome ideas are needed. In the 'miracle economy' of Korea in the 1960s, for example, the government intervened to ensure that a company, the LG Group, could not enter the textile industry but had to focus on electronic cables. That is now the basis of its entire business.

Then, take this whopper of a conundrum: in the next ten years, 1.2 billion people will enter the labour market. However, in the next thirty years, the rise of automation (most visible in things like driverless cars, drone deliveries and the like) will place up to 30 per cent of jobs at risk.[62] How will the free market respond to that? Our economy has already shifted from manufacturing to services; what happens when those services become automated?

One mooted solution is to consider something called the Universal Basic Income. The idea is that the state pays – to everybody, without means-testing – a basic income, which can then be supplemented by other sources. This does not necessarily disincentivise aspiration or work, because those seeking to improve their financial lot could still do so. What it would do – in theory – is allow people to live in dignity without a job, freeing them up to pursue training and education, to enable them to search for employment that was either socially useful or personally satisfying. As we know, nobody can agree on the economic cost–benefit analysis of anything, and there is debate about whether such a scheme could work.[63] One would have to try to measure the benefits in health terms (people no longer subject to the stress and strain of working somewhere they hate), social terms (the end to the indignity of the dole queue) and economic terms (reduction in the bureaucracy of the welfare state), set against their possible costs (fostering laziness, shrinking the tax intake, freeing up people to pursue malign activities). Given what is coming over the next few years, these are equations worth sweating over.

Another solution, espoused by the Labour Party, is to compel companies who benefit from disruptive technology (Amazon, Uber and the like) to spend money on retraining people whose jobs disappear. Tories and free marketeers call this a tax on innovation, which is one way of looking at it. Another is that it is a necessary step to preserve social order and happiness. The first Industrial Revolution was a brutal moment in time for the luckless and the poor; we do not want the next one to be so callous, do we?

In any case the purpose of this book is not to define for you the possible future, but to help you (and me) to understand the systems that underpin any such decisions. Can economic interventionism be sustained within a capitalist framework? The answer is yes. But are we still left with the free-market creation of out-of-control banking? The answer is also yes. Our economy is a precarious, misunderstood thing; that is unlikely to change in the future.

2

Politics

In our age there is no such thing as 'keeping out of politics'. All issues are political issues, and politics itself is a mass of lies, evasions, folly, hatred and schizophrenia

George Orwell (1903–50)

One winter's day, I decide to kick my heels in the shabby environs of Westminster and Whitehall, that curious corner of central London that devotes itself so utterly to the running of the nation, so I can speak to various political types: special advisers, journalists, politicians themselves. The weather is suitably Dickensian: sputtering rain, glowering sky; the city animating itself as a muttering, scowling grouch. I end up in the shared office of Lord (Paddy) Ashdown, the former leader of the Liberal Democrats, who always retains a gleam in his eye whatever the political – or indeed the literal – weather. He is contemplative about the mess of British politics, sometimes urgently practical ('Westminster would be ten times better if it did ten times less'), sometimes plangently rhetorical: 'I am scared to death about the world; I am very worried about my country: politics breaks my heart.'

Ashdown is – as we shall see – somewhat triply marginalised: a Liberal Democrat, a Lord and an ardent Remain campaigner in the EU referendum. The Britain he perceives through those still gleaming eyes is not recognisably his Britain. And that itself represents a crucial point for us all to wrestle with: the extent, in our creakingly representative democracy, to which anyone speaks for the nation, or truly controls its destiny. 'Who governs Britain?', Heath's unanswered question, may not be properly answerable at all.

If you visit the British Parliament,[1] say to watch the weekly questioning of the Prime Minister,* you are immediately confronted by a paradox: this is living, breathing democracy, urgent and angry, at which the pulse of our ruling government can be seen visibly to throb and quicken; it is also an act, a show at which all the players are complicit in impressing upon a largely uninterested country their own symbolic importance.

I've visited PMQs more than once, and always come away with a combination of excitement and mild dismay: the hooting and braying, all the naked tribalism within that Gormenghast of an old building (mice occasionally scurrying between your legs, as you veer into a Gothic nook or creaking corridor). It is, like everything we have seen and shall see in this book, a very British mess.

In early autumn 2017, I show up on a Wednesday to watch Theresa May, clinging limply to power, hold forth against questions from the Leader of the Opposition, Jeremy Corbyn. All that theoretical excitement has faded already. She stands to muted cheers and jeers, her own side sullen and unforgiving of her disastrous decision to have a snap election; the Labour benches opposite her torn between relishing her weakness and self-conscious regret that their own leader has proven too popular to unseat. The Prime Minister gives the standard answer to the first standard question: if she will list her formal engagements for the day.[†] And then . . . well, not much happens. There is some desultory sparring. MPs bob up and down like clockwork creations, trying to catch the Speaker's eye so they can get their moment of televised glory. The political journalists, seated up high, take few notes, instead tweeting instantly evaporated thoughts about the proceedings. Civil servants emotionlessly watch

---

* Tony Blair, who was good at them, called Prime Minister's Questions 'the most nerve-racking, discombobulating, nail-biting, bowel-moving, terror-inspiring, courage-draining experience'. A serious of epithets he could have more profitably applied to the decision-making process of going to war, a cynic might say.
† Here's why the PM always has to answer this question. Before Margaret Thatcher, Prime Ministers could dodge questions by referring them to someone else in government. So a ruse was cooked up: the PM had to be asked about his personal schedule, which only he could answer; the real question could then be asked in supplementary fashion, with no dodging possible.

in the corner, careful to note whether any of their work was being destroyed in an idle answer. A miasma of bored desperation hovers above proceedings.

When it is over, I troop with other journalists into a back room where spokespeople first for May, then for Corbyn, take turns to be encircled and prodded. There are hardly any women there; there are hardly any non-white faces. Everybody is comfortable in their role: the reporters asking questions they don't expect to be answered; the spokespeople confident in their ability not to answer them. I potter off to lunch in an echoey chamber, where I get the sort of cabbagey, starchy meal you might imagine people were served at a minor public school in the 1930s. A minor scene, all in all, in the great play of our parliamentary democracy, endlessly repeated across the days and weeks and years. Repeated in the devolved parliaments of Scotland, Wales and Northern Ireland; in the council chambers of towns and counties across the country. The fruits of our democratic activity, our votes, their promises, and all the old structures that creak but just about hold British politics in place. Let's try to explain them, if we can.

The Palace of Westminster – where Parliament is physically located – was once a real palace until Henry VIII fancied a bit more swiving room and moved further into west London. Its current fixtures and fittings are not as old as they look: the fire of 1834 destroyed much of the site, and the chamber of the House of Commons took another blast during the Second World War. The only old bit remaining is the wonderful Westminster Hall, a magisterial cavern of a place overarched by an ancient beamed roof, dating back to the medieval period, used mainly for show now. But the institution itself is, of course, venerable. Parliament really dates back to 1265, when representatives of towns were summoned by Simon de Montfort on behalf of Henry III. By the fourteenth century, there was a clear division based on status: the men from the shires and boroughs (the Commons), the magnates (the Lords Temporal) and the clergy (the Spiritual). The class divide was formalised into two locations, which we still preserve: the House of Commons and the House of Lords.

By the end of the seventeenth century, following the two revolutions of the preceding 100 years, the sovereignty of Parliament was fully asserted in the Bill of Rights (1689). This document set out, to the incoming monarchs William and Mary, how the country was to be run.★ In essence, it made clear that taxes could only be levied, or laws suspended, with the consent of Parliament. The sidelining of the monarchy in terms of actual government was set in place, although – as we will see – not entirely.

How we vote: a very brief history

And so we started to see the beginnings of the democracy we enjoy and endure today. It has been a slow, painful journey to the current position. In the eighteenth century Parliament was the preserve – more or less – of the elite in terms of who could vote and who could be elected, and, if we believe William Hogarth, who painted *Humours of an Election* in 1754, an opportunity for everyone else either to ignore it, or spend the time getting drunk and copping off with one another. We might profitably recall Edmund Blackadder here: 'Marvellous thing, democracy. Look at Manchester; population 60,000, electoral roll, 3.'

Blackadder was, if anything, understating the problem. Electoral reform became unstoppable (although plenty of people, especially in the House of Lords, tried to stop it) in the nineteenth century, when campaigners confronted the fact that major cities like Manchester, Leeds and Birmingham (all at the forefront of the Industrial Revolution) had no political representation at all. The nomination of half of all seats in the country was in the hands of single individuals. Change, laboriously fought for, started to happen. In 1819 a crowd of 80,000 gathered to protest in St Peter's Field,

★ The Bill of Rights also – due to sectarian concerns – gave Protestants the right to 'bear arms' within the law. Notice how we have never clung to this power. Contrast the Americans with their Second Amendment: a piece of legislation designed to allow an eighteenth-century militia the right to uphold state rights is fetishised to enable modern-day barbarians to have machine guns. The British lack of a proper constitution (the Bill of Rights being a faint imitation) is often criticised, but look what the Americans sometimes do with theirs.

Manchester, and were charged upon by cavalry. The resultant Peterloo Massacre, named after the recent battle in Belgium, led in the short term to strong measures of government suppression, but became emblematic of the fight for enfranchisement.* The First Reform Act of 1832 allowed many of those with property to vote; the Second Reform Act of 1867 increased the franchise to 2.4 million men; the Secret Ballot Act of 1872 changed the psychology of voting, by making it a private act, thus enabling people to shift sides more easily; the Third Reform Act of 1884 brought the franchise up to 5.7 million, about six in every ten men. It wasn't until 1918 that universal suffrage for men over twenty-one arrived, though, along with that of women over thirty. Full enfranchisement of all women came ten years later. Today, of course, almost everyone over eighteen can vote in general elections[†] (the exceptions being prisoners and the severely mentally ill), although it is striking that 6 million adults are currently not registered to do so.

When we do vote, we use the First Past the Post System (FPPS), a phrase nobody in hundreds of years has managed to improve into something more elegant. In each of the 650 constituencies in Britain, the outright winner with the most votes is elected as an MP. The party with the most MPs becomes the government. It is simple and comprehensible. It is also, at one reading, deeply unfair. Look at UKIP in 2015: they had 4 million votes, but spread thinly over multiple constituencies, and ended up with one MP. In the same election, in Scotland, the SNP won just under half of the total votes, but had the majority in 95 per cent of constituencies. In that election, it took 27,000 votes to elect one SNP MP; and 4 million to elect one UKIP MP. This system can disenfranchise voters, because

---

* It also prompted the creation of the *Manchester Guardian*, later just the *Guardian*, which may be regarded as a mixed blessing.
† In 2015, Scotland voted to lower the voting age to sixteen in Scottish and local elections (having lowered the age for the 2014 referendum). Wales is now following Scotland's lead. It is fair to say that Conservatives, not exactly popular with the politically engaged teenage demographic, are reluctant to see this spread further. That is why David Cameron was unwilling to countenance it for the EU referendum, although it probably would have won it for him.

it creates safe seats where crushing majorities render dissent mean-ingless. About 26 million people live in safe seats; that's a lot of frustrated voters.

So what are the alternatives?

I'll be as brief as I possibly can. There is Alternative Vote (AV), in which a voter puts a number by candidates by order of preference. If no candidate gets more than half of the first votes, second preferences are counted. This way means that, generally, either the most popular or a compromise candidate overall will win. It is still based on indi-vidual constituencies, though, and so does not create a proportionate result to the nation as a whole. There is Single Transferable Vote (STV): voters in larger areas rank candidates in order of preference, and groups of MPs are elected as a result. This tends to help independent candi-dates, who can sneak into the group by virtue of individual popularity (and so organised parties tend not to favour it). It is used in Northern Ireland and Scottish local elections, and in Australia.

How about proportional representation, which is the most popular method in the world, and is the means by which we (used to) elect MEPs to the European Parliament? Essentially, the ballot paper lists political parties, and the number of MPs reflects the percentage of the overall vote won by their party. Each vote counts, but there is little relationship between the elected MP and the community, and very often the result is a broad coalition of parties (which, as we shall see, may or may not be a good thing). Finally, there is the Additional Member System (AMS), used in the Scottish Parliament, the Welsh Assembly and the London Assembly. Under AMS, voters get two votes: one for a candidate and one for a party. The former allows single-member constituencies to be elected, but those figures are buttressed by regional representatives that reflect the overall party vote. This seems like the most sensible one, if you think about it.

It should be obvious that voting reform is of great interest to small parties, and a bother to the larger ones. It has not had an entirely happy history as a result. Under Tony Blair, flush with a huge majority and an appetite for name-making change, a proposal was raised to develop something unappetisingly called AV Plus, not dissimilar to the AMS system described above. He got cold feet, presumably when he thought about its impact on his majority. The idea lingered, though. When time for coalition arrived in 2010, the Liberal Democrats made a referendum on AV electoral form a condition of their membership of government.

You may have been forgiven for not paying attention to the wrangle that ensued, but it remains one of the very few referendums in our national history, and is useful in its tactical foreshadowings of the recent Brexit campaign. On 5 May 2011, 42 per cent of people voted, and the outcome was clear: 68 per cent said no to AV, and 32 per cent said yes. The central thrust of the 'no' campaign (many of whose agents resurfaced in the Leave movement five years later) was that any change was too expensive and disruptive. They put forward a figure of £250 million as the cost of AV: it was based on dubious accounting, was widely discredited, widely remembered and probably won the day. They didn't put it on a bus, at least. But the debate wasn't so much Project Fear as Project Meh: the BBC modelled every election since 1983 and concluded that the result would have been more or less the same under AV, and nobody – apart from the Lib Dems★ – got very excited about it.

So we have been left with a system by which 650 constituencies get individual, discrete Members of Parliament, but as a nation we get ruled by one of two (or occasionally up to three) parties. Let's look at the history of the party system.

Party games†

Britain has had a two-party system for much of its political history, but real tribalism has been a twentieth-century invention. By the eighteenth century, the two groups were the Whigs and the Tories,

★ Paddy Ashdown is still angry about it: 'Referendums never work; Hitler benefited from four of them.'
† Yes, I did take this from the title of a *Yes Minister* episode, and yes, I am trying my hardest not to fill this chapter with *Yes Minister* quotes.

both rooted – and this is a much overlooked factor in the development of British politics generally – in sectarianism. The Whigs were originally Protestants, who eventually developed policies leaning towards religious tolerance (and so evolved into the Liberal Party). The word Tory comes from a Gaelic term *toraighe*, which means 'pursuer', describing the Catholic Irish who wished to cling to their lands. As the term developed, it lost its Catholic meaning, and came to describe people who stood for Church and country (especially the rights of landowners) more generally. When Ireland joined with the United Kingdom in the Act of Union (1801), most Tories actually argued against full Catholic emancipation, their ideological focus shifted and they became the Conservative Party as a result (the nickname stuck, though).

The eighteenth and nineteenth centuries were dominated by great individuals, rather than great political tribes.[2] What united politicians was their share in the vested interests of the land they felt they possessed: they had more in common with each other than they did with the people they scarcely purported to serve.[3] Governments joined in coalition, and then fell apart; personalities squabbled and schemed. In 1809 the Minister of War, Lord Castlereagh,[4] actually fought a duel with the Foreign Secretary, George Canning, over (true) claims the latter had been trying to overthrow the former. When Castlereagh sent a long letter demanding satisfaction, Canning replied he would rather fight than read it. At 6 a.m. on Putney Heath, the two met. Both fired shots; both missed. Canning refused to back down, and fired again, his bullet striking a button on Castlereagh's coat and bouncing harmlessly away. Castlereagh then shot Canning in the thigh. The two remained colleagues, but Canning's career, like his leg, was blighted thereafter.

The Conservative Party itself is said to have been birthed in the Tamworth Manifesto of 1834, in which its leader Robert Peel (whom we'll meet again, in his role as father of the modern police force, in Chapter 6) set forth his definition of conservatism. Essentially, it was the idea that the party should be 'strong and stable' under competent leadership. Do feel free to make your own jokes here. The journalist Walter Bagehot called Peel a 'very good administrator', which is what all Tory leaders since have aspired to be.

Meanwhile, the Liberal Party was being established as an alternative to Conservatism. Lord Palmerston, a man who dominated the mid-Victorian period, had been a Whig and a Tory before becoming the first Liberal Prime Minister, after the party was formally recognised in 1859. The division in politics was based on two key areas: free trade vs protectionism (the Conservatives favouring the latter); emancipation vs suppression of Catholics (ditto). It was Peel, however, who repealed the protectionist Corn Laws in 1846, which heralded – in the minds of some – the beginnings of globalisation. Individual men shaped policy more than party ever did. It is not a coincidence that it is a Victorian historian, Thomas Carlyle[5] (whom we will regrettably meet later in this book), who said that 'the history of the world is but the biography of great men'; it is an accurate summary of the politics of his age.

The next Liberal Leader was William Gladstone, who eventually served as Prime Minister four times.* He had been (as the history of these islands always has been) vexed by the Irish question. By the end of the century, there were around eighty Irish nationalists in Parliament, often controlling the balance of power. In 1886 Gladstone pushed the first Home Rule Bill, seeking to give Ireland political autonomy. It was voted down; another was kicked out by the House of Lords seven years later. But the die was cast: Ireland was going to get some power in some way. The Conservatives became ever more the party of union, if not with the whole of Ireland, at least with its northern province. By 1912, the Tory leader Andrew Bonar Law was willing to foment violence in support of this stance, stumping around the region with hints of sanctioned uprising: 'I can imagine no length of resistance to which Ulster will go, in which I shall not

---

* I write with heavy heart that his legacy has already been challenged by Liverpool students who wish to remove his name from a housing block. This is on the basis that Gladstone, whose father made his money from slavery, was insufficiently vocal in his career in condemning the institution that had given his family wealth. Liverpool University in 2017 campaigned to hold a 'preferendum' into the name of the Roscoe and Gladstone halls of residence, with a proposal to commemorate *Channel 4 News* presenter Jon Snow instead. A fine reader of news, but not – it must be said – one of the greatest leaders of the nation in our history. I hate modern life sometimes.

be ready to support them, and in which they will not be supported by the overwhelming majority of the British people.'

A Home Rule Act was passed in 1914, but was suspended by the advent of the First World War. Frustrated at the delay and the historical intransigence of the British, a handful of Irish republicans initiated the famous armed insurrection of 1916 (the Easter Rising), which was brutally suppressed by the British government in a way that, eloquently, was to make the case for independence even stronger. In 1920 (with the Irish nationalist party Sinn Fein holding seventy-three seats), the Government of Ireland Act was passed, which split the island into two provinces, both of which were intended to remain part of the Union. A revolt ensued (the Irish war of independence), which led to the creation of the free Republic of Ireland in 1922. Irish influence in British politics simmered down for a while, only to return (as we shall see) in recent times.

In any event, by the turn of the twentieth century we had a Liberal Party that supported an independent Ireland and free trade,[6] and a Conservative Party that didn't (but soon would concede both points). And a new party was on the horizon, spurred both by the gradual enfranchisement of working men and the rise in the second half of the Victorian period of the trade union movement.

Modern politics: the rises and falls of Labour

The Labour Party began as a mechanism to get trade union voices heard in Parliament, and its origins lie in something called the Labour Representation Committee of 1900. As manual workers got the vote, the thinking was that such a force would become unstoppable in British politics. Marx wrote, in regard to universal suffrage, that 'its inevitable result, here, is the supremacy of the working class'. As so often, he was wrong. And as we shall see, the 'working class' (however we so define it; and we'll have a go in Chapter 8) has often voted Conservative, sometimes predominantly so. The story of Labour in the twentieth century is one of some success (eight out of twenty elections since the war), amid many failures, but it is not a story solely based on elevation by the tears and toil of the working classes.

And the reasons for that go right back to the beginning. The ideals of Marx, for example, were internationalist, regarding working men as the same around the world. The ideals of many of those men themselves, though, were resolutely nationalist: suspicious of intruders into their already strained economy, proud of their local backgrounds.* Labour has often found itself drifting into debates that move away from the basic principles of their audience: in the early years, it flirted dangerously with pro-temperance;† in later years, with anti-military, pro-disarmament rhetoric that sounded feeble in the ears of the patriotic. Meanwhile, the Conservatives have remained ever clear on their imperialism, their jingoism, their unionism, a consistency that has attracted at least a respectable amount of white working-class voters.[7]

In the beginning, Labour was a cuckoo in the Liberals' nest. The former joined with the latter in Parliament by 1906, contributing twenty-nine MPs to a sort of coalition of opposition. Members today will recognise the tensions that existed from the start: was the Labour Party compromising itself in search of power; was socialism being betrayed?‡ Progress was slow: when women got the vote in 1918, they did not flock to the Labour cause especially (not helped by Labour leader Ramsay MacDonald calling suffragettes 'pettifogging middle-class damsels', it must be said).

However, after Conservative Prime Minister Andrew Bonar Law[8] died of throat cancer in 1922, his successor, Stanley Baldwin, decided to call a snap election to get a personal mandate. It went disastrously wrong. A hung Parliament ensued, with Labour on sixty fewer seats than the Conservatives, but theoretically supported by a strong Liberal Party. The King asked MacDonald to form a government, and Labour sneaked into power for the first time.

It did not go well. Churchill, groping as ever for a killer phrase,

---

* We see this tension in the party today: Corbyn is ideologically pro-immigration; many of his party are, to say the least, not.
† It may or may not have been Marx who said that 'drink is the curse of the working classes'; it was certainly Oscar Wilde who offered more correctly that 'work is the curse of the drinking classes.'
‡ Had Twitter existed the clarion call would have gone out from chippy socialists: 'Why don't you just fuck off and join the Liberals' etc.

called it 'a national misfortune such as usually has befallen a great state only on the morrow of a defeat in war'. The left of the party immediately accused Labour of not being socialist enough in government. Meanwhile, the right-wing press accused it of being at the vanguard of a communist conspiracy. This was a *Daily Mail** headline just days before the 1924 election: 'Civil war plot by socialists. Moscow order to our reds. Great plot disclosed yesterday'. It was an early example of #fakenews, though: the *Mail* was publishing a letter purportedly from Gregor Zinoviev, President of the Communist International, which called upon all socialists to unleash a class war; it was actually a forgery by Russian aristocrats, trying to get support for their own anti-communist crusade back home. No matter: it symbolised the threat of the left to the status quo.

We can see all the elements of the modern Labour Party at play here: a fear it cannot be trusted with serious government; its own self-loathing for wanting to try; the desire to be socialist but not too socialist. In any event, the Tories romped home with the largest majority of the century: 210 seats. The damage was not, however, permanent. Labour had been the party of power, and that could now never be erased. When the economic crash of the 1930s happened, a National government was formed of all three parties, but was led for the first five years by MacDonald. Again, the practicalities of being in charge were too much for the ideologues on the left: the party split once more. It was the Conservatives who led the coalition into the end of the decade and the war: under Baldwin, Neville Chamberlain† and, of course, Winston Churchill.

---

* Yes, the *Mail* has been publishing splashes aggravating the left for at least a century!

† Chamberlain has been badly treated by history, and probably correctly so. The Liberal leader David Lloyd George said he was like 'a good mayor of Birmingham in an off year'. He will for ever be known for the policy of appeasement towards Hitler, culminating in the Munich Agreement of 30 September 1938, by which Germany was allowed to annex part of Czechoslovakia. Chamberlain famously said the deal meant 'peace for our time'. He was widely praised (*The Times* pompously said 'no conqueror returning from a victory on a battlefield had come adorned with nobler laurels'). He was utterly wrong. He was forced to resign, following British defeat in Norway at the beginning of the war (although much of the blame for that, ironically, was Churchill's).

The war was crucial for the future success of Labour: suddenly there was a remorseless confluence of factors in its favour. Most obviously, conflict is ever the bloody herald of change; it smashes the status quo. Nye Bevan (the architect of the NHS, whom we shall meet properly in Chapter 3) said this: 'War opens minds that were sealed, stimulates dormant intelligence and recruits into political controversy thousands who would otherwise remain in the political hinterland.'

In 1942 a survey showed that 40 per cent of people had changed their minds about their political allegiances. The sands were shifting for the first time in British society in decades. The First World War had not unseated a government, because the National Coalition (dominated by Liberals and Tories) had stood in 1918 on a stability ticket, indeed had fused together so successfully a permanent alliance of parties had been on the cards. The situation in 1945 was different. Labour continued to politick hard throughout the war, developing ideas and staging party conferences. The Tories under Churchill focused on the war itself, and wanted the coalition to continue in the immediate aftermath. Labour refused, sensing an epochal opportunity. Churchill was exhausted,[9] his party was still tainted by the appeasement of Hitler under Chamberlain,[10] and socialism was on the rise again. Communist Russia had been a recent ally (and murmurs of Stalin's brutality had not become deafening) and its successful industrialisation an example of the value of collective effort; Britain's own wartime nationalisation had demonstrated that state-led projects could be efficient and productive; and ultimately a country that had sacrificed so much for so long wanted something back in return.

There was the largest ever swing (12 per cent) towards Labour in the 1945 election: Clement Attlee became Prime Minister with a majority of 146, and set about changing the country for good, nationalising industry, creating the welfare state and the NHS in what the sociologist T. H. Marshall called 'a British revolution'. What is surprising is not that his government's legacy was so great (we live in a country still shaped by Attlee), but that its survival was so short. Just five years later, the majority was slashed to an unworkable twelve, and by 1951 another election saw the return of Churchill with his own small majority.

It is slightly hard to fathom the collapse at this remove: it would be akin to Blair being booted out in 2001. In fact, the very causes of the original landslide counted against Labour: it overstretched on nationalisation, failing to show that it had brought increased prosperity, now having the sugar industry needlessly in its sights; communism began to cast a longer and creepier ideological shadow from the East; and the continuation of rationing became intolerable as the war receded into the past. The first two points are illustrative more generally: Labour is always torn between ideology and practicality, the left and the centre; it can balance them for a period, but ultimately is sundered at some point.

Meanwhile, the Conservatives prospered along with the nation, winning three elections on the bounce, the last of which in 1959 under Harold Macmillan increased their majority (the only third-term government in British history to do so) to more than 100 seats. Labour was uncomfortable with the rise of consumerism (Bevan said 'This so-called affluent society is an ugly society'); the Tories gloried in it. Their slogan in 1959 stands for their clarion call in every election since, not involving Tony Blair: 'Life's better under the Conservatives. Don't let Labour ruin it'.

Labour was meanwhile brawling about nuclear disarmament and Europe, and internal divisions about the direction of the party. Thank God it has stopped doing that. Macmillan was eventually brought down by a sex scandal[11], the Profumo affair, and the sense he was too heavily influenced by Old Etonian cronies. Labour, upon the death of their leader, elected a centrist with real ambition,[12] destined to transform the fortunes of the party. Here is one golden rule of British public life: everything has happened before in politics.

Harold Wilson took office with a tiny minority in 1964, and a load of financial woes. As James Callaghan assumed the role of Chancellor, his predecessor Reginald Maudling stuck an insouciant head around the door to say: 'Sorry to leave such a mess, old cock.'*

---

* You might recall the note left by Liam Byrne, Labour Chief Secretary to the Treasury, in 2010 to the new government. It simply said: 'I'm afraid there is no money.' He subsequently has claimed that he still 'burnt with shame' about it and apologised. I am not sure it was that bad, honesty and gallows humour being distinctive British traits.

But the new Prime Minister was brave: he called a snap election in 1966 and got a healthy enough majority to become a legitimate heir to Attlee. It was under Wilson that Britain started to modernise, culturally: the death penalty was abolished; abortion was legalised; homosexuality was decriminalised;* the iniquitous system of grammar schools – as we shall see – was permanently damaged. He went in to the 1970 election ahead in the polls, which turned out to be catastrophically wrong, and the Tories entered the decade in government under cheerless Ted Heath.

The seventies was a time of poor government and economic crisis, in which the Conservatives eventually found unity and salvation behind the first female Prime Minister in our history. Labour divided and argued, its militant left agitating with more abandon, the consequences of its economic policies perceived as ruinous. Thatcher took power with a majority of forty-three and an inflation rate of 21 per cent; by her second re-election, inflation was down to 2.4 per cent and her majority remained above 100. She had an ideology and opportunity: an opponent riven by internal discord and a mandate fundamentally to change economic conditions to kick-start a revival.

It is here that the Liberals return briefly to our story. The twentieth century (as indeed is true of its successor) has not been kind to the party. The establishment of free trade, the answering of the Irish question lost them their ideological point of difference; the role of providing a home for anti-establishment protest was then taken by Labour. The Liberals were without purpose; they had been shouldered out of history.† In 1981, though, they formed an alliance with a brand-new party: the Social Democrats, created by a 'gang of four' disgruntled Labour grandees, who were concerned about Labour militancy over disarmament and anti-European sentiment. The SDP took twenty-eight MPs with them (twenty-seven from Labour, a solitary soul from the Conservatives), and began to

---

* With much holding of noses it must be said. Labour's deputy leader, Lord George-Brown said at one point: 'I don't regard any sex as pleasant. It's pretty undignified.'
† One of my favourite political quotations is from the poet Robert Frost: 'A liberal is a man too broadminded to take his own side in a quarrel.' It captures the self-nullifying essence of it as a political movement.

campaign. The net result was that the SDP-Liberal axis took 25 per cent of the vote in 1983, splitting the natural enemies of the Conservatives and essentially handing Margaret Thatcher the keys to the country for a decade. In 1988 the SDP and Liberals merged to form the Liberal Democrats, which has been resolutely the third party of politics since, the damage to the left done.

The damage to the right soon followed. Thatcher's government was crippled by hubris and the European question (which I have been putting off; but which is on its way in this book). In the waning years of the empress's court, financial woes came in the form of spiking inflation (further compromised by Britain's entry into, and then humiliating exit from, the Exchange Rate Mechanism)[13], political disasters in the form of the poll tax,[14] and internal enemies finally willing to stop Thatcher from going 'on and on' indefinitely. Against all odds, the Major government that followed won the 1992 election, which was about the worst thing that could have happened to it (it began with a majority of twenty-one, and ended with a minority of four). The stage was set for the arrival of Tony Blair, and a newly invigorated Labour Party, seeking to rule from the centre of British politics.

This Labour government led to improvements on the domestic front, as we shall see in much of the pages that follow. It was lucky too, as it presided over an economy ready to boom once more. By 2001, it had held on to a vast majority, and was spending money all over the place on public services that were being reinvigorated as a result. Blair was Attlee and Wilson combined, and on amphetamines, if without the social conscience. The left of the party, sidelined and chuntering as they had been for decades, were more or less silenced: Labour was in power and popular, so what traction could they have? Their plight was personified by a scruffy, bearded nobody on the back benches, a cross-legged CND activist, always ready to vote against the government, while harping on about things like an independent Ireland and a predatory Israel, happiest when earnestly debating disarmament and disparaging America. A true believer, a crank. Oh, Jeremy Corbyn. An anachronism whose time – though nobody knew it – was about to come.

Abroad, Blair was as bad, as catastrophically, damagingly bad as

Neville Chamberlain. The decision to go to war in Iraq in support of America, without proper evidence of a clear and present threat from Saddam Hussein's government, was – and will be ever – Blair's Munich moment. It has destroyed his legacy,* which indeed started to slip from his hands even when in power. In 2005 the majority was halved, and the anti-war Liberal Democrats were in the best position to profit for almost a century. Blair handed over power to Gordon Brown in 2007, as he had promised to do,[15] but things were swiftly souring. Brown did not do a Wilson and call a snap election, which he might have won. He smouldered instead within Number 10, and became a victim of what Harold Macmillan had winningly called 'events, dear boy, events'. In this case the banking crisis, which crippled the economy (as we now know, more or less permanently) and meant that – whatever else might happen in the 2010 election – there was not going to be another Labour government.

By now, of course, other parties were stirring, sensing the chance to seek popularity amid the disruption. UKIP, under charismatic (to some) leader Nigel Farage, grew fat and dominant on the twin questions of Europe and immigration. Nationalism in Scotland, a generally more inclusive version of its southern cousin, took on a post-devolution, pre-independence-referendum (we'll get to both of those things) sense of urgency, as the Scottish National Party, dominant in its own Parliament, sought to become more influential in the national version. The Scottish question became the Irish question of the day, for a while. The votes splintered everywhere: Tories lost some to UKIP, Labour to the SNP, both (a bit) to the Liberal Democrats. The dominance of the Blair years, in a totemic party led by a totemic figure, seemed long ago.

Disraeli once said that 'England does not love coalitions', and there was some truth in it. We certainly have a voting system, in

---

* I spent three years hosting political phone-ins on LBC Radio, and can say without fear of contradiction that Blair is now the most toxic character in the history of modern British politics. If you did an hour on Margaret Thatcher, you got a balance of (agitated) opinions; the same was true of Putin, Trump, Corbyn et al. With Blair, you had to screen the screeching calls carefully, and even then still ended up with a procession of angry people demanding that he be executed for war crimes.

the UK as a whole, that means it rarely happens, except in emergencies. Coalitions were present through both world wars and the economic crisis of the 1930s; before that they were even more common. So it was perhaps unsurprising that our own Great Depression created a climate for a government in the national interest: this time the Conservatives and the Liberals clubbing together. For a while, it was then said that the future of British government would *only* be that of coalitions, thus conforming to a major law in political reporting: the broader the prediction, the more likely it is to be disproved quickly. In 2015, therefore, the Conservatives scraped a small majority, and David Cameron was compelled to honour his promise of a referendum on membership of the EU (which he almost certainly felt would never happen, because he thought it would be blocked by a future Lib Dem coalition partner). Britain and its politics were set to change for ever. The most revolutionary, and simultaneously most enervating, issue in our domestic political history had arrived: Brexit.

We are almost up to date with our party politicking, and we have not even touched upon funding. In brief: parties must declare all annual donations over £7,500. The cliché is that the Tories are 'funded by the elite' and Labour is 'in hock to the unions'. There is more than a grain of truth in both claims. What is clear is that large donations from vested interests have the capacity to create undue influence in our political system. In 2011 the parties were asked to consider how to fix this; they couldn't even remain in the same room together when they tried.

In 2017 there came another general election, when Theresa May tried to do a Harold Wilson and ended up doing a Stanley Baldwin, or an Edward Heath. 'Who rules the country?' she might have asked. 'Nobody at all,' came the testy reply. Before we explain that, we should first focus on what the aim of it all has been: the process of government, the actual practice of power.

How Parliament works

The Conservative Prime Minister Arthur Balfour called our system of democracy 'government by explanation', suggesting that power lies in the hands of the ruling party, which merely uses Parliament as a conduit for making clear more or less what it is up to. This has a deal of truth in it. When I spoke to Paddy Ashdown, he pointed out with grim relish that a dominant government could 'send all the Jews in Britain into a gas chamber', and there would not be a ready constitutional means of stopping it.

At present, Parliament operates within a fixed term of five years (following legislation from the Coalition government in 2011, concerned that their flimsy marriage would not last long enough to create stability). As we saw in 2017, this was merely a polite fiction. Theresa May was able to have an election simply by indicating that she would like one. Labour could have refused to co-operate, of course, but would have looked terminally frit (to use the parliamentary phrase).[16] Parliaments have generally been supposed to last five years, but – before 2015 – none since 1945 had actually done so (the average is a little over three years).

The government every year sets out what legislation it wants to achieve, but, being British, it does so by ventriloquising the Queen, who reads out its plans amid much pomp and pageantry. We are, after all, a constitutional monarchy in this country: Parliament is both a sovereign body and advises – in formal terms – the Sovereign herself. This manifests itself mainly at the level of colourful display. The day of the Queen's Speech is set-dressed like Hogwarts on PCP; there are processions and mummery displays, involving characters like Black Rod[17] and the Rouge Croix Pursuivant.[18] Parliament itself, lest we forget, is still summonsed every year as if the Queen had the power to invade Spain or harry the north: 'And We being desirous and resolved, as soon as may be, to meet Our people and have their advice in Parliament, do hereby make known unto all Our loving subjects Our Royal Will and Pleasure to call a Parliament.'

The Queen does, though, still wield some power, at a level that may make a republican quail a little. The Victorian journalist Walter Bagehot suggested that 'The sovereign has under a constitutional monarchy such as ours, three rights – the right to be consulted, the right to encourage, the right to warn.' Queen Elizabeth II has known thirteen Prime Ministers, and meets them on a weekly basis, able to cajole and communicate without scrutiny. It is the Queen who formally asks a Prime Minister to form a government, and can be the person to break the deadlock of a truly hung Parliament.[19] As a nation, we still crook the knee to inherited power, in a faintly puzzling fashion. Why should the opinion of an unelected figure, a figure selected by the simplest freak of birth from a family especially unlikely (due to its narrow gene pool) to produce someone of genuine brilliance, matter at all? Apparently, we should not examine this too closely. Bagehot again on the monarchy: 'Its mystery is its life. We must not let in daylight upon magic. We must not bring the Queen into the combat of politics, or she will cease to be reverenced by all combatants; she will become one combatant among many.'

Daylight is disinfectant, one might say, but let's not labour the point. The monarch has an odd role in our public life, but not a dominant one. Parliament, once it has licked all its spittle, is free to do its main job: allow the government of the day to make laws; otherwise make the government of the day as discomfited as possible. Most parliamentary business is government business: it will set out each year the bills it wants to see passed,[20] and then a clear process is followed to pass them, which I will summarise as briefly as I can.

Government bills can be proposed in either the House of Commons or the House of Lords. A bill is given a first reading without challenge. It then gets a second reading, prompting debate on the general thrust (rather than any specific detail), which can lead to amendment and vote (although this would generally be a disaster; the government last lost a vote at such a point in 1986). The bill then goes to committee stage, where it is scrutinised line by line, by either the whole house or a designated committee (whose make-up mirrors the party split in Parliament). Amendments are proposed* and either accepted or voted down. Then comes the report stage when it returns to the full chamber, and everyone can comment once more. The third reading is the final vote.

Once a bill has been passed by one house, it goes to the other. If significant changes are made, it will then 'ping-pong' between houses until a final version is agreed. Finally, it proceeds for Royal Assent[21] and becomes a law. What is clear is that a government with a huge majority (and a disciplined set of MPs) has the power to do whatever it likes. Votes (called 'divisions' because MPs literally divide themselves into 'Aye' and 'No' groups and pass through opposing lobbies) are controlled by party whips,† whose job it is to make sure people show up to vote the way they should.

The House of Commons

The House of Commons provides other diversions than the legislation of government business, however. Some time is allotted to opposition days, in which the other side can raise embarrassing issues and propose motions. A strong government can simply then whip its MPs to vote against them. Amazingly, as Theresa May has shown, a weak government can simply ignore them. In October 2017 the Labour Party proposed that the roll-out of the much derided Universal Credit system should be paused. It was a real policy proposal, but in a meaningless forum. The Tories could not be sure

* This process (detailed examination of complicated subjects by non-experts) is the reason why lobbyists have such power. An MP cannot be expected to understand every industry, so legitimately seeks the views of those who do. The consequence is a huge increase in the opportunity to influence legislation by those most affected by it: they pay companies to get in touch with politicians, give them briefings, write their speeches and so on. And MPs have occasionally got caught up in scandals as a result: the 'cab for hire' claims in 2010 that senior Labour former ministers would use their influence in return for fees; the 'cash for questions' scandal of 1994 in which Tories were alleged to have taken brown envelopes in return for asking questions in Parliament.
† Named after 'whippers in' who were responsible for driving the direction of hunts. We really are a funny country.

that some of their members would not agree with Labour, and so instructed them not to vote at all. The motion was passed unanimously; and literally nothing happened.

There is plenty that goes on in Parliament that is full of sound and fury, and not much else.[22] Most Private Members' Bills (ideas for laws that come from individuals, not government) begin and then run out of time before they have any chance of becoming laws; there are Ten-Minute Rule Bills, in which a doughty MP raises an often-worthwhile idea to no avail; there are Early Day Motions (EDMs), which are written proposals to which MPs can add their signature of support, and which then just sit there effectively dormant; and there are endless debates in Westminster Hall on non-binding issues.

The Speaker can make life harder for the government by controlling the business of the house in such a way as to require it to justify itself more often. This post officially dates back to 1376, and used to be the rather fraught role responsible for maintaining relations between Parliament and a growling, obstreperous monarch. Six were executed between 1471 and 1535. The job retains perks (salary of a Cabinet minister; no opposition in their constituency in a general election) and pomp (MPs are expected to bow as he passes), and also a sense of purpose. John Bercow, the incumbent* in 2017, may seem to the world to be a tiny, teak-toned show-off, but to backbenchers he is a hero: he regularly calls them to speak, he allows them urgent questions that might embarrass the government, and he makes sure respect is paid to their position.

The other area of parliamentary activity is the select committee. This institution used to be irregular and contingent on major events: one can imagine the pressures within the Committee for the Uniformity of Religion in 1571, for example, or the importance of the Sebastopol Committee of 1855, charged with looking at failures in the conduct of war.[23] The current formal system is recent. It was established in 1979, and agreed by Margaret Thatcher in a moment of early-inning nerviness, which I am sure she regretted. Now select

---

* The post has only been elected since 1992. MPs use a system of AV to select the Speaker, an irony that nobody seems to notice.

committees are formally attached to departments, and scrutinise their work and the issues that dominate their area. The government has to respond to their reports, and therefore is kept on its toes a little.

I have appeared before a select committee, and it is an odd experience. You sit before a semicircle of MPs, who are either leaning forward, ready to throw out a question, or almost recumbent, staring at their phones and wishing they were elsewhere. Behind you sits the audience (in my case, a single civil servant and an old lady who looked lost); to the left some reporters. The aim of the committee members is to say something so memorable it will be quoted on Twitter, TV or in newspapers the next day; the aim of the interrogated party is to say nothing interesting enough to be remembered at all. The latter, I am proud to say, happened with me.

I am being a little unfair, of course. These committees do much to challenge in public the major institutions of British life. They have free rein (and legal privilege) to poke and probe; and they mean that government departments always have to be conscious of their spending and their behaviour. They are part of the almost endless meetings to which hard-working MPs subject themselves when Parliament is in session.

The House of Lords

But what of the 'other place'? According to Paddy Ashdown, the House of Lords is a 'disgrace', an institution to which people are sent 'only if you are a friend of the Prime Minister or your great-grandmother slept with a king'. It is the second largest assembly in the world,[24] and full of people unelected to fulfil the important task of scrutinising the legislation of the country. Reform has been discussed, literally, for centuries, but without ever any genuine prospect of lasting change. Tony Blair in 1999 managed to remove most hereditary peers (the landed gentry) leaving a rump of ninety-two for tradition's sake.* When a hereditary peer dies, a mini by-election takes place, and a replacement is voted in by the others. It is a weird

---

* He also left twenty-six Lords Spiritual, who are Church of England bishops.

and typical irony that the only elected members of the House of Lords, then, are the hereditary ones.

The remainder get their ticket largely due to the patronage system: nominated by the Prime Minister, and by opposition groups. Around 50 per cent are there for purely party political reasons, as a reward for services rendered. This includes, of course, the donation of funds to specific parties. The Blair administration got caught up in the 'cash for honours' scandal, in which Tony Blair became the first Prime Minister to be interviewed by police in the course of a criminal investigation. No charges were filed. But the suspicion persists that, if you chuck a large amount of cash at a political group, you will first get influence then reward somewhere down the line. The House of Lords is a House of Rewards, without a doubt. Many are former MPs, 'kicked upstairs because they're so fucking useless', according to Ashdown, himself a Lord.* It is not a diverse bunch: 25 per cent of the Lords are ladies; 6 per cent are from ethnic minorities; and the average age is comfortably more than seventy. It wasn't until 2014 that Lords were allowed to retire; before that they seem to have simply expired in the role.

The power of the Lords is critical, if slightly circumscribed. It cannot, by tradition, amend bills from the Commons regarding 'aid and supplies', like Finance Bills following the budget. Nor will it vote down bills originating from policies set out in the elected government's manifesto. The House of Commons is, in the final analysis, sovereign: the two Parliamentary Acts of 1911 and 1949 (not coincidentally passed by reforming Liberal and Labour governments, worried about the truculence of a largely Tory House of Lords) mean that a bill passed in successive sessions by the Commons can be presented for Assent without the Lords' approval. This happened notably in the banning of fox-hunting in 2004 and the reduction of the age of gay consent to sixteen in 2000.

It is not entirely fair to see the Lords as a bastion of gouty conservatism, though. It was in this chamber that the Blair government's desire to hold terror suspects for forty-two days was defeated; that identity cards were rejected; and that the proposal to criminalise

---

* 'I'm here to bring down the system from the inside,' he tells me.

'insulting' words about religion was removed from the Racial and Religious Hatred Act. The Lords can act as the nation's conscience, especially in the face of a powerful government able largely to get its own way in the Commons.

It is not a bad life, either. Peers get £300 a day for attending, plus other expenses, and can leave as soon as they have clocked in. In 2016, 115 did not speak at all in the chamber, and 72 did not offer written questions or work on a committee either. At the moment, it is too easily dismissed as a retirement home for the politically entitled, whose vital role in our democracy is performed by the undemocratically unelected. The House of Lords is, and for ever will be, a cushier, dodgier number than the Commons.

Indeed, one question in British politics is never satisfactorily answered: why would anyone be an MP in the first place? Almost anybody can try to become one,* but why would you bother? They get paid well, but not amazingly so (around £75,000 a year)[25] plus expenses. The latter, indeed, got them into trouble in 2009, when a *Telegraph* investigation revealed the extent to which their incomes were being supplemented by outrageous claiming. Since then, this part of their income has been regulated by the Independent Parliamentary Standards Authority (IPSA),[26] which also sets their pay. MPs are held responsible in their local constituencies, but are really often powerless there: most pressing issues (schools, bins, roads) are controlled by the local authority, not Westminster. MPs can pass on letters of complaint, and fulminate on constituents' behalf, but not always help them. Meanwhile, they must spend their time when not in Parliament more or less pleading for votes: attending fetes and events, listening to bum-numbing speeches at schools, pandering to local members. Their job security is limited to five years at most.[27] Their every action is susceptible to scrutiny by the old media, and abuse on social media.

* You cannot be an MP if you have been bankrupt, in prison for more than a year, in the House of Lords or work as a paid agent of the state. The latter is why MPs who wish to resign are given meaningless state jobs: steward of one of 'Her Majesty's three Chiltern Hundreds of Stoke, Desborough and Burnham' or of the 'manor of Northstead'. There is no reason why MPs can't just resign, of course, but our public institutions do nothing simply if they can be done picaresquely.

The greasy pole[28]

Of course, MPs can seek to climb into positions of authority. Almost 140 make up the 'pay-roll' vote, which means that they are formally connected to the government as either ministers, or private parliamentary secretaries (junior MPs who support ministers). Their loyalty should be guaranteed, and their positions are contingent upon their supportive voting.

As a Secretary of State, in charge of a large department, an MP can expect more money, more prestige and an almost exponential increase in work. Each night, they are given a red box of material from their department, which will contain letters to sign, briefings to read and policy proposals to approve. It is almost impossible to handle with accuracy and promptness. This was Blairite minister Alan Milburn in 2004:

> It wouldn't be unusual for me to work an 18-hour day and be away from home for 6 days a week. I would return home on Friday night, having tried to spend Friday in my constituency in Darlington. So you walk through the door at 8 o'clock at night and the phone's already ringing and the fax machine is whirring and the emails are arriving . . . And you want to see the kids, and the kids want to see you, but actually there's a lot of business to be dealt with, and then you wake up on Saturday morning and the boxes arrive bright and early, and they sit there like a nagging toothache in the hallway, reminding you that actually you might be at home physically but mentally your mind is elsewhere.

It is not difficult to see how such pressure is neither good for an individual, or for government. Gladstone remarked that 'swimming for his life, a man does not see much of the country through which the river winds', and most successful politicians ultimately end their careers lacking a sense of proportion or even realism. Meanwhile, the very British mess gets messier, as each incumbent enters, demands change, becomes slowly more aware of the issues at hand, and then departs, never to return. The Labour demagogue Tony Benn said that 'new ministers come in with very little knowledge and a great deal of energy – and leave with a great deal of knowledge and very little energy.' Institutionalised entropy, followed by periodic chaos, is the result.

The government is supported by the Civil Service, who do their best to advise upon, and then implement, all this policy-making. Its numbers get trimmed every year, but still amount to more than 300,000. No matter how talented, and how numerous, the service is seeking to do the impossible: manage a massive system of implementation, the direction of which changes at least every five years, and often much more frequently. The government now spends £800 billion every year on trying to do things; it cannot – and does not – do them very well. The Labour MP Stella Creasy said that 'governments should not just start projects or policies – the public expect them to be able to finish them too. Essentially, implementation is as important as ideology in politics.' But ideology is easier, it always triumphs; implementation is always the next government's problem, or the next generation's.

Devolving powers away from the centre

In September 1997, in the aftermath of the Blair revolution, there were referendums held in Scotland and Wales on the subject of the putative expansion of their powers. In Wales the response was pretty muted: just 50 per cent turned out to vote, and just 50.3 per cent of them voted for a National Assembly, a Parliament of their own. The Scottish response was – and is – more vigorous on the subject: nearly 75 per cent voted for a Scottish Parliament, and 64 per cent for one with some degree of tax-varying powers.

The Scottish system led to the creation of 129 MSPs, selected using our old chum the Additional Member System, who themselves elect a First Minister, in turn creating an executive Cabinet. The government has powers – as we shall see in this book – over health, education, local government, transport, law and order and more. It does not have devolved responsibility for foreign policy, defence, benefits and pensions and macroeconomic decisions. Or, of course, membership of the EU (ouch). Ninety per cent of its budget comes from Westminster,[29] 7 per cent from local business rates and 2 per cent from Europe. It was initially given the power to vary income tax by 3 per cent but has never used it. In 2016 a new Scottish rate of income tax was introduced: of the 20p paid in every £1 of basic rate income, 10p would be levied by the Scottish Parliament (and they could vary it themselves).

Devolution has led to two obvious areas of Scottish departure from Westminster policy: (mostly) free social care for the elderly, and the abolition of tuition fees.[30] Its freedom, generally speaking, has not made the nation more prosperous than its southern neighbour. It has, of course, unsettled notions of union. Blair was reportedly contrite on the subject: 'You can't have Scotland doing something different from the rest of Britain . . . I am beginning to see the defects in all this devolution stuff.'

This 'devolution stuff' was the culmination of agitation for independence that has bubbled around in Scotland, if not since the Act of Union in 1707, at least in the century afterwards. There was never quite a 'Scottish question', though, as there was for Ireland, not least because the historical basis of the union between England and Scotland had never been one entirely of colonial subjugation. A Scottish king had sat upon the English throne in 1603, and although one of his successors, the Catholic James II, had been subsequently eased out in 1688, the principle of mutual connection had been established.

By the 1970s, the Scottish National Party had got an act of sorts together, North Sea oil had been discovered (offering a sense of a viably independent economy), and Westminster politics was being serially mismanaged by both major parties. In 1979 a devolution referendum was held (as the Labour government under Jim Callaghan was desperate for support above the border to cling on to power), and Scotland voted for devolution by the iconic figure of 52 per cent to 48 per cent on a turnout of 64 per cent. This meant that fewer than 40 per cent of the electorate had voted yes, and – by the conditions of the referendum – the result was void.* The SNP

---

* Yes, it is possible to put threshold levels into referendum votes of massive constitutional significance. No, there is no reason why this was not done with Brexit.

spat out the dummy, refused to prop up the government and Callaghan was forced to call an election. Unhappily for the SNP, and many Scots, this heralded more than ten years of rule by Margaret Thatcher.

It took another Labour government to reopen the debate,[31] and it immediately delivered on devolution. The Scottish Parliament building was constructed in Edinburgh and opened in 2004: three years late and – at a cost of £414 million – some 1,000 per cent over budget. It is an oddly beautiful structure, designed to fit in with the land 'in the form of a gathering situation: an amphitheatre, coming from Arthur's Seat', the big carbuncled hill at the centre of the city. It is worth a visit: it is very *designed*, probably not worth the money, but an aesthetic experience nonetheless.

Scottish devolution did not lessen the clamour for full independence; it accelerated it. The SNP marched to success in the new Parliament, and took an overall majority in 2011. Its demands for a referendum became unignorable. David Cameron – still a candidate for luckiest politician in Britain back in 2014 – oversaw the process, and the verdict came in on 19 September 2014: 55 per cent said no to independence on a turnout of a whopping 84.5 per cent. Why had it failed? Ultimately, the SNP could not credibly posit a strong enough economic future for the nation: oil was running out, the country had a large economic deficit propped up by Westminster, it had no answer to the currency question,[32] and its reliance on the internal single market of the UK meant departure was too much of a risk. The phrase Project Fear was coined for the way in which the Unionists fought to preserve the status quo; and its success in this referendum ultimately fixed it as the preferred tactic for the next one, over the fate of membership of the EU.

Meanwhile in Wales, the devolution question, barely answered by its own original referendum, has produced a quiet peace. It elects sixty Assembly Members (AMs) using the same system as Scotland. They get to spend a budget given to them by Westminster, which retains control over all primary legislation that affects the region. It has a few discrete policies (free school milk for the under-sevens; free bus travel for the over-sixties), but remains more or less content as the economically weaker sister of England.

Northern Ireland, of course, has always been an area of pointed, perfervid political dispute. Since the Good Friday Agreement* of 1998, there has been a Northern Ireland Assembly in Stormont. It has 108 members, elected using the Single Transferable Vote System, and with broadly the same powers as the Scottish Parliament† (although security and law and order remain the preserve of Westminster). The system has led to mandatory power sharing between whichever of the major parties (Ulster Unionists, Democratic Unionists, Sinn Fein and Labour) are successful. The losers can voluntarily enter opposition. Such coalitions seldom get on, inevitably, even when compelled. The two largest parties have to provide the First Minister and Deputy First Minister positions: if they refuse, the system of government falls, as it did in 2017. As we shall see, the tensions of Brexit make this feeble structure even weaker.

Let's talk about local government; no wait, come back . . .

Centralised government in the UK is tremendously powerful, but many decisions that affect our lives take place a long way from it.‡ Schooling, social services, fire protection, roads, waste disposal are all the preserve of local government; when major tragedy strikes, it is the local services run by local authorities that are most involved in the response. I am not going to lie, though: the system is a

* This was signed by the British government, the Irish government and the parties of Northern Ireland on 10 April 1998. It brought a conclusion to the Troubles, the bloody battle over the position of Northern Ireland that dated back to the 1960s (and, in reality, centuries before that). The outcome was a great credit in the UK to the Major administration initially, and then to the efforts of the Blair government. Characteristically, he empurpled his rhetoric accordingly: 'A day like today is not a day for soundbites, really. But I feel the hand of history upon our shoulders.' That pivot between the sentences is a thing of genuinely absurd beauty.
† In 2018 it has the power to reduce corporation tax in order to allow it to compete with its southern neighbour (the UK rate is 20 per cent; the Republic of Ireland is 12.5 per cent).
‡ We are a unitary government, formed from the top downwards. Countries like the USA, Canada, Australia and Germany are federal states: formed from the bottom up, as individual regions that have clubbed together.

confusing, often sphincter-clenchingly boring, tangle of structures and arrangements. I shall be brief.

For years, local government was an archetypal example of the great British mess. The country was divided hugger-mugger into shires, counties, boroughs, parishes, all of which had varying degrees of responsibility. As the Victorians got their act together, a degree of rationalisation took place; after 1945 central government became more interventionist and started to clarify, and reduce, the amount of local rule. Scotland and Wales led the way towards simplicity: by the 1990s, all their councils had become 'unitary' in the sense that they were uniform and covered everything from urban to rural areas. In England we have been left with a top tier that is weirdly mixed: unitary councils in some big urban areas; county councils; and metropolitan district councils. These are all big beasts that provide the basic structure of government. Beneath the county councils sit some district councils. Beneath them all sit parish councils, which are informal, hyper-local committees with no real powers, and nothing to do with the parish church system.

Before 1970, there were 1,246 councils in England, 430 in Scotland and 181 in Wales; there are now respectively 388, 32 and 32. We have the highest ratio of voters to councillors anywhere in Europe; and – not coincidentally – one of the highest rates of voter apathy.

Councils used to be bodies that were responsible for the *delivery* of local services; they now are responsible for the commissioning of them. In that elision of management-speak, there is a summary of the move towards free-market capitalism that has taken hold of this country, for good or for ill. What it means is that councils used to run schools, housing schemes, the police and the like. Now they partner with free schools, housing trusts, development agencies, police authorities and so on. In the West Midlands, somebody worked out that £22 billion was spent by fifty different public bodies, none of which was directly elected.

A council is ultimately organised by five directorates: chief executive's, children's services, adult social services, transport and environment, and corporate. They are either run by an elected mayor, with a cabinet or council manager; or an executive leader (elected by the council), and a cabinet. Blair's government, as we have seen, was big on devolving power to the regions. Few people have since shared his enthusiasm. Under Blair, nine Regional Development Agencies were introduced, to support a series of Regional Assemblies (mini parliaments) that were also envisaged. One referendum on the latter was held, in 2004: 78 per cent of the stout folk of the north-east voted against it. By 2010, all the RDAs were closed down.

Blair wanted elected mayors, but not many schemes to get them have actually been approved by voters. There were eleven initial mayoral contests in 2002, none pursued with especial enthusiasm. In Hartlepool the local football club mascot H'Angus, a furry monkey, became mayor. He was re-elected in 2005 and 2009. In 2012 Hartlepool voted to abolish the institution. Few areas want to ape the Hartlepool experience.

What we are seeing consistently is that British people do not value local government at all. Turnout in elections is under 40 per cent; most of us do not even know when elections take place★ and whom we are really electing. And yet this stuff is important. Around 10 per cent of the national workforce are employed by local government; we have 22,000 local politicians, largely unpaid, very often in their sixties or older, with what charitably might be called a broad range of abilities; together they spend more than £90 billion of our money. When we talk about the crisis of social care, the elderly immured in hospitals, growing feeble and dying of infection because there is nowhere to tend to them, we are talking about a local government issue. When we bemoan fire safety negligence, as with the conflagration of Grenfell Tower on 14 June 2017,[33] we are talking about a local government issue. When a child dies, abused and unprotected by local services, we are talking about a local government issue.[34]

Britain is a paradox (as we shall see in the NHS shortly): we experience life locally, but we only discuss it nationally.† It is no

---

★ More mess: some council elections happen every four years; some elect a third of the council almost every year.

† Compare Switzerland, in which there is no national health or education policy. Each canton makes its own decisions according to the demands of its own voters.

wonder that we end up tolerating muddles and mess. And if our nationalistic approach causes us problems internally, just imagine what it does when we look outwards.

Yes, alas, it is time to discuss Europe.

EU-turn if you want to

I know, I know. We have left. Brexit means Brexit. But wranglings about Europe have gone from a national pastime to the predominant influence on our national politics and identity. We are defined by what we seek not to be: European, proximate to our neighbours, part of a wider whole. This is not a value judgement; it is a statement of what our country is: Britain is now Brexit.

The briefest of trots through the history of the argument. In 1957 (the legacy of the Second World War still prevalent; the need for economic development, not solely financed by the US, apparent) the Treaty of Rome formed the European Economic Community of Belgium, France, Germany, Italy, Luxembourg and the Netherlands. Britain remained aloof: it was a gang, noted Clement Attlee, 'of six nations, four of whom we had to rescue from the other two'. But by 1973, it looks like a gang to join; and by 1975 we had voted to do so in a referendum that was passed by 67 per cent to 33 per cent.

As Brexiteers will never tire of telling you, this was an economic community we were joining, not a political union. But union was soon on the cards. In 1986 the Single European Act was passed, perhaps surprisingly, by Margaret Thatcher, which committed to the establishment of the single market. In 1992 the Maastricht Treaty was battled over, tearing up the Tories, but eventually leading to the creation of the European Community, and the beginnings of monetary union (the creation of a single currency), customs union and the further development of the single market. Britain began the process of opting out of some of it.

The single market is, of course, critical. It allows the EU to act as a massive internal market for member nations to trade freely among themselves. It is based on four freedoms: goods; services; capital; and people. The heart of the EU debate is that we cheery capitalists all love the first three,* but many resent the fourth, because it means untrammelled immigration. The customs union is a separate free trade idea: it abolishes internal restrictions on trade; and it agrees tariffs and quotas on external trade. It also means that goods passed within the EU do not need further checks by individual member states; it is based on block deals by the EU with other nations. Britain cannot stay within it and do its own bilateral trade deals, so a full Brexit means we lose the benefit of it (which may come at a cost of up to £25 billion, depending on who you listen to).

Britain helped to found the European Free Trade Association (EFTA) in 1960, which in turn created the European Economic Area (EEA). It now exists as a halfway house for countries (Iceland, Liechtenstein, Norway) who want to be in the single market, but do not wish to be in the EU[35] or the customs union. To be a member you simply have to follow the rules and regulations of the EU, and agree to having no say in their development. That means accepting freedom of movement, which is why such a sensible – even British – muddle as this is vehemently rejected by Brexiteers.†

In 1997 the Treaty of Amsterdam moved decision-making further into the European structure. It also formalised the Schengen Agreement of 1985, by which European countries agreed to operate with internal open borders, allowing the possibility of mass

---

* I don't include Jeremy Corbyn in this. He is suspicious of capitalist institutions, but believes genuinely in unfettered immigration, so loves the fourth freedom but dislikes the first three.

† Remember, as a quick primer: you can be in a version of the customs union but not the single market (as are Turkey or the Isle of Man); and you can be in the single market but not the customs union (as are Norway or Iceland). Being in a customs union with the EU is not much use for Turkey, and means it has to accept whatever deal the EU gets on imports from other nations without benefiting from reciprocal deals for its own exports. It puts up with it, because it wants to be part of the EU one day.

migration.* Two countries opted out of that deal: Ireland and the UK. By 2007, the Lisbon Treaty created the European Union: a centralised body with a strong Parliament, firmer in its hold over national institutions. Ironically, it also contained Article 50: the first formalised piece of legislation to enable a country to leave the EU. It was not envisaged that it would be triggered, of course. Indeed, its architect, Giuliano Amato, a former Italian Prime Minister, said this: 'I wrote Article 50, so I know it well. My intention was that it should be a classic safety valve that was there, but never used.'

This is often cited by Remainers as evidence of the illogicality of Brexit, but it – to my mind – reveals one of the dominant problems of the EU. A 'classic safety valve' is actually a necessary piece of kit to remove a build-up of tension or toxin; it is not designed to be 'never used'. One of the legitimate criticisms of the EU is its overcomplicated, often otiose machinery. This is perhaps best symbolised by a valve not designed to work.

Anyway, as you know (or should do if you voted in the referendum), the EU has three power structures: the European Council, comprising all the heads of state, as the highest decision-making forum beneath its President, in 2018, Donald Tusk; the European Commission, a weird combination of civil service and policy-makers, comprising twenty-eight commissioners under President Jean-Claude Juncker; and the European Parliament, comprising 751 elected members[36] (seventy-three from the UK) under President Martin Schulz. Through this unwieldy model, the Commission proposes legislation, which needs to be agreed by a majority in the Parliament and the Council. There are a couple of notable areas of veto, though, for individual states: new membership, new rights to EU citizens, the creation of an EU army. If somebody said to you in the referendum debate that the UK could be forced to join an EU army, or welcome Turkey into the EU, they were misinformed or – shock – lying.

---

* This became especially concerning in the refugee crisis that arose in the last several years, following political turmoil (some of it Western in origin) in the Middle East. If Europe is seen as one giant land mass, then it must share the impact of the arrival of those seeking refuge. Put that way, from a moral point of view, it does not seem so bad, does it?

In any event, and as we shall see more in Chapter 5, EU legislation supersedes national laws, and must be enforced by member states. Nobody can agree on how much EU legislation has become law, because in many areas it would be UK law already (due to the subject needing to be covered by something): estimates vary between 15 and 55 per cent.

So much for the structural points. The state of play before the referendum in Britain was this: a gradual frustration with the overall direction of the country; the displacement of blame for this upon a vast, faceless bureaucracy. We were an insular country, whose national identity came from colonisation not collaboration. We were frightened often by immigration, and in 2004 we had witnessed a genuinely large influx of Eastern European nationals across our borders. We had suffered economic shock in the form of the banking crisis, which transmuted naturally into a widespread distrust of globalised institutions that appeared to bring us nothing but grief (not least because we have never been interested in examining their benefits). What Prime Minister David Cameron had called the 'fruitcakes, loonies and closet racists' of UKIP were actually folk representative of a wider national sentiment, waiting to have its moment of manifestation.

David Cameron misjudged the national mood, like he did so much else in the tail-end of his time at the top. In 2010 he said that he 'didn't want Europe to define my Premiership'; in the end it did in the way that the Munich Agreement has defined Chamberlain's, that Iraq has defined Blair's. When Cameron promised a referendum in 2013 he probably thought, if a further coalition didn't kill it, he would luck his way through it, and lance the boil that had suppurated on the buttocks of the Tory Party for decades. When he was forced to see the promise through, he said to the British public that he would deliver a better relationship with Europe, and went off and renegotiated very little.

In the negotiations of 2015 with the EU, which preceded the referendum, he failed to get a means to put a brake on immigration, or to prevent child benefits leaving the country to go to EU citizens. These were two talismanic points. When the issue of immigration came up in the subsequent debates, he had no argument to make other than the (true) statement that it benefits our economy and we shouldn't worry so much about it. That was not, inevitably, a winner. He could have insisted on a threshold of 60 per cent of votes for a referendum involving such a significant change, rather than a bare majority. But he was ever at the mercy of events, instead of controlling them.

I will not go into detail about the appalling (on both sides) referendum debate.[37] What is striking is that, although the referendum was in some senses a battle of metropolitan elite vs provincial revolt, it was conducted in the same way as all our political disputes: angry white men in small rooms trying to outdo one another. It is a story of special advisers (spads) and wonks, grids and TV hits, micro-targeting on Facebook, private polling and message discipline, a Battle of the Bubble. Do not ever let Brexiteers recast it into a revolution of the people. The Leave gang had professional campaigners from within Westminster: men like Dominic Cummings and Matthew Elliott, elite narcissists like Boris Johnson and Nigel Farage, intellectual dabblers like Michael Gove, big media like the *Mail* and the *Sun*, even an owner of an actual diamond mine (the UKIP donor Arron Banks).

And the devil, of course, had the best tunes. This was the campaign leader Dominic Cummings on the message approach of the Leave campaign: 'We want to win, therefore whatever we've just talked about now, what we're going to talk about in the campaign is 350 million quid, immigration, Turkey, and we'll win.'

The fact that only one of these points is accurate in the real world is irrelevant. Welcome to the political age of the double-down. If something is wrong, do not change it, repeat it louder. Take the infamous quote on the side of the bus: 'We send the EU £350 million a week; let's fund our NHS instead.' The figure is wrong, unquestionably.* In case you care, we paid about £17 billion a year into the EU budget, and got a discount of £4 billion in the form of a rebate. So we sent £13 billion. We also received £4.5 billion in terms of EU spending on our public sector. All this amounts to

---

* The UK Statistics Authority called it 'a clear misuse of official statistics'.

a lot of money, still: about £230 million a week, with £80 million spent on us in return.

Here's the critical point: if Leave had used the £230 million figure (a massive amount of money), it would have been accepted too quickly. By using the wrong figure, it had to be rebutted by the other side; and dutiful broadcasters had to cover the rebuttal. It became an iconic number, not merely a useful debating point: propaganda alchemised into something more real than the truth. Trump is an expert in this sort of double-down. All power-hungry people are.*

Allow me to declare an interest: I voted Remain. But not because I could not see validity in the arguments for Brexit; I could and can. The sovereignty question is a true and vital one: why should we have policies (on, say, immigration) set by people who we really cannot vote out if we think they are wrong? The EU is a vast bureaucracy, peopled by plenty of mediocrity; it is full of concealed self-interest and monstrous inefficiency. So I voted Remain for pragmatic reasons: I believe achieving Brexit is too difficult, too costly, too time-consuming in a period where – as we saw in the last chapter – so much is in flux. We are experiencing change at a rapid rate; we picked the wrong time to undertake a massive logistical exercise that may end up improving things either a little or not at all. So my vote was on a cost–benefit analysis, judging the former to be greater than the latter.

But the Brexit vote overall was about more than just pragmatics. It revealed the most obvious political truth about Britain: we are an utterly divided country. Sundered. Riven. Indeed, this book will often

---

* Norman Mailer tells the story in *The Fight* (1975) about what happened when President Mobutu came to call his country Zaire:

> Then they discovered that Zaire is not an African word. It happens to be Old Portuguese. Be certain, he's not about to admit the error and open himself to ridicule. On the contrary, that's probably the moment he decides not only the country but the money and the gasoline and the cigarettes and, for all I know, the contraceptives are going to be called Zaire. The first rule of a dictatorship is reinforce your mistakes.

I thought about that quote a lot during the Brexit campaign.

chart the gouging of that divide over recent times. We can see some
of it in the patterns of that vote. The old outvoted the young in
number and in appetite to leave.[38] The educated wanted to stay, the
under-educated to leave.* The poorer wanted change; the more
comfortable wanted the status quo. Those with passports wanted to
stay, those who have never travelled wanted to leave. People who saw
themselves as 'English' wanted to leave, the 'British' wanted to stay.†

And what of British identity in this post-Brexit era? Well, Scotland
voted by 62 per cent to stay in Europe, and although – for economic
reasons – demands for independence have quietened recently, it is fair
to say that dislocation between the two countries has widened. The
Irish question has returned with a mournful vengeance. Since 1998
the border between Northern Ireland and the Republic had been
pacified, was nominal in many senses. It has now become the one
land border between Britain and the EU: something solid, awkward,
symbolic; an affront to decades of comparative peace following years
of bloodshed. Here is the Irish historian Roy Foster: 'The days of
contraband checks, identity interrogations and angry queues of vehicles on approach roads had been long gone. To assume that they
cannot return after Brexit is yet another instance of wishful thinking.'

This is neither the time nor the book to contemplate how the
eventual Brexit uncoupling will happen, and what it will mean for
the economy and unity of our land. We know it will be difficult
and costly to disentangle decades of administrative, legal and trade
deals.[39] We know that any damage to our economy will bite against
not the moneyed few, but the impoverished many. We know that
issues of nationalism, some fine, some ugly, will rise up; there will
be tension within and without our united kingdom. We know that
the opportunity cost will be great: all those hours spent on unloos-
ening us from the EU, all the millions and millions of pounds.‡

---

* Researchers from Leicester University argued that, had 3 per cent more people
gone to further education, the vote would have been to remain.
† Stewart Lee satirised the sense of polarised anger with this gag: 'Not everybody
who voted to Leave was racist. Some of them were cunts.'
‡ We will continue to owe the EU £40 billion in the initial years after we leave,
which will be an outright cost to the taxpayer. But the real cost is in the money
spent on changing systems in the brave new world.

Government, at the best of times, is inefficient and wasteful; a distracted government, overwhelmed by a single issue, has no chance. Brexit changes everything, including our politics itself.

Post-Brexit politics: A personal view

This change was most starkly revealed in the election of 2017: a strange and unsettling business. Samuel Beckett once said: 'To find a form that accommodates the mess, that is the task of an artist now.' It is becoming abundantly clear that it is the task of the British political classes now, too. And, it must be said, they are not very good at it. Nor, it must also be said, are many of the people who are paid to analyse and discuss it either.

Theresa May's consistent response after her electoral embarrassment and inability to win an overall majority (leading to her government being perilously propped up by ten Democratic Unionist Party MPs, to whom she had to promise a big chunk of Northern Irish funding), astonishingly, was more or less to pretend that the mess did not exist at all. 'Nothing has changed,' she unconvincingly intoned. Indeed, May's performance as Prime Minister has been typically characterised by its absences: no humility; no soul-searching; no human touch; no real change. The audacity of nope.

In this nation of Brexit, we often reach for imported terms when we are confronted by events of magnitude. The leaders of the EU, for example, consistently delighted at the prospect of negotiating with a weak and wounded UK, have been likely to confess to *Schadenfreude* about our electoral confusion (just as we may do the same about Angela Merkel's in Germany). You will also see the term 'hubris' rightly bandied around in reference to the Prime Minister, which has drifted from its original meaning of shameful violence to the overweening sense of pride so strong as to invite a mischievous intervention by the hands of fate. C. S. Lewis called it 'the complete anti-God state of mind', ironic in the context of a God-fearing vicar's daughter like May.

The Greeks, of course, also gave us the word *hamartia*, which may be helpful to us too, both in its eventual meaning of 'tragic flaw' and in its root from *hamartano*, 'to miss the mark, to fall short'. Theresa May's electoral flaw was arrogance, that she felt she could take a democratic process for granted; her true sin was failing to deliver any meaningful form of success in spite of it. She missed the mark badly. Politics is notoriously forgiving of flaws; it punishes failure very severely.

The 2017 election can be considered the election that everybody lost, or at least nobody won. Theresa May demanded a mandate from the nation to negotiate a firm Brexit deal; she ended up losing a mandate to rule at all. She spent more than £130 million of public funds (the cost of holding an election) simply to reduce her own majority to a nugatory level.

The autopsy on her campaigning has been a brutal and bloody one, focusing on its unsurpassable, yet still barely credible, incompetence throughout. The Conservatives' manifesto, cooked up by the tiny cabal of May's advisers without the input or sanction of many of the Cabinet, was a disaster unparalleled in modern politics. May committed the unpardonable sin of calling a surprise election that surprised her own party. The proposal for the funding of social care by taking funds from the post-mortem sale of houses (dubbed witheringly the 'dementia tax') alienated older voters, without enticing any younger ones, who now have never been more likely to vote Labour. May was correct that the taxation of assets rather than income was a reasonable policy to entertain, as we argued in Chapter 1, but she was neither strong nor stable enough to see it through.

Her failed U-turn became a symbol not only of the wobbly campaign itself, but also of her failure to emulate the sort of strong female leader the Tories once happily supported (whose position on U-turns was rather well articulated). Martin Amis called the love of Tories for Margaret Thatcher (shared by Philip Larkin, for example) 'a clear example of UK toilet-training run amok', and apparently more than one senior Tory has referred to May in the past as 'mummy'. But no Thatcher is she.

Not that the issues were properly tackled either. The Prime Minister found herself engaged in rows about fox-hunting, free school meals and her track record on security. In retrospect (as in real time), the decision to stand on a platform based on attacking furry creatures and the nutritional well-being of five-year-olds was a very strange one. Since then, in the unlikely shape of Michael Gove, the Tories have tried to reposition themselves as the friend of the animals and the environment. The response has been one of suspicion, it must be said. The fact that Jeremy Corbyn was seen by some to be the pro-police candidate was yet another indictment of accustomed stances being doubted.

Other losers abounded, of course, in 2017, but none whose fall was so painful. The Scottish National Party lost a third of their MPs (and clung on to six seats by a collective majority of just 629 votes), including the talismanic former leader Alex Salmond. In an election of ironies, it was thanks to this SNP shift to Conservatives* (unthinkable ten, or even two, years ago) that May remained in power at all.

Elsewhere, UKIP, the lifelong losers of British politics, will surely cease to exist. Its followers used to protest about the scale of the popular vote and its minuscule representation in Parliament. Now it has ended up with neither.

It is easy to mock UKIP, though that – of course – does not mean we should not do it. In its recent history, its highlights have included: a councillor blaming flooding on God's wrath against same-sex marriages; the decision to ban the burka on the grounds of it causing vitamin D deficiencies; a leadership candidate, John Rees-Evans, revealing that a gay donkey had tried to rape his horse; the then-leader of the party, Henry Bolton, claiming he could strangle a badger with his bare hands (he later became more famous for his on–off relationship with a racist model many years younger than him); the 2010 election pledge to 'turn London's Circle Line into a circle' and to ensure people wore 'proper dress' when going out for the night; and many, many more. Here is the peculiarly British kicker, though: for all of this cloth-eared absurdity, UKIP still has been one of the most significant forces in our politics over

---

* The SNP were suffering unquestionably from dominance fatigue, and were being held to account for the poor performance of its devolved government. The Tories benefited from having a charismatic, youthful leader in the form of Ruth Davidson. The future government of Britain may now find a central battleground in Scotland: fifty-nine seats are up for grabs, and winnable by SNP, Tory or Labour.

the last two decades, and – with Brexit – its central figure, Nigel Farage, has a claim to be one of the country's most influential politicians since Tony Blair. We live in UKIP Britain whether UKIP exists or not. The party has lost its status by winning the overall argument about Europe. Another irony.

Naturally, the Liberal Democrats lost. They actually increased their number of seats to twelve, an insignificant number even for a party historically comfortable in the skin of its own insignificance. The idea that this election could be a re-run of the referendum, with an enlivened 48 per cent of the population demanding a centrist, Europhile party, proved illusory. People who voted to stay in the EU were not willing to vote for the only significant party (in England at least) willing to stand up for them.

'It's pretty clear we won the election,' said an understandably exuberant Jeremy Corbyn in its immediate aftermath. Well, up to a point, Lord Copper. His campaign produced the largest increase in vote share since 1945 (a whopping 9 per cent), and thirty extra seats. His personal standing increased, as more voters saw a man resolute in his beliefs and attuned to the rigours of stumping. Yet Labour did not emerge the party of government, any more than it did in 2010 or 2015. It still had (as it still has) no durable or agreed position on Brexit. Had the Tories won 287 more votes between four areas, they would have retained a majority. Labour's centrist adherents (the same MPs who demanded Corbyn's resignation less than a year before) emerged from this election with their seats intact, but their party lost to them for ever. Corbyn may not have been elected, but he was no longer to be considered unelectable. A left-wing populist party has demonstrated that it can gain widespread approval; the ghost of Blair can be exorcised for good.

Indeed, one inescapable conclusion of this election is that some of our recent political verities need rapidly to be jettisoned. The notion that people always vote out of fear rather than hope was comprehensively undermined, for example. It was a version of hope that led to Trump's triumph over Clinton, Brexit over the status quo, Sadiq Khan over Zac Goldsmith as a multicultural mayor of London. The Conservatives approached politics as a negative exercise, 'wading through doubt and dishonour', as Anthony Trollope once said. They treated this election as if it were 2015; the country, and the world, have changed since then.

It was once axiomatic that Britain feared socialism, and would never embrace a party truly of the left. It was once axiomatic that it would not warm to a figure like Corbyn with radical roots and connections to extremist organisations such as the IRA and Hamas. Instead, his consistent position on the surrounding issues (a united Ireland; Palestinian rights) was at least respected, or a younger electorate simply did not care. It was once axiomatic that the young do not vote. It was once axiomatic that the right-wing press would see its party home with relentless electioneering. The *Sun*, not much keen on May, was actually never hugely engaged at all in the 2017 process (although it did become more excitable in the final week), and the *Daily Mail* felt like nothing so much as a parodic, Blimpish uncle, harrumphing through its moustaches in a way more liable to produce a smile than a landslide. More crucially, the dirty media war for Corbyn was conducted on the internet, via Twitter, Facebook and hyper-partisan sites. The proudly biased and rambunctious British press now has an online cousin, apparently capable of cancelling it out (as we shall discuss in Chapter 7). That will be a feature of all elections to come.

I remember texting a politically neutral (but senior) journalist on voting day, inquiring about his thoughts on the expected result. I got this: 'Labour pal says Tory maj. will be 100+; north is a bloodbath, apparently.' Everybody was saying the same thing; everybody was wrong. The problem with election prediction is that you are forced to rely upon past performance and the patterns of history, and so you are caught out when history shifts.

In this case, young people were more mobilised than they had been in years,* and they were inspired by Jeremy Corbyn. Among first-time voters, according to YouGov, the Labour lead was 47 per cent. In contrast, older people came out for the Conservatives: there

---

* The term 'youthquake' was coined (although I have never heard anybody use it) to describe this revolution of the young. As ever with statistics, the level of youth vote is disputed: the British Election Study revealed that young people voted in about the same numbers in 2017 as in 2015; other pollsters disagree. The point is that more of them voted Labour than expected.

was a fifty-point gap over Labour. But it is not just callow teenagers who made the difference: the age at which a voter was more likely to vote Labour was thirty-four at the start of the campaign; it rose to forty-seven at the end. They were the people squeezed by the financial crisis (especially outside London), the people for whom the current system was not working, who feared that the future will not surpass the past. As with Brexit, education makes a difference: with people educated only to GCSE level, the Tories led by 22 per cent; with people educated to university level, Labour led by 17 per cent.

The current political trend is unquestionably towards polarisation: 35–40 per cent of the country (older, less educated, more nationalist) are Tories; 35–40 per cent (younger, more educated, more internationalist) are Labour. The collapse of the Liberal Democrats and UKIP (and the inevitable fatigue towards the ruling SNP in Scotland) has left the UK an effective two-party state. Even a disastrous election for the Conservatives gave them the best share of the vote since 1983. And, as we have previously said, it is clear that a large rump of the traditional 'working class' remains stubbornly blue: a truly striking feature of British life, which tends not to be replicated in other countries. If we are seeing the rise once more of the ideological left, we are also seeing the entrenchment of the ideological right. And that either concerns you or reassures you. Many will agree with the nineteenth-century philosopher John Stuart Mill,[40] who may have actually coined the phrase 'dystopian' to characterise Tory policies. He also said this: 'I did not mean that Conservatives are generally stupid; I meant, that stupid persons are generally Conservative.'

Others will be content with the definition of conservatism by a twentieth-century philosopher, Michael Oakeshott: 'To be conservative . . . is to prefer the familiar to the unknown, to prefer the tried to the untried, fact to mystery, the actual to the possible, the limited to the unbounded, the near to the distant, the sufficient to the superabundant, the convenient to the perfect, present laughter to utopian bliss.'

This is almost a mission statement for Theresa May. But it would not have been to Margaret Thatcher, who at least asked the question as to how radical a conservative could be. Such arguments are as old as British politics, as old as the difference between established interests and the desire for change. We always feel as if we are living in unprecedented times, but precedence is one of the unyielding laws of our political system. Even as we experience the shock of the present, we are forced to recognise that there is nothing new under the sun. Indeed, here are ten rules of our national politics, which I promise will hold good until something happens to alter them:

1. Everything has happened before.
2. All politics ends in failure.
3. Change always comes too late: 'the commonest error in politics is sticking to the carcasses of dead policies' (Lord Derby).
4. Politicians always become popular when they resign, apart from Tony Blair.
5. There is always a loser in a coalition.
6. Polls have often been wrong, sometimes spectacularly so.
7. It is impossible to take politics as seriously as politicians and officials (and lobby journalists) do.
8. Politicians who say 'let me be clear', never then are.
9. Politics can only continue as it does because memories and attention spans are equally short.
10. No victory is everlasting; no defeat for ever: 'the pendulum swings' (Disraeli).

The pendulum swings, a comment from more than 150 years ago; it should still be the dominant metaphor today. Meanwhile, the business of stable government gets ever more difficult. The incumbents have to spend all their energies and capital on the process and aftermath of Brexit, a thankless and perhaps unwinnable challenge, the result of which will annoy or disappoint at least half of the nation. They are expected to tackle the most complicated trade negotiation in modern political history, without any clear authority to do so. Meanwhile, the other problems we face as a country (healthcare, social care, low wages, education etc.) must either be ignored or, worse, further compromised in the negotiation.

It is clear, at least, that Jeremy Corbyn's Labour Party should *want* to stay out of power until 2020, to let the Conservatives be damaged by the fall-out of our most divisive vote. 'I got us into this mess,' said May to her MPs in the first weekend after the election, 'and I'll get us out of it.' The first part is true.[41] Labour should allow her to attempt the second part, betting confidently on her probable failure. The Brexit mess of 2016 only became messier in 2017, as it will in 2018, 2019 and so on. The form to accommodate it may yet be undiscovered.

A British Mess could, of course, have been the subtitle to this book.⋆ And it is indeed a familiar mess. In 2017 events that felt seismic, but were not that extraordinary, took place: European wrangling; the rise of the hard left; weak leadership at the centre of the state; hubris; the return of the Irish question. The pendulum will swing once more, but beneath it much of our political world remains the same.

⋆ In fact, I should have totally gone with this. *Stuck in the Muddle* was another good option.

3

Health

Wherever the art of medicine is loved, there is also a love of humanity

Hippocrates (460–370 BC)

In 2011, when I was thirty-one, I stood holding my newborn son – an hour old; a crinkled hodgepodge of grimacing skin and sinew – as my wife spasmed on the scuffed floor of the birthing room. Her eyes were rolled back in her head; there was blood everywhere. The midwife, hitherto the model of brisk efficiency, blindly ran to the wall and pressed a button. No sound emerged, indeed in my memory I can remember no sounds at all. But two minutes later, a whole team of doctors poured into the room, moving all non-essential figures (me especially) to one side. I leaned against a cold wall, rocking from left leg to right,* murmuring nothings to my heedless son, whose eyes were screwed tight shut like he was trying to remember something. The doctors prodded, set up drips; my wife was still lifeless before me. And then, slowly, the situation seemed to calm, the room's panic subsided. My wife opened her eyes, smiled faintly, but didn't seem to know where she was. My son started pawing at my body with his mouth, the instinct for feeding stirring. As my wife was stretchered and prepared to move, I pushed through the crowd and plopped him on her chest, where

---

* This was my second child, so I had the conditioned response of bouncing gently whenever I had a child in my hand. It is now impossible for me to stand still and hold a baby. As I write this book, my third child is, somewhat dauntingly, on the way.

he latched on to her, simultaneously seeming to take life from her and give it straight back. Upstairs, in a curtained annex, the haemorrhaging stopped and my wife could speak again. Five hours later, I could leave the hospital (to check my three-year-old daughter had not destroyed the sanity of my parents), knowing that her life had been saved.

A short coda to this story: I returned to the hospital the next morning to find my wife lying in bed, surrounded by bloodied cloths and tissues. She had not eaten since the birth. She had scarcely been spoken to, could scarcely be comprehended, by a succession of non-native nursing and auxiliary staff. Nobody had helped her get clean, nobody had removed the baby wipes she had used to clean herself. She was dangerously anaemic, and – while I was there – a doctor arrived to say she should stay another couple of days and have a blood transfusion. I could not, in conscience, leave my wife in that unforgiving environment: we checked her out and I took my family home where we could look after each other in a cleaner and more appropriate place.★ While the hospital could cure her, they were not able to care for her.

In 1983, when I was three, I lay lifeless in a hospital bed, in a coma. I had had a febrile convulsion, a rocketing temperature not uncommon in young children, but sufficient to shut down my entire system. I had been rushed to hospital, and my temperature brought down, but I had not regained consciousness. The consultant doctor had told my parents that my brain could have been irrevocably damaged, that I might never recover. For twelve hours I lay in a coma. When I stirred, my parents still could not know what lasting impact I might have suffered. I looked up at the decorated walls of the children's intensive care unit and whispered the words 'Mr Tickle', one of the characters immediately above me. Still my mum's favourite phrase, as it happens. My life had been saved.

In between the two events (saving the lives of the two most important people I know), I have needed the NHS to help me

---

★ It turns out that eating steak, eggs and kale three times a day is like having a blood transfusion in terms of treating anaemia. I followed this diet too, just for the sake of solidarity.

when I suffered another convulsion a year later, for three broken bones, a head wound and the birth of my daughter. I have rushed to the hospital when my daughter fell off a wall and hurt her head; I have rushed to the hospital when my baby son slid off the sofa to the ground.★ My uncle, a former smoker, had a cancerous tumour so toxic it pushed one of his eyes almost out: he had to have half his face removed and rebuilt to excise the malignancy; an operation costing tens of thousands of pounds for which he never had to pay a penny. My grandfather died of Parkinson's, shipped to a hospital from the foul stenches of a nursing home. Two other grandparents were treated for the ailments of old age (broken hips and prostate cancer), and died from the superbug MRSA contracted within the hospital precincts. First things and last things: always the NHS.

I tell the stories not because they are exceptional, but because they are not. Virtually everyone in this country owes their life to the doctors, nurses and staff of our National Health Service. But it is for that reason that it is almost impossible to be objective about it, to examine its flaws and problems, as well as celebrate its successes. Nigel Lawson, the Conservative Chancellor at the time of my coma, said that 'the NHS is the closest thing the English have to a religion, with those who practise in it regarding themselves as a priesthood.' His next sentence was key: 'This made it extraordinarily difficult to reform.'

As we shall see, Lawson's Conservatives will often play the villain in the story of the NHS. But his point is a valid one. How can we examine the NHS rationally, and consider its parlous future, while still recognising both its actual and symbolic significance to the country? This chapter will try to find a way to do precisely that, to help us understand how and why the NHS is structured the way it is, how we got here precisely, and what is going to happen in a country where everybody is getting older, fatter and living longer, with more costly and chronic illnesses along the way.

★ My wife was looking after him at the time, although we never mention this.

The pre-history of the NHS

Before we trot through the story of the last seventy years or so, a brief word on what there was in terms of healthcare before the NHS was created in 1948. This is necessary, because most people living in the country can remember no time when the NHS wasn't a permanent feature of our lives. Professor Raymond Tallis, the philosopher and former doctor, once told me that the NHS 'is like the air', an essential but unremarked-upon necessity of existence. We should recall that we had coped oxygen-free for virtually all of our collective history before it.

The Second World War changed everything. Before that, since 1911 at least, healthcare was paid privately or by state health insurance. If you earned less than £160 a year, you were placed on a 'ninepence for fourpence' system by which the worker paid 4d, his employer paid 3d and the state chipped in a generous 2d per week. This got you some medical treatment, but no right to hospital care. No women or children were covered at all. Hospitals were generally funded by charities and generally broke.* Thanks to the war, not only was there massive upheaval which demanded social change in all areas of life, but an 'Emergency Medical Service' for everybody was created. As people were maimed by German bombs, the concept of the state treating them became an urgent one.

The person credited for the conception[1] of the NHS is William Beveridge.[2] He was tasked by a reluctant government with examining the issue of how to extend the principle of social insurance. What resulted was perhaps the biggest mismatch between title and content in the history of publishing: his 1942 report *Social Insurance and Allied Services*.[3] In it, he recognised the Zeitgeist was upon the nation: 'a revolutionary moment in the world's history is a time for revolutions, not patching'. And so he declared war on the five 'Giant Evils' of 'Want, Disease, Ignorance, Squalor and Idleness'. Like an updated *Pilgrim's Progress*,[4] it personified these enemies, and sought to present itself as an attack: 'Upon the physical Want with which it is directly

* Unlike today. Oh.

concerned, upon Disease which often causes that Want and brings many other troubles in its train, upon Ignorance which no democracy can afford among its citizens, upon Squalor . . . and upon the Idleness which destroys wealth and corrupts men.'

Breathe deeply the pungent sense of morality here. The report shocked the government – who had been perhaps expecting something a little less revolutionary, a little less rhetorical – but directly led to calls for the creation of the National Health Service, as part of the welfare state. Once the war ended, a Labour government was elected with a crushing 146 majority[5] (more than ever possessed by Margaret Thatcher) and a mandate to get started.

The heroic mantle then passed from Beveridge to Aneurin Bevan,[6] the Labour Secretary of State for Health. In 1946 an Act of Parliament was passed under his auspices with this in mind: 'The establishment of a comprehensive health service designed to secure improvement in the physical and mental health of the people of England and Wales and the prevention, diagnosis and treatment of illness.'

It was here, in the very beginnings of the NHS, that its central principles were articulated: that it meets the needs of everybody; that it is free at the point of delivery; and that it is based on clinical need, not the ability to pay. As we shall see, such principles, much weathered and battered, remain at the heart of the debate today.

It is worth noting, however, that not everyone was excited about the prospect of a National Health Service. Doctors, for example. They were terrified that a centralised system would rob them of the ability to charge privately (a source of much of their wealth). When the BMA* had a ballot in 1947, 84 per cent of doctors voted and 86 per cent of them voted against joining the NHS. One surgeon commented that the prospect of joining the NHS was making the medical profession unwell: 'I have spent a lot of time seeing doctors with bleeding duodenal ulcers caused by worry about being under the State.' Another doctor, and former Secretary to the BMA, wrote: 'I have examined

---

* The British Medical Association is the trade union for doctors and represents 150,000 across the UK. It is either a unifying voice for the industry, and brave defender of the NHS, or an over-politicised, socialist enemy of change (depending on your politics). Interestingly, in the early years of the NHS, it spent its time sticking up for the right for doctors to practise privately and so get rich.

the Bill and it looks to me uncommonly like the first step, and a big one, towards National Socialism★ as practised in Germany.'[7]

Famously, the Tories were also not in favour of the NHS, thus beginning the tradition (not entirely false) that, as an institution, it is only safe in Labour's hands. They voted against the 1946 Bill, not because they did not believe in the need for a 'comprehensive health service' (they agreed with that), but because they were worried about too much state interference as a threat to private practice. The notion of private health interests being over-represented by Conservative politicians has a long tradition, too.

In any event, the Act was passed, and the NHS came into existence on 5 July 1948. An epochal day in the country's history. Especially for women, children and the unemployed, who had been largely left to fend for themselves and die untreated. The idea that, before 1948, most women had no recognised right to casual medical treatment is mind-blowing, yet true. Dr John Marks tells this story of that first week in July: 'There were women with prolapsed uteruses literally wobbling down between their legs that had been held in place with cup and stem pessaries – like a big penis with a cup on it. It was the same with hernias.'

The use of a penis metaphor to describe a uterine collapse is striking, but the social implication more so. The country had changed for ever. People could expect to get treated when they needed it. The state was now on the hook for all of our health and well-being; and that altered our relationship with it permanently.

The history of the NHS

In one sense, this is a very tangled affair. In another, it is very simple, because almost every issue at stake in the NHS was present at its inception, almost every problem has gone unsolved since the

---

★ An astonishingly early example of Godwin's Law from the pre-internet age. The Law (proposed by Mike Godwin in 1990) states that 'as an online discussion grows longer, the probability of a comparison involving Hitler approaches one.' So credit to Dr Bill Cox for being fifty years ahead of his time, using the letters page of the *BMJ*!

beginning. As the journalist Nicholas Timmins noted: 'It is quite important to know that virtually every day since 1948 the NHS has been in crisis, and for the last forty-five years morale within it has never been lower.' Let's just focus on the big areas of change that have taken place.

There have been six major restructures in NHS history ('endless redisorganisation' in the words of Professor Tallis), five under Conservative governments, the last in 2012 following a promise that there would be no more restructures of the organisation (we'll get to that). Essentially, the structural changes have been made to address a fundamental issue: the NHS is funded nationally, but experienced locally. This begs the continuing question of where the power should be vested.

The first restructure in 1962 came under the stewardship of Enoch Powell* as Secretary of State for Health, who split the NHS into three sectors: district hospitals, general practice and local health authorities. This began a tension unresolved to this day between different types of medical care (hospitals and GPs) and social care. At the same time, Powell spent £500 million on 90 new and 134 refurbished hospitals, thus establishing the precedent of throwing money at the NHS that would be keenly followed by Tony Blair thirty-five years later.

In 1974, under Keith Joseph,[8] a decision was taken to transfer decision-making, taking power away from the hospitals and placing it in the hands of regional health authorities, who had their own supervisory management teams. This had the effect of ensuring that nobody was left to run the hospitals. In three years, 30 per cent more clerical staff were needed to administer a system designed to reduce red tape.†

---

* History will pass over his sometimes creditable performance as Health Secretary to focus on – legitimately enough – his divisive race hatred. We shall meet Powell again later in Chapter 8, when we look at race and British identity.

† As ever, the TV programme *Yes Prime Minister* was acute on the issue of inefficiency in the NHS, when it imagined a hospital staffed with 500 administrators, but containing no doctors, nurses or patients: 'one of the best hospitals in the country . . . up for the Florence Nightingale Award . . . won by the most hygienic hospital in the area'.

In 1983 Margaret Thatcher commissioned the managing director of Sainsbury's supermarket, Roy Griffiths, to consider the issue of organisation once more. His aversion to bureaucracy was such that he did not wish to take formal evidence, or bother with reams of civil service prose. Memorably, his eventual text said that 'action is now badly needed and the Health Service can ill afford to indulge in any lengthy self-imposed Hamlet-like soliloquy.' So he took a week off to write a letter to the Prime Minister, framing seven pages of recommendations, thirteen of diagnosis, and none of evidentiary support.

In essence, Griffiths wished to reverse the 1974 reorganisation and return authority to managers and doctors working together, responsible to a centralised NHS management board. More managers, more control over budgets. His famous line was that 'if Florence Nightingale were carrying her lamp through the corridors of the NHS today she would almost certainly be looking for the people in charge.' Placing people in charge, creating accountability, have become the clichéd watchwords ever since. As in 1974, the management reorganisation was ugly and bureaucratic. Around 435 early retirements were expected at a cost of £9 million; around 2,800 were accepted to the tune of £54 million. Many were subsequently re-employed. Remember when you read about another NHS red-tape screw-up: nothing happens for the first time in the NHS.

By 1990, the Conservatives realised that they had not had a time-consuming reorganisation for several years, so decided to opt for a big one. They pushed through another Act of Parliament, this time for the purposes of creating an 'internal market' for the NHS. This meant there was a split between purchasers and providers of healthcare; the idea being that purchasers could shop around for the best deals and there would be competition, hence declining prices and rising efficiency. NHS Trusts and GP 'fundholders' (groups of GPs together) were created as providers, to have their services purchased by local authorities.

The thinking behind this (which, despite changes of government, has remained integral to the NHS) is that – in the absence of genuine paying customers – an artificial market can be created by using institutions as proxy customers. It is, if you think about it, a weird sort of pretend capitalism. Its supporters say it will lead to greater efficiency; its detractors that it makes an institution that should be caring and altruistic obsessed instead with a confected bottom line. Many people also believe that this step, in the early 1990s, was the beginning of a deliberate path to dismantle the NHS and turn it private. In any event, at the time, Margaret Thatcher remained committed to the governing principles that 'the NHS will continue to be available to all, regardless of income, and to be financed mainly out of general taxation.' That is still the case thirty years on.

Regardless – or perhaps because – of these changes, the NHS lumbered on in continual crisis. When Tony Blair stood on the brink of his electoral landslide in April 1997 he memorably said: 'We have twenty-four hours to save the NHS.'* His solution was less a reorganisation than a commitment to chucking a lot more money at the problem, including an immediate extra billion pounds in the first budget and a commitment† to match European spending on healthcare. There was then a restructure, but one that built upon previous efforts rather than reversing them: Labour replaced GP fundholders with Primary Care Trusts, responsible for commissioning care from providers; and created Foundation Trusts, which are semi-autonomous hospitals, given responsibility for managing their own budgets. The latter looked a lot like private operations, indeed are regarded as such by the government,‡ and were held accountable not by the state, but by a financial regulator (since defunct) called Monitor. All this is worth bearing in mind when people tell you it is the Tories desperate to privatise the NHS: Labour's time in government actually tightened the private grip even further.

* You are shocked, *shocked*, to recall that Tony Blair occasionally lapsed into inflated rhetoric at the expense of meaningfulness.
† Made, apparently without much planning, on one of those Sunday morning political shows watched mainly by political journalists who need to dredge up something for the Monday papers. When he got back, apparently Gordon Brown (who already hated him with that dark Presbyterian passion of his) raged: 'You've stolen my fucking budget!'
‡ Perhaps extraordinarily, Labour created a body in 2009 called the Cooperation and Competition Panel to ensure that the competition between Foundation Trusts was functioning properly and there were no monopolies. But wouldn't a monopoly be okay, given that it is funded by the state and has an altruistic purpose? A good question indeed.

Look, I realise that this is complicated, unrewarding stuff. Analysing the structure of the NHS is a depressingly confusing business. And we have one more insanely Byzantine restructure left to come. The general direction of travel, though, is this: managing the NHS centrally, when it is consumed locally, creates an unbearable bureaucracy; governments have successively (if not successfully) tried to push responsibility ever further away from themselves, on to managers, doctors, trusts and semi-autonomous bodies nobody really understands.

In 2010, when David Cameron had failed to defeat a Labour Party that had supervised an illegal and unpopular war and one of the greatest financial crashes in human history, his new Coalition government made a surprising promise: 'We will stop the top-down reorganisations of the NHS that have got in the way of patient care.' Unsurprisingly, it was lying. The subsequent reorganisation (from the top down) was so big the NHS chief executive said it was 'visible from space'. The NHS's own website still calls it 'the most wide-ranging reforms of the NHS since it was founded in 1948'. The legislation necessary for it, the Health and Social Care Act, was longer than the original Act to establish the NHS in the first place.

Considering it charitably, the intention was to return (in a similar way as Griffiths tried in the 1980s) some degree of control to the medical profession, while retaining a centralised management. Examined more forensically, it was designed to continue the process that absolves the government ever further from the mess that is the NHS. In essence, it replaced Primary Care Trusts (PCTs) with Clinical Commissioning Groups (CCGs), whose members include GPs and other clinicians. At the top is NHS England, an independent body, which manages the overall budget and gives the resource to the CCGs. Foundation Trusts remain, running hospitals independently as businesses; they are free to raise cash where they can (including from the private sector, and also by borrowing) and aim to make a profit to plough back into the business. Other trusts exist too: hospitals that haven't qualified for Foundation status yet; Ambulance Service Trusts; Mental Health Trusts; and so on.

All this is regulated by a body you've never heard of: NHS Improvement, which judges trusts on their financial and operational performance, and incorporated another regulator you've never heard of (until four paragraphs ago) called Monitor. Other regulators are the Care Quality Commission, an independent body that monitors and inspects providers (not always brilliantly) to see if they are maintaining standards, and the General Medical Council, an independent body responsible for the training and disciplining of doctors.

Confused? You should be. You will also notice that I have used the word 'independent' four times in the last two paragraphs.* It is clear that the government wishes to get off the hook for the failures of the NHS: to privatise responsibility if nothing else. This is apparent from the new legislation it has passed: wording of the 2012 Act cynically removes the original phrase from the 1946 Act that 'it shall be the duty of the Minister of Health to promote the establishment in England and Wales of a comprehensive health service', replacing it with 'the Secretary of State must continue the promotion in England of a comprehensive health service'. Nationalised healthcare is no longer a duty of government. In short: don't blame me, bruv.

A short history of NHS scandal

Attributing and escaping blame have been the vigorous activities of those in government and the NHS ever since its inception. For all the many triumphs, it is inevitable that individuals – and groups of individuals – have failed in their responsibilities over the last seventy years. And, as with everything else in the NHS, nothing ever seems to happen for the first time.

Before Harold Shipman in 2000 became the only doctor to be successfully convicted of murdering his patients, for example, there

---

* Fear not: this was deliberate. I also am wary of that pernicious example of journalese: elegant variation. You see this in tabloids particularly: a visceral fear of using the same word twice leads to a flurry of increasingly elaborate synonyms. The 1930s American journalist Charles Morton gave a name to this: 'elongated yellow fruit writing', after a periphrastic colleague struggled to describe a banana. Other examples he cited include: 'rubber-tired mastodon of the highway' (a truck); 'hen-fruit safari' (an Easter egg hunt); and 'the azure-whiskered wifeslayer' (Bluebeard).

was the strange case of Dr John Bodkin Adams, known as the wealthiest GP in England. Altogether, 160 of his patients died in his care between 1946 and 1956; 132 of them left him money or items in their will. Despite being almost certainly guilty, he was let off in deeply suspicious circumstances,[9] and returned to private practice.

Clearly, impropriety by individual doctors is not common[10] and offers little in the way of general lessons. Institutional scandals have historically been the more damaging to the NHS, such as Alder Hey in the 1990s (where dead children's organs were illegally harvested) or of various mental institutions in the 1960s and 1970s such as Ely Hospital in Wales. This was exposed as inadequate by the *News of the World* in 1969, which ran stories of abused patients and delinquent staff. Such scandals prompted Keith Joseph to say in 1971: 'This is a very fine country to be acutely ill or injured in, but take my advice and do not be old or frail or mentally ill.' The same advice could be given with rueful confidence today.

Such episodes tend to reveal a sort of institutionalised mentality that can be toxic and fatal: an indifference to individual suffering, a focusing on the mundane or unimportant, a lack of direction or accountability due to weak leadership, a demotivated and harassed staff.

We saw this with what has become the emblematic scandal of the modern NHS: the failure of Mid Staffordshire NHS Foundation Trust. Nobody will ever know how many people died in Stafford Hospital as a result of poor care between 2005 and 2009,[11] but the scale of neglect and suffering was laid bare by two inquiries,[12] both by Robert Francis QC. He told a 'story of appalling and unnecessary suffering for hundreds of people': patients left without pain relief; patients left unwashed for up to a month; food and drink left out of reach for the incapacitated, some of whom resorted to drinking from flower vases in desperation; 'families forced to remove used bandages and dressings from public areas and clean toilets themselves for fear of catching infections'; patients left with no access to the toilet, lying in their own filth or left sitting on commodes for hours 'often feeling ashamed and afraid'.

Francis's recommendations (largely but not entirely accepted by the government) were designed to improve regulation, to improve the mechanism for reporting problems, to emphasise compassion and care in nursing training. To make clear that individual patients, whatever the financial pressures, have to be treated with respect at all times. In 2015 another inquiry took place, this time into Morecambe Bay NHS Trust (a 'second Mid Staffs' according to the Secretary of State), where the unnecessary deaths of eleven babies and one mother were uncovered, in the 'dysfunctional' maternity unit of Furness Hospital, in which 'substandard' care was offered by staff 'deficient in skills and knowledge'. Again, there had been a failure of regulation, accountability and compassion. Babies died as a result. Joshua Titcombe was nine days old when he died of sepsis that had been ignored and untreated. His dad welcomed the inquiry, but made the unanswerable point that 'when we talk about missed opportunities in this report, that for me means not having a six-year-old.'

What is clear is that, across its history, there has been a huge variation in quality of care across the NHS. In 2013 the Keogh Mortality Review examined fourteen trusts 'that are persistent outliers on mortality indicators', which is to say more people died in them than should have done. It found that, in several places, there was no culture of listening to complaints or acting in response to them; instead there was isolationism and mistrust and a desire to obscure accounts of bad practice.

Individual scandals have certainly been a spur to improvement, but they are also a reminder of the sheer scale of the overall organisation, trying to persist in the Sisyphean task of maintaining good practice and service across the whole country. Another reminder is the increased cost of medical negligence, which has grown from £1 million in 1974 to £1.4 billion in 2015. If all the outstanding claims were paid out at once, the liability would be up to £30 billion. Much of this is down to legal costs (which have quadrupled over the last decade, as bloodthirsty lawyers get the scent of prey in their nostrils),* but it also reflects a culture in which much is expected of the NHS, and a better recognition that it is not always delivered.

---

* Like the BBC (as we shall see), the NHS seems to be determined to be complicit in its own assault. Some hospitals currently rent space to claimant lawyers (and, for some reason, do not take the opportunity constantly to give them diarrhoea bugs).

How does the devolved health service work?

Briefly, Scotland, Wales and Northern Ireland have responsibility for their own NHS. Scotland has had this from the beginning (treated as such in the original 1946 Act). NHS Wales was created in 1969 as part of the responsibility of the Secretary of State for Wales, and was handed over to the Welsh government following devolution in 1999. Health and Social Care in Northern Ireland (HSC) was established in 2009.

In Scotland and Wales there is no purchaser–provider split, no internal markets or purchasing of care from the private sector; there are also free prescription drugs.[13] But it is striking that performance is largely similar everywhere. Wales (run by a Labour government for many years) has bigger problems with waiting times, much to the glee of English Tories. NHS England has fewer nurses proportionally than its counterparts. But in most metrics differences are negligible. The problems of the NHS travel across the internal borders of the UK, as do its successes. It also might suggest that seemingly huge structural issues (like the creation of internal markets) make little practical difference to the overall provision of care. Endless reorganisation has tended to fill a political rather than a practical need.

The cost of the NHS

We have a sense of the vastness of the institution, so let's examine the spending on it, which is perhaps its most commonly discussed aspect.* Bare figure first: the expenditure of the NHS in 2016 was around £120 billion. Is that enough? The answer – as we shall see – is almost certainly no.

---

* Enoch Powell said in 1966: 'The unnerving discovery every Minister of Health makes at or near the outset of his term of office is that the only subject he is ever destined to discuss with the medical profession is money.' This is true, and also true of the wider public at large.

Another way of considering spending is as a proportion of GDP. Historically, this percentage has been fairly low: around 4 per cent in the 1950s, 1960s and 1970s, going up to 5 per cent in the 1980s. When Labour supercharged the spending under Tony Blair and Gordon Brown it got to around 8 per cent in 2009, not coincidentally a time of much improved performance for the institution. It has been waning ever since, and is likely to continue to do so, probably dropping to around 6 per cent by 2020. The UK GDP is forecast to increase by around 15 per cent by 2021; our spending on the NHS by only 5 per cent. In Britain, we spend less on healthcare than most other civilised countries: we rank thirteenth out of the fifteen countries that originally made up the EU; we spend less than the EU average now as a whole. To match the average of EU spending, the NHS budget would have to be increased to £185 billion.

This is important to bear in mind when you listen to government platitudes on the subject of NHS spending. Yes, the NHS budget is ring-fenced and not subject to cuts; yes, spending has increased in cash terms every year. But it is also clear that we spend less than most other countries, spending is not growing in line either with our economic performance (i.e. the amount of money available to the government) or in line with the increased demand of an expanding, sickly population.

In 2016 the government published its Five Year Forward View, which revealed a £30 billion black hole between its spending and its allocated budget. So the NHS, as currently constituted, will cost more than the government is willing to pay. The report says: 'It is implausible to think that over this period NHS spending growth could return to the 6%–7% real annual increases seen in the first decade of this century.' Translation: we are not returning to the Blair years. It is worth pondering that a little: Labour took a decision to channel more money into the NHS to make it better. The current government is not willing to do this, pleading austerity and belt-tightening. It believes that there is no more money left to give, which – as we saw in the last chapter – depends on what your priorities in government are.

This begs another question, then: if the current system is over budget and out of money, should we look at other ways to provide healthcare to the nation?

Other models of healthcare

It is, of course, a heretical subject. The core principle of the NHS is that the cost is shared by everyone, paid for out of general taxation. The upside of this is that the rich are compelled to support the poor in a communal effort; the essential inequality of human society is removed from the equation. That is why Nye Bevan called it 'the biggest single experiment in social service the world has ever seen'. The downside is that everybody takes the NHS for granted: it sits there, automatically funded in the background, without anybody thinking too much about it.

One new approach might be to keep the overall model, but clarify the funding. You may have heard the notion of a hypothecated tax, which simply means one ring-fenced for a specific purpose (in this case the NHS). National Insurance used to be a hypothecated tax, designed to provide a safety net in the event of illness, unemployment and retirement.[14] Now that is forgotten and it is just an adjunct of income tax (it accounts for about a fifth of tax revenue collected).

A solution would be to convert NI contributions into a hypothecated tax earmarked for funding the NHS and social care. Alternatively, a specific part of income tax could be used to perform the same task. In October 2016 research by the broadcaster ITV suggested that 70 per cent of people would happily pay an extra penny in the pound if it was guaranteed to go to the NHS.

This is heartening, in a sense.* And a hypothecated tax would have the effect of making people value how their money is being spent more: we might be less likely to miss hospital appointments,

---

* It recalls the dictum of the American jurist Oliver Wendell Holmes that 'Taxes are the price we pay for a civilised society.' More taxes, more civilised. Somewhere, a right-wing economist just exploded.

more likely to appreciate our GP, if we feel we have paid extra for them. It may not be enough, though, to deal with the issue of our ever increasing requirements for healthcare. It is unlikely that people would consent to a spiralling tax system designed always to match demand.

Perhaps we should consider the first principle and question whether general taxation is the right approach. Have you ever considered that the world is full of progressive, successful countries, not all of which (indeed not many of which) have a national health service? Well, consider it now, as we look briefly at how everybody else does it.

Healthcare models in other countries

Essentially, most other parts of the world follow a system that is – to a lesser or greater extent – a combination of health insurance and backstop state support. In France and Germany social insurance is paid by a combination of employer and employee, with the government handling the unemployed. In France 85 per cent top up the healthcare package with voluntary extra insurance; in Germany only 16 per cent do.

In Switzerland there is no employer contribution, but everyone has to contribute to their own health insurance. The government subsidises 75 per cent of hospital provision, and a third of the population buy top-up insurance. In Holland there is greater collaboration between individual and state: a central tax funds long-term or catastrophic care; compulsory individual health insurance funds acute treatment; and people can opt out for private insurance or purchase add-on individual insurance for things like dentistry.

Outside Europe, Australia has a hypothecated tax that funds a Medicare system, but almost half of Australians have top-up private insurance (incentivised by tax breaks). In America everything is based on private health insurance, largely paid by employers. The now defunct Obamacare improvements were designed to make coverage more affordable, make companies better with their coverage and make insurance companies less mercenary and venal. As a backstop,

US Medicaid purportedly supports those without health insurance and – in absolute terms – constitutes a larger free health system than the NHS.

The European examples are the most telling. What is striking is the belief that a combination of health insurance and some (lesser) state support is very common. And effective. The idea is that those who are earning pay directly for their own care, and the state supports only those who need it. Those with money buy private health insurance far more readily than in the UK, which in return lessens the burden on shared services. In the UK, about 12 per cent of people have private health insurance: theoretically that could be increased relatively easily.

Now campaigners will (correctly) tell you that the joy of the NHS is its democratisation of risk and payment for all citizens; it is fair: a banker is treated the same as a butcher. But compulsory health insurance is fair too, provided that those without the ability to pay for it are also looked after. As in Holland, say, or Germany. One question follows: well, how does the performance of the NHS compare with these other places? Glad you asked.

Healthcare performance in other countries

As we saw from our economics chapter, wherever there are metrics, there are arguments. Not everyone agrees about how best to measure healthcare performance.

But, if we look at doctor numbers per 1,000 people we see that Australia has 3.3, Germany has 3.9, the Netherlands has 3.2, France has 3.1 and the United Kingdom has 2.8. If we look at hospital beds per 1,000 people we see: Australia 3.8; Germany 8.3; the Netherlands 4.7; France 6.4; and the UK 2.9.[15] The UK comes twenty-seventh out of the thirty-five OECD[16] countries by this metric. In terms of spending as a percentage of GDP: Australia 9.4 per cent; Germany 11.3 per cent; the Netherlands 10.9 per cent; France 11.5 per cent. As we know, the UK peaked at around 9 per cent (when you count private and NHS together) and is now declining away from the average.

So, broadly, with our NHS, we spend less on care, with fewer beds tended by fewer doctors than many other rich countries in the world. When it comes to cancer treatment, while things have improved over years in absolute terms, we still do not compare well with other countries. According to OECD data, the UK ranks twentieth out of twenty-three countries in bowel care five-year survival rates; generally speaking we are – according to the *European Journal of Cancer*★ – the worst country in Western Europe for all cancer survival. In 2010 the OECD said that 'the quantity and quality of UK healthcare services remain lower than the OECD average.' In 2016 the Euro Health Consumer Index judged the UK to have the fifteenth best health system in Europe, saying that 'the NHS urgently needs further reform if it is to match the services offered by Western Europe's leading health systems.'

There is one outlier analysis, which you may have heard something about. In 2014 a Washington-based organisation called the Commonwealth Fund did extensive comparative research about healthcare systems using data from patients, doctors and the World Health Organisation. The UK came top out of eleven countries, doing well in terms of quality, access and efficiency. This is despite the fund judging the UK to come tenth in its 'healthy lives' score, which measures infant mortality rates and cases in which patients would have survived had they received timely intervention. Call me a cynical so-and-so, but I would say that 'keeping people alive' should count as a more significant metric than this in an overall examination of a health service.

Taken together, such measurements are probably a fair portrayal of the NHS's performance: even when it does well, there is a suspicion that it is doing badly. Indeed, its central quality remains the fact that it is free for everybody. The expectation isn't that it will perform well; the surprise is that it performs at all.† And the situation is getting ever

---

★ Not a cheery read, it must be said.

† The Labour adviser John McTernan once pointed to this original attitude to the NHS: 'Be patient, join the queue, wait your turn, be glad that it is free.' We are impatient and angry now, but there is a lingering relic of this sentiment. It made me think of the Samuel Johnson quote: 'Sir, a woman's preaching is like a dog's walking on his hind legs. It is not done well; but you are surprised to find it done at all', minus the sneering misogyny.

bleaker, not simply due to underfunding, but because of ever increasing demand. Any consideration of the NHS needs to become a consideration of the health of the nation: the NHS is not necessarily failing us; we are persisting in failing it.

Health of the nation

Let us begin by noting this miscalculation by William Beveridge: he predicted that 'there will be some development of the service, and as consequence of this development a reduction of the number of cases requiring it'; in other words, demand on the NHS would shrink over time. This was plausible, I suppose. Beveridge saw around him a nation hugely disadvantaged in terms of treatments and care, and was entitled to think that a democratised, fully-functioning service would bring health and well-being to a deprived populace. Instead, of course, it has brought longer lives, and more survivable chronic ailments. Enoch Powell spotted this in 1966: 'Every advance in medical science creates new needs that need not exist until the means of meeting them came into existence . . . there is virtually no limit to the amount of medical care an individual is capable of absorbing.'

We are unquestionably getting older as a nation, and – although there is some cautious talk of life expectancy levelling off or even slightly decreasing overall – we are collectively sticking around for more than was once considered natural. Life expectancy for a man in 2018 was around 79, for a woman 83. The number of over-85s is going to double to 3.6 million people in the next twenty years. At present, two-thirds of people admitted to hospital are over 65; and more than a quarter of hospital inpatients have dementia.* The nature of entropy within our bodies means that we can do little to

---

* One in three people over sixty-five will develop dementia before they die. My grandma did, lingering incapable and nonsensical for months before the end. Terrifyingly, when we looked through her belongings after her death, we found a diary charting the moments of lucidity she had had amid the madness. She was compelled to live not only with a disintegrating consciousness, but a periodic awareness of the disintegration. Dementia is a truly dreadful condition.

combat the fact that, as we live longer, we will contract more ailments. Seventy per cent of the NHS budget is spent on long-term health conditions, rather than one-off illnesses susceptible to a cure. But our age is not the true threat to the NHS: our lifestyle is.

So we may start with this proposition: the future of the NHS lies not in the hands of politicians and economists, but in our own. When former banker Derek Wanless was asked to review funding in the NHS in 2002, his answer was that people needed to be more 'fully engaged' with their health. Because, in some ways, a dystopian version of Beveridge's vision has actually occurred before our eyes: a fully-functioning, free health service has provided tacit encouragement for ill-health. If you know you are going to be treated whatever happens, you may take warnings about salt, or sugar, or booze or cigarettes less seriously; you may not bother to turn up to an appointment on time, or at all. As it stands, 40 per cent of the NHS's workload is related to 'modifiable health risk factors'. In other words, if we behaved ourselves, then the NHS budget could stand at £75 billion, and be both affordable and efficient.

Here are a couple of obvious areas where we as a nation are killing both ourselves and the health service. Today, a majority of adults in this country are overweight or obese;[17] by 2035 the figure could be as high as 75 per cent of every grown-up in Britain. We spend our time sitting on our bottoms or lying on our backs,[18] eating pre-prepared pap from a packet.* Of course, the problems start early: 9 per cent of children are obese by the age of five. And not only is obesity unhealthy and unattractive,† it is incredibly costly to the economy and to the NHS. One accounting method says that obesity costs the overall country £47 billion a year, more than armed violence, war and terrorism. We know that it costs the NHS £16 billion every year, of which £10 billion is the cost of treating diabetes.‡

---

* Britain's first chilled ready meal was probably a Marks and Spencer Chicken Kiev in 1979.
† I realise that, statistically, many of the readers of this book will be chubby, so I don't mean you!
‡ There are two types (1 and 2) of diabetes; the latter is by far the most common (90 per cent of all cases) and can be caused by lifestyle factors.

Add in smoking, which costs the NHS between £3 billion and £6 billion a year,[19] and boozing, which costs £3.5 billion a year,[20] and you can see the scale of the problem, and the theoretical possibility of a solution if we only acted more responsibly. This is, of course, not just an issue of healthcare economics, but of societal well-being. I did a phone-in on my LBC Radio show once, discussing the 2.5 million children living in the homes of alcoholics, and was overwhelmed with stories of alcohol-maimed lives. One woman was drinking so much she got septicaemia from an untreated cut and entered a nine-month coma. She had to learn to walk again, but the first thing she did with her regained mobility was limp to the off-licence. Alcoholics called the station to demand more governmental action: less availability; higher prices; even prohibition.

Taxing and behavioural change

Of course, the government already uses tax and legislation to modify behaviour, on alcohol and – more effectively – on tobacco. By banning smoking in public spaces, requiring health warnings and plain packaging, stopping advertising and continually taxing the product, the government has reduced smoking in the UK by about two-thirds. In 1974 over half of all men and 40 per cent of women smoked; now it is less than 20 per cent and 15 per cent respectively. Could a similar approach be taken to obesity?

Well, the government has already begun the process of what is being considered to be a 'sugar tax'. It makes soft drink companies pay a levy for drinks with a sugar content of more than 5g per 100ml, with the amount rising if there are more than 8g per 100ml. A can of Coke has around nine teaspoons of sugar or around 35g, which is more than double the recommended daily amount for a child.

The positives of this approach? Britain has the highest consumption of sugary soft drinks in Europe. Soft drinks contain needless calories, and offer no nutritional benefits. Two years after Mexico introduced a 'soda tax' of 10 per cent per litre, sales of fizzy drinks were down by 12 per cent and 17 per cent in poorer households.

Purchases of water and non-taxed beverages went up by 4 per cent. Tax hurts and works.

The negatives of this approach? First, it is weirdly narrow. It excludes fruit juices, which are often filled with natural sugars that – guess what – are just as bad as artificially added sugars. Taxing one product may not improve health, it may just drive people to other unhealthy products.[21] The Institute for Fiscal Studies has noted that 'if people have a strong taste for sugar, they could switch to fruit juices, milkshakes, chocolate or confectionery'. Denmark has had a soft drink tax since the 1930s, but actually repealed it in 2014 (having also repealed an unpopular fat tax). It found that Danes were simply crossing over to Sweden and Germany to fill their cars with butter, ice cream and cakes.

People are also suspicious of government-led health schemes, with good reason. While it is unlikely that sugar will ever be judged to be good for you, for years its dangers were overlooked in favour of scare stories about natural fats. Eggs were said to be bad for you, as were butter and milk. Cholesterol was the killer. As a result of this, people were changing to low-fat products that actually were full of sugar.

There is also the regressive nature of product taxation. VAT is a regressive tax, for example, because it charges everybody the same whatever their income or wealth. It hurts poor people more than rich people. So a sugar tax will hurt those on low incomes especially, for whom an extra ten or twenty pence on a can of Coke would affect the affordability of the weekly shop. Good, you might say: poor people are more likely to be fat, diabetic and have sclerotic hearts; taxation is the most efficient way to drive some sense into their lifestyles. Before we accept this argument, recall this passage by George Orwell:[22]

> A millionaire may enjoy breakfasting off orange juice and Ryvita biscuits; an unemployed man doesn't. When you are unemployed, which is to say when you are underfed, harassed, bored, and miserable, you don't want to eat dull wholesome food. You want something a little bit 'tasty'. There is always some cheaply pleasant thing to tempt you.

Nannying and sneering are peculiarly unattractive, given that they avoid empathising with the lives of those most affected by these problems. It is easy for a millionaire to eat Ryvita. It is, perhaps, at least rather charmless to tax a poor person into making the same choices.

Inequality of health

We should reflect on the accurate assumption we are making here: poorer people are unhealthier than their richer counterparts. The number of fast food outlets in the UK has increased by 4,000 (8 per cent) in the last three years; and there is a correlation between an area's level of deprivation and its reliance upon fast food shops (twenty-five out of thirty councils with most takeaway outlets are in the poorer north). By the age of five, poor children are doubly likely to be obese than their well-off peers. Rates of excess weight are highest in the north-east, and lowest in wealthy London. Life expectancy actually fell between 2011 and 2016 in post-industrial (northern and Midland) towns; in London and the south-east it continued to rise. As we saw in the economics chapter, we are an utterly divided nation.

It has ever been thus: and, worse, it is not only that poorer people have worse health (due to lifestyle and education), but they experience poorer healthcare too. In 1980 the Black Report on inequalities in healthcare was published, noting that 'a class gradient can be observed for most causes of death', that the death rate in 1974 for unskilled workers was nearly twice that of the professional classes, and that, while working-class people used GP services more than middle-class people 'they may receive less good care'.[23] When a similar study was done in 1998 by Donald Acheson, a similar picture of inequality was noted: health disparities were still related to economic success.

In 2010 the Marmot Review* again found the same sort of

* That's three major pieces of work over a period of thirty years making – in essence – the same points.

ingrained problem: people in the poorest neighbourhoods of England will die seven years earlier than those in the richest; they will spend seventeen years more of their lives with disability. The same factors are always cited: a combination of housing, education, social isolation, culture. Such a concatenation of issues means that no single policy can be offered up as a solution; that is why the problem remains stubbornly unsolved. We also have seen that the government's decision, since 2010, to pursue a policy of austerity means an overall reduction in the size of the welfare state, which is unlikely to ameliorate the condition of the most disadvantaged in our society.

Physical well-being is affected by economic factors, but as pressing are issues around mental well-being, perhaps the biggest health threat we face as a nation, and yet another area of increased pressure on the NHS.

Mental health problems

Mental illness is the single largest cause of disability in the UK. You will hear this statistic often: one in four people will suffer from a mental health problem at some point in their life. This figure has almost no basis in research, and is likely – if anything – to be an understatement of the problem.* We can say simply this: the condition will undoubtedly touch you or someone close to you in your lifetime. It costs the economy, in terms of treatment and lost productivity, £100 billion every year: more than smoking, alcohol and obesity combined. It is a pandemic, but scarcely regarded as such.

When I was in my mid-twenties, I went through a period where I would wake up in the middle of the night, shaking uncontrollably, anxious and implacably terrified. My brain and my body felt

---

* Mental health charities and the government use the statistic quite often, but – as the journalist Tom Chivers has explored – there seems to be no specific source for it; it has simply become shorthand for 'many people'. In fact, if you consider all forms of mental unwellness (diagnosed or otherwise), it is extremely unlikely that three in four people will live their entire lives free from problems.

disconnected. Every time I sought to control how I was feeling, that sensation of being in command slid away from me. Physically, I was healthy; but my mental distress was creating physiological symptoms of panic. At work, I would feel nauseous at the prospect of speaking or meeting someone for lunch. I felt not only paralysed, but horrified at the notion that this might become the rest of my life. You see, physical ailments and their treatments have a straightforward relationship: a cut gets stitched, bacteria get blasted by antibiotics, a break gets set. Treatments might not work but they are in the realm of the logical, the causal.

With mental health, answers are seldom clear-cut. We are entering into the murky waters of the mind–body problem, still a contentious area for both scientists and philosophers:[24] how do ineffable concepts like fear and emotion have a physical basis in the brain? When you feel mentally unwell, you are both ill and cut adrift from orthodoxy and understanding. Uncertainty is piled upon uncertainty.

In the end, my health improved with the support of my wife, and a regular programme of exercise and reading P. G. Wodehouse.* But, as with all of you reading this book, I am only ever a short step away from lapsing into mental agitation once more. I feel the peril every day.

The NHS speaks about achieving 'parity of esteem' between physical and mental health, but currently does not allocate it parity of resources. Mental health – as we have seen – accounts for a considerable part of the total burden of disease, and receives 13 per cent of the funding to treat it. Direct funding to mental health trusts decreased by 8 per cent between 2010 and 2015, while demand has increased by 20 per cent. The government would say that overall funding is increasing, but money is channelled into other areas like education. However, although recognition is rising, it is clear that insufficient attention is being given overall to the problem.

And we are living in a culture in which social and work pressures[25]

---

* I am not being glib here: finding physical exhaustion, and the comfort of familiar books, was a critical factor for me in feeling better. Reading about Bertie Wooster's entanglements with Honoria Glossop or Florence Craye or Madeline Bassett seems to place real-world cares at bay.

are increasing like never before. We are living in a culture where one in ten people feel lonely* (both the bereaved old and the listless young). We are living in a culture, then, in which strain on our collective mental health is going to burgeon rather than contract. We must think of that pressure – not just drunks in A&E, or the elderly rotting in hospital beds – when we consider the true pressures on our national health service.

Weight of numbers

Of course, another pressure on the NHS is simply the number of people in the country using it. In the last ten years the population has increased by about 4 million people. Increases in NHS staffing mean that there has been one new doctor for every extra 120 people; one new nurse for every additional 216 people; and one GP for every additional 700 people.[26]

It is correct to say that immigration is a major cause of overwhelming demand on the NHS, in the sense that our population expansion over recent years has indeed owed a lot to patterns of migration. But beware of confusing this with health tourism. The latter – for all the bluster of MPs, and huffing and chuffings of *Telegraph* and *Mail* splashes – is not a vastly significant factor in the story of the NHS.

The government itself estimates that the use of the NHS by people who are not 'ordinarily resident' in the UK costs about £1.8 billion a year. This is a significant sum, but it does not constitute the amount by any means that pure 'health tourism' – deliberate entry into the country for the purpose of obtaining healthcare – costs. The majority comes from holidaymakers, temporary workers and people from countries with reciprocal health arrangements. These people are perfectly entitled to care. Deliberate health tourism costs us between

---

* Loneliness is a good example of an unhealthy mental state that can exacerbate physical ill-health. It has been estimated that its impact is equivalent to smoking fifteen cigarettes a day, although – like all catchy statistics – one probably shouldn't rely entirely on the science behind that.

£100 and £300 million a year, around 0.3 per cent of the total budget.

It is certainly the case that the NHS is unsurprisingly bad at recovering costs from those who should pay. The government wants to claim £500 million a year from patients not eligible for free service, or from their countries of origin. This is laudable, and correct, as a point of principle and as an example of good financial management. But it is not going to alter the overall picture of the finances a great deal: we are still talking about only around a sixtieth of the likely underspend in the next five years.

As we saw in an earlier chapter, the overall impact of migration on public services is an area of dispute. Broadly, anti-immigrant bodies produce statistics that paint a catastrophic picture; cuddly liberal institutions like universities do the opposite. However, it is hard to credibly assert that immigration – as a whole – creates an unbearable burden on the NHS. Say, to take one figure,[27] EU migrants cost the NHS £160 million in 2014. This is small beer in the context of the overall budget, and it is likely that the tax and other contributions made by those migrants came close to or surpassed that total. There seems to be little scandal to see here.

And the NHS is not only a place where immigrants come to get treated, but where they come to work. Ten per cent of doctors and 4 per cent of nurses come from elsewhere in the EU; and, overall, 11 per cent of staff and 26 per cent of doctors are not British. It is, therefore, not uncommon to sit in a hospital waiting room surrounded by patients whose first language is not English, and then to be treated by medical staff with a similar background. How angry this makes you is a matter of politics and social beliefs,* not really of economics.

The truth is that the greatest human burden on the NHS is our naturally growing[28] and ageing population, which according to the government added an extra £1.4 billion to the cost in 2015. As we have seen, getting older (and fatter) is now a national problem. And

---

* Some might say that the NHS's problems with ongoing care are, at the very least, compounded by having staff who are neither native nor ready speakers of English. While I support the right of immigrants to work here, I am disconcerted when I cannot make myself understood to a nurse failing to look after my wife.

we cannot do anything about the former; although we can change how we respond to it.

The problem of social care

There has always been a grey area between care that is the responsibility of the medical profession and that which is covered by other aspects of government support. Our old friend Roy Griffiths produced a report in 1988, which made the case for 'community care' as the responsibility of local government authorities. He said, with customary turn of phrase, that this sort of care had always been 'everybody's distant cousin but nobody's baby'. His recommendations were not uniformly followed but the direction of travel was clear: social care should take place away from institutions and, where possible, with people living at home; it should be the responsibility not of the NHS, but of local councils; they should be able to contract with both public and private providers to support those in need, primarily the elderly and the disabled.

So who pays? The taxpayer still in many areas. In the case of elderly care, in England, it must be privately funded if you have the means (either in cash or in sellable assets, like your home). Those who cannot pay are supported by the government. Local councils are, since 2016, allowed to add a 'precept' to their council tax bill, an add-on of a few percent to be used solely for the funding of adult social care. In Scotland, the government pays for most from its existing resources, but additional charges still be must be privately met.[29]

So social care has nothing to do with the NHS. Except that it does.* Because a failing social care system leaves vulnerable people – who cannot be looked after in the community – stuck in hospitals.[30] It is simple: the less care that takes place outside hospitals

---

* 'Of course you have to bring the fucking care system into health,' as Paddy Ashdown put it to me when I met him. In 2018, it was announced that the senior politician in the area would be the Secretary of State for Health and Social Care. It is not clear what this change in terminology would mean in actual practice.

and GP surgeries, the more that takes place in them. And healthy people stuck in hospital soon become unhealthy, sick and infected, escalating demand for treatment even further. Now, as we have seen, one of the tricks successive governments have played is to absolve themselves from the responsibility for the unsolvable problem of healthcare. Social care is a classic example of the phenomenon: it is not our fault; it is the fault of the local councils.

Well, successive periods of austerity measures have led to cuts in council budgets. That in turn has led to a predicted shortfall in social care funding of around £2.5 billion by 2020. According to Age UK, net expenditure on social care had dropped from £8.1 billion in 2006 to £6.3 billion in 2015, at a time when demand is certainly increasing. As spending decreases, costs of running care homes have increased[31] and so many have closed. There were 20,000 fewer residential beds in 2016 than in 2010.

Ultimately, we have a fundamental problem in how we think about our ageing population, which we are studiously ignoring. Ros Altmann, the former Pensions Minister said this, which is acute:

> In the 1940s, the concept of millions of chronically ill older people needing a little help with their daily lives on a long-term basis was unthinkable. Either their families or local communities would look after them, or they would not live very long. Life in the twenty-first century is totally different, but our social care system is stuck in the past.

Other cultures espouse multi-generational living, families caring for themselves and only needing support either at the margins or as last resort. We do not have that culture in the UK, and cannot acquire it by osmosis, even if we wanted (and I, to be honest, do not want to live with my parents, lovely people though they are). So one answer may be more cash,[32] but with it has to come a new sense of our collective responsibilities. We have to recognise that looking after ourselves and our families is something we have to contemplate ahead of simply demanding its universal delivery by the state; and we have to recognise that we will need to pay more money in taxes to support these services.

The politics of the NHS

There are easy political narratives, as we have seen, for our National Health Service: Labour wants to protect it; the Tories want to privatise it.★ And there is enough truth in those claims for the story to stick. But here is a striking thing to ponder: every political party in England has had a hand already in privatising parts of the NHS. The Tories privatised cleaners and cooks under Thatcher, and launched the internal market. Under Labour, radiology and transport services were privatised, and Foundation Trusts were created. The Liberal Democrats were part of the Coalition that attempted the last restructure, which again cemented the notion of the marketplace of healthcare. By 2011, private hospitals were taking £1 billion of NHS money to perform treatments; under new rules up to 49 per cent of NHS hospitals can be used for private patients. UKIP has made the clearest clarion cry for more privatisation, not less. Every party has supported the idea to some extent. Perhaps a truly left-wing government would be different; that has not been tested.

Consider the Private Finance Initiative (or PFI) in healthcare, which was established under the Major government of the early 1990s but pursued enthusiastically under Labour† and the Coalition too. The idea is simple enough: the government does not build and maintain hospitals, but contracts with a commercial outfit to do the job. That outfit then leases the buildings back to the NHS, with an ongoing contract for support services. Remember my point about privatisation of responsibility? This is another example of it; and it is also privatisation of visible liability, because the hospital costs come off the national books. Current PFI projects are valued at £11 billion, and the contracts are index-linked[33] and

★ See the decision to introduce something called 'accountable care organisations', umbrella bodies in local areas with the purpose of co-ordinating various medical services more efficiently. Stephen Hawking joined a chorus of observers to declaim that this will lead to subcontracting to private companies, as a vanguard to widespread privatisation.
† It has been openly reviled by the Corbyn administration, which misses no opportunity to disparage the Blairite past of the party.

must rise by at least 2.5 per cent every year, so the total cost for the lifetime of the projects may be up to £65 billion. There is no evidence to suggest that health PFI schemes are any more efficient than nationalised ones.

While Margaret Thatcher considered more brutal forms of privatisation in the 1980s, she was too fearful of public outrage to do anything seismic, and there is now a hardened political verity that challenging the NHS's funding is a public relations disaster. In 1982 a Tory think-tank produced secret plans to replace the NHS with private health insurance and charges for doctors' visits. The document was leaked to *The Economist*, and the outcry swiftly ended the debate. But here arises another paradox: the NHS is not actually important in electoral terms. The NHS has never won or lost anybody an election, except for perhaps its first one in 1945. While people express anger at the failing services, they do not vote based on those feelings. In April 2015 Ed Miliband had commanding poll leads on his trustworthiness about the NHS (37 per cent to Cameron's 22 per cent). And, contrary to the opinions of the Twitterati, he did not become Prime Minister.★ In the 1980s Shadow Health Secretary Robin Cook had 70 per cent approval rating for Labour's health policy and − as he himself noted − he did not actually have one. The 1980s were not good years for Labour from an electoral perspective.

What we can say, though, is that the performance under Tony Blair's government seems to be among the most impressive in this country's history. When Labour took power in 1997 (with their twenty-four hours to save the NHS), waiting lists were huge.[34] Heart surgeons had to warn patients that they stood a 5 per cent chance of dying while waiting for surgery. By 2010, Labour's commitment to delivering treatment within eighteen weeks of seeing a GP was almost universal; and half of people needing inpatient surgery were seen in eight weeks. Labour did two things: centralise targets and shoutily enforce them; and throw lots of money at the NHS. NHS spending doubled to more than £100

★ Jeremy Corbyn did not win the 2017 election either. Although it is hard to get many of his followers to admit it.

billion in its tenure, and there was an unsurprising corollary in improved quality of care.★

It is fair to say that things have declined since the acme point of 2009. The Coalition's mendacious restructure of 2012 has not improved matters, and the Conservative Department of Health's relationship with the medical profession has been abysmal. Again, though, it is worth pointing out that doctors have always been in dispute over the NHS, starting from their initial (and visceral) objection to its very existence and continuing with their periodic demands over pay. In 1965, 18,000 GPs sent letters threatening resignation, until their rates were increased by a third. In the 1970s consultants fought to keep the distinction between gentlemen (those who did a lot of private work) and players (those who mainly worked on the NHS). In 1990 a new contract had to be imposed on GPs by the then Health Secretary.

But the decision by Jeremy Hunt to impose a contract on junior doctors in 2016 in order to achieve a seven-day NHS created a vicious row even by NHS standards. Hunt believed that – as mortality rates were higher at weekends[35] – there needed to be the same medical coverage across the whole week. The problem was that he did not want to employ more doctors, he wanted to change their shift patterns and payment structures so that Saturdays and Sundays were treated as normal days. The medical profession, almost en masse, disagreed. No rapprochement was reached: doctors went on strike, repeatedly.

Doctors are, of course, much beloved people, who work incredibly hard[36] for not that much money,[37] and so they retained a lot of popularity, especially in contrast to the politicians (who are, of course, a much reviled people). Yet the dispute lingered, with confusion about whether the detail of the row really mattered; whether the doctors were out for cash, not the best for the NHS. In the end it petered out, an exchange emblematic of the modern treatment of the NHS: politicised and angry, passionate and impractical.

★ Worth noting that inequality was not defeated by this splurge, suggesting British society's deep-seated unfairness requires a different approach to shift, if it will ever do so.

Today's NHS

Certainly, while we remember that the NHS has always been in crisis, we look around us and feel that this crisis is worse than ever before. And we may be right. In 2016 the British Red Cross said that there was a 'humanitarian disaster' in English hospitals, that its own charitable services were needed, as if England were some sort of benighted Third World country. Statistical evidence of misery abounds. Numbers of people waiting longer than they should for treatment have more than doubled in five years since 2012; the eighteen-week pathway in 2017 was being missed for more than 350,000 people; we have 3.7 million people on an NHS waiting list. In 2016 more than 4,000 life-saving operations had to be cancelled, a record high. A majority of NHS Trusts in January 2016 declared a major alert, which meant they were overstretched to the point of breaking. In January 2018 all non-urgent operations were postponed due to pressure on resources. If a 'Winter Crisis' is an annual event, is it even a crisis any more, or simply a recurrence of a systematic problem?

Outside emergencies, we may simply all be using the NHS excessively, too, desperate to medicate ourselves at all costs. Healthcare does not guarantee health, though. Interestingly, a review in *Social Science and Medicine* (2008) of relevant literature concerning five doctor strikes around the world between 1976 and 2003 uncovered this notion: an absence of doctors in some cases reduced hospital deaths, and in no cases increased them. The reasons? Fewer elective surgeries, better prioritising of cases, fewer people lingering in dirty beds. Patients were safer when doctors were absent. An American Medical Association investigation of 2014 examined what happened to heart patients at times when there were national cardiology conferences (i.e. when all the specialists were forced to be absent from hospital). They found that high-risk patients had a lower thirty-day mortality rate (so fewer died in the next month) when they were admitted at such times; they were less likely to receive surgical treatment, and lived longer as a result.

My point here is that some of our reliance on medicine – apart from life-saving treatment – may be potentially both wasteful and counter-productive. And it imperils the whole institution. Of course, the NHS has never quite broken down, despite the protests and legitimate wails. 'You must go on, I can't go on, I'll go on,' is its Beckett-like refrain.* This is because our collective love for the NHS both binds us to it, and blinds us to its perhaps irrevocable flaws. Nye Bevan once said that the NHS 'will last as long as there are folk left with the faith left to fight for it'. And he was right: like Nigel Lawson said, it is a faith, a religion that will inspire adherents and votaries for ever. But the NHS may also be like a religion in that it is impractical and struggling to respond to modernity.

One factor, unquestionably, is money and our priorities for spending it. The NHS improved when Labour hugely increased the funding for it. Is it possible for the government to do something similar: say increase investment in the NHS by £30 billion annually? That would more than fill the current black hole, and give the chance to ensure that cash flows down to the places that need it. The government could fund it with more borrowing and tax rises: a percentage point rise in all income tax would net £5.5 billion; a percentage point rise in National Insurance would net another £5 billion; our progressive tax on the idle rich (floated in the earlier economics chapter) could garner another £5 billion, perhaps.

At the same time, the government could pass laws limiting compensation against the NHS (saving perhaps half a billion), truly crack down on both health tourism and recovery of owed charges (another half a billion); it could find efficiencies across standard practices[38] (up to £5 billion over several years); it could swallow deeply and stop doing some elective treatments like cosmetic surgery or IVF[39] (maybe clawing back half a billion here).

Yet, the time will come when a cash influx and savings drive will not alter a basic truth: demand will always expand, pressure will

---

* This is from Beckett's novel *The Unnamable* (1953), which is bleakly beautiful but pretty hard going. The other Beckett quote with a universal application you can pull out is: 'Try again. Fail again. Fail better.' That comes from the novella *Worstword Ho* (1983), which virtually nobody has read. I once saw Andrew Marr drop this quotation on the Jonathan Ross chat show, and Ross nearly had an orgasm over its intellectual heft.

always grow again. Bevan himself said it: 'We shall never have all we need. Expectation will always exceed capacity.' Either we put up with it, or we have to look again at first principles. This doesn't mean shouting about the NHS being privatised by the mercenary Tories. But it might mean looking again at systems like the Netherlands and Germany – fair, civilised societies – where compulsory health insurance, supported by government, means that healthcare is focused on the needs of the individual, not the demands of the nation state. Where people value their healthcare because they actively contribute to the cost of its upkeep. Where health is not a passive experience, kindly subsidised by a benevolent superpower, but something that needs to be worked at, shaped, contributed to, safeguarded. The NHS is a wonderful religion, a beautiful idea born out of the utmost ugliness of war and want; it may not be the future for an ageing, wobbling nation, however much we believe, however hard we fight.

4

Education

The roots of education are bitter, but the fruit is sweet

Aristotle (384–322 BC)

An attentive reader will notice the connection between health and education (improvements in the latter leading to benefits in the former). We spend around £60 billion less on our education system, and generally are even more complacent about it than we are with our health service. It is another muddle of restructures and embellishments; another example of the great British mess; another thing we put up with, but do not regularly challenge.

I was a little nervous about meeting Michael Gove, the former Education Secretary. Not that he is especially imposing as a public figure, even when in high office; when I met him, he was temporarily no longer a front-line politician: his Machiavellian scheming after the Brexit vote ended up with the knife embedded in his own bony back.* I was nervous because I had once written an article in the *New York Times*, in which I had referred to him as 'halibut-faced' and his wife (a columnist for the *Daily Mail*) as 'a Lady Macbeth of middlebrow letters'.

I see him on a stifling late spring morning in Westminster, the sort of day when the shirt sticks to your back and your spirit sinks to your knees. He bounds into the hotel where we are meeting, his

---

* In autumn 2017 he returned to be Secretary of State for the Environment, where his initial actions were broadly well received. Gove is intelligent and well-read, and willing to countenance large structural change. This was welcomed in the Ministry of Justice, and Environment. Rightly or wrongly, it was not welcomed by the education establishment.

piscine face (sorry) bedewed with perspiration. But then he is unflaggingly polite. Sure, he occasionally drifts into political automaton mode, rolling set phrases around his mouth that he has used on his stump speech a million times. He scarcely blinks when I ask him why he was so universally reviled as Education Secretary (one head teacher had told me of the occasion he was showing Gove the school roof-garden and seriously considered pushing him off). 'No Education Secretary leaves the job popular with teachers,' he concedes, not exerting himself greatly in the service of humility, it must be said.

But he is right: the politics of education in this country is both perilous and poisonous. And all education is political, because it is about the possible; it is about the potential of what a country will look, think and talk like in the future. It is political because it is about values, and the application of them in practice upon mouldable individuals. It is political because it must answer questions of secularity and religion, morality and pragmatism, attainment and vocation. It is political because it is an endlessly shifting mess. It is an endlessly shifting mess because it is political.

Who could disagree with Disraeli when he said that 'Upon the education of the people of this country the fate of this country depends'?[1] And yet the education of the people is something upon which almost nobody can really agree: how to do it, how much to pay for it, or how to measure its success. The theme of this chapter, indeed, is a theme of this entire book: Britain has been built largely, layer by layer, upon an accumulation of short-term, often conflicting and contingent policies. When we try to understand them, at least, we understand ourselves a little more.

Kenneth Baker was a determinedly reforming Tory Education Secretary, as we shall see, and set out the problem he faced with clarity:

> Our education system is not the product of a single directing mind – a Napoleon or a Bismarck – let alone the expression of a single guiding principle. It has grown up by a process of addition and adaption. It reflects a good many historical compromises. In short, it is a bit of a muddle, one of those institutionalised muddles that the English have made peculiarly their own.

Needless to say he went on to muddle things even further. I'll try to explain some of the key historical compromises along the way, but for now let's pretend that we are visiting this country for the first time and have asked the question: how does British education work?

Of course, education is a devolved subject, and so is pursued in different ways by different home nations (we'll get to that), but many of the issues are universal and the facts and figures for England are indicative enough for our purpose. In 2016 there were 8.56 million pupils in English schools, and the number is on the increase. In primary schools alone, there have been more than 500,000 additional pupils since 2009, and more than 100,000 since 2015. Since 2011 the average size of a primary school has increased by thirty children, a whole extra class.* The children entering the system are, increasingly, coming from an ethnic background: English primary schools have almost a third non-UK-born children, and the proportion has increased every year since 2006 (when it was 20 per cent).[2] More than a million pupils in our schools are classed as having Special Educational Needs.

School spending is on the slide, alas.† Until 2015 it was largely constant,[3] but recent proposals have seen increases dip below inflation. This means that, in real terms, schools in England are having budgets cut by £3 billion between 2015 and 2020.[4] Civil servants expect that schools will need to make efficiency savings of £1.3 billion through better purchasing, and save another £1.7 billion by using staff more efficiently. Bitter experience suggests this will not happen easily. The government has also been seeking to share resources better, by developing a new funding formula that will not focus as much on cities, although this may come to nothing.[5]

So lots of children; no more money: where do they all go? Here is where the muddle comes in. Most children are taught in schools funded and directed by the state. But it is not as simple as that.

---

* The number of schools has not increased hugely due to population rises; rather the size of schools has expanded. In fact, in 1947 there were more than 20,000 primary schools in England; now there are under 17,000.
† Ellen Wilkinson, the Labour Education Secretary in the late 1940s, said: 'Whenever government hits trouble, education is the first casualty.'

Some schools are run by local authorities, which is a legacy of an older system. The new system involved the creation of academies, and has been around since 2000: state-funded but free from local authority control, they are non-profit charitable trusts, which do not have to follow a national curriculum but do have to submit their students to national examinations.

This was Tony Blair's justification for the system, as set down in his memoirs: 'Freed from the extraordinarily debilitating and often, in the worst sense, politically correct interference from state or municipality, academies have just one thing in mind, something shaped not by political prejudice but by common sense: what will make the school excellent.'

Free schools are types of academies, but the trusts are set up by groups such as parents, education charities and religious bodies. They came about in David Cameron's doomed Big Society[6] phase of 2010, with the idea that interested and motivated individuals will demand higher standards than town-hall bureaucracies. Since 2015, there has existed something called the 'free school presumption', that first dibs, as it were, will go to a free school proposal over anything controlled by the council. As of March 2017 there were more than 6,000 academies and free schools teaching more than 3 million pupils.[7]

Are they better than state comprehensives? The answer is, inevitably, a muddle. Some do very well, others do not. There is not overwhelming evidence that academies outperform their local authority counterparts.

Now let's throw into this mix faith schools. To this bemused sceptic it seems odd to relate that a modern society should prioritise education based on parental beliefs in mythological beings, but it is a key factor in our education system (and has been from the very beginning). Faith schools can be run by the state[8] or privately. They are allowed to give priority to applicants of a particular faith if they are oversubscribed (which of course they generally will be), but must admit other applicants if there are places available.[9] For years, all state faith schools were Christian or Jewish, but since 1997 they have expanded to include all other religions.[10] And the numbers involved are surprisingly high: there are nearly 7,000 state faith schools in England, mostly primary (accounting for about one-third of all schools). Pupils at faith schools tend to do a bit better than those without God's blessing, either because (S)he is helping them out with tricky questions, or because they have been through a selection process first and will necessarily have more engaged parents (who care enough about education to have a view on its religious aspect).

A lengthy digression on grammar schools and the history of our education system

So: we have council-controlled, free, academy and faith schools. Let's add the really divisive poster-child for politicised education: grammar schools. To explain them, we are going to have to briskly explore the story of how schooling has been historically organised in Britain too.

The origins of grammars, as it happens, are religious. They were originally attached to cathedrals and monasteries as a way of teaching Latin. This explains the name: Samuel Johnson's[11] dictionary defined the term as 'a school in which the learned languages are grammatically taught'. But, even by Johnson's time, they were more than that: in the sixteenth century they had become institutions, charitably funded by either individual sponsors or the Church, offering tuition to local children.[12] As time progressed, they became increasingly more academic, and some became fee-paying by Victorian times.

Until the 1830s, grammar schools were the main educational establishments available, alongside 'dame schools' taught by individual women on a very limited basis. There were just ten 'public',★ fee-paying schools and four universities. The education revolution began quietly: in 1833 Parliament voted to spend a few thousand pounds[13] on supporting Church schools (an amount less than it was willing to spend on the Queen's stables for the year, as it happens).

★ They were called 'public', despite being private, in order to distinguish them as open to the fee-paying public, rather than under the patronage of the Church. The term has grown rich in irony since that point.

In 1870 the Elementary Education Act introduced the first state schools, which could offer free places to the poor.[14] Ten years later, state schools were made compulsory up until the age of ten; by 1902, Local Education Authorities were created to fund elementary schools (which taught children up to the age of fourteen), as well as primary and secondary schools. In 1918 an Education Act was passed that abolished all fees in state schools, and raised the school leaving age to fourteen.

Just before the Second World War, England had gone (in 100 years) from no organised system of education to one teaching 3.5 million children compulsorily and freely up until the age of fourteen. Most people went to elementary school covering that whole period. Some boys went to the new public schools that had sprung up in the Victorian age: these followed the example of Thomas Arnold,[15] the renowned headmaster at Rugby, and were the sort of flog 'em and bugger 'em, teach 'em a bit about Latin and a bit about life, cold showers and rugger, muscular Christian institutions that have passed into our cultural identity.

In 1941 Rab Butler was appointed Education Secretary by Winston Churchill* and presented with the opportunity to overhaul completely the education system once the war was over (provided he did not upset the public schools or the Church too much, that is). A national education service to go alongside the National Health Service was in prospect. Butler largely blew it. Churchill, in Butler's words, had an interest that was 'slight, intermittent and idiosyncratic' and had a prejudice in favour of public schools. The resultant system left them intact (free to grow again when Britain became rich once more) and did not simplify the complicated relationship between Church and schooling.

Instead it created a new framework called the 'tripartite system', all under local education authorities, by which children would be educated to the age of fifteen: grammar schools ('for those interested

---

* Butler recorded in his diary how he went to see Churchill when the latter awakened 'after his afternoon nap and was audibly purring like a tiger'. Two days later, he met the Archbishop of Canterbury; three weeks later he met him again, this time with a load of bishops. The influence of religion on our current schooling system is hard to overstate.

in learning for its own sake'); technical schools (for those whose skills 'lie markedly in the field of applied science or applied art'); and secondary moderns (for those who 'deal more easily with concrete things than ideas . . . interested only in the moment'*).

So children, based on selection via examination at eleven, would be split into the clever, the handy and the disdained. Much was made of a desire for 'parity of esteem' between these institutions, which was a lie then, and will be a lie in the mouths of anybody who now praises the grammar school system. Technical schools never got more than 2 per cent of the school population at any point (and we have no successful tailored education in applied science today). Grammars were for those judged successful; the rest could go somewhere worse.

The system persisted in this form until a Labour government of 1964, which appointed Anthony Crosland as Education Secretary. His position was not a subtle one: 'If it's the last thing I do,' said he, 'I am going to destroy every fucking grammar school in England. And Wales. And Northern Ireland.' He did not quite succeed, but put such a dent into the system that it has never recovered. In 1964 there were 1,298 grammar schools, teaching more than 700,000 pupils; today there are 163, teaching a bit more than 150,000. In acutely British fashion, the counter-revolution wasn't accompanied by pomp and flag-waving: Crosland sent something called 'Circular 10/65' to local councils requesting[16] that schools should go comprehensive. Harold Wilson called it 'grammar schools for all', which in practice meant nothing whatsoever.

Enter the lists Margaret Thatcher, a grammar-educated force of nature, who became Education Secretary five years later.[17] Her response was swift and without consultation, and still within the thrilling medium of a circular request to councils. 'Circular 10/70' countermanded Crosland's and allowed grammar schools to remain, and their number possibly to expand. The force of nature failed. Crosland's system was too firmly established: more comprehensive schools were created and more grammar schools closed under Thatcher's tenure than under anyone before or since. In 1970, 32

* These deeply patronising and inane quotes come from the education committee responsible for helping to create the system.

per cent of children were at comprehensives; in 1974 it was 62 per cent; in 1979 it was 85 per cent.

Today, just ten Local Education Authorities (LEAs) run selective programmes involving grammars, and a further twenty-six have at least one grammar school in the area. These are concentrated in the wealthy south-east. The north-east is the only region with no grammar schools. So why talk about them at all? It is a good question, actually. Grammar schools are statistically insignificant, but are talismanic, especially for the Conservative Party. Prime Minister Theresa May has been a fervent adherent to the cause, and her Thatcherite desire to expand them is indicative of an educational philosophy worth pausing over.

So are grammar schools fair?

I once spoke to a middle-aged woman called Chris, who lived in the Midlands, about her experience of trying to get into her local grammar school. It was clear that her failure, as she saw it, aged eleven still lingered in her mind. This is how she could instantly picture it:

> Our home stood in the middle of a row of rented houses; there was very little to distinguish them from each other save different coloured front doors. From our house a short walk either way, left or right, would take you to a school bus stop. Nothing strange about that you might think, but you are wrong. If you went left each weekday morning, you donned a grammar school uniform. If, however, you went right, then everyone knew you had failed the eleven-plus and were off to the village college. As a young child, so inexperienced in life, it felt as though the entire village watched me make that journey each morning and evening as I returned. As an adult I realise now that of course they weren't watching, they were simply getting on with the business of life. But this is my point, this damning experience of what I perceived to be humiliation ruined my general happiness for years to come.

Both my parents passed the eleven-plus, as it happens: working-class children who were being given an opportunity to better

themselves. But my mum's central memory relates to the consequences of division:

> When we got the results (read out in front of everyone by the
> headmaster), those who had passed were allowed to go home to
> tell their parents; those who had failed had to stay in school. I
> usually had to go a certain way home but, because I had passed
> the eleven-plus, I was allowed to cross the road by myself and take
> a short cut home.

It was indeed a system of short cuts for some, long ways round
for others. Clearly, it was enforced with a typically British combination of ineptness and emotional constipation. Clearly, it benefited
those who were selected: prioritising their educational needs, helping
them to prosper. Generations of senior figures in politics, the Civil
Service, medicine and law (and so on) achieved their success due
to the social mobility granted to them by their free and high-quality
schooling. But it was social mobility for some that came at the cost
of the (emotional, educational) status of others. And this was known
from the beginning. Here is a quote from the White Paper that led
to the 1944 Education Act: 'There is nothing to be said in favour
of a system, which subjects children at the age of eleven to the strain
of competitive examination on which not only their future schooling
but their future careers may depend.'

That was the very system about to be put in place. There is no
evidence that the age of eleven is a propitious time to judge the
potential of children to learn. There is ample evidence that testing
can be gamed:[18] it is the children of wealthy, pushy parents who get
the right tutoring to enable them to pass exams. There is global
evidence (we will come to this) that selection and streaming is
damaging to a country's education system.

Today's grammar schools are likely to be single-sex, have a sixth
form and – despite being free – attract people from more wealthy
backgrounds (just 2.6 per cent of grammar school pupils qualify
for free meals, paid for by the government for families below a
certain earning threshold, against the average of 14.6 per cent).[19]
Let's reflect on that latter statistic for a moment. Why are these
free institutions not genuinely open to all? One reason is that, by

The scale of the NHS

So here we are: that is how the NHS – in very broad terms – reached its current, largely incomprehensible state. Could you tell your PCTs from your CCGs? Have you ever thought about Foundation Trusts? Do you know who is the regulator of the NHS? Of course not. The NHS is both a simple, fetishised ideal, and a complicated, borderline inexplicable bureaucracy.

Its size – its comprehensiveness – is of course both its strength and its fatal weakness. When Nye Bevan said 'administration is going to be the chief headache for years to come', he was absolutely right. The NHS is now the fifth largest employer in the world, with a staff population the size of Botswana. Statistics are overwhelming so I shall try to cherry-pick a few to give you the sense of the job done by the NHS. It deals with over 1 million patients every 36 hours; 23 million people attend Accident and Emergency departments every year. There were 3.1 million emergency 999 responses in 2015; 1.9 million people were in contact with mental health services in the same year. At the end of September 2016 there were 3.7 million people on waiting lists. The NHS employs 149,000 doctors, 340,000 nurses, 25,000 midwives, 19,000 ambulance staff and 31,000 managers. Taking staff all in all, it employs just under 1.5 million people (more than ten times as many as the next largest employer, the army).

And this is just England. Remember – if you consume London-based media* – it is the English NHS that is generally being described, although it is fair to say that the principles and indeed the processes are fairly universal across the United Kingdom.

* A good rule of thumb is that the closer to London an issue is the more it will be covered. Hence Tube strikes being massive stories in the way that, say, a bus strike in Leeds would be ignored. The BBC tries to fight this by making programmes outside London wherever possible, largely by sending disgruntled London broadcasters under protest to the provinces to slum it for a story.

eleven, social inequalities have already kicked in: 60 per cent of what is called the 'disadvantaged attainment gap' exists already between impoverished children and their better-off peers. That is equivalent to ten months' schooling, and stops many poorer children from passing the exams. Another reason is that house prices rise abruptly around grammar schools, where entrance is based on a small catchment area, as middle-class parents seek the benefits of private education without the direct cost. Poorer people are pushed out of the area entirely.

Worse still, the existence of grammar schools contributes to the gap widening after the selection process has finished. According to the Education Policy Institute, 'pupils eligible for free school meals in wholly selective areas that don't attend a grammar school perform worse than the national average.' Those left behind, stay behind. This is perhaps not surprising: the expectations from teachers will be less towards those already judged to be academically ungifted; and the better teachers in the area will inevitably gravitate towards the 'better' school. The proportion of teachers with academic degrees in their teaching subject is significantly higher (especially in science) in grammar schools than in comprehensives.

A quick digression on expectations (we'll return – almost as a recurring theme – to the importance of teaching and teachers later). In 1968 Robert Rosenthal conducted an experiment in America where teachers were told that randomly selected pupils had actually performed in the top 20 per cent of a test that identified 'potential'. This was, of course, untrue. But here's the thing: when those pupils' IQs were tested at the end of the year, they had increased relative to everybody else. Expectations improved performance. And the tragedy of low expectations is crystallised – as we saw with Chris – in the grammar school system.

Of course, grammar school pupils tend to do well in exams, but probably no better than those of similar backgrounds in comprehensive schools. In other words, it is not the schooling that helps, it's the privilege that precedes it. The Education Policy Institute in 2016 found 'no overall attainment impact of grammar schools, either positive or negative'. It is a fuss about nothing.[20]

So where does the fuss come from? A Tory friend of mine told me that this is an idea that prospers at the individual, not the societal, level. 'Yes, comprehensive education should be better, but I want the best for my children; I want them to be considered to be high achievers, getting the best opportunity.' And the policy is persistently popular. A poll in 2016 showed both a majority agreeing that grammars were a good way of increasing the quality of schooling (38 per cent to 28 per cent), at the same time as recognising that they would leave too many children 'feeling like failures' (41 per cent agreeing, 26 per cent disagreeing). Another poll in the same year saw more people thinking that the schools were 'good for social mobility'. The trend on this is pretty unwavering: people will back grammar schools largely because they hope one day they will benefit from them.

That is why they are, and have been for decades, the aim of Tory actual policy or crypto-policy. Prime Minister Theresa May has talked about 'building a great meritocracy so that children from ordinary working families are given the chances their richer contemporaries take for granted'. Noble words, populist words; but hard to see how grammar schools will achieve this. Indeed, we must also remember that the number of grammar schools in existence is tiny. Say that, under a future Tory government, they were to double (which is a stretch in itself): we are still talking about only around 300,000 grammar school pupils (less than 10 per cent of the 3 million attending state secondaries). Michael Gove, careful not to rubbish the concept (which he felt 'reinforced the sense of Theresa May as a meritocrat'), concedes that it 'sucks all of the energy out of the education debate'. It is an issue of footling significance, but loud lobbying; something full of sound and fury, but signifying nothing.

In any event, our hodgepodge of educational options is almost complete: council-controlled, academy, free, faith, grammar. Finally, there is the independent sector. This grew out of the grammar school system, when parents were asked to take up the burden of payment from charitable benefactors.

Another digression, which perhaps should be considered a declaration of interest. I attended a school of this stripe: Loughborough Grammar School, founded in 1492 and for a long time a genuine, free grammar; it became independent before I arrived. My family was not wealthy, but was becoming increasingly more comfortable, as my parents shifted economically upwards. To pay the school fees, my mum took a job as a lab technician in an inner city school in Leicester. In a structural way, then, my schooling is a testimony to the inequalities of the system: a school of little resource funded my education in a school of greater.

Loughborough Grammar combined some of the pretensions of a public school with a resolutely mediocre execution. I hated it.* It favoured the sons of the local elite, who tended to be brainless and gifted at rugby. It crushed individuality and undervalued academic thought. I pretty much learned everything from the teachers of two subjects (history and Latin),† and did well enough to get into Cambridge to do English (although I was told, formally, by my school that I was not good enough for that).‡ Digression over.

About 7 per cent of school children go (like I did) to a fee-paying school: it's about 625,000 pupils in 2,600 schools. The number is pretty stable, although there is cautious talk of it falling due to prohibitively rising costs. Surprisingly, these schools have charitable status, which is worth about £150 million a year collectively to them. It means they are VAT-exempt (so their bills are 20 per cent cheaper than they would otherwise be) and they can claim an 80 per cent reduction in business rates.

Why are private schools charities? An increasingly pointed question. Private schools educate 40,000 children from low-income families on means-tested bursaries. That's around 6 per cent of their intake, and worth about £350 million a year. To varying degrees, private schools also have partnerships with state schools and offer use of their facilities. It seems that one could legitimately argue that this is insufficient to justify the tax breaks, to say the least.

Should private schools be abolished? Such an idea would only be

* Many years later, the school approached me to hand out prizes on Speech Day; my teenage self joyfully endorsed me telling them to bugger off.

† Latin, it seems to me, is one of the critical academic subjects, because it teaches formal structures of language in a way that your own language instruction never does. It teaches you how to spell. It teaches you the basis of literature. Almost everything I know about reading and writing comes from the study of Latin.

‡ And, no, I will never fucking forgive them for it.

possible if the entire education system were utterly revamped from scratch (as Butler could theoretically have done in 1944). As it stands, they save the taxpayer around £3 billion every year by educating children who otherwise would have to be reabsorbed into the state system. They represent evidence of an unequal society; but that evidence subsists and persists in almost every aspect of it anyway. Certainly, they produce children who are good at exams: private pupils represent 13 per cent of all A-level entries, and account for almost 30 per cent of all A-star grades. However, there is some suggestion that the advantage (as with grammar schools) resides with the socio-economic-cultural background of the families, rather than the quality of the schooling. And, perhaps happily, the advantage flattens further at university: research in the *Oxford Review of Education* in 2015 found that 'students from independent schools were less likely to achieve either a first-class degree or at least an upper second . . . than students from comprehensive schools with similar prior attainment.' Cleverness will make itself apparent in the end, we hope.

Measuring standards

If the entire education system in England (and elsewhere) is a patchwork, there have been attempts to bring about central standards in the form of exams and inspections. General Certificates of Education (GCEs) were introduced into England, Wales and Northern Ireland in 1951. They were split between O-level and A-level ('ordinary' and 'advanced'), and were deliberately made too arduous for any but those at grammar schools to take. Pupils at secondary moderns mostly left school without any qualification at all. In 1965 Certificates of Secondary Education (CSEs) were introduced to be taken in secondary moderns at the age of sixteen; however, as the optional school-leaving age was still as young as fifteen,* many still did not take them. Essentially, O-levels were taken by 20 per cent of children at sixteen, CSEs by 40 per cent.

---

* School-leaving age was finally raised to sixteen in 1972, in the teeth of opposition from the Treasury who wanted more people in work.

The remaining 40 per cent were not considered capable, and were ignored.

In 1988, amid a raft of changes, this structure was simplified with the introduction of one set of exams at sixteen called GCSEs. We all accept them as inevitable now, but we should recall that their origins relate to a time when many children left school at sixteen. What is their current purpose? Around 10 per cent of seventeen-year-olds are in work or work-based learning, so is there a reason to be testing so heavily at sixteen? The historian Tristram Hunt, when Shadow Education Secretary in 2015, made a sensible case for a programme of education focusing on the period between fourteen and eighteen, with both academic and non-academic qualifications for school leavers its target: 'I would not be saddened,' he said, 'if that meant in a decade's time we were beginning to phase out GCSEs.' This is so sensible it almost certainly will not happen.

GCSEs were introduced by Kenneth Baker as part of his Great Educational Reform Bill (or GERBIL, for short), which also compelled testing at 'Key stages' (age seven, eleven and fourteen, as well as sixteen), gave targets for schools and introduced the national curriculum. In doing so, he established the framework for our system today: neither major political party has sought radically to resile from a notion of centralised testing and measurement.

A note on testing

This has become an increasingly divisive educational issue, especially around SATs (Standard Assessment Tests, although the term is no longer formally used; they are called National Curriculum assessments) taken at the ages of seven and eleven (the test at fourteen was dropped in 2008). These were made more formal (and difficult) in 2016.

To someone like Michael Gove, testing is critical to education. He says that tests 'embed knowledge', drive standards, stretch children (to prevent them becoming 'snowflakes'). How else, his question goes, can we enforce improvement, if we do not know how schools are performing? Indeed, his party introduced optional testing at age four: in order to understand what the baseline levels of pupils are, so their progress can be accurately monitored.[21]

The rebuttal can be summarised in an old American farming phrase: you don't fatten a pig by weighing it. Teachers are concerned that testing places undue pressure on schools and pupils, and creates artificial targets* to hit in place of a genuine drive for actual education. Some parents have taken their children from school in protest, with reports of children tearfully suffering from stress at the thought of their prospective performance. The extent to which that is down to the conduct of their teachers and parents is a legitimate debating point. My seven-year-old daughter did her tests almost without noticing it. Her school managed the process with little fuss at all. Her headmaster is not especially concerned about testing (as he admires rigour and measurement); he made sure that it did not impact negatively on the pupils. Is it that simple? In any case, the principle of a one-size, centralised approach to education is not going anywhere.

It may be a surprise that a one-size curriculum is such a late development. Or that it would be controversial. But it had been resisted for years on the grounds that it represented state intrusion into an area that should remain non-political. It was not uncommon for the spectre of fascism to be invoked in discussions. Robert Cook, the general secretary of the National Association of Head Teachers said in 1976: 'I was teaching in Nazi Germany in the thirties and saw what happened where the curriculum was nationally controlled. My history books were taken out and replaced.'

So far the threat of mass indoctrination has been averted (although don't say that to a Brexiteer). But the national curriculum has regularly raised good questions on which nobody can reasonably agree: what sort of subjects, covering what sort of areas, must be taught in what sort of way? Politicians and educationalists continually clash over this, and two philosophies have emerged: the neo-traditionalists,

---

* Some head teachers responded to the rise of testing with letters to parents and children (practically begging to go viral), arguing that intangible aspects of education are important. One said: 'The people who create these tests . . . do not know your laughter can brighten the darkest day,' and so on.

who believe in teacher-led interaction based on the dissemination of facts and details; and the progressives, who believe in the child-led development of critical skills. In any event, the curriculum is now focused on a number of core subjects, which includes – alongside obvious staples like English, maths and science and so on – 'citizenship'. In a shiver of patriotic fervour, schools are expected now to 'actively promote British values', if there are such things.

The national curriculum, and the regularisation of testing, has led to league tables, first published in 1992 and now the go-to guide for parents when selecting schools. They are a triumph of the Tories' free-market philosophy that we saw in the area of health, and have been embedded with relative success. In 1993 OFSTED (the Office for Standards in Education) was created* with the brief to assess every school in England and help to raise standards. Between 1993 and 2005, schools were inspected for a week every six years (with two months' notice); this then became a two-day visit every three years, with two days' warning. Schools are judged on a scale of 1–4 (outstanding; good; requires improvement; inadequate). Since 2015, schools ranked good became subject only to 'temperature checks', short inspections every three years; outstanding schools have become formally exempt from further inspection unless concerns arise.

OFSTED has real powers. Poor-performing schools are inspected at least every two years and can have the governance completely altered without agreement, including: suspension of budget; appointment of new governing body; requirement to join federations of other schools; conversion to academy status. It is for this reason that OFSTED is feared and bemoaned by many involved in education. It certainly is open to parody for its jargon and virtue-signalling waffle: schools should be 'user-focused'; 'the primary focus will be on learning, rather than teaching, with students working in partnership with teachers, asking questions and reflecting on the learning strategies that work best for them'; and so on. I spoke to a head teacher at an 'outstanding' school, who railed against the 'worship of the OFSTED god'.

---

* Replacing a system of local inspectorates that had been in place since 1876. Again, it is surprising how recent all this innovation is.

What does devolved education look like?

The overarching framework of education[22] differs in different parts of the country, but the similarities are far more substantial. The national curriculum is the same for England, Wales and Northern Ireland, as is the examining system of GCSEs and A-levels.[23] The grammar school system is even more embedded in Northern Ireland (about 45 per cent of children attend selective schools; the top five schools in the country are Catholic grammar schools), as is the lingering debate about its fairness.

Scottish state schools are fully comprehensive and non-selective. It has its own Curriculum for Excellence, which rests upon three pillars: health and well-being, literacy and numeracy. Scottish pupils are tested far less frequently over their school careers than anywhere else in Great Britain. They sit National 4 and 5 exams at sixteen, followed by Highers at seventeen and Advanced Highers at eighteen, the middle of which can qualify you for university. That is the reason you meet seventeen-year-old Scots at university, drinking illegally (as is their birthright).

Welsh schools perform the worst in every subject in the whole UK by most international metrics. It may be that the distraction of compulsory Welsh-speaking impacts on broader learning (Welsh is also used as the main language of teaching in 15 per cent of its schools); it may be that a greater tradition of manual or rural labour across the country has historically downplayed the value of academic education. It is now a priority for the Welsh government to fix, although it is always a priority, and it is seldom fixed. Education, education, education:* the hopeful clarion of the politician that echoes throughout our modern history.

---

* The words, of course, of huckster superstar Tony Blair during his pre-landslide party conference of 1996. The Blair years did see – as with healthcare – an increased investment in education that has been dwindling since.

Now what about higher education?

Like everything in the area of education, the widespread attendance of British young people at universities is not as recent as you would think. Oxford and Cambridge have great claim to antiquity, of course, the former slightly older than the latter,[24] but both up and running in the medieval period. They held more or less a duopoly in England all the way up to Victorian times, when finally other great city institutions began to emerge, beginning with University College London in 1826 and Durham in 1832. Scotland, as so often in matters of the mind, had rushed ahead: St Andrews University was founded in 1411, Glasgow in 1451, Edinburgh in 1583. By 1938, though, just 50,000 students in this country were enrolled in universities; and they were essentially finishing schools for the elite.

Indeed, the function of universities was similar to that of public schools: to focus on both moral development and study of the classics.★ They were avowedly not vocational, or technical; they did not seek to improve the scientific knowledge-base of the nation. This was John Stuart Mill in 1867: 'What professional men should carry away with them from an University, is not professional knowledge, but that which should direct the use of their professional knowledge, and bring the light of general culture to illuminate the technicalities of a special pursuit.'

In other words: let's educate a nation of generalists. And we have. In any event, the real explosion of tertiary education, the notion that the opportunity to advance your academic learning after school was a mark of civilisation and democratic entitlement, came in the

---

★ A slight digression: in the history of tertiary education, the course I would have most liked to attend is that of Literature 311–312 in Cornell University (in America) in the 1950s. It was taught by Vladimir Nabokov: one of the greatest writers, in English and Russian, of any era, teaching young Americans about classic books. Before each exam he said this: 'One clear head, one blue book, ink, think, abbreviate obvious names, for example, Madame Bovary. Do not pad ignorance with eloquence. Unless medical evidence is produced nobody will be permitted to retire to the WC.' Those exams were then peculiarly Nabokovian. Sample question: 'Discuss Flaubert's use of the term "and".'

1960s. The Robbins Report of 1963, commissioned to determine the future of the sector, said that 'courses in higher education should be available for all those who are qualified by ability and attainment to pursue them and who wish to do so.' Massive investment followed,[25] and a golden era of sorts began. A distinction, though, was drawn between universities and technical colleges: the former allowed to be autonomous; the latter kept within the public sector. This was the birth of the polytechnic, theoretically designed to ensure that scientific and practical knowledge would be given its due. It was not. As with technical schools, there was never any parity of esteem: Mill's view of universities as arts-based improvers of character persisted.

The 1980s brought with them huge budgetary pressures, and cuts in spending, which fell largely on the newer, less august universities.[26] Student loans were introduced as top-ups to the maintenance grant system (by which the government gave students money to support their living and education costs), a herald of a political storm that was to emerge over the next decades, as more and more students availed themselves of higher education. The number hit 31 per cent in 1993: 1 million young adults attending university. The figure had flourished because this was the year that polytechnics were allowed to become universities, ending the arbitrary and unsuccessful division of previous years.

In 1997 one of the first acts of the Tony Blair administration was to receive a special report into the state and future of higher education.* This made clear that there was an unignorable funding crisis, and more money needed to be spent on research, teaching and technology (about £2 billion, actually, over a twenty-year period). But it also changed the face of universities when it said that students should contribute to the cost of their own education. It recommended that undergraduates should offer up £1,000 per year as a fee, repayable once they started work, and that means-tested grants

---

* This was the Dearing Report, the most significant piece of work on funding for thirty years; it ran to 2,000 pages and broke the foot of someone who dropped it while reading on the day of publication. It contained ninety-three recommendations, but will be largely remembered for one.

should remain to support poorer students. Amazingly (given subsequent events), the principle of fees was scarcely opposed. Dearing, the report chairman, spoke to a collection of student union leaders about his plan; he was quietly heard and then applauded as he left.

In the end, the government scrapped the grant system, but introduced means-testing to a system of fees[27] (which were payable up-front). In 2004 universities in England could charge variable fees up to £3,000 per year to students, a policy soon followed in Northern Ireland and Wales. The cost of going to university was rising; but so was the number of students attending.[28] Seeking to avoid a political row in the run-up to the 2010 election, Labour commissioned a further report into higher education funding to appear after the election was over. This was to prove treacherous to the Liberal Democrats, who campaigned hard on the principle of free higher education, and whose leader signed an NUS pledge not to increase tuition fees.

As it turned out, the Lib Dems were unlikely kingmakers and entered government with a Conservative Party absolutely committed to fees. The Browne Review reported in October 2010, and gave the Tories more or less what they wanted. The eventual policy proposed tuition fees capped at £9,000,[29] supported by student loans to be repaid once a graduate earned at least £21,000 per year (and written off in thirty years if not paid in full by then). The Lib Dems were in a terrible position: to get into the Coalition government they had promised the Conservatives not to block this policy (but to get elected in the first place they had promised the electorate to do the opposite). In the end, they conceded quietly: twenty-eight Lib Dems voted for the policy, twenty-one against and eight abstaining. The damage to the party's credibility was long-lasting,* on a policy that was probably inevitable anyway. Its leader Nick Clegg apologised in 2012, but to little avail.[30]

So are tuition fees reasonable? There is some good news and bad news. The bad news is that it is incredibly hard to get the loans

---

* Whenever I did LBC phone-ins on the subject of the Lib Dems (which I occasionally did for reasons of masochism), this broken promise came up over and over again.

paid back. In 2010 it was predicted that 28 per cent of student loans would never be repaid; in 2014 the *Guardian* calculated that the figure was now more like 45 per cent.[31] At 48 per cent, it is calculated, the government starts to receive less money than it did before the increase in 2010. By 2044, the unpaid student debt could hit the vaguely incomprehensible figure of £330 billion.[32] The Business Select Committee said in 2016: 'We are concerned that the Government is rapidly approaching a tipping point for the financial viability of the student loans system.' Rising inflation also means that the interest rates on the loans has been on the increase, and hit 6.1 per cent by September 2017 (it is worked out by taking inflation figures and adding 3 per cent), amounting to more than £5,000 of interest charges for a three-year degree. This is unfair and demoralising.

Pretty bad news, then. However, the gloomy prognostications about the damage to social mobility caused by higher tuition fees have not proven entirely correct. Paying for university education does not deter people from applying. Since 2010 the rate of poorer students applying to English universities for full-time study★ has actually increased; and the gap between rich and poor students has declined. One theory is that the extra money from tuition fees has enabled universities to increase investment in bursaries and outreach schemes. English, Welsh and Northern Irish universities do better at attracting disadvantaged students than Scottish universities, where there are no tuition fees at all.[33]

The system may be failing for practical reasons; it is not necessarily failing for ideological ones. The abolition now of tuition fees would benefit many middle-class families, arguably without improving the lot of the poor.[34] It would also leave an even greater hole in higher education funding (approximately £10 billion) than already exists.

Fees have, inevitably, turned students into consumers. This is yet another example of how the philosophy of the free market has

---

★ There is a crisis, however, in part-time applications for university, which declined more than 50 per cent between 2010 and 2016. Many universities are no longer offering the option of part-time study, which is a problem for mature students and many from less privileged backgrounds who combine education and paid work.

ineluctably entered British life. The Conservative government is naturally unrepentant about this: in 2018 it launched a market regulator for further education, the Office for Students (OfS), designed to test for value for money, and ensure proper competition, within the sector. Universities are no longer to be considered as secluded cloisters of learning for its own sake, but part of the consumable economy, subject to performance pressures and market requirements. The verdict on this may be dependent on your politics: either you applaud a drive for efficiency, which will act as a bulwark against complacency and scandals like inflated salaries for vice-chancellors; or you deprecate yet another bid to remove notions of altruism and moral purpose from a bastion of public life.

How much should the state take a benevolent role here? In the debate about tuition fees, the question of the maintenance grants has sometimes been lost. Dearing, we recall, suggested introducing fees and retaining grants. As it now stands, poorer students are likely to have to borrow more than richer students. According to the IFS, the poorest 40 per cent of students will emerge with an average debt of £57,000; the richest 30 per cent will have a debt of £43,000. A happy medium of policies here may be fees, loans and grants targeted at the most indigent members of society.

And there you have it: the British education system from beginning to end. A muddle and a mess of state support and private funding. A lottery of opportunity based on where you live, what your parents earn, and what ideological spasms have entered party politics over a century. Should we really expect any more? To consider that point, let's look at how some other countries do it.

How does British education compare worldwide?

Any comparison comes with a caveat: different countries have different cultures that are not replicable, even if their education systems may be. Many educationalists will visibly sag when you mention countries like Finland and Korea (as I am about to do now), saying that they cannot offer complete solutions to our problems, and may be overrated anyway.

Certainly, we know that the national characteristics of countries are vastly important to their behaviour, including in the classroom. There is – without being racist – a recognisably Asian mentality towards learning, for example. In the 1990s there was an experiment involving American and Japanese children designed to test how long they would try to solve an insoluble maths problem. It was cancelled when it was clear that the Japanese children would never give up on it. Asian children tend to be more conditioned to believe that effort is one of life's most important attributes, and that failure is a spur to success.* In 2001, a survey found that European Americans thought effort accounted for 36 per cent of intelligence; for Asian Americans it was 45 per cent; for Japanese children it was 55 per cent.

There is, happily, a way at least to assess comparatively how well different countries seek to educate their children. You may have heard (as the media talks about it once every three years) of the PISA test: the Programme for International Student Assessment. It is a set of exams taken in seventy-one countries, involving more than half a million fifteen-year-old children. It was devised by a scientist called Andreas Schleicher in order to test not just the pupils' reproduction of knowledge, but the development of their critical abilities in the areas of literacy, numeracy and science.

The UK performs in resolutely average fashion, and has always done so: last time up, it ranked twenty-seventh in maths, twenty-second in reading and fifteenth in science. The tests reveal that about a fifth of British students are classed as low performers, failing to reach baseline levels of proficiency in the three subjects. Around 20 per cent of our students are regarded, then, as failures by global standards.

The top performing country is always Singapore, joined generally by Japan, China, South Korea, Vietnam, Canada, Finland and Estonia (the latter three the only non-Asian countries ever to get into the top five of any subject). You will note that Britain, by GDP, is richer than all but two of them. I will try to give you a whistle-stop

---

* One experiment tested how Americans and Asians performed in tests taken after a prior failure and after a prior success: the Asian children performed better after a failure, the American children performed worse.

(avowedly non-exhaustive) tour of some of the systems that might give us some pointers for the future. You will spot some themes emerging fairly quickly.

Finland

In 1963 Finland embraced an entirely comprehensive system (ending a system of selection based on an exam taken at the age of ten). Instead, all children attend the same school for nine years, having not started formal education until the age of seven.* At fifteen, children decide whether to pursue an academic or vocational path until eighteen. There are no national exams until the very end. Streaming of children based on ability became outlawed in 1983. Private schools were forced to become part of the system, and cannot charge fees or select based on ability. It is a legal requirement in Finland for schools to have multi-disciplinary support teams in place, including psychologists, social workers, speech therapists and family counsellors. The Finnish government has calculated that the cost to the state of a school drop-out is more than a million euros over a lifetime, so it should be avoided in the first place if possible. (Evidence from the US, by the way, shows that two-thirds of children who cannot read by the age of ten end up in prison or on welfare.)

In many ways, this is a system that Britain could have adopted in 1945; a means of addressing 'ignorance', one of Beveridge's five giants that needed slaying. It is a system that requires massive government support, existing in a historic moment in which the status quo will not be tolerated. The Finnish government managed to do this, and was very dictatorial in the beginning about how to achieve it. It is now the opposite: there are no national inspections in Finland, no OFSTED equivalent and no teacher evaluations. Teachers instead are trusted, not least because they are so well trained: primary school teachers have to do a five-year master's degree in education in order

---

* Interestingly, evidence suggests that – by fifteen – there is no difference in reading ability between children who start school at five and those who start at seven.

to qualify, including a thesis on a pedagogical subject. Finland regards its teachers like we regard doctors: high-achieving professionals selected from the very best of the graduate pool.

It is worth noting that Finland's stellar performance has slipped in recent years* (while still outperforming Britain comfortably). One argument is that increased numbers of immigrants – with additional language and social needs – have brought major challenges to bear on the system. The immigrant population of Finland has indeed increased by 1,000 per cent in twenty years. However, the most likely reason is the system of austerity in place since 2008: Finland has reduced its spending on education, leading to merged schools, increased class sizes and the reduction in those extra support systems. As Pasi Sahlberg, a Finnish educator, told the *Washington Post*: 'What Finland should learn from these recent results is that reducing education spending always comes with consequences.' We might learn that lesson too.

Japan

In Japan, there is no setting or selection based on ability until the age of fifteen. Teachers are paid more than other civil servants, and are regularly rotated so that no schools monopolise the best educators. They share lesson plans, and ensure that first-time teachers enter the profession with the opportunity immediately to succeed.

School in Japan is also (and not attractively) about instilling respect for authority and the value of hard work and endurance.† It is also seen as a contract between the state and families: parents are often given lists of things to do with their children (including marking

---

* The Finnish government is not overly impressed by its PISA score (in the way much of the rest of the world is) and is not panicking as a result of any slippage. Contrast Germany, whose poor performance led to such national debate that *The PISA Show* was created for television, in which contestants competed to answer exam questions.

† A Japanese concept and motto for you. The concept of 'Gaman' is defined as 'the importance of enduring the seemingly unbearable with patience and dignity'. The motto: 'The nail that sticks out will be hammered down.'

their homework); they are discouraged from both holding jobs that might interfere with the business of child-rearing.

Singapore

This is the country that has become the world superpower in education, at some moral cost.★ Singapore recognised that, as a nation without obvious resources, it had to make use of its human potential, and has used education as a means to that end. It now has the third highest GDP per capita in the world.

It values teachers hugely, attracting them from the top 5 per cent of its graduates. They then have a defined system of training targets to reach, which determine their eventual salaries. They teach in a system that rewards ability and crushes failure. The Primary School Leaving Exam (taken at twelve) utterly determines pupils' future life: 8 per cent enter a stream that will lead straight to university; the remainder are divided into other categories that will take them to junior colleges, polytechnics or the creepy-sounding Institute of Technical Education. It is a brutal case of survival of the fittest: in 2000 a survey by the *Straits Times* found that a third of ten- to twelve-year-olds were more afraid of exams than their parents dying.

There is a recognition, incidentally, that vocational training is important and valuable. Lee Yock Suan, Education Minister, said this in 1994 (which will resonate with UK policy-makers too): 'Singapore will be poorer if everyone aspires to and gets only academic qualifications but nobody knows how to fix a TV set, a machine tool or a process plant.'

There seems to be a trade-off that Singapore has embraced: early selection into academic and vocational streams is unfair from an educational perspective, but good for an employment perspective (especially among the young). The possibility exists for a middle ground here, of course.

★ It is a nation that believed firmly in eugenics, for example. In the 1980s there were state-sponsored cruises for clever graduates to meet their future spouses.

China

The idea of an absolute and determinative exam is taken to an extreme with the Gaokao: a nine-hour, two-day monster taken by Chinese students at eighteen to decide their professional future. It is the sole purpose of their schooling.

You will, as I do, have images of robotic Chinese children learning endlessly by rote. And there is some truth to that thought. But PISA tests show that Chinese students are also taught to make use of that information: they do well on questions designed to show critical thinking as well as memory. As we shall see in a moment, traditional learning methods still have their place in the modern world.

South Korea

As with China, South Korea takes its final examination absurdly – and dangerously – seriously. During school finals planes are grounded in Seoul airport in order that the noise does not disturb the English-listening section. Honestly. In exam season, libraries have to sell tickets for spaces in order to prevent arguments.

Indeed, the central strength of the Korean system comes from the inordinate desires of parents to drive their children. This takes place in its shadow education world of *hagwons* or extra-curricular tutorial classes: seven out of ten Koreans take after-school lessons of some sort in an industry worth $18 billion★ in 2011. The government has to employ enforcers to ensure that agreed curfews are followed (and the *hagwons* are not running past 10 p.m.): government officials – acting on tips from informers – do surprise visits every night.

Is this healthy? Of course not. It places unbearable pressure on young people to succeed.† And it is based on fundamental inequality:

★ Amanda Ripley tells, in *The Smartest Kids in the World* (2013), of a super-tutor who – due to market demand – earns $4 million a year.
† Ripley also tells the cautionary tale of Ji, a teenager who stabbed his mother in the neck to stop her going to a parent–teacher conference where his bad grades would be revealed.

the students with rich parents get the best *hagwon* tuition. But it does reveal something: when a society recognises the value of education, when it sees that its own citizens are its best resources, it can take societally altering steps to remould itself. In the 1980s South Korea was known – as journalist Michael Breen puts it in his book *The New Koreans* (2017) – for 'war, dictatorship, tear gas, riot police in Darth Vader outfits, MASH, dog eating, the Olympics'. Now it is seen at the forefront of high-end tech development, skyscrapers and multinational conglomerates. Why? Because the state intervened in its approach to capitalism (as we saw in the economics chapter); and the state recognised that it needed to value education more.

The importance of the teacher

Valuing education means valuing teachers. A striking similarity in all the successful education systems around the world is the primacy they place on those doing the educating. Here is a thing about Britain: we do not value teachers as much as we should. Or, at least, we may say we value teachers, but do not show it in any meaningful way.

In 1902, Arthur Christopher Benson (a schoolmaster at Eton) wrote a guide to teaching called – in true patriarchal Victorian fashion – *The Schoolmaster*, which still has its merits now. And he noted: 'There clings about the profession of schoolmastering a certain slight social disability . . . it is not held to be a profession for a very capable or ambitious man.'★

In Britain, we do not feel that our brightest graduates should be directed towards teaching, and we seem never to have done. Benson feared teaching 'is more apt to be entered by those who have no particular vocation for anything else than any other profession'; a large number 'have a vague feeling at the back of their minds that

---

★ Benson's footnote on the hierarchy of jobs is amusingly anachronistic now: 'It may roughly be said that the professions which stand highest in the social scale are the army, the navy, the bar, land agency and the civil service. We may perhaps include with these artists, architects and literary men. In the second rank come the solicitor, the engineer, the doctor, the schoolmaster.'

if everything else fails they can always be teachers'. Teaching is seen as a soft option, with gentle perks: 'a life of regular work, with possibilities of physical exercise tending on the whole to health and activity; it means the prospect of marriage;* and it means also the interest which always attaches to dealing with human beings at a lovable and interesting age'.

Teaching is now, largely, a gendered career: it may be seen to fit in well with child-rearing (due to school holidays); it may be seen – wrongly – as a soft, maternal occupation. There is also the issue of sex scandals. In July 2016 a man called Kato Harris was cleared of anally raping a fourteen-year-old at a girls' school, his life damaged for ever by a false allegation. This is what he said in an interview some time after the case, with understandable bitterness:

> If you become a male teacher, you are buying that lottery ticket, whether you like it or not. Now, you might win the £10 lottery prize – there might be a false allegation that you called a child a rude name, or swore at a child.
>
> You might win the £1,000 prize, where a pupil suggests that you had inappropriately touched them passing them in the corridor. Or you might win the £1 million jackpot prize: that you took a pupil into a classroom on three separate occasions, in full view of the entire school, and anally raped them.

Whether or not this is statistically correct,† it will be a factor in the career choices of individuals. Narratives matter.

As well as the risk of false accusation (which one in five teachers say they have experienced in their careers), there is the lack of risk money to compensate. Teachers have never been paid well. In Benson's day, the average salary was £128 for a man and £86 for a woman (around £11,000 and £8,000 in today's money). Things are a little better now: the average salary of full-time, qualified teachers

---

* You laugh, but in 2016 the Tinder dating app released its list of 'most-swiped' professions. The top three for women were: teacher, dentist and speech pathologist (whatever the hell that is). For men: lawyer, actor and creative director.
† In 2011 a Department of Education study examined the nearly 3,000 allegations made against teachers in the previous year. Forty-seven per cent were found to be unsubstantiated. Three per cent led to a criminal conviction.

in state schools was £34,700 in 2011. That means, of course, many teachers earn considerably less than that. Indeed, British teachers work eight hours more per week than the OECD average, and are paid 16 per cent less.

I went to see a head teacher at one of the best state schools in the country: Mark Hartley, of Barnes Primary School in London. He is small, with salt-and-pepper hair, and a stubbornly regional accent. He has the bustle and swagger of a man used to dominating his surroundings, and not only because they are filled with pint-sized human beings. He is passionate about pedagogy and the value of teachers. He frequently videos lessons and then discusses them with his staff on Tuesday evenings for a couple of hours. He has developed his own guide to education (he wielded a thick, laminated document in front of me in an animated fashion). As a result, he has retained some teachers at the school for more than a decade, constantly supporting their ongoing improvement (one was in Shanghai when we met, learning about maths from the Chinese). Primary school teachers are, to him, 'renaissance men and women', who need to ever expand their skills.

He is not the norm; his school – in a privileged area of west London – is not the norm. England ranks thirtieth (out of thirty-six measured countries) in terms of number of days spent by teachers on professional development: five days per year, compared to an average of more than ten. In Shanghai, teachers spend forty days. In Singapore, teachers are allowed to take up to a hundred. Teachers in Japan only spend seventeen hours a week in the classroom actually teaching: the rest of the time is spent collaborating on lesson plans, observing other classes, sharing knowledge and pedagogic approaches. When a British teacher is not teaching, they are often doing admin or starting lesson plans from scratch or marking.*

It is not surprising, then, that we do not keep people in the teaching profession. Almost a third of all teachers leave their jobs within five years of starting; with more than one in ten not even lasting a year. This has been a fairly constant figure for a long time,

---

* I spoke to a teacher who called my LBC show. She was earning £18,000 and working a seventy-hour week. She was getting out of the profession.

and it is down to a combination of low salaries, long hours, high stress and collective ingratitude. Mark Hartley thinks – as we discussed in Chapter 1 – that the problem will get worse in London, as teachers cannot afford to buy the ever more expensive houses in the capital, and will have to move away.

We also cannot agree how and what teachers should be teaching. This takes us back to that philosophical split in the profession between neo-traditionalists and progressives. To the latter the former are no better than Gradgrind, the monstrous pedant of Dickens's *Hard Times*, who symbolised the soullessness of the Industrial Revolution:

> 'In this life, we want nothing but Facts, sir; nothing but Facts!'
> The speaker, and the schoolmaster, and the third grown person present, all backed a little, and swept with their eyes the inclined plane of little vessels then and there arranged in order, ready to have imperial gallons of facts poured into them until they were full to the brim.

A progressive teacher would argue that lessons should be guided by the children themselves, who should be assisted not with facts but with skills. It makes no difference, the argument goes, if a child knows the date of the Battle of Waterloo; she would be better learning to be a problem-solver in the real world. This is from OFSTED's guide *Making English Real*: 'The primary focus will be on learning, rather than teaching, with students working in partnership with teachers, asking questions and reflecting on the learning strategies that work best for them.'

Daisy Christodoulou, a neo-traditionalist educator, wrote a book called *Seven Myths About Education*, largely to rebut this approach. She recalled 'one teacher trainer telling me that if I was talking, the pupils were not learning'. There is little evidence to support such an approach in its entirety. All but one of the top fifteen PISA countries have higher than average teacher-led instruction; Gradgrind could probably get a job in Finland or China.

The problem here is that there has been no philosophical consistency in education. In the last fifty years there have been twenty-four Secretaries of State for Education, each with his or her own ideas, each – since 1988 – with a national curriculum to fiddle with. And fiddle they unapologetically all do.

Take the example of Knowsley in Liverpool,[35] one of the poorest areas of the country. In 2005 the Labour government launched a Building Schools for the Future programme there. Eleven secondary schools were flattened, and seven new institutions built at a cost of £157 million. Education officers decided that most children were 'kinaesthetic learners', who needed to be away from desks, using their bodies and senses, trial and error, as a means of receiving information. The schools were called 'centres for learning', teachers 'progress leaders'; classrooms became 'base areas' with curtains separating them into different zones. The result: parents demanded to send their children out of the borough; funding was reduced; the schools were depopulated. In September 2016 it became the first local authority to cease offering children A-level education *at all*. A deprived area (where 15 per cent of adults have no qualifications at all) became more deprived.

The problem of inequality

Knowsley is not alone in being educationally sub-normal. The former OFSTED chief Michael Wilshaw has publicly (in 2015) warned of the 'significant discrepancy in performance between North and South'. He judged there to be sixteen weak local authorities (where less than 60 per cent of children attend good or outstanding schools) and thirteen of them were in the north and Midlands. We should not be surprised: regional inequality is another theme of this book. It exists in health, in education, as it does with the economy as a whole.

Indeed, economic inequality and educational inequality go together. Using PISA data, we learn that our gap between the highest and lowest achieving pupils in science is bigger than the average in the industrialised world: the equivalent of more than eight years' schooling. Think of that for a second: at the age of fifteen, some children are already eight years behind. And there is a clear correlation between parental income and educational performance: poor kids do worse.

This is a recognised, not a disputable, fact. We should recall that idea of the 'disadvantaged attainment gap', which is the difference between the academic performance of those children eligible for free school meals and their peers. In 2014 the percentage of disadvantaged children getting at least five good GCSEs was 36 per cent; for all other pupils it was 64 per cent. That is a colossal difference. Indeed, we see that the gap gradually expands over time, and is more pronounced at the end of schooling than the beginning. According to the Sutton Trust, two-thirds of pupils on free school meals who are among the top fifth of performers at age eleven are not there at age sixteen: they are falling out of the system.

So, if you want children to prosper: don't be poor, don't be northern. And don't be all those things and have boys. The worst demographic, bar none, for educational achievement in this country is working-class boys. Under a quarter of poor white boys get five good GCSEs; meaning that the visible majority leave school classed as failures. And, while we are seeing a slow improvement in attainment by poor Bangladeshi or Chinese or black African children, we see none in the white working class. We see the consequence at university: poor white boys are the least likely to reach further education too.★

Why is this? Nobody knows entirely. Often in poor, white communities, there is a lack of male role models both in family life and in schools themselves. Primary schools in Britain are hugely gynocentric: just 15 per cent of teachers there are men.[36]

Another narrative is perhaps relevant here: immigrant families tend to have a comprehensible narrative arc from poverty to success, a story of hard work and striving against the odds. Education is seen as life-changing, story-changing. It is not clear that this is true for white working-class families, where aspiration can be crushed, where examples of educational failure are overwhelming and all-encompassing.

We also know that vocational, non-academic schooling is undervalued in this country: it has never survived the ghetto of the tripartite system of 1944. If (as in Finland) options of attending good

---

★ UCAS (the university admissions service) has said that white working-class men are 50 per cent less likely to attend university than white working-class women.

vocational schooling after sixteen were widely available, would non-academic children have a better focus and sense of their own prospects? The answer is almost certainly yes.

The value of parents

When we consider environmental factors outside the schools them-selves, we must pause on the most important: mums and dads. One of the reasons why inequality is so hard to break is that we inherit much of our potential for schooling from our parents, not simply in terms of our genetic abilities, but in the context they provide for our education. Parental engagement – listening, reading – can, according to the OECD, improve a child's examination performance by up to 29 per cent. Students whose parents regularly talk to them are two-thirds of a school year ahead in science. All around the world, children who are read to become better at reading. Talking, using words, is a key to education.*

This should be more clearly recognised than other parental effects. Clearly, wealthy parents who provide tutors and pressure make a differ-ence: the tiger mums of Korea and Tokyo. But all parents could readily find more time to show an interest in their children's educational welfare. It is, of course, getting harder, which is why perhaps we are seeing such stagnation in school performance. In Britain 58 per cent of households contain two working parents; the average working week is thirty-seven hours; three in five children will see their parents split before they become teenagers. Family life is further fractured by screen-time: four individuals, hermetically sealed by headphones attached to iPads, not talking, not connecting with one another.[37] The future.

---

* When I was at school, every Sunday my dad and I would sit at the dining room table and work together. He would plan his week (he was a logistics manager at an American company), and I would write essays or do other homework. We listened to music at the same time, and thanks to him I have an odd predilection for progressive rock and heavy metal (Genesis, Black Sabbath, Deep Purple, Led Zeppelin and so on). But thanks to him, more importantly, I have had an unshake-able work ethic, a willingness to get things done. He (with my mum) cared that I worked hard, so I did.

So what have we learned?

Do not worry, there will be no tests at the end of this chapter. But there do seem to be some principles that have been nudging their way to the surface throughout. Parental input is undervalued and hugely important. Adults need to recognise the impact they can have on their children, and try to help them. Our pupils neither perform as well as many in the world, nor are as happy[38] as them. That is all our fault.

Teaching is undervalued and hugely important. We should start to treat teachers like we treat doctors. Indeed, teachers need to help by regarding themselves in the same way: they need to demand high standards of one another; demand that better continuous professional development is a requirement of their career. Michael Gove said to me that 'there is too much educational homeopathy', too many poor teachers dragging down the brilliant, vital educators of our young. And he is not wrong (although it is perhaps understandable why teachers hate him for saying it). We should require the government to find more money to pay them better, to give them more time to improve and collaborate; but teachers need to set higher standards for themselves too.

Our patchwork system of selective education is unfair and unequal (most notably in the form of grammar schools and private schools). Almost everywhere, we stream and set children by ability, even though virtually no other successful country does this. In doing so, we cement inequality, we tolerate under-performance. As the sage Bart Simpson noted, when he was placed in a remedial set: 'Let me get this straight. We're behind the rest of the class and we're going to catch up by going slower?' When Poland delayed academic selection by just one year (from fifteen to sixteen), its PISA performance went up by 120 points. There needs to be some recognition, by disinterested observers, that a universal approach benefits more people, more significantly than a patchwork and selective one.

Some policy suggestions, then, are clear: remove the tax breaks for private schools, so they become gradually less economically viable; end grammar schools in favour of genuinely comprehensive education, uniform until the age of fourteen; end GCSEs, instead allowing children to select a path at fourteen that focuses on either academic or vocational routes towards employment; value those vocational paths far more than we have ever done historically; have one final exam at eighteen ahead of tertiary education; reintroduce maintenance grants for poor students attending university.

This is all going to become more important in the future. We have discussed the rise in automation, and its impact on jobs. One impact will certainly be the growing technical demands on all workers at whatever level. Even the lowest-paid, starter jobs will need more capabilities around health and safety, report writing, compliance and so on. Education will become more important, not less. And technical skills will need to be more advanced, not less. We need to be able to produce citizens at eighteen in possession of them.

In 1944 the government had the opportunity to reboot the system, be radical and (true to say) comprehensive. We have been living with the consequences of its failure ever since.

5

Military

Every gun that is made, every warship launched, every rocket fired signifies, in the final sense, a theft from those who hunger and are not fed, those who are cold and are not clothed. This world in arms is not spending money alone. It is spending the sweat of its laborers, the genius of its scientists, the hopes of its children . . . This is not a way of life at all in any true sense. Under the clouds of war, it is humanity hanging on a cross of iron

Dwight D. Eisenhower (1890–1969)

I still feel that I let my grandfather down. He was always cagey about his experience in the Second World War, always reluctant to give specifics or tell stories. One of four brothers, he lost two to German gunfire, one in France and the other in the African desert. They had asked him to join their regiment, so they could look after him, but he had preferred to stay with the friends he had made in the 51st Highlanders. He survived; they did not.

When I was at school, I was forced – under some considerable protest – to join the CCF: the Combined Cadet Forces, that miniature toy army for teenagers. It was dominated by the sort of towel-flicking, insecurity-riddled jocks for whom the sexual awakening of puberty could best be expressed by the firing of loud guns. I hated it, needless to say. But so did my grandparents, who saw a boy in uniform, and were taken back to the generation of boys who got all dressed up for war, and often never returned home.

I studied English at university, and got it into my head that it would be nice one day to tell my grandfather's wartime story, which was at once horribly typical (he was a squaddie, a driver; not a quirky British major with a double-barrelled name and an exotic pedigree)[1] and yet also peculiarly replete (he served all the way from the beaches of Dunkirk to the invasion of Germany). He remained reticent, was not opposed, but not eager either. He was uncomfortable talking about it, and thinking about it. Then one day he mentioned that he was making notes about his experience, and would record them for me on a dictaphone. I was pleased, but, amid the selfish maelstrom of my early twenties, thought too little of it.

After he died we found the recording, forty-five minutes of stream-of-consciousness about the Second World War, narrated by an old man with no literary pretensions or interest in posterity. I should have sat with him while he did it; I should have asked questions; should have given the narrative an arc, a shape, filled in the nagging spaces of the story. But I was a couple of hundred miles away, heedless and foolish. When writing this book, I listened again: his voice a soft, faltering, feathery thing, with the traces of the Welsh valleys not quite obscured by the roughening effects of sixty years in the Midlands; a litany of facts and events, and emotions suppressed by force of habit.

It is a story of Great Britain and the military, a story in compressed haste of the whole Second World War; a tale of how armies function, and of how they always involve human beings, flesh and blood, being exposed to peril and somehow coping with it. When we talk about British military capability, or the future of the armed forces, the threat of Russia, or the folly of Afghanistan, it helps sometimes to hear the voices of the people who have submitted themselves to mental and physical danger in the name of their country. This is a ghost voice from the past, but still speaks to the present.

This is not the place to transcribe the entire narrative, but I do want to reflect what happened to my grandad, Jim Spence, especially as he stood waiting to be evacuated in Dunkirk,* a young man up

---

* The evacuation of Dunkirk remains one of the greatest triumphs of logistics and of volunteering in the history of warfare. A thousand vessels sailed across the Channel, many manned by civilians who wanted to help, with the aim of rescuing 45,000 soldiers. By 4 June 1940, they had saved 200,000 British, 130,000 French and 10,000 Allied soldiers. Churchill rightly called it a 'miracle of deliverance'; he also rightly said that 'We must be very careful not to assign to this deliverance the attributes of a victory. Wars are not won by evacuations.'

to his chest in water, bombs screaming around him, thinking he was going to die. So I give here an abbreviated account of that adventure in Jim's own words. It takes place at the beginning of the war, when the underprepared British forces were shocked by the surrender of Belgium:

They moved us into this farm, where we got a little bit of shelter from the snow, but that was a miserable time. The journey across France was uneventful, really. Paris was nice. We were all given a night out in Arras, once a week, which was all right, though we had nobody, so we just roamed around a bit. Then we got to Lille. We got very friendly with a café owner there and he used to do us egg and chips about twice a week for next to nothing. So we had a good friend with him, there. Then, of course, from then on when we moved into Belgium, it was hard work with loading the guns, loading the shells on to the lorries, because every shell weighed 100lb and it was off and on, off and on, night in, night out. It was damned hard work. Then when we started retreating, we came back and then the roads got absolutely chocker with civilians. We just couldn't move. We went up off the road, but in that area in France there's a lot of ditches, so you couldn't go off the road a lot because the ditches were too deep. So in the end, we got permission to burn our vehicles, which we did. Through the chaos, terrible crowds, and being strafed we soon lost touch with each other. There was only Jack, myself, Jack Williams and myself, who stayed together. We were like two lost souls. Jack was older than me because in the end I was only nineteen.

Well, we were frightened. Not a bit frightened, damn frightened. Jack held us together. After we burned our vehicles and set off on foot, it was funny really because every time the planes came over and strafed, Jack and I, straight as they'd gone, we'd get up and run like hell up the road before the civilians got back on and blocked the road. You know, because we couldn't move any faster than they could. So that was the way we, I think, lost our regiment. Getting into Dunkirk, well, getting near Dunkirk, we were diverted then to the west of Dunkirk by these MPs. There were a lot of naval MPs and they were a bit of a bugger, really, but they had a job to do and that was to keep us out of Dunkirk, which thankfully was a good thing in the end. Then we ended up on the sand dunes. I'm not quite sure of the dates. I think it was nearer June 1st, June 2nd when I got out. Yes, it was. It was June 2nd when RSM picked us up. He took us to the front of the queue because we'd been up at the back with this gun and weren't allowed to join the queue, and the RSM saw the Beachmaster, told him, and he allowed us to go to the front of the queue, but not right to the front. There was about fifteen hours there. Went through, walked into the sea, couldn't get on that boat, walked back again, then the Germans came and fired on us. So we ran, but where we ran to, there was nowhere to hide. You just ran, got your head down, your backside in the air.

I don't think there's much more I can tell you other than being on the beach was horrendous. The Germans used to come down regularly, three or four times a day, strafing. All you could do was bend your head into the sands and hope to God that they missed your backside. There were hundreds killed that way. You see, you used to run away, but where do you run to? No trees. You used to get under a lorry and then most likely the lorry would blow up. So it was frightening, really frightening. After that, things weren't so frightening. Right throughout the war, you know, you had your, I don't know, your fears, all at once. So after that, you know, when we went on the other invasions, they didn't seem as bad because you'd had your share of shocks. Anyway, I'll finish now and then Stephen and I can go through it also later on. Okay.

We never did go through it (I am the Stephen here, of course; something only my grandparents and parents called me), and now there is much I will never know. But there is much here of the general, as well as the specific. The human response to danger. The importance of food to a soldier. The value of friendship, of camaraderie.* We live in a world where that proximity of life to death, and the closeness between people it creates, will only ever be known by a few. Each passing generation is tested less by conflict and duty. Our proximity to one another is confected and artificial, the over-connectedness of technology. That creates a different society in terms of thoughts and actions, of what we value most as a nation.

* I have a copy of Jim's release certificate. Under military conduct, it says 'exemplary'. And these handwritten remarks: 'has performed the duties of butcher and M/T driver, both of which he has carried out in an efficient manner. Honest, sober, hardworking and reliable.' British understatement at its best.

Jim's history tells of a silent heroism, of obeying orders to stand at his post on the beach at Dunkirk, even at the cost of his own life. Such conformity – and such bravery – is one of the central purposes of the military establishment, one of the aims of its training. Is such training, are such aims, now anachronistic? And what is the purpose of the military in a world where the wars are largely over? Where would a serving Jim Spence now be sent, and why? This chapter aims to answer those questions, and before we linger on the present, we shall return briefly to the past in order to understand how the British military machine has developed over the years.

Because I remain fascinated by soldiering: its cost in lives and psychic trauma; its value in building character and protecting freedoms. My stance echoes that of Tolstoy: 'I was more interested to know in what way and under the influence of what feeling one soldier kills another than to know how armies were arranged at Austerlitz and Borodino.'

I am a child of the unmilitary, who has no direct experience of that feeling. I am a man conscious of ideals of virility and masculinity that are – atavistically at least – connected to concepts of martial valour and physical strength. Yet the world that most valued those attributes has changed, perhaps for ever. How exactly did we get here?

A brief history of the British army (and navy)

The development of the military has, in essence, been one of increased organisation and technological sophistication. The arrival of the longbow in the fourteenth and fifteenth centuries led to English success on French battlefields, notably at Crécy (1346), Poitiers (1356) and Agincourt (1415); of gunpowder and artillery led to the massed battle lines of the eighteenth century and then the defensive warfare of the twentieth.

Until the seventeenth century, England had no full-time army. When military action was necessary, individual militias were formed, and people compelled to serve (or buy their freedom from service).[2]

It took the Civil War* and the creation of Cromwell's New Model Army for the recognition that a regular army, of full-time soldiers, could be a battlefield asset. By 1660, it was accepted that the same was true for the Royal Navy, which was formally established at that time (including by the notable diarist Samuel Pepys).[3] Until that point, ships had been 'borrowed' by the Crown for the purposes of transporting soldiers and for armed engagements. The great Elizabethan age of sailing had also included her reliance on 'privateers' (pirates of sorts) like Sir Francis Drake[4] to conduct self-aggrandising raids on the Spanish.

It was the Napoleonic Wars that saw the true professionalisation and dominance of the British military. At sea, culminating in the Battle of Trafalgar (1805), Britain asserted a naval dominance that it did not lose (arguably) until the end of the Second World War. In 1889 the Naval Defence Act demanded something called the 'two-power standard': the British navy had to be as strong as the next two largest navies combined. In 1913 Britain was spending half of its defence budget on the navy. This dominance is a critical point to any understanding of the development of this country. Consider this: Britain is a tiny island at the corner of Europe, blessed with an average climate, a smallish population, and some – but not an overwhelming – amount of natural resources. And yet it has been by any estimation the most influential nation upon the world in the modern epoch: it has provided the lingua franca of business and diplomacy, the principles of parliamentary government; it constructed an empire covering a quarter of the world,[†] whose disintegration

---

* It is perhaps a peculiarly British thing that this armed uprising (1642–51) against a ruling institution, which involved the entire nation in internecine conflict, is never called a revolution. And yet the transfer of power in 1688 from a Catholic to a Protestant King *is* called the Glorious Revolution. But there it is: the Civil War was a revolution; it was a battle against the authority of the Crown; it was a step towards parliamentary democracy. The fact that Charles II returned with many of the same powers his father had does not mean the prior conflict was somehow not 'revolutionary'.

† Between 1815 and 1914 the British Empire expanded by 10 million square miles and 400 million people. Britain enforced a (more or less stable) Pax Britannica, modelled after the Pax Romana of the Roman Empire, the notion that there could be global peace under a dominant leadership.

still dictates almost all modern political conflicts; it spawned the successful countries of modern America, Australia and Canada.

The primary reason, the underpinning factor, is historic naval superiority: the country's ability to move its inhabitants, goods and ideas across vast swathes of territory; its ability to stand alone against the might of foreign foes (such as Napoleon and Hitler). Vast land masses can look inwards for success;[5] small islands can only push outwards if they have the ability to do so. From the seventeenth century onwards, the global superpower was Britain, and its dominance of the seas was the reason.

One summer day, I visit the Ministry of Defence in Whitehall to talk to Rear Admiral Nick Hine, the Assistant Chief of the Naval Staff. He is a tough-looking former submariner proud of the naval history, but cautious of fetishising it too much (he dismisses the Patrick O'Brian novel I show him with a gruff 'I don't have time for books'). The purpose of the navy has not changed, he says, since Nelson: 'forward deployed; assurance; reassurance; trade and aid'. Even in the modern era, it is the only branch of the military that retains scale and global reach: it is 'the most political of the services', because it will be the most visible and mobile presence in any trouble spots. It also protects the 95 per cent of all global trade that comes by sea, and so is closely connected to our collective economy.

Hine makes clear that to be a 'premier league' navy in the modern world, you need only two things: aircraft carriers as a conventional strategic deterrent; and submarines as a nuclear strategic deterrent. He has captained the latter ('doing stuff we shouldn't be doing in places we shouldn't have been'), observing without engaging a similarly silent phalanx of prowling Russian subs.* It is a stressful but necessary existence: ninety days under water; six hours on, six hours off; the professional embrace of icy claustrophobia. Much of the work, of submariners and frigates, is protective, preventative. Nelson began his career protecting fishing

---

* I take to Hine very much, being impressed by people who have placed themselves in harm's way and can talk with bluff offhandedness about it. 'The thing about submarines with ballistic missiles' – he leans forward to tell me at one point – 'they are just really fucking hard to find.'

grounds from squabbling Europeans; he would recognise much of the naval activity today.

Back on land, the British army moved – during the Napoleonic Wars – from a collection of often ragtag squabblers, drunks and minor criminals to a military force respected for its courage and organisation. Lord Wellington,* who rose to lead them, famously said of his troops: 'They are the scum of the earth – it really is remarkable what fine fellows we have made of them.' Pride in their regiments and camaraderie were held to be the dominant sign of British soldiers, and those ideals remain in the military today. One of Wellington's opponents, Marshal Soult, remarked: 'There is no beating these troops. I always thought they were bad soldiers – now I am sure of it. I had turned their right, pierced their centre and everywhere victory was mine – but they did not know how to run.'

The nineteenth century saw no truly major wars to test these troops, but continued (and bloody) skirmishes thanks to the onward encroachment of the British Empire in places like South Africa, Aden, Persia, Burma, China (over the rights to trade opium) and New Zealand (with the native Maoris). Britain's major rival at the time was Russia, and the manoeuvrings on both sides were termed the 'Great Game', a sort of Victorian cold war. Two conflicts stand out as important: the Crimean War (1854–6) and the Indian Mutiny (1857–9).

The Crimean War came from the desire of Britain and France (now allied) to support Turkey against Russia, which wanted a toe-hold in the Mediterranean. It was a conflict that provided lasting testimony to the bravery of soldiers, the incompetence of generals and the appalling conditions of warfare. About half a million people died on both sides, mainly due to disease.

---

* Arthur Wellesley (1769–1852) was born in Dublin, educated unhappily at Eton, and drifted into his early twenties with little distinction, his mum saying, 'I don't know what I shall do with my awkward son Arthur.' As it happens, he went on to become arguably Britain's greatest military leader, often dominating Napoleon's army in battle, culminating in victory at Waterloo. The *Letters of Private Wheeler* (1809–28), written by a soldier who fought throughout the Napoleonic Wars, paint a picture of a man – Old Nosey – beloved by his troops: 'We would rather see his long nose in the fight than a reinforcement of ten thousand men.'

Our ideas about this war are shaped thanks to journalism, incidentally, and the advent of the first truly embedded reporter.[6] It was William Howard Russell of *The Times* who described 'that thin red streak tipped with steel' of the 93rd Highlanders under Colin Campbell, facing down the massed Russian cavalry at the Battle of Balaclava, which became known for ever as the 'thin red line'. It was the prose of Russell, describing the fateful charge of the Light Brigade in the same battle – 'a more fearful spectacle was never witnessed than by those who, without the power to aid, beheld their heroic countrymen rushing to the arms of sudden death' – that led to Tennyson's immortal poem. Finally, it was Russell's reporting of the appalling conditions of military hospitals and the failure of supply lines that brought down the government and led to improvements in the care of soldiers.[7]

The Indian Mutiny is perhaps little discussed now, but it stands as an example of the barbarism of empire, even notwithstanding the heroism of the military. The British establishment,* superior and racist, failed to recognise the religious concerns of Indian soldiers, who were frightened that they were being asked to grease their weapons with pig and cow fat, as a deliberate means of beginning their conversion to Christianity. Revolt spread across the country; it was a civil war of appalling violence (committed by both sides).[8] In some ways, it was representative of the conflicts of the age: Britain set against indigenous people amid a desire to maintain its hegemony across much of the world. That was the context of fighting in Afghanistan,† in Africa against the Zulus,[9] and the two Boer Wars – over an attempt to annex the Boer Republic in South Africa (1880–1) and a fight over Transvaal (1899–1902) – that ended the century.

---

* There is a considerable linguistic legacy from the army in India, incidentally. 'Khaki' comes from the Urdu word for dust; 'Blighty' from the Urdu word for 'foreign'; 'sniper' in the sense of sharp-shooter comes from the practice in the eighteenth century of officers hunting snipes in the Indian hills.

† Afghanistan was very much a proxy for geopolitical squabbling (sound familiar?), this time seen as the 'back door' for Russia in India. Dr Watson, of *Sherlock* fame, interestingly, was a veteran of the Second Anglo-Afghan War of 1878–80: he was wounded by a 'jezial bullet', suffered 'enteric fever' and was invalided back to England. His leg continued to pain him in wet weather.

War changed for ever after 1900: the power of mass slaughter came with the advent of the machine gun, the tank* and airborne warfare;† the ability to defend equalled – and sometimes surpassed – the power to attack. In the First World War, the British army was at its largest, and suffered its worst ever casualties. In the first couple of months of war, both sides lost half a million people. The Western Front was established after the first Battle of Ypres (November 1914), and scarcely moved for the next three and a half years. On 1 July 1916, at the Battle of the Somme, the 57,000 casualties were the highest daily butcher's bill in British military history. War became about endurance, prolonged torment. Shell shock became properly recognised for the first time, because so many men were experiencing the terrors of conflict not for hours or days, but for months and years.

And the First World War represents, in many ways, the birth of our collective consciousness of the horrors of war, and our modern response to it. We discuss warfare today using the mental grammar established by portrayals of the trenches: we recognise its ability to cause mental trauma and devastation, not just physical harm. This war provoked arguably the greatest artistic response to conflict in human history, in the poetry that sought to make sense of it, to challenge its orthodoxies and to berate its stupidities.

Take the figure of Wilfred Owen, who was invalided out in 1917 with shell shock and sent to a Scottish hospital where he met (and idolised) another leading poet, Siegfried Sassoon. The latter helped

* Originally called 'landships', their development was pursued more vigorously by the British than the Germans, who thought they would always prove unreliable. Planning was secret, so the rumour was spread that the things under construction were water cisterns for the Russian army; hence 'tanks'. The first tank-on-tank battle was near Amiens on 24 April 1918.

† During the First World War, there were two air forces: Royal Flying Corps (part of the army); and the Royal Naval Air Service. Initially, they dropped bombs by hand over the side of the planes. By the end of the war, they had gunners and engaged in dogfights. The RAF was created on 1 April 1918. Its greatest achievement came in the Second World War and the Battle of Britain (1940), when its supremacy of the skies over the more numerous Luftwaffe meant that Hitler could not risk an invasion. Churchill famously said in response: 'Never in the field of human conflict was so much owed by so many to so few.'

him with his poetry, including perhaps the greatest of war poems, 'Dulce et Decorum Est'. Its title comes from a line by the Roman poet Horace ('the old lie' that 'it is sweet and right to die for your country'), and, with mordant bitterness, uses it as the kicker to a poem about the appalling experience of a gas attack. The poem ironically bastardises the sonnet form (it is two sonnets crumpled together), and tells the story of the soldiers, lame ('blood-shod') and tired ('like old beggars under sacks'), and their attempt to get the 'clumsy helmets' of gas masks on with 'an ecstasy of fumbling'. It contains this sight of a man dying, 'his hanging face, like a devil's sick of sin':

> Dim, through the misty panes and thick green light,
> As under a green sea, I saw him drowning.

> In all my dreams before my helpless sight
> He plunges at me, guttering, choking, drowning.

We are all 'helpless' at such a sight, the futile repetition of the word 'drowning' enacting the encompassing swell of toxic gas that takes life from the soldier and agency from the observer; the hard syllables of 'guttering' and 'choking' playing out the rattle of a dying man; the word 'guttering' itself a metaphor taken from the flickering of a candle before it is extinguished for ever. Poetry of the First World War like this established an idiom – whether people have read the poems or not – to measure in words the horrors of war; and it is an idiom used today when we consider the deaths of soldiers in Afghanistan or the risks of any future conflict.

Siegfried Sassoon articulated it further in a statement he wrote called 'Finished with the War: A Soldier's Declaration', which was read out in Parliament in July 1917, and stands as an urtext for conscientious objection:

> I believe that the purposes for which I and my fellow soldiers entered upon this war should have been so clearly stated as to have made it impossible to change them, and that, had this been done, the objects which actuated us would now be attainable by negotiation.
>
> I have seen and endured the sufferings of the troops, and I can no longer be a party to prolong these sufferings for ends which I believe to be evil and unjust . . .

On behalf of those who are suffering now I make this protest against the deception which is being practised on them; also I believe that I may help to destroy the callous complacence with which the majority of those at home regard the continuance of agonies which they do not share, and which they have not sufficient imagination to realise.

As it happens, it is thanks to the writing of people like Sassoon that all of us lucky enough never to have shared the agonies of war can begin to have sufficient imagination to realise them. Sassoon, already a decorated hero known for his suicidal feats of bravery, did indeed return to the war from hospital. He was accidentally shot in the head by a British soldier who thought he was a German. He survived. Wilfred Owen also went back to fight and was killed in the final week of the war; his mother received the telegram informing her of his death on Armistice Day, when every bell in England was pealing in joy.

Those peals echoed once more twenty-seven years later at the end of the next massive global conflict. Nearly 400,000 British military died in the Second World War; more than 800,000 had been lost in the First World War. After 1945, though, nobody really knew whether another war was on its way, and what the military establishment should be to meet it.

Why did Britain have national service (and should we have it now)?

Our country's dalliance with national service is worth examining, not least because periodically the notion of its return pops up in public debate. As our society loses its grip on ideals of martial valour and self-sacrifice, a nostalgia can set in for an age when everybody shared both the agonies and the benefits of military service. It is, needless to say, a nostalgia for an age that never existed, as conscripted troops were compelled to serve in the dying era of a 'ramshackle Empire',[10] often in violent and illegitimate conflicts.

Over 2 million men* were conscripted into the British armed forces between 1945 and 1960; the last were finally demobilised in May 1963. They were entering a chaotic military,[11] unsure of the demands it needed to meet, but fearing a third global conflict with the communist Soviet Union. Most conscripts stayed in the UK, often in a misery of freezing dormitories and mind-sapping chores, but some were called upon to see battle. Indeed, in terms of casualties, the era of national service was the bloodiest of all periods after the Second World War: Korea, Kenya, Palestine, Malaya, Cyprus were all fields of violent dispute in this era.

The primary lesson for today is that at no point was national service considered to be necessary for public good. Quite the opposite: Anthony Eden (then Shadow Foreign Secretary) said, 'I have never heard anyone defend conscription for the sake of conscription'; Churchill's doctor Lord Moran thought that it 'interferes with the building up of character', while a contemporary RAF report called it 'a kind of initiation into virility', that was not necessarily felt to be a positive step. The experience tended to be one of coarseness,[†] violence and incomprehension: 'That two years matured me physically, and I do not just mean my body. The way you bear yourself involves more than the body. I mean a kind of manhood. In the old phrase, I went in a boy and came out a man. But not a very nice man.'[12]

At the remove of several decades, the concept of national service remains stubbornly popular. A YouGov survey of 2018 showed 48 per cent support for reintroducing conscription (against 36 per cent objection) for all healthy people between the ages of seventeen and twenty-one. Such a stance tends to ride a wave of public sentiment that today's teenagers are ill-disciplined, mentally and physically flabby, weakened by the ease of technology and the comforts of

---

* Only clergymen, the insane and the blind (make your own joke about tautology here) were granted exemptions, although public schoolboys with university places were allowed to start and finish early.

† The stories of swearing in the army are funny: one conscript counted 'fourteen fucks' in one minute; another heard a corporal try to maintain discipline during a church visit by saying, 'Oi! You take off your hat in the house of the Lord, cunt!'

home. The notion of muddy marches, ironed sheets and being shouted at sounds appealing (especially to those who will never have to experience it themselves). But the military, in the end, is a place of killing in the national interest; it is not – although it may seem that way sometimes – a superannuated nursery for moral education. Had it existed in 2009, conscripts would have been sent to Afghanistan, to a foreign field where an IED could leave them smeared across an unforgiving landscape.

We'll consider briefly the wars of the national service, not least because they get forgotten now, our perspective distorted by the world wars that preceded them and the contingent conflicts of the present day. The Korean War (1950–3)* started when the communist, Chinese-backed North Korean army invaded the US-backed South. It felt very distant to the UK, whose support for it was never particularly eager (the war was first discussed in Cabinet in June 1950; it was a small item on the agenda below a bid to restore the white fish industry). The primary consequence was, perhaps, the recognition that the US was now the dominant military force in the West, and Britain at best a supporting actor. For a nation that once held sway over the world, and provided the ever present bulwark against the enemy in global conflicts, this was a humbling experience.

In this period, Britain was being humbled elsewhere, as the empire disintegrated all around it. There were four key 'Imperial emergencies' over fifteen years. In the Middle East, Britain was seeking to divest itself of control in the area, in time for the creation of the two independent states of Israel and Palestine. Fighting started immediately – which indeed has never stopped – and the British army was attacked by both Jewish and Arab militants until it was withdrawn in 1948.

In Malaya (1948–60), a guerrilla insurgency was waged against British rubber plantations by the Malayan Races' Liberation Army, which was dominated by the Chinese. The MRLA were eventually destroyed by the British (a rare example of a standing army defeating

---

* Keen students of history will note that there is still a hostile division between North and South Korea. No formal peace treaty has ever been signed, so technically the two countries are still at war.

motivated insurgents),★ and independence for Malaya was actually achieved with consent. The Kenyan emergency (1952–60) was a far uglier affair, in which the Mau Mau resistance movement was brutally suppressed by the British establishment. More than a million people were forcibly moved; more than 150,000 were detained without trial. As we shall see later, allegations of brutality and war crimes were credibly made;[13] the behaviour of British troops was often disgusting. The same could be said in Cyprus (1955–9) in which the EOKA movement fought a campaign for unification with Greece. Again, there was pointless and bloody violence.[14] And, as with Kenya, the results were the same: both countries obtained their inevitable independence by the mid-1960s.

There was, in this time, the continued reduction of the British military from a large-scale force to a (sometimes morally questionable) peacekeeping body. That has been the direction of travel for the last seventy years. Perhaps the most notable example of our loss of 'major power' status was the Suez Crisis of 1956 when the Egyptian President Colonel Gamal Abdel Nasser nationalised the Suez Canal, which had been run by an Anglo-French consortium. Britain and France came to a secret deal that Israel would attack Egypt, allowing our two countries to intervene and reclaim the territory. The then Prime Minister Anthony Eden, who had lived a political life hugely in the shadow of the bulldog Winston Churchill, was hot for Nasser's blood and misled Parliament about the Israeli involvement. The whole enterprise was slapped down forcibly by the Americans; we retreated chastened back to our island in the corner of the sea. The age of empire was over.

And the age of large-scale armed intervention seemed to be, too. The Sandys Review of 1957 was a report into military efficiency, whose words could still stand today: 'It is now only a matter of a few years before there will be missiles steered by electronic brains capable of delivering megaton warheads over a range of 5,000 miles or more . . . sensational scientific advances in methods of waging war have fundamentally altered the whole basis of world strategy.'

We would never again need to witness the heroics of painstaking advances on enemy positions by warriors hopped up on adrenalin,

★ See Vietnam, Afghanistan etc.

eyes ablaze with battle lust, primitive bayonets steaming with hot blood, would we? Well, actually, yes we would.

Before we return to the primitive world of modern warfare – of the Falklands, Iraq and Afghanistan – the most significant peace-keeping venture of the British military in the post-war era should be recorded: Northern Ireland.

The period known – with typical British and Irish understatement – as the Troubles began in 1969, with the escalation of violence between the largely Catholic nationalists (who wanted a united Ireland) on the one hand and the largely Protestant unionists (who wanted Northern Ireland to remain part of Britain) on the other. This was a conflict of ideas, including sectarian ones, that were – and are – ultimately irreconcilable. We saw some of their political causes and consequences back in Chapter 2. The nationalist campaign expressed itself in terrorist violence by the Irish Republican Army (IRA); the unionist response by loyalist paramilitary forces. The role of the British army, under the name Operation Banner, was purport-edly to keep the peace and support the civil authorities. In doing so, it became enmeshed in the politics of the nation, and complicit in the promulgation of violence.[15]

At one point in 1972 there were 30,000 British troops in the province, and 10,000 additional police. In that year, 131 British personnel were killed and 578 wounded. The conflict in Northern Ireland was the third bloodiest for the British army since the Second World War.* In January 1972 came the notorious Bloody Sunday

---

* The full list here, breaking down the 3,639 fatalities in the British military between 1945 and 2017:
Palestine: 784
Korea: 765
Northern Ireland: 763
Afghanistan: 453
Malaya: 340
Falklands: 255
Iraq (after 2003): 179
Cyprus: 105
1st Gulf War: 47
Suez: 22
Kenya: 12

massacre, in which British troops fired on unarmed protesters, killing fourteen. The eventual public inquiry called these killings 'unjustified and unjustifiable'.

As we have seen throughout, warfare of any sort brings with it questions of endlessly disputable morality. We can never now empathise entirely with British soldiers patrolling Irish streets, terrified of the cowardly attacks of car bombs or bullets, and understand how their reactions were supposed to be controlled. We can never now empathise entirely with the families of innocent protesters – who had the perfectly credible aim of creating a united nation in which they fervently believed – killed by gunfire of the British establishment, which had for centuries neglected or mistreated that same nation. The Troubles formally ended with the Good Friday Agreement of 1998, and the entry into the Northern Ireland political process by Republicans, including those – such as Gerry Adams and Martin McGuinness – who had once been terrorists.*

The death of McGuinness in 2017 illustrated the conflicted moral response to the entire situation: he was heralded by Tony Blair as a 'formidable peacemaker' for being willing to take part in the armistice; he was excoriated by former Tory politician Norman Tebbit (who had been attacked by the IRA) as 'a coward who never atoned for his crimes'. The answer, as ever, is some muddled combination of the two. From 2017 onward, somewhere between 1,000 and 2,000 troops will remain in Northern Ireland, about the same level as before the Troubles began.

Before 1982, it would have been a reasonable question to ask whether the British military was capable of a successful and sustained operational attack away from its bases. The conflict in the Falkland Islands provided an answer. Argentina had invaded this British territory for a combination of reasons: geographical sentimentality; the desire of its ruling junta to gain domestic popularity; a feeling that

---

* As we confront the newish spectre of Islamic terrorism, often with hysteria, it is salutary to note the scale of devastation wreaked by the Troubles. These are civilian deaths in the UK from terrorism in the last nearly fifty years:
2000–2015: 90 deaths
1985–99: 1,094 deaths
1970–84: 2,211 deaths

– post-Suez – Britain was a diminished military force and would protest but do nothing. As it happened, Britain was run by a Prime Minister who had her own eye on the ability of external conflict to quell domestic disquiet, or at least a burning desire to demonstrate her nation's ability to be strong on the world stage. The military response was swift and efficient, and the Argentinians surrendered in seventy-four days.

It is a matter of dispute whether the wars that have followed are relics of empire or not. Certainly, instability in the Middle East has some of its roots in historic British conquests. Iraq was a British protectorate in the early twentieth century. Afghanistan has – as we have seen – ever been a proxy battleground for great powers; it has ever proved a graveyard for British soldiers too. In 1991, the First Gulf War, the might of Western powers drove back Saddam Hussein's invasion of Kuwait with 100 hours of fighting; another example of military efficiency and expertise that seemed to be the keynote of modern warfare.

After 9/11, the format of warfare changed again. In both Iraq and Afghanistan,[16] British troops were once more forced to fight wars of insurgency, of guerrilla assaults and suicide bombs; what American General Charles Krulak called a 'three block war' in which all the tactics of combat would be tested within the space of three city blocks. Modern warfare was all about paranoia and claustrophobia, collateral damage and hostile inhabitants.

The job of the British and Americans was to dismantle a country's structures and then help to rebuild them. A military force can assist with the former; it can never achieve the latter.★ That is the function of politicians, and it always seems to fail. And, while operations formally ended in Iraq in 2009 and Afghanistan in 2014, our presence remains in these countries, and will do for a long time to come. Between 2007 and 2014, 128,000 troops were deployed in Afghanistan at a cost of £22 billion; at one point we had 10,000 soldiers permanently stationed there.

That said, it is interesting to note that the violence and terror of

---

★ One American commander put it succinctly: 'The longer I stayed there, the more I realised I didn't understand.'

war in Afghanistan was not so far removed from that of the First World War. Both were wars of prolonged shellings and firefights, of bayonet[17] charges against well-defended positions. The scale is different, of course, but the essentials persist; there is something uniquely visceral about conflict that connects combatants across the eras. This is Colonel Richard Kemp, who retired in 2006:

> Every soldier from 1916 would immediately recognise the basic tools of the modern infantryman's trade: rifle, bayonet, bullets, grenades – and a murderously heavy pack. Infantry soldiers must still be able to march for miles over harsh terrain in searing heat, bent under the weight of 100 pounds of combat equipment, and then fight face-to-face with a ruthless, tough and determined enemy.

Patrick Hennessey was a young, Oxbridge-educated man who signed up to be an officer, fought in Iraq and Afghanistan, and wrote a book about it called *The Junior Officers' Reading Club*,[18] in which he tried to convey the sensation of sheer excitement of being a soldier. He tells of 'an evening of roaring with homoerotic bloodlust at [the film] *300*', the training in which everyone is 'going mad with horrible, big fuck-off knives' and the 'guys punching the air and hugging each other with delight' at the prospect of going to war.

We must remember that people who volunteer for the military want to fight, and to take the lives of the enemy. 'There's not a soldier of us all, that, in the thanksgiving before meat, do relish the petition well that prays for peace', as a gentleman in *Measure for Measure* puts it. Regular soldiers are not Jim Spence or Wilfred Owen, compelled to serve for a greater cause; they are – increasingly – volunteer aggressors, willing killers. Here is a startling statistic (in respect of the US army): in the Second World War, only 15–20 per cent of combat infantry fired their weapons in any given battle; in Korea it was 50 per cent; and in Vietnam it was 90 per cent. It comes from the book *On Killing* (1995) by Lieutenant Colonel Dave Grossman, which has this as its thesis: 'The history of warfare can be seen as a history of increasingly more effective mechanisms for enabling and conditioning men to overcome their innate resistance to killing their fellow human beings.'

This seems compelling as an argument: technology has allowed a lot of modern combat to be remote (in the form of bombs and long-distance artillery); and those who are engaged in close-range battle are now more than ever geared to be killers. The professionalisation of the military sets a course towards a greater efficiency of its practitioners, in this case by equipping them mentally and physically to kill.

Over the course of recent years, I believe that those in the armed forces of Great Britain are more sinned against than sinning; give for our benefit far more than they subtract from our common bank of morality. Of course, the cost of violent warfare is paid both by those who practise it as well as those who are harmed as a result. This notion takes us into two areas, both of which require further discussion: can we measure the immoral conduct of the British army; how much have those who have served themselves suffered?

A brief history of British war crimes

It is axiomatic that warfare throughout the ages has been brutal and unforgiving. Until the nineteenth century there was no accepted standard of universal conduct when it came to the battlefield or the treatment of prisoners. Enemies were tortured, citizens were slaughtered. There is a moment in Shakespeare's *Henry V*, when the French troops have seemed to rally during the Battle of Agincourt and the King says:

> But, hark! What new alarum is this same?
> The French have reinforced their scatter'd men:
> Then every soldier kill his prisoners:
> Give the word through.

And this is scarcely remarked upon. To dub the conduct that of a war criminal is anachronistic; to condemn its morality, though, is eminently justifiable. From the times of Henry through to Wellington, soldiering was an unruly and unfair business. As the early nineteenth-century diarist Private Wheeler (a decent man, and shocked observer) put it: 'If you knew but the hundredth part of the atrocities committed by men calling themselves British soldiers, it would chill your blood.'

No, the modern story of war criminality must begin a few years later, in the Victorian age, with the development of the Geneva (and Hague) Conventions. It starts with a Swiss businessman called Henry Dunant, who went to visit wounded soldiers after the Battle of Solferino★ in 1859, where conditions were so appalling that he published a book on the horrors of war, established the charity Red Cross and called for an international set of standards in the area. In doing so, he established the first Convention for the Amelioration of the Wounded in Time of War (1864), attended in Geneva by all the great powers, by which nations agreed that the safety of medical personnel during warfare was sacrosanct. A Second Geneva Convention in 1906 extended this approach to naval, as well as land-based, conflicts.

Taking this spirit of benign co-operation further, the Hague Conventions (of 1899 and 1907) sought to develop rights for combatants and prisoners of war.[19] They forbade the use of torture, the killing of prisoners, the use of poisoned gas in conflict, the forced conscription of civilians and the looting of captured towns. These two conferences were attempts to show that countries could co-operate in peace on the major issues of civilisation. A third conference was scheduled for 1914, but by that time – alas – everybody was at war again.

And, in any case, everybody immediately ignored the previous agreements. The German invasion of Belgium was a violation of Convention III, which stated that hostilities should not commence without explicit warning. Poison gas was introduced by the Germans and then used by all major belligerents, in breach of Convention IV, which explicitly prohibited 'poison or poisoned weapons'.

The Third Geneva Convention (1929) focused on the humane treatment of prisoners. It was expanded further in the Fourth Geneva Convention of 1949, which is the one we all refer to now. The

---

★ This was between the French, led by Napoleon III, and the Austrians, led by Emperor Franz Joseph I. It was the last time in which two opposing sides had their monarchs in command during the battle. The dispute came in the run-up to the recognition of Italy as a nation state. As my old history teacher told me once, you should always remember that Italy is younger than Notts County Football Club.

definitions around the treatment of prisoners were expanded to require humane treatment, adequate feeding, no discrimination, torture or 'outrages on personal dignity'.[20] In 1977 two further protocols were added to make clear that the convention covered all wars, including of self-determination and civil conflicts. The United States refused to sign them,[21] and still does not accept their authority.

By now, though, the conventions have the weight of universal moral acceptance and of international law, enforced by the International Criminal Court in[22] The Hague since 2002, which has prosecuted around forty individuals for war crimes. It is clear how they have coalesced, over the last 150 years, as a set of rules to form an established standard of behaviour. It is equally clear that the British military have broken both the letter of these laws, and their moral basis, on a very regular basis.

Some examples to ponder. The mass destruction of property in the Boer War was followed by the creation, by Lord Kitchener,[23] of concentration camps[24] for more than 100,000 citizens, detained without trial. In the same conflict, two soldiers were court-martialled in 1901 for the murder of civilians without justification; other abuses went unpunished. In the First World War poison gas was used in the full knowledge of its evil, but for pragmatic (and perhaps understandable) reasons.* On the home front, British servicemen killed Irish civilians following the Easter Rising of 1916. Ireland, more generally, has been the home of British military brutality for many years, including the torture of suspected IRA members.†

The Second World War saw attacks on civilian shipping, and the indiscriminate bombing campaigns of civilian homes, most notably

---

* This is Lieutenant General Sir Charles Fergusson: 'It is a cowardly form of warfare which does not commend itself to me or other English soldiers . . . We cannot win this war unless we kill or incapacitate more of our enemies than they do of us, and if this can only be done by our copying the enemy in his choice of weapons, we must not refuse to do so.'
† A notorious case was in 1971, when detainees (held without trial) were subject to 'deep interrogation' using the 'five techniques' of wall-standing, hooding, subjection to noise, deprivation of sleep, and deprivation of food and drink. These were accompanied by beatings and verbal abuse. Interestingly, while the British government came to accept their illegality, the European Court of Human Rights found them to be 'inhuman and degrading' but not torture.

in Dresden. Prisoners were also, it now appears, tortured by the British. Alexander Scotland, the head of the Prisoner of War Interrogation Section of the Intelligence Corps, wrote a memoir in 1950, which had to be heavily censored by the government (before being published seven years later) because it would help 'persons agitating on behalf of war criminals'. In fact, it contained evidence that Scotland was a war criminal himself. He ran the institution called the London Cage, sited incongruously in one of the gilded streets of Kensington, and detailed in his book numerous breaches of the Geneva Convention, including prisoners forced to kneel while being beaten; to stand to attention for up to twenty-six hours; and being threatened with executions or damaging surgical procedures.

Now we might argue that war is no picnic, that the Nazis deserved no special treatment (not least because, via the Gestapo, they were meting out far worse to our citizens). But civilisation requires order, even – perhaps especially – in wartime. Scotland's defence – that his detainees were criminals, not combatants, and therefore outside the rules of war – is exactly the same dubious argument used by the CIA and the American establishment to justify torture in Afghanistan and Iraq, and no more plausible. And, let us be clear, torture and abuse involving the British has continued throughout the rest of the century and onwards, from the killings of the Mau Mau in Kenya or the insurgents in Malaya, through to the wars of the modern period.

Take the case of Baha Mousa in Iraq, arrested by members of the Queen's Lancashire Regiment in Basra in September 2003. He was a receptionist in a hotel where suspected bomb-making equipment had been discovered, and was detained without charge. In prison, he was beaten to death by the British army, with ninety-three sites of injury across his body. A public inquiry, under Sir William Gage, eventually ruled that his death had been caused by 'factors including lack of food and water, heat, exhaustion, fear, previous injuries and the hooding and stress positions used by British troops★ – and a final struggle with his guards'; it had been, it was ruled, 'an appalling episode of gratuitous violence'. We know it was not isolated: the

★ The 'five techniques' of torture resurfacing after thirty years, we note.

MoD has paid out, quietly, £20 million to the victims of abuse in Iraq, based on 326 cases.

Of course, there is another side here too. There is no question that soldiers, operating under unimaginable stress, have been subject to false accusations and unreasonable demands. In 2010 the government set up IHAT (the Iraq Historic Allegations Team), which was immediately hijacked by ambulance-chasing lawyers.[25] Until it was disbanded in 2017, it cost £60 million and led to only one prosecution: against one of its own representatives for falsely impersonating a police officer.

The extent to which normal standards of human behaviour can be held to apply in wartime fosters a legitimate ethical debate. In 2013 the Supreme Court of the UK ruled that the government could be sued for negligence under the Human Rights Act, because it had failed to provide adequate equipment to ensure soldiers' 'right to life'. This is a sensible notion in the end: responsibilities and obligations should exist, if anything, more rigorously in situations of extreme peril. However, at the same time, special understanding should be given when judging the actions of those who are suffering that peril.

This potential conflict was demonstrated in the case of Alexander Blackman, known originally (when his identity was protected) as Marine A. In 2013 he was found guilty of murder when – and the facts are scarcely disputed – he took a disarmed Taliban fighter to the edge of a field and shot him in the chest, saying: 'There you are, shuffle off this mortal coil,* you cunt. It's nothing you wouldn't do to us.' He added: 'Obviously this doesn't go anywhere, fellas. I've just broken the Geneva Convention.' No psychological assessment of Blackman was admitted to his trial. Following a campaign, led by the *Daily Mail*, an appeal was heard, and the charge was changed to manslaughter, on the grounds that Blackman was suffering from

---

* The line is taken from Hamlet's 'To be or not to be' speech, where he ponders suicide and the uncertainty of what follows death. It is striking that this hymn to inaction, to complexity, should be used by a soldier at the moment of doing what Hamlet spends much of the play not doing: taking a life. A sign that, at least subconsciously, Blackman recognised the magnitude of his actions and their moral dubiety?

diminished responsibility. At the time of the killing, he had reached the point of psychic stress that he could not tell right from wrong.

There is much to unpick here. First, that the system – in the end – worked: Blackman's conduct was only known because of the army's own recordings; the Geneva Convention was recognised as a moral and actual law, and upheld; and the amount of pressure placed on a young man was finally taken into consideration. The British military is a proud organisation, based on remarkable achievements, and also carrying the burden of occasional moral error. It has done much good, and some evil, in the world. Blackman is not unfairly a symbol of that.

Indeed, the one constant of all human conflict is the soldier, sailor or pilot who is expected to temper aggression with restraint, to take part in bloody struggle but not be controlled by it. This can be an impossible task. Neil Greenberg, a psychiatrist called in Blackman's appeal, said that everybody has a 'breaking point': 'there is no such thing as a Rambo type, an Arnold Schwarzenegger soldier, who can face all sorts of stresses and appear to be invulnerable. That sort of person only exists in the cinema.'

What do soldiers suffer, and how are they supported?

In 1944 Sydney Jary led 18 Platoon of 4th Battalion Somerset Light Infantry, and thought about the qualities that made the ideal soldier:

> Firstly sufferance, without which one could not survive. Secondly, a quiet mind which enables the soldier to live in harmony with his fellows through all sorts of difficulties and sometimes under dreadful conditions . . . Thirdly, but no less important, a sense of the ridiculous which helps a soldier surmount the unacceptable. Add to these a reasonable standard of physical fitness and a dedicated professional competence, and you have a soldier for all seasons . . . If I now had to select a team for a dangerous mission and my choice was restricted to stars of the sports field or poets, I would unhesitatingly recruit from the latter.

As a piece of idealisation, this is unimprovable; as a demonstration of reality, it is perhaps more dubious. But let us focus for a moment on the 'quiet mind' of a soldier, because that seems to me to get to the heart of the problem: peace of mind is precisely what is often lost in the military, and its absence can become a curse back on civvy street.

On my LBC Radio show one day, I was called by Cody, who had served two operational tours in the army before being discharged with mental health problems. He had no home or job or sense of purpose; he had been 'living in a bubble' in the army and that bubble had popped.

Cody told the story of how, following his discharge, he got himself into a situation where he had just £3 left in the world. He went to a phone box to try to find a hostel where he could stay. Two pounds down, his last coin was rattling through the machine, not being accepted; he resolved then that, if the coin did not take, he was going to hang himself. Thankfully a hostel picked him up and offered him a bed. An army charity got him a flat and he lived to tell me his story: 'If that hadn't happened, I'd be homeless and honest to God I'd be dead, because there is no way I was going to continue living that life.'

It is estimated that there are about 4.8 million veterans in the UK, and around 20,000 leave the services each year. Most are fine, and live normal lives. Many are not. It is important that we do not overstate the problem, of course. Generally speaking, the incidence of poor mental health in military personnel is probably similar to that of civilians: about one in five for common illnesses (such as depression or anxiety); about 3 per cent for cases of post-traumatic stress disorder. But there are some caveats. First, the complexity and the severity of the mental trauma is likely to be increased by those who have been in the military. Second, those who have actually seen combat are more likely than average to suffer from PTSD (indeed the rate more than doubles). Third, we are still in the aftermath of Iraq and Afghanistan, and there may be a long tail of those seeking treatment* still to come. Fourth, many mental conditions

---

* We do know that awards for compensation in mental disorder cases have increased by 379 per cent between 2009 and 2015 (from 121 to 580), which may suggest an increase in claim-worthy conditions as a result of Afghanistan.

are augmented or affected by substance abuse, especially alcohol: a 'chronic problem' according to General Lord Dannatt; the 'damnable poison' according to Private Wheeler more than a century earlier. Patrick Hennessey offered this as a description of the post-army life he experienced: 'No one wanted or chose to be a scotch-drinking, night-spoiling, glass-smashing, relationship-bashing cliché, it was just as unavoidable, as slamming on the brakes in a car on ice and watching the wall come sliding towards you anyway.'

You see: not all moments of despair and angst can be pathologised. A night of teary boozing is unlikely to fetch up in a mental health statistic. But it is an example of the consequences of trauma that we must, as a society, recognise.

Because we are all complicit in the care for our military. We all know the causes of many of these moments, many of these illnesses: us. It is our country that has sent these men and women to serve; we are responsible for the health of those who come back. This is literally the case, too. Military personnel are treated in NHS hospitals, both for physical★ and mental ailments. In 2000 the Ministry of Defence instigated the Armed Forces Covenant, an agreement between the military and the nation that sought to emphasise the moral obligation of the latter to the former to provide support and care at all points during and after their service. It is recognised that governmental support to service personnel has improved ever since.

But it is striking how much work is performed by charities such as the Royal British Legion,[26] Help for Heroes, Combat Stress, the SSFA (which rescued Cody and gave him a home) and the like. This used to bother me: why, the logic goes, should our country send out people to be broken up in war and fail to cover all the costs in helping fix them up again? There is some sense in this argument. However, the value of charity is that it commits all of us, not just civil servants who allocate budgets, to the assistance

---

★ I have focused largely on the mental, because it seems to me less tangible or visible. There were 790 people judged to be 'seriously injured' in physical terms between 2002 and 2012 (the period of Iraq and Afghanistan). There were 150 amputations that have been officially recorded in that time.

of veterans. Our donations – if we choose to make them – become part of our own covenant with the military.

And that is the covenant that needs work, will always need our attention. More than one military source has said to me that the amount of care now available to injured veterans is acceptably high (indeed there is talk of furnished complexes going under-used, especially as we now enter a period of comparative peace). But the cost of service will be ever present, and it cannot always be paid in financial terms. Far more important is our collective recognition of the issues affecting the military and those who serve in it.

What is the current state of the armed services?

A notable statistic for you: in 2016 no British military personnel was killed in operations; the first year this has happened since 1968, which was the only other year since 1945. The disasters of Iraq and Afghanistan – in the sense of their human cost and limited strategic success – have led to an environment in which British interventionism has become politically less acceptable. This means that services will need to be smaller, and more mobile. Some numbers for you, courtesy of the 2015 Strategic Defence and Security Review: the plan for the next five years was for the army to have about 82,000 regulars (and 35,000 reservists); the navy around 30,000; and the RAF 34,000. This is about a third of the size of the military in the 1950s.[27] Some in the military worry that its cost-cutting has gone too far.

About 9 per cent of the armed forces are women, and in 2016 the decision was taken to allow women to fight in close combat units (the cavalry, the infantry and armoured corps) for the first time. Women will need to pass the same requirements as any man to do so, which involves an eight-mile forced march in under two hours carrying a 25kg pack.* Evidence suggests just 5 per cent of existing service women will be able to achieve this. The notion of

---

* In case you were wondering, the basic fitness test for all applicants to the army is a 2.4km run in less than fourteen minutes, together with forty-four press-ups and fifty sit-ups within two minutes. Not that difficult.

women serving with men at the front has attracted dissent, inevitably including blimpish parps of objection in the pages of the *Daily Telegraph*. Colonel Richard Kemp said he believed the 'price for this social engineering experiment will be paid in blood'.

This seems odd, on the face of it. In the Second World War 600,000 women served in auxiliary services, and were recognised as a permanent part of the armed forces in 1949. Women were eligible to fly combat aircraft in 1989, and serve on Royal Navy warships in 1990. Of course, the physical demands of close combat may be difficult, but – in the event that women can pass them – there seem to be little moral or practical grounds for rejecting them. One person's 'social engineering' is another's evolution of equality.

Not that the military is necessarily a beacon of equality. Just 7 per cent of the military is from an ethnic minority,★ compared to 13 per cent of the entire workforce. There is an atavistic sense that the services are one of the last bastions of escape for the traditional white working class, which they struggle to shift.†

The military, whatever its constituent parts, is certainly cosmopolitan in terms of its deployment: we have a new naval base in Bahrain; an increased presence in the Baltics, especially Estonia; two permanent bases in Cyprus; bases in the Falklands, Gibraltar and Kenya; and small numbers remain in Iraq and Afghanistan to continue the training of indigenous military. Since 1945, Britain has maintained

---

★ That's 9.4 per cent of the army, compared to just 3.4 per cent in the navy and 2.1 per cent in the RAF; a striking discrepancy. There were just 480 Muslims in the army in 2015, just over 0.55 per cent of the regular force (about 4 per cent of the UK population is Muslim).

† There is one ethnic aspect to the army we must reflect: the Gurkhas, military recruits from Nepal. They were first recruited into the army after the British were impressed by their conduct in the Anglo–Nepalese War (1814–16). Today, up to 30,000 Gurkhas apply to join the British military every year; and only around 200 are accepted. Shamefully, until recently, Gurkhas received smaller pensions than their British counterparts and were not guaranteed citizenship. The law was changed in 1997 to remedy this, and then made retroactive in 2009. Gurkhas are awesome fighters: 'murderous in the battle line', recalled Jim Spence; 'if a man says he is not afraid of dying, he is either lying or he is a Gurkha,' said Field Marshal Sam Manekshaw; 'bravest of the brave, most generous of the generous, never had a country more faithful friends than you', said Sir Ralph Lilley Turner, who served with them in the First World War.

a permanent base in Germany, but a decision has been taken to relocate all troops there by 2020. The Cold War is now over.

Or is it? Arguably, the most pressing military threat in nation state terms comes once more from Russia. And the body organised to meet it remains NATO, which was created decades ago in the face of Soviet expansion.

What is NATO?

It is a political and military alliance of twenty-nine member countries from Europe and North America, established (with twelve countries) following the signing of the North Atlantic Treaty on 4 April 1949. At that stage, the greatest threat to the Western world was perceived to be communism (the Soviet Union had test-detonated an atomic bomb in 1949; the Chinese-backed North Koreans invaded South Korea a year later) and a strong military alliance was seen as the best means of keeping it in check.

The key article of the treaty – critical still today – is Article 5, which states that 'an armed attack against one or more [member] . . . shall be considered an attack against them all'.★ For the entirety of the Cold War, the alliance of NATO countries counterbalanced those of the Warsaw Pact (the Soviet Union and its satellite communist states). With some bumps along the way,[28] this maintained an uneasy peace until the collapse of communism in Eastern Europe, with the fall of the Berlin Wall, and then in Russia itself.

Today, NATO has the capacity – in extreme circumstances – to provide 3.4 million military personnel, including 1.7 million soldiers and 22 nuclear submarines; its members spend nearly $1,000 billion on defence every year. It has a small amount of equipment itself, and relies on the troops and the gear provided by its members being

---

★ Without wishing to trivialise this, the principle is the same as the '99' call used by the British and Irish Lions rugby team in South Africa in 1974. In the face of continued violence by the home team (ignored by the referees), it was decided that if someone was involved in a fight, '99' would be called, and every player would hit the nearest opponent. This is the same principle as that of 'massive retaliation' that was the NATO policy in the 1950s.

placed under its unifying authority. NATO offers, in theory, a dominating threat that no single country could countenance facing. But its value remains open to question.

The US thinks that many European members have failed to show requisite support for NATO. Donald Trump, speaking colourfully and (typically) without full knowledge of the facts during his presidential campaign, suggested it was 'obsolete'. Some of his objections, though, are not unfounded. A pre-condition of NATO membership since 2006 has been an undertaking to spend 2 per cent of GDP on defence. The US more than meets this, and spends 3.6 per cent; the UK just scrapes in, and spends more than £30 billion annually. But most countries do not meet their requirements: in recent years, Germany has spent 1.2 per cent, Italy and Spain around 1 per cent, France just below 2 per cent, Canada 1 per cent.

Indeed, by 2017 the only other countries who met their defence-spending responsibilities are Estonia, Poland, Turkey and Greece (with Latvia and Lithuania on track to do the same). It is no coincidence that these countries are on the eastern side of Europe, close to the incipient Russian threat. Incidentally, the extent to which Russia is a real, rather than a theoretical, enemy remains open to dispute. Russia certainly has shown its willingness to expand westwards and to meddle militarily in other states: it fought bloody campaigns in Chechnya; it annexed Crimea; it supported militants in eastern Ukraine. It has amassed a significant force, including with nuclear capability, to the east of Estonia. It has – all the evidence suggests – assassinated its enemies on British streets.

How seriously you take this depends a bit on your politics. If you are anti-EU and anti-American, you regard Russia as more sinned against than sinning. It is European expansion eastwards, the argument goes, taking Ukraine out of its natural Russian orbit, that is to blame for creating uncertainty and dispute. NATO expansion is readily criticised for raising the military stakes. An opposing – and, to my mind, more rational – view sees Russia, under its volatile President Putin, as more of a threat to world peace. Russia made itself the kingmaker in Syria, propping up the tyrant Assad with illegal airstrikes that would reasonably be seen as war crimes; Russia's actions in eastern Ukraine were violent and in breach of international law; it was

Russian-backed forces that plucked the passenger jet MH17 from the sky in July 2014, killing 298 people, including eighty children. As we have seen elsewhere, military action has a way of increasing domestic popularity, and Putin has shown a willingness to buy popularity at the cost of human life. He has done so thus far with impunity.

It is, then, unlikely but not impossible that Putin's Russia will test the NATO alliance; the willingness of countries to fight back on the eastern fringes of Europe will then come into question.

What about the UN as a force to prevent military problems?

The UN was also forged in the heady aftermath of the Second World War: the term 'united nations' was invented by American President Franklin D. Roosevelt as a description of the 'goodies', those fighting the Axis Powers; it came into force in 1945 with fifty-one member states. Big decisions are made by the Security Council of the UN, which has fifteen members, five of whom are permanent: Russia, Britain, France, China and the US. Germany should be a permanent member (it contributes the third largest amount of money to the UN) but isn't for the simple historical reason that it was once a 'baddie', that it lost the war.

The permanent members of the Security Council have the right to veto any decisions.* In practice, this means that the UN can do nothing in the face of misbehaviour by China or Russia, which represent two of the most significant threats to world peace. That is why the UN has achieved so little in Syria.[29] The United States' support for Israel similarly blocks any significant intervention in its illegal occupation of Palestinian territories.

There are certainly significant grounds to criticise the UN, mainly because it tries to accommodate peaceably so many opposing ideologies. It has 193 member states, fewer than half of which are free

---

* More than half of all vetos have come from Russia, though mainly before 1965. In 2017 China and Russia vetoed UN sanctions against Syria for the use of chemical weapons. Russia has used its veto in relation to Syria seven times in the previous five years.

democracies.[30] It has a country like Saudi Arabia sitting on its Human Rights Council,[31] despite its appalling record in that particular area.

All that said, the UN has mandated intervention in conflicts with some success, as we saw in Yugoslavia and in Sierra Leone. It, correctly, argued against the invasion of Iraq. An American policy think-tank, RAND, once judged that the UN was successful in two out of three interventions, which is not a terrible record at all. Over the last seventy years, the world has been at comparative peace, and the number of people dying in conflicts has been reduced to a vast extent. The UN has played a considerable part in that.

So what is the point of the military as the world gets more peaceful?

The world is – taken with a long perspective – not only getting more peaceful, but we may be entering an age of military non-intervention by the UK. The costly war in Afghanistan seems to have finally ended the last spasms of our imperial mindset, of the sense that we – as a nation – are responsible for the world's problems. When military action in Syria was first discussed in the UK Parliament in 2013,[32] it was rejected (following polling suggesting that the population was opposed).

However, it seems that the price of non-intervention is both ceaseless vigilance and the persistent threat of retaliation (the latter being a succinct summary of the NATO approach). The argument for our continued development of nuclear weapons is not that anybody expects to use them, but rather that they continue to act as balance and counterbalance on all sides. Mutually assured destruction has a long pedigree, because it seems – largely – to work.

Britain's nuclear deterrent, Trident, consists of four submarines, each of which can carry up to sixteen Trident missiles, each armed with eight nuclear warheads (each one eight times as powerful as the atomic bomb at Hiroshima). There is one submarine at sea patrolling at all times. The system will be replaced by 2030, and the government has approved the spending to do this. Labour leader Jeremy Corbyn – who is anti-nuclear – proposed keeping the submarines, but losing the missiles. Not many people agreed with him. Admiral Hine told me that a nuclear arsenal is essential to maintaining our status as a global player of military significance.

However, it is right to acknowledge that the shape of the UK's enemies has changed in recent years. The greatest threat to our democracy and to our citizens comes from terrorism, and the response to that lies more in the hands of our security forces than our military. The rise of the Islamic State, amid the ravaged badlands of Iraq and Syria, still presents a military target, though a diminishing one, which is why airstrikes against it were approved in 2015. It does not present a force that will require boots on the ground, a large-scale, infantry-based response. The UK will support the forces in Iraq that are battling IS, for example; it will not fight this war for them.

So the current purpose of the British military is to maintain peace, and support the fighting of others. Warfare comes down to training other nations' combat troops, and providing long-distance (safer distance) backing, assurance and reassurance. The former Defence Secretary Michael Fallon called 2017 the 'year of the navy', as the UK becomes the only nation other than the US to have two aircraft carriers,★ with the arrival of the HMS *Queen Elizabeth* and HMS *Prince of Wales*, two symbols of this remote fighting. A re-established naval base in Bahrain, HMS *Juffair*, will be the first east of Suez since 1971.

When we look at the 2015 review of the armed forces, we see small increases in navy and RAF personnel, and the continued de-powering of the army. That seems to reveal the projected course of modern warfare: short, sharp action by aircraft launched from mobile ships; a smaller army to be deployed only where necessary. We are also seeing a tremendous shrinking of the Ministry of Defence, which employed 41,000 in 2016, down from over 61,000 the year before. In 1980 it employed 316,700. The army is entering a phase of existential self-assessment, and the government's answer seems to

---

★ Rear Admiral Nick Hine called them '65,000 tonnes of UK territory; the real Royal Yachts', a visible presence in troubled waters. They are relatively efficient, too. Eighty per cent of the size of an American carrier, they are run by 1,000 personnel; the Americans use 5,000 people on board.

be that its reserve should be built up for emergencies and its standing force reduced to account for the predicted diminution in workload.

But inertia will always rule for a long period. We still have a parachute regiment ('Elite forces, but not fucking dropping out of any aeroplanes any time soon,' said a senior military figure to me), the ability to stage an amphibious landing of marines (last attempted decades ago), and the like with a diminished strategic purpose. We have fifty-one airfields in Britain, and a vast landbank of property owned by the Ministry of Defence, all the relics of a bygone age. We still spend £36 billion on our military, even if much of that is on resources we probably do not need. 'Is it value for money?' asked Admiral Hine. 'No, it is not.'

But whatever the economics, we will always need some investment in our armed forces. The existence of the military will always mean that our nation is putting our people in harm's way for what it considers to be our benefit. Whatever policies are pursued – and however much we agree or disagree with them – it is right and proper, *dulce et decorum*, that we acknowledge and understand what has been done, and will continue to be done, in our name.

6

Law and Order

The end of law is not to abolish or restrain, but to preserve
and enlarge freedom. For in all the states of created beings
capable of law, where there is no law, there is no freedom

John Locke (1632–1704)

Most Saturdays when I was growing up, I would be driven past
Leicester Prison on the way to watch the Leicester Tigers rugby
team. It is an extraordinary building: it looks like a theme-park
vision of a medieval castle. Crenellated towers and battlements; an
oaken wooden door at its heart. Sometimes, I used to half imagine
Robin Hood, a lively flash of green in a thicket of arrows, mounting
a daring sally inside. In the maudlin damp of a winter afternoon,
though, it was ever an imposing, depressing sight. On Saturdays,
there was always a forlorn line of people outside, heads bowed,
clutching plastic carrier bags. The car tended to fall silent as the
shadow of the prison fell upon it. 'Who is in there? What did they
do?' I often asked, not for the knowledge but for the childish thrill
of discussing the transgressive. My gran, who attended rugby games
into her eighties, with a tartan rug and a hip flask, would always
set her jaw, and utter some condemnatory words. There were villains
in there; there were robbers. It was a horrible-looking place, because
it needed to be; the walls were thick and cold, with moisture seeping
down them like a death-sweat, because they had to withstand the
wiles of the criminal classes contained inside.

The image of the prison has never left me, nor the vagrant straggle
of those waiting by the gate. I think about Leicester jail when I

visit another, even older prison* recently, to see an Alpha[1] course being taught there. The walls are similar: high and forbidding; a repeating whorl of rusting barbed-wire atop, like a child's handwriting exercise. A chaplain, the lovely and optimistic Sarah (not her real name), purple-haired and full of tea and cheer, walks me briskly to the chapel (recently refurbished, she notes with pride; the previous building having been riddled with asbestos), and then to stand at the centre of the prison, the hub into which all the wings lead. It is still lockdown time. The only movement comes from prison officers, bustling around with cartoonishly large sets of keys swinging down from their generally over-ample frames. They look imposing, but tired, unagile. 'That woman there used to throw the shot or the discus or something for Great Britain,' Sarah says happily.

She is full of praise for her colleagues, but dismay at the conditions in which they work. There were too few guards: some days just seventy were available when the full requirement was double that. Fewer guards meant more prisoners left in the cells for the whole day. There was an effective pandemic of mental illness in the place too, as across the entire system: 28 per cent of all prisoners in this one building were on anti-psychotic medicine of some sort.

A bell rings, shouts are raised; harsh noises echo around the concrete and metal structures. It is 'free-flow' time, when prisoners can leave their cells and spend twenty minutes moving around the prison ahead of their planned activity for the afternoon (work, say, or meeting their solicitor). I think my five-year-old son's school uses the same term, free-flow, to denote the time between specific classes when the children can control their own activity. And there is – it is clear – something infantilising about imprisonment: I see it in the way the prisoners talk to the guards, seek permission from them, worry about being in the wrong place at the wrong time.

Men approach the chapel, at first warily, then with increasing confidence as they see Sarah's face. Everybody shakes hands with me, makes the same joke about me being 'the Stig' (the racing driver

---

* I have been asked not to say which one, because there is a general reluctance to allow journalists (even ineffectual ones like me) into prison at all. When we discuss the system in more detail, you will see why.

from the *Top Gear* TV show); I make the same joke back (pretending not to be able to confirm or deny it). Laughs, nods and arm clasps. I talk first to a young black guy (and even the most youthful figures appear older than they are; prematurely wizened and distressed by the environment), who has a year to go before release. 'Ask him about his arm!' calls Sarah over her shoulder. He holds it up: I see a long scar stretching down, and three pronounced bumps, little hillocks of scuffed skin.

He tells me the story of Christmas Day this year. In his cell, wanting a cigarette, and seeing that a cellmate is already smoking a roll-up. He gets two tokes, realising too late it is not tobacco, but the once-legal high Spice★ that has pervaded British prisons. He hallucinates; sees devils; feels no sensations in his body. He feels the unutterable conviction that he can break the metal around him with his strength. He shouts and screams. By the time the guards get there, he has woven his arm between the unflinching bars and pulled with all his might. The bone shattered in four places, white spars protruding out of his black skin. Today, he muses on Spice and its dangers. I say he must be fairly annoyed with his cellmate. 'What can I do? I can't make it not have happened.'

Drugs get into the prison via drones. There is a public footpath that skirts one side of the complex; there are plenty of unfixed, open windows within range. Up to ten times a day in the past (I am told), little packages (containing drugs or mobile phones or SIM cards) are buzzed into range. There is a flourishing micro-economy in place based upon it.

We are now sitting in the chapel to hear the last talk of the course, which has been running for seven weeks. There are maybe twenty of us there: the prisoners in sweatpants, despite the oppressive heat of the day, the sun's rays magnified through the gaudily stained glass. One guy is painfully old and thin; his trousers keep slipping down

---

★ This drug is a collection of synthetic cannabinoids, i.e. chemicals artificially designed to mimic cannabis. It was made illegal in 2016, but − by driving its production underground − it has become even more potent, unpredictable and dangerous. Many believe that it is as addictive as heroin: it is certainly cheaper (£5 for half a gram, or about twenty joints worth), and is commonly found in prisons and among the homeless.

and so when he walks he has to clutch them tightly to his waist. He is a former rough-sleeper, used to being outside amid the elements; he can't sleep at night in prison. I don't get to speak to him, as throughout the two-hour session he sits and slumbers deeply, unwakeable.

The theme of the day is making better decisions, making sure that each person changes their life – through God – so that they never return to this seemingly forsaken place. The speaker is a man called Paul Cowley, a pioneer of Alpha in prisons, and an ex-army man who has had his own brush with the law, his own misfortunes with family. He is empathetic; he can look tough cons in the eye while he talks. Prisoners nod; occasional muted cries of 'Amen' punctuate the discussion. During a break, another prisoner approaches, clutching the Bible. He wants to talk theology. I ask him if he believes in the possibility of God helping him: 'Gods, plural,' he says with a glint. He grabs my hand and points to a passage in Genesis that refers to the 'giants in the earth', the 'Nephilim', which he believes is a reference to the Sumerian account of creation. In his view, the Sumerians were confronted by gods from another planet (connected to ours by an orbit that brings it into proximity every 3,000 years), who have been living here ever since, desperate to collect the gold necessary to regulate their home environment. 'Look at the cuneiform inscriptions,' he says, 'there are spaceships drawn on them!' I ask where the gods live now; he looks wryly at me and tells me the government did not want us to know.

My new friend (who graciously acknowledged my scepticism) has been in prison for the last five years, because he had offended again while under licence (essentially the agreement on his last release that he would follow a certain set of rules). By his account, he has lost his liberty simply for missing a curfew in a hostel and having been seen with alcohol. Later he refers to the fact he had been termed 'unmanageable', which may be closer to the mark. He had been in more than ten prisons in his life, and was broadly content with this one. You must, though, always be able to look after yourself, he says: not all parts of this prison, even now, have CCTV cameras; in other places, there were hundreds of dark corners where you might face attack or abuse. He tells me about 'spooning': if a gang believes that you are concealing contraband in a body cavity, they hold you down, and use a spoon to probe your anus. 'I'd fight pretty hard to stop that happening,' he points out. I agree readily.

This is a reminder that, for all the calm in this soporific chapel, there is the threat of danger and angst never too far away. The prisoners are asked why they come: 'For fellowship,' says one, and everybody agrees instantly. Now I am an atheist of long standing, and religion makes me uncomfortable. I feel uncomfortable at the end of this service, when people stand and sing of their love for God; I feel uncomfortable when we lay our hands on three men who are set to be released, so we can join in prayer for their rehabilitation. Like an unwelcome Macbeth, I cannot say 'Amen' when everyone else does. But I am touched nonetheless. The volunteers behind the course, and their charity Caring for Ex-Offenders, clearly offer something: not only care and love (they use the term 'love' unembarrassedly with one another, even the hard-nosed prisoners), but also practical help for the future. One of the organisers tells me how they undertake to meet a prisoner at the gates of the prison and help them find home and work. Sometimes they are competing directly with the drug-dealers who congregate outside prisons, waiting for an easy mark: a man with fifty quid in his hand and an overwhelming sense of uncertainty and excitement within him.

Such figures of charity are a small light in the prevailing dark, though. Almost every prisoner I spoke to had no home to return to, no job to return to, no family willing to welcome them back. Their lives in the prison were grim; their prospects would be – without external help – not much better. As I leave, back to the real world of permissible mobile phones and free movement, one guy grabs me. He wants to make the 'Stig' joke again. He is excited, bubbling over, because he is released tomorrow. What will he do? Get some clothes, see where his belly takes him, and walk the streets, for there is nothing so beautiful as the city at night.

Such positivity, such articulacy. Sarah steers me away: he is under observation until he leaves, because of serious mental health problems. He is about to go into that beautiful, anonymous city with no help other than God's or – at least – that of a couple of people who believe in Him. He may well be back some day.

Some key developments in our justice system

The men I met are in prison as a result of a process that has been around 800 years in the making. Our legal system today is full of hocus pocus, mystery and flummery, but it is more efficient and rational than it used to be. In Britain there was once a point where guilt of a crime was determined by how quickly your skin could recover from holding a burning piece of metal ('trial by ordeal') or whether you could defeat your accuser in armed combat ('trial by combat'). The former was condemned by the Pope in 1215 and abolished; the latter was, somewhat surprisingly, still on the books in 1819.[2] Soon a system of being judged by peers became common, although early juries were not independent arbiters of the evidence, but members of the community asked to use their own knowledge to establish guilt. By Tudor times, they were expected to be impartial and decide cases on the facts presented to them.* Juries remain to this day fickle and unpredictable, able to convict out of prejudice, or save out of pity. Indeed, juries in modern Britain are more likely to do the latter than the former: they acquit 65 per cent of the time. Magistrates (we'll get to them), judging cases without juries, acquit only 20 per cent of the time.

In the aftermath of the phone-hacking scandal, twenty-seven journalists working for the *Sun* newspaper were arrested, following allegations that they had been involved in paying public officials for stories. Their company, then News International, had handed over a cache of apparently incriminating emails that revealed knowledge or involvement in transactions. Homes were ransacked, devices were confiscated. The process took more than four years: children were born, marriages were broken, while the accused were charged and suspended from work. It was an example of the tremendous cost and delay inherent in the system. But when prosecution of nineteen journalists followed, juries almost universally refused to convict them:

---

* Court records show the long history of judges telling off jurors for inappropriate behaviour, including a Tudor example of one member being fined for eating sweets when he should have been concentrating on proceedings.

because either the law was not clear[3] or they felt that paying for stories should not be criminalised. Either way, the bloody-mindedness of British citizens★ was seen by those involved as their greatest saviour.

In similar fashion, a jury in 1985 refused to convict Clive Ponting for a breach of the Official Secrets Act (he had leaked documents about the sinking of the *Belgrano* in the Falklands War), despite the judge telling them that Ponting had no defence in law. Juries have the freedom to reflect what they consider to be the public mood, or the prevailing standards of morality, and they cannot really be prevented from doing so. In 1960, Penguin Books was prosecuted for publishing *Lady Chatterley's Lover* by D. H. Lawrence on the grounds of its obscenity.[†] The prosecutor listed some of the most shocking elements ('the word "fuck" or "fucking" appears no less than 30 times . . . "cunt" 14 times; "balls" 13 times; "shit" and "arse" six times apiece; "cock" four times');[‡] the jury was unmoved; the book was published and went on to sell 3 million copies in the next three months.

Very few will make the case that the jury system is a poor one,

---

★ One of the trials lasted over the Christmas period. One day, the jury passed a note to the judge asking if they could wear Christmas jumpers on the next Friday, as part of a nationwide charity day. The judge asked the defendants, who reluctantly acquiesced, and spent the day having their fate determined by twelve people with protruding red noses and antlers on their sweaters.

† The test, according to Geoffrey Robertson QC (who has written about this for the *Guardian*), was what was acceptable for a fourteen-year-old girl to read. In 1928 Radclyffe Hall's *The Well of Loneliness* had been destroyed by a magistrate thanks to one line ('and that night they were not divided') that would 'induce thoughts of a most impure character and would glorify the horrible tendency of lesbianism'.

‡ Here is a sample of Laurentian sex writing from the book:

> He too had bared the front part of his body and she felt his naked flesh against her as he came into her. For a moment he was still inside her, turgid there and quivering. Then, as he began to move, in the sudden helpless orgasm, there awoke in her new strange thrills rippling inside her. Rippling, rippling, rippling, like a flapping overlapping of soft flames, soft as feathers, running to points of brilliance, exquisite, exquisite and melting her all molten inside. It was like bells rippling up and up to a culmination.

No writer is as screamingly, helplessly open to parody as Lawrence.

though legal professor Brian Hogan has cogently argued that it is, at least, somewhat illogical:

> If we'd never had trial by jury in this country and our practice had been to try cases by judges, rationally finding the facts and drawing inferences, and I were to come boldly along with the suggestion that this professional judgment should be replaced by an almost inscrutable verdict, by the first twelve men and women you meet in the street, I think any sensible person would believe that I had gone out of my mind.

In any case, juries and legal independence have become synonymous in the national narrative. The beginning of the rule of law[4] – it is often said, and is largely true – in Britain coincides with the signing by King John of the Magna Carta (the Big Charter)[5] in 1215. This has two key chapters, which make clear that a person cannot be punished without due process, and that such a process cannot be bought, delayed or denied. These are critical principles in our judicial system today. As it happens, Magna Carta was in force for precisely two months (when Pope Innocent III annulled it on the grounds it had been obtained by compulsion, calling it 'illegal, unjust, harmful to royal rights and shameful to the English people'), and did not directly lead to modern jury trials in any significant way. As an articulation of principles of justice, it owed much to existing texts, such as the coronation oaths of Anglo-Saxon kings and the law codes of Henry I. The Pope also called Magna Carta 'void of all validity forever'. He was wrong. It has survived as both a romantic gesture and a useful precedent[6] to cite as our courts became more professional and individual rights became more established.

The more significant, but less heralded, legal development came a couple of centuries later with the articulation of the principle of habeas corpus. The full phrase is *habeas corpus ad subjiciendum*: 'may you bring the body before the court', which sounds pompous or funereal. What it means, though, is that everyone has a right to be tried in person before being imprisoned. If someone is held by the state without trial, a petition using this phrase should get them either freed or at least their status interrogated by a judge. Two Latin words contain the most effective measure against tyranny in existence.

As time progressed in this country, then, we see the development of ideas of fair trial, and of judge and juries. We also see the early abolition of torture as part of the judicial process. It was banned by the Pope in 1215 (who seemed to be rather busy that year), and judges had established that it could not be used in English courts by the fifteenth century. Yet you will be familiar with the rack[7] and thumbscrews; you will have – at some point – shuddered in empathy at the plight of the helpless victim described in your history books. Torture was used in England only in the exercise of the royal prerogative: i.e. if the king or queen demanded it for the prevention of terrorism.* Guy Fawkes was tortured when he was uncovered planning to blow up the Houses of Parliament in 1605 (the effects of his racking visible in his almost illegible signature to his confession). The only woman to be tortured in the Tower of London was called Anne Askew, in the last year of Henry VIII's reign. At that point, Henry – fat, gouty and fearing for his soul – was tempted to return to the Catholic faith, and heretical Protestants were at risk. Askew was taken to the Tower, and placed on the rack by the Constable (or chief warder). After a few minutes, he sobbingly refused to continue, so his place was taken by two of the king's advisers, who turned the rack so hard that Askew's hips and shoulders were pulled from their sockets, her elbows and knees dislocated. When she was subsequently burned at the stake, she had to be carried to her fate on a special chair.

Before she died, Askew's account of her torture was sneaked out of prison and published, to much horror. By the time of the Civil War, sanctioned abuse was regarded as one of the signs of improper power in the hands of the monarch. In 1640 the royal court allowing[8] torture was abolished. A further development then occurred, crucial to our wholesale rejection of the practice today: in 1670 rendition – the removal of people to other jurisdictions for the purpose of torture – was made illegal in this country. One of Charles II's ministers, Lord Clarendon, had been accused of sending prisoners 'to remote islands, garrisons and other places, thereby to prevent them from the benefit of the law'. In 1679 Parliament passed the Habeas

* Modern parallel alert!

Corpus Amendment Act by a very small majority* to make such practices illegal.

By the end of the seventeenth century, there were processes in place to enforce the laws of the land that are broadly recognisable to this day. The language of the courts was still inaccessible,[9] their manner rigid and unforgiving, but some sights and sounds were beginning to look familiar.

Where do laws come from?

There are three places. The first is the 'common law', the collected precedents formed by judges' rulings built up over many centuries. The second can be summarised in eight words, thanks to the constitutional expert Vernon Bogdanor: 'What the Queen in Parliament enacts is law.' This is the source of the vast majority of new, modern laws: Parliament – via its royal figurehead – is responsible for the creation of laws,[10] which are then applied in the legal system by our judges. This means we trust politicians to understand what areas of our life should be formally regulated, and to conceive of the most efficient means of achieving that. It is a touching act of faith in many respects. To complicate matters further, the third source of laws in this country is the European Union (until Brexit, as we shall see later, changes this further).

Certainly, the charge can be brought that we have too many, too little-understood laws. Recent years have proven to be a golden age of superfluous legislation. In the decade from 1997 under Tony Blair, 2,685 new laws were created every year (a little over one every three hours); there were 382 Acts of Parliament (including ten Health Acts, twelve Education Acts and twenty-nine Criminal Justice Acts). Laws, of course, do not only denote what is and is not criminal behaviour, but set out responsibilities for public bodies and denote our civil rights too. They can be incredibly dense to the point of nonsense. The late Tom Bingham[11] nominated this sentence (from

---

* The story goes that it was only passed because the teller in the House of Lords counted one very fat lord as ten people. Huge, as they say, if true.

the Banking Act Appeals Procedure of 1979) as his favourite piece of legal gibberish: 'Any reference in these regulations to a regulation is a reference to a regulation contained in these regulations.'

You got that? The problem is that so many pieces of legislation, sometimes so poorly drafted, make life difficult for judges. In 2008 one judge complained that 'the courts are in many cases unable to discover what the law is, or was at the date with which the court is concerned.'

How do the courts work?

The court system for England and Wales is slightly different to Northern Ireland and Scotland,[12] but can be used as broadly indicative of the British concept of how justice should be transacted. The court is the place where disputes are settled: either in a criminal matter between the state (representing society) and the defendant; or in a civil matter when two parties (or more) cannot agree on an issue.

Connected to this but separate are the coroners' courts. Coroners must be qualified lawyers or doctors, and hold public inquests into any violent, suspicious or unnatural death, or any death in custody. They can involve a jury, and must decide on the manner of death: suicide, unlawful killing, misadventure or accident. If there is uncertainty, they record an open verdict.

Ninety-five per cent of criminal cases go to the magistrates' court.* Magistrates are the key pillar of the criminal justice system: they are a body of mostly unpaid, largely untrained volunteers numbering little more than 21,000 in total,[13] who deal with around 2 million cases every year. Criminal cases are divided into three categories: summary; either-way; and indictable-only. The first are the preserve of magistrates, being less serious (such as motoring offences and minor assaults); the second are more serious (such as theft and handling stolen goods),

---

* The decision to prosecute a person is taken by the Crown Prosecution Service, although until 1986 it was, surprisingly, just in the hands of the police. The CPS, technically a public authority, has broad discretion whether to proceed with a prosecution, and must take into account the public interest, the likelihood of a conviction and a sense of proportionality.

and can instead be referred to the Crown Court by discretion; the third are of such gravity that they can only be determined in the Crown Court. The role of the magistrates★ is to try the case or kick it up to the Crown Court. Defendants can ask for an either-way case to be tried by a jury (where they will stand a better chance at acquittal), although there are some who think that right should be removed from them. Magistrates send around 50,000 people every year to prison (their sentencing power is capped at twelve months).

Crown Courts have existed since 1972,[14] and are presided over by High Court judges for the most serious cases, and circuit judges or recorders for the others. The Central Criminal Court for England and Wales is the Old Bailey in London, which sits on the location of the old Newgate Prison. Its presiding statue is, famously, the female figure, holding the scales of justice.

Separate to the system of criminal justice is that of its civil equivalent (the settlement of contractual or other non-criminal disputes). That takes place at a low level in the magistrates' or county courts, but more seriously in the High Court, which itself is a typically British hodgepodge of responsibilities. The High Court is divided into three divisions: the Queen's Bench; Family; and Chancery.

The last court is probably the most obscure, although it was given notoriety (and much entertaining opprobrium) by Charles Dickens in *Bleak House*. Its task is to rule on issues to do with financial or property holdings. It is now rather efficient (if unglamorous), but Dickens's judgement lingers in posterity:

> This is the Court of Chancery, which has its decaying houses and its blighted lands in every shire, which has its worn-out lunatic in every madhouse and its dead in every churchyard, which has its ruined suitor with his slipshod heels and threadbare dress borrowing and begging through the round of every man's acquaintance, which gives to monied might the means abundantly of wearying out the right, which so exhausts finances, patience, courage, hope, so overthrows the brain and breaks the heart, that there is not an

---

★ They sit in panels of three, with as broad a range of diversity as possible. The chairman is the only one to speak in court; the two other magistrates are known, brilliantly, as his or her wingers.

honourable man among its practitioners who would not give – who does not often give – the warning, 'Suffer any wrong that can be done you rather than come here!'

As often throughout the book, Dickens's deliberate build-up of dependent clauses echoes the cumulative effect of the legal process, the idea that everything is swept up by an inexorable advance of words and phrases until nothing is left but exhaustion. The famous case described in the novel is *Jarndyce v Jarndyce*, a 'scarecrow of a suit' over a large inheritance that has 'over the course of time become so complicated that no man alive knows what it means': 'innumerable children have been born into it; innumerable young people have married into it; innumerable old people have died out of it'. It ends – spoiler alert – with an outcome that ceases to matter because 'the whole estate is found to have been absorbed in costs'. However unrepresentative of the modern Chancery Division it is, it stands as a fitting demonstration of the insatiable maw of legal financing to this day.

The largest division of the High Court is the Queen's Bench, which hears civil claims for money, breach of contract, personal injury, commercial disputes and so on. The relative fairness of the British legal system is one of the reasons businesses choose to come to this country; it is a place where commercial activity can be reasonably regulated. This approach goes back centuries. Lord Mansfield,* a prominent jurist of the eighteenth century, said that

---

* William Murray, the Earl of Mansfield, arguably set Britain on the path to abolishing slavery. In 1772 he issued a ruling on the case of an escaped slave, James Somersett, in which he made clear that – as England did not have a law supporting slavery – slavery could not be supported in this country at all:

> The state of slavery is of such a nature, that it is incapable of being introduced on any reasons, moral or political; but only positive law . . . it's so odious, that nothing can be suffered to support it, but positive law. Whatever inconveniences, therefore, may follow from a decision, I cannot say this case is allowed or approved by the law of England; and therefore the black must be discharged.

Jane Austen called the location of her novel Mansfield Park because it discusses the slave trade briefly, and she may have been signalling her disapproval of it. We shall return to this subject in Chapter 8.

'the daily negotiations and property of merchants ought not to depend upon subtleties and niceties; but upon rules easily learned and easily retained.' The ideal is still pursued, albeit not always successfully, today.

The Queen's Bench is the forum for libel cases too. I worked at the *Sun* newspaper for three years, and only had to go to the High Court once. That is because the price of British justice is so cripplingly high, you never wish to get into court if you can help it. Most libel claims are settled in advance with an apology, payment of damages and a settlement of costs. The latter is always the hardest pill to swallow: an argument over a single newspaper article can cost £100,000 in legal fees in eight weeks; a case taken all the way to court costs in the millions. If people tell you that newspapers deliberately libel people, knowing they can make the money back on increased sales,★ they know nothing about the media or the British legal system.

The first thing we do, let's kill all the lawyers†

Britain has two types of lawyers: barristers and solicitors.[15] There is no good reason for the distinction, which does not exist in many other countries (and is now starting to blur even in this one). In essence, the solicitors are the GPs of the legal system: they meet with their clients, organise the case, establish the facts. If the case is going to court, they will refer up to a barrister or barristers, who

★ In my three years at the *Sun*, the most any story ever added to a sale was probably 100,000 copies. I think it was the case involving the Labour peer who became known as Lord Coke, thanks to him disporting with prostitutes and snorting cocaine. The image of him mischievously wearing a bra (beneath the headline 'Busted') is seared into my memory. Say it put on 100,000 sales at 50p a sale: that generated an extra total revenue of £50,000. That would scarcely pay the lunch bill for a claimant's legal team in court. And most stories add nothing to the sale at all; the tragedy for newspapers is that almost nothing adds to sales these days.
† The most famous quote from Shakespeare's *Henry VI* plays, spoken by Dick (a butcher), as the common people contemplate armed insurrection. *Henry VI* has three parts, but the first was written last, as a sort of Hollywood-style prequel, by Shakespeare in collaboration with others.

will represent the client before the judge. Some barristers are hugely expensive: the most high-profile charge thousands of pounds first for a view of a case (called an opinion), then as a daily fee. The senior barristers are called Queen's Counsel,[16] having 'taken silk' (because they get to wear silk gowns), which means they can charge even more.

The quality of legal representation is critical, as Britain operates an adversarial legal system:* both sides are given leave to make their best argument, competitively and sometimes aggressively. H. L. Mencken summarised the British court thus: 'a place where Jesus Christ and Judas Iscariot would be equals, with the betting odds in favour of Judas'. This has led to the cult of the barrister that still persists, perhaps the greatest example of which was Edward Marshall Hall.

Marshall Hall was a criminal defence barrister at the time that George Orwell called the 'Elizabethan period' of British murders, which provided 'the greatest amount of pleasure to the British public'. Orwell was referring to the turn of the twentieth century when there was a proliferation of stabbings and poisonings, of affairs brimming with great passion, of scurrility and scandal. Take the case, in 1894, of Marie Hermann, a prostitute who battered her seventy-two-year-old client to death with a poker and stuck him in a trunk. Madame Tussauds saw the schlock potential of the case and hired Marshall Hall to defend Hermann; he obtained her acquittal on the grounds of self-defence. This was his peroration: 'These women are what men made them . . . there was a time when this woman was as pure and good as any child . . . Look at her, members of the jury, look at her; God never gave her a chance. Won't you? Won't you?'

Hermann was saved because a waxworks tourist attraction was

---

* Contrast this with France: there, a *juge d'instruction* is appointed as an inquisitorial magistrate, who can talk to witnesses, supervise police and look for evidence. They then make a recommendation about the need for a trial. In the French system, 90 per cent of tried cases result in a conviction; in England it is 40 per cent. In France a defendant is entitled to a jury trial only when prosecuted for a felony that may bring at least fifteen years' imprisonment.

willing to pay for her representation,* which is a reminder of the role of money in the system. As the saying goes, British justice is open to all, like the Ritz Hotel.

If the system is so adversarial, how can it be impartial? That is, of course, where judges and juries can come in. But problems undoubtedly exist in how the police and Crown Prosecution Service prepare cases against individuals in the first place. There has arisen over the years, thankfully, a process in all legal disputes called 'disclosure': the need for both sides to see all relevant material upon which either side might wish to rely. In criminal cases there is a responsibility on the police and prosecution to share and explore evidence that might help the defence. Only, often they do not. A report in 2017[†] by the government found that police disclosure was 'poor' or 'fair' (in the sense of just about acceptable, not equitable) in 78 per cent of cases, and the CPS's handling of it was 'poor' or 'fair' in 77 per cent of cases. Does this matter? Of course it does. The police's role is to present fairly a case against an accused; the CPS's role is to consider the possibility that it might not be a valid charge. A failure to do either places a disproportionate amount of pressure on the ability of the defence, which inevitably favours those capable of affording a good one.

Legal aid: access to justice

As part of the foundation of the welfare state – that post-war consensus that equality was an achievable aim – attention was turned to access to justice. The system of legal aid was introduced in 1950 to put the law in reach of people with 'small or moderate means'. In practice, almost all defended[‡] criminal cases that go to the Crown

---

* Newspapers, too, used to pay Marshall Hall, in order that juicy cases could get the full treatment at trial.

† This book is full of recommendations of other books to read, but here is one for a Twitter account to follow: @BarristerSecret. An anonymous blogger, he reveals issues within the legal system and corrects erroneous reporting. Although he has a book out too.

‡ Seventy per cent of defendants in these courts plead guilty immediately.

Court are covered by legal aid, because their prosecution is so expensive. I know of a multimillionaire accused of insider dealing, whose defence was entirely paid by the state because even he could not afford lawyers for three years of wrangling. When people are arrested, by the way, they are automatically entitled to free legal representation in the police station (though just 40 per cent take up the offer).

Legal aid also covers these areas: family disputes; housing (including evictions); asylum and immigration claims; education; and others. However, since 2010 it has been a target of budget-slicing within the austerity-inclined government, culminating in the 2013 Legal Aid, Sentencing and Punishing of Offenders Act (LASPO), which intended to cut funding by around £500 million a year. As a result, in 2012 there were 925,000 legal aid cases; in 2014, 497,000.

People are now, without doubt, going unrepresented, having their access to justice denied. For example, legal aid is no longer available in family disputes unless one of the parties is the victim of domestic violence; family law advice on matters like child contact has been curtailed. In magistrates' courts, more than a quarter of defendants may be unrepresented, with the likelihood of guilty pleas to avoid court costs on the rise. Meanwhile, many solicitors and barristers – at the lower end of the food chain – who already received a pittance for their work are getting even less.

When national tragedies like the conflagration of Grenfell Tower in June 2017 happen, attention is paid briefly (but normally inconclusively) to the problem that the complaints of the impoverished in Britain so often go unheard. The LASPO Act restricted legal aid to actions where the aim is the 'removal or reduction of a serious risk of harm to the health or safety of the individual or a relevant member of the individual's family', but can generally only be triggered where there is evident 'disrepair'. Getting advice on this question is itself unlikely now to be covered by legal aid.

The reason for restricting legal aid was to prevent ambulance-chasing claims (often against the state) being subsidised by the state. The risk is that, by restricting unmeritorious chancers, the government has silenced the vulnerable. Objections were also made to lawyers getting rich in the defence of criminals: in 2010 the top ten legal aid earners were paid almost £7 million between them. The argument for the defence: ensuring proper representation, and a fair trial, is the hallmark of civilisation, even if the cost of it can be hard for some to tolerate.

On the bench

Successful barristers (and a few solicitors) get to become judges, the most senior of whom is the Lord Chief Justice, asked – as Shakespeare said in *Henry IV* – to uphold 'the majesty and power of law'. He sits atop of the entire judiciary. Judges are now (since 2005) chosen by an independent Judicial Appointments Commission,[17] which convenes special panels for the most senior positions. They tend to be largely privately, then Oxbridge, educated (a little more than 70 per cent of them, in fact, and the number is pretty stable), white and male. However, by 2016, a quarter of all judges, and more than half of those under forty, were women. Five per cent of court judges are from ethnic minorities (9 per cent of all those under forty).

Judges get criticised for being out of touch, and either too soft or too unfeeling. They are easily caricatured in their wigs and robes (although, in 1993, an inquiry found that most people in Britain preferred their judges bewigged), but they are a vital part of our legal system. More so than in other countries, in fact. Thanks to our adversarial legal system, judges need to be above reproach. They act as referees in the game: they decide what is admissible in court; in criminal trials, they sum up the case as fairly as possible★ and direct the jury; they issue sentences and award damages. As we have seen, their words form the common law for the future.

Judges can have their decisions appealed, indeed appealed twice over. Britain[18] has two senior courts: the Court of Appeal; and the Supreme Court.[19] There is not a convincing reason why we need two, actually, as it effectively means senior judges second-guessing

---

★ This fairness has, it must be said, improved over time. Judges used to be rather more obviously placed on the side of the establishment. In 1840 the jury was told by one judge: 'Gentlemen, I suppose you have no doubt? I have none.'

each other. Thus, a unanimous Court of Appeal verdict by three judges can be overturned by a majority decision in the Supreme Court (three judges overriding the other two). That would mean five of the land's most senior judges disagreeing with the eventual decision. It would be far cheaper to have one court.[20]

The sentences[21] given by judges are subject to endless second-guessing by the public and media. Judges follow tariffs, which provide the range of acceptable outcomes based on a combination of precedent, Court of Appeal judgements and specific guidance by a public body called the Sentencing Council. When judges are criticised for being too soft, they are very often merely following the guidance handed down to them (a failure to do which would itself be grounds for appeal). Generally speaking, tariffs have increased in recent years (thanks to public anxiety about serious crime), which is a contributing factor in the increase in prison numbers.

Take the decision in 2003, under Home Secretary David Blunkett, to introduce Imprisonment for Public Protection sentences. IPPs were designed to ensure that, while convicted people would be given specific tariffs, they would only be allowed out at the end if they no longer posed a threat. By 2010, there were more than 10,000 people serving IPP sentences, until the power was abolished in 2012 (following a European Court ruling that it was a breach of human rights). In 2017 there were still 3,500 serving what amounts to an unlimited sentence, most of them having already served their allotted time, but without any clear hope of release. It sounds like something out of pre-Revolutionary France, but it is happening in Britain today.

The Attorney General is allowed to appeal a sentence on the grounds of its leniency, if he receives at least one complaint from a member of the public. In 2015 he received 713 such complaints and referred 136 (more than a third of which related to sexual offences). Our punishments are seldom too lenient, if we are honest.

European courts

Few things get EU-bashers' blood boiling more than its infliction of garlic-stinking, unashamedly foreign laws and so-called ''uman rights' on proud British folk. The picture is, needless to say, a little more nuanced.

Our membership of the EU (now ending) has meant that the European Court of Justice in Luxembourg has been the final arbiter on disputes involving laws affected by that EU membership. There are more than 12,000 EU regulations in force in the UK, touching on things like: the free movement of labour; child benefits to the offspring of migrant workers; the working time directive, limiting the working week to forty-eight hours; equal access to fishing waters; clean water rules; the requirement for VAT on energy bills. British national courts can only refer issues of EU law to Luxembourg; the ECJ cannot hear appeals on matters involving national law.

In 2008 (when data was last recorded) the ECJ heard more than 1,300 cases; in 2014 it had a budget of more than 350 million euros. Brexit will not change the fact that EU laws exist: most are likely to be incorporated into the British system. Furthermore, we cannot avoid the need for a supranational arbiter because – whatever happens – we would like to have a close trading relationship with the EU, which will likely mean a congruence of regulations, and the acceptance of an authority to rule on disputes arising from them. The ECJ will have to remain involved in British justice, or a body very like it to be created.

The ECJ is often confused with the European Court of Human Rights. The latter has no formal connection to the EU, and is part of the Council of Europe of more than forty-seven countries (from Russia to Iceland). It enforces the European Convention on Human Rights, which was ratified by the UK in 1951 and was incorporated directly into UK law via the Human Rights Act in 1998.[22] Leaving the EU will not alter this.

The root of this human rights legislation is the Universal Declaration of Human Rights, which emerged from the wreck of the Second World War and the creation of the UN. During the war, the Allies had articulated the need to fight for four freedoms: of speech; of religion; from fear; from want. The UN subsequently empanelled a committee, under Eleanor Roosevelt,[23] to write the formal articles of the declaration. The resulting, heavily Christian, document represented the clearest articulation of inviolable rights and protections in human history.* Our current human rights legislation owes much to this document and philosophy and covers some fundamental issues (that date back to Magna Carta and before): prohibition of slavery; right to personal liberty; right to a fair trial; no punishment without law; right to privacy; freedom of expression; freedom of thought, conscience and religion; freedom of personal assembly and the right to join trade unions; the right to marry; the enjoyment of rights without discrimination; the protection of property.[24]

Set down so baldly, it is hard to argue with the ideas behind such legislation. It is thanks to the HRA, for example, that the Hillsborough inquest was reopened. The first inquest into the deaths of ninety-six people at a football game between Liverpool and Nottingham Forest on 15 April 1989 returned a verdict of 'accidental death'. This was quashed in 2012, and a second inquest ordered, largely on the basis that Article 2 of the HRA (right to life) meant that the state was bound to ensure that suspicious deaths were properly investigated. The outcome was a vindication for those who campaigned for twenty-seven years: deaths at Hillsborough were unlawful, caused by the neglect and negligence of the state.

But fundamental rights are not always so absolute. How do you balance privacy, for example, with freedom of expression (a decision taken by journalists every day)? How important is religious freedom, if the consequent religious practices (like female genital mutilation) are barbaric or harmful to the common good? How do you stop terrorism, if you are burdened by a legal process that allows dangerous people to slip away? These sorts of questions are considered by the courts, and can be ultimately appealed to the ECHR, which is asked to decide where the balance should lie. It can lead to poor decisions; it can prioritise individual welfare over national concerns. That is

---

* Interestingly, eight UN countries abstained from accepting the declaration: the Soviet Union; Ukraine; Belarus; Yugoslavia; Poland; South Africa; Czechoslovakia; and our old friend Saudi Arabia. Communist countries did not really believe in personal freedom and thought the text was too soft on Nazism; South Africa was concerned it might end apartheid; and the Saudis presumably wanted to be free to get up to no good in the name of religion.

why it falls into disrepute with those, say, who wish for the UK to be able to deport dangerous people more easily.[25]

The law on terror

Terrorism places the most stress on a country's legal and moral systems: its force is more than just physically destructive. It makes us think about what steps we are willing to take in the name of self-preservation. At the one extreme, we could sacrifice all liberty and live in a military state under curfew without public gatherings. We would be safe but not free. At the other, we could neglect all security intervention, instead allowing personal inclination to dictate behaviour. We would be free but not safe.

Our collective position is likely to be closer to the former of those scenarios: few people object to the loss of liberty when faced by the widespread loss of life. Cicero spelled this out when he said 'salus populi suprema est lex': our safety is the ultimate law. This can be used as a justification for increased restrictions on behaviour, communication and congregation. That was the thrust of Tony Blair's speech in the aftermath of the 7/7 London bombings in 2005 ('let no one be in any doubt, the rules of the game are changing'); the thrust too of Theresa May after the attacks on Manchester and London Bridge in 2017 ('enough is enough').

In many ways, we are all living in a world fundamentally altered by the terror attacks on America in 2001. Not only did that lead to a misguided and mishandled war in the Middle East, it changed how we regarded societal security, and the behaviour of an entire religious grouping; it changed how we regarded the presumption of innocence. In 1997 a person could be detained without charge for four days; in 2003 that became fourteen days; in 2005, twenty-eight days (the government was twice defeated going for ninety days, then forty-two days). It is not clear that any interrogation has been thwarted by the lack of time available for detention, but – like so many things – the policy is a political rather than a judicial issue.

With that in mind, between 2001 and 2010 there were six anti-terrorism Acts of Parliament. The aim of the government was to be able to detain without trial, and deport without due process. But the law – in the form of the higher British courts, backed by the European courts – would not let them. 'Control orders' were means of curtailing the actions of those suspected of malign intention, for the purpose of 'protecting members of the public from the risk of terrorism'. As a result, individuals could have curfews imposed, be tagged, be told whom they could meet or where they could not go. The more extreme of these were found to be in breach of Article 5 of the HRA (the right to liberty). In 2011 they were replaced by Terrorism Prevention and Investigation Measures (or TPIMs), which allowed a reduced suite of powers of surveillance to the state. Terror attacks in 2017 are likely to result in these powers being expanded.

In 2018, in Britain, there were around 3,000 extremists of interest to the British state, of whom 500 were actively monitored. Some 400 jihadis returned from Syria in 2016, tired of the monotonous life of rape and pillage with ISIS; others will follow. There may be tens of thousands of others on the spectrum of radicalisation, who may or may not prove to be dangerous. The troubling question, for those who think deeply enough on the subject, is what do you do to people who have not yet committed a prosecutable crime?[26] Benjamin Franklin offered to my mind a humane answer when he said: 'Those who would give up essential Liberty, to purchase a little temporary Safety, deserve neither Liberty nor Safety.' But try telling that to people who have witnessed scenes of horror and indiscriminate violence on British streets. Try telling that to the parents of teenagers torn apart by the shrapnel of a home-made bomb in a pop concert aimed at the young and innocent. Liberty is a hollow notion, perhaps, set against the real-life ravages of flesh and blood.

Crime and punishment

The role of the state in regard to those who wish to damage it is at the heart of our consideration of law and order. Crime in the UK has probably been falling ever since the mid-1990s. We measure crime in this country in two ways: the Crime Survey (which asks people what they have experienced in terms of criminal behaviour that year); and police statistics (which rely on what is reported). Not many people are aware of the former – which is probably an accurate reflection of mass crime – and it is worthwhile looking for its figures if you want to compare yearly crime rates.

In 2017 the Crime Survey had its lowest ever figure: 5.8 million crimes experienced,* set against a figure of 18 million in the early 1990s. The police figure was 5.3million (a rise on the previous year, but that has been attributed largely to better reporting).

There is, though, clear evidence that violent crime is in the process of staging a resurgence, better reporting or not. In 2016 there was a rise of 13 per cent in gun and knife crime reported to the police; in London, police reported that gun crime was up 42 per cent and knife crime 24 per cent. This trend continued to increase in 2017. The phenomenon of acid attacks has sadly arisen, and assaults involving corrosive substances more than doubled between 2012 and 2016. All this has been politicised as the consequence of inequality and austerity, which may be true to some extent. Whatever the cause, it is likely to lead to more aggressive policing in future and more pressure to incarcerate.

A brief history of punishment

Prisons, as we know them today, are essentially a Victorian invention. The idea of putting someone inside for a prescribed length of time as a punishment would have seemed odd to most people in British history. Prison was a place where people were kept secure until they received their punishment (corporal or capital) or paid their debt. Punishment was largely meted out in a desire for revenge, deterrence or compensation,[27] not out of a need to remove people from public intercourse or to rehabilitate them.

Corporal punishment was once a societally satisfying means of taking painful revenge. It was abolished in 1861, but brought back

---

* This excludes computer-related crimes which skew any comparisons with the past. If you add them in, the total number is over 10 million (which is down 10 per cent since 2016).

only three years later due to a moral panic over 'garrotting', a form of street robbery that had become widespread. It lingered – the cat-o'-nine-tales for adults; the birch for juveniles – for almost a further century. Indeed, it was surprisingly widespread until relatively recently: in 1917 there were 6,135 cases of juveniles being birched, often on the authority of no more than a policeman. In 1948, another example of the post-war consensus, corporal punishment was banned except in prisons, where it was kept as a punishment for striking an officer. It was finally abandoned in prison in 1967.

The legal expert David Friedman has said: 'It is only a slight exaggeration to say that, in the early years of the eighteenth century, English courts imposed only two sentences on convicted felons: either they turned them loose, or they hanged them.' A third option had also been transportation. From 1718 to 1775 around 30,000 convicts were sent to America. The independence of the US the following year stalled the process, and the government had to consider other options. Amazingly, they retained the concept of putting people on ships, and simply undertook not to send them anywhere: these were the hulks, rotting and motionless, an odd combination of transportation and incarceration. Dickens in *Great Expectations* (1861) said they were 'like a wicked Noah's ark. Cribbed and barred and moored by massive rusty chains'; Robert Hughes in his magisterial book about the founding of Australia, *The Fatal Shore* (1986), called them 'a rookery of sea-isolated crime . . . like floating Piranesi ruins, cramped and wet inside, dark and vile-smelling'. In 1784, though, Australia became the new destination for troublesome convicts: by 1830, 5,000 were being moved every year (and 165,000 overall were transported by the end of the policy in 1868). There was, however, a nagging feeling that sending people to another (beautiful, resource-rich) country was not a brilliant idea. This is the Reverend Sydney Smith in 1826: 'You shall be immediately removed from a very bad climate and a country overburdened with people to one of the finest regions of the earth, where the demand for human labour is every hour increasing, and where it is highly probable you will ultimately gain your character and improve your future.'

The solution was to develop a prison system that could cope with a national programme of incarceration. The philosopher Jeremy

Bentham[28] developed the idea of the Panopticon, a prison built around a central viewing tower, and sought to be the owner and governor of it. He nearly got his way, but eventually just received compensation from the government for the concept. His ideas were used in the construction of Millbank Prison (built in 1816, designed to be an imposing place of punishment and dread). The prisons that followed used either the 'separate system' by which inmates were completely isolated from one another, or the 'silent system' by which nobody was allowed to communicate. They amounted to the same thing: these were institutions of retribution, of 'hard labour, hard fare and a hard bed' as the Prison Act of 1865 put it.

These were the conditions into which Oscar Wilde fell when he was imprisoned in 1895. He had been convicted – in perhaps one of the most famous criminal cases in British legal history – of indecency and sodomy.* The issue had originally arisen because the Marquess of Queensberry,† outraged at the rumour that Wilde and his son Lord Alfred Douglas were lovers, had left a card at Wilde's club saying 'For Oscar Wilde, posing as a somdomite [*sic*]'. Wilde, insanely in retrospect, sued the marquess for libel in a civil court, which led to the latter paying detectives to amass evidence of Wilde's homosexual activity. Wilde abandoned the libel case, but the damage was done and he was subsequently prosecuted in the criminal courts. The first trial failed to convict him; the second sent him inside for two years.

* The full piece of legislation dealing with this was not repealed until 2003. In 1967, sodomy between consenting adults over twenty-one was decriminalised in England and Wales (this happened in 1980 in Scotland; 1982 in Northern Ireland). The anniversary is celebrated now, but the victory was somewhat sourly granted: the Archbishop of Canterbury denied that this 'change would legalise homosexual behaviour'; Lord Arran called it 'no occasion for jubilations . . . any form of ostentatious behaviour, now or in the future, any form of public flaunting, would be utterly distasteful'. Gregory Woods said in the *TLS* in May 2017: 'all the new state of the law grudgingly allowed was hugger-mugger buggery between two bodies, hidden away in shame.' The age of consent was not reduced to eighteen until 1994, sixteen in 2000.

† Yes, the same man who gave his name to the rules of boxing, although he did not write them. Two of his sons were gay, which must have perturbed him. He died with symptoms suggestive of syphilis.

Ironically, just as he was convicted, Parliament was about to consider improvements to the penal system, and reconsider its purpose, recognising that 'recidivism is the most important of prison questions', and that the aim was 'wherever possible to turn [prisoners] out better men and women, both physically and morally, than when they came in'. This was no consolation to Wilde, who suffered the spiritual and corporeal agonies of hard time, in Pentonville and then in Reading, the latter run with military brutality by Colonel Isaacson (whom Wilde described as having 'the eyes of a ferret, the body of an ape, and the soul of a rat').

Wilde's experience, of course, bequeathed us his wonderful *Ballad of Reading Gaol*, which still acts as a polemic against the indignity and inhumanity of mass incarceration:

> This too I know – and wise it were
> If each could know the same –
> That every prison that men build
> Is built with bricks of shame,
> And bound with bars lest Christ should see
> How men their brothers maim.

Gone are the days of hard labour,[29] of enforced silences and separation for the general prison population. But most modern prisoners are housed in Victorian prisons, and Victorian prisoners would recognise many of the rituals of the current age. After an odd period of decarceration before the Second World War, when prison numbers fell to just 11,000,* prisons filled up again, reaching 40,000 inmates by 1970. The next thirty years were marked by escapes and riots, and a growing public recognition of some of the problems within the institution.

One notable escape (this is such a startling story to me) involved a man called George Blake. He had been a British spy, captured in the Korean War and converted to communism by the North Koreans:

---

* The roots of this improbable improvement may have lain with Churchill (Home Secretary in 1910), who had been imprisoned in the Boer War and did not like it, or the rise in middle-class prisoners thanks to the suffragette movement and conscientious objection. Such people were able – like Wilde – better to articulate the misery of prison.

'It made me feel ashamed of belonging to these overpowering, technically superior countries,' he recalled, 'fighting against what seemed to me defenceless people. I felt I was on the wrong side . . . that it would be better for humanity if the Communist system prevailed, that it would put an end to war.' He subsequently was sent to Berlin by MI6, where he betrayed British agents to the KGB; he was caught and sent to prison for forty-two years – then the highest tariff ever awarded, and said (probably wrongly) to be one year for every agent who died as a result of his betrayal. In October 1966, abetted by two prisoners who shared his political values, he constructed a rope ladder made out of knitting needles and escaped from Wormwood Scrubs, during prisoners' film hour. Blake eventually got to Russia, where he lived happily ever after, winning the Order of Friendship from Vladimir Putin in 2007, and remaining unrepentant: 'To betray,' he said, 'you first have to belong. I never belonged.' Tell that to the families of the dead spies.

Blake's escape alongside other high-profile examples (like that of train robber Ronnie Biggs) led to a report by Lord Mountbatten in December 1966 into prison security, which advocated a tightening of regimes still in place today.[30] In turn, the tightened regimes led to increased prisoner unrest, which culminated in era-defining riots. Like the case of Michael Hickey, who climbed on to the roof of Gartree Prison in November 1983, and came down ninety days later, having protested his innocence for the murder of a thirteen-year-old paperboy called Carl Bridgewater. His conviction was overturned in 1997; he received nearly £1 million compensation, which was then reduced by 25 per cent on the inexplicable ground that he had enjoyed the cost of 'board and lodgings' during his incarceration.

The most memorable riot, and the biggest in British penal history, occurred at Strangeways in 1990. The prisoners held control for twenty-five days, injuring 147 staff in the process. Eventually, twenty-three prisoners were convicted of involvement, and collectively received an additional 140 years of imprisonment. The protest began in the prison chapel, and there is a tape recording of its early explosion of anger:

NOEL PROCTOR (CHAPLAIN): After that remarkable message that has . . .

A PRISONER (LATER IDENTIFIED AS PAUL TAYLOR): I would just like to say, right, that this man has just talked about the blessing of the heart and how a hardened heart can be delivered. No it cannot, not with resentment, anger and bitterness and hatred being instilled in people.

A PRISONER (*speaking over noise*): Fuck your system, fuck your rules.

PROCTOR: Right lads, sit down.

(*More noise*)

PROCTOR: Right lads, down. Down. Come on, this is no way to carry on in God's house.

(*More noise*)

A PRISONER: Fuck your system.

PROCTOR: Right lads, sit down. This is completely out of order. Sit down.

A PRISONER: Why is it [out of order]? It's been waiting to happen for ever. It will never change.

Prisoners were objecting to the standard of food and accommodation, the existence of 'slopping out' (pouring the contents of a chamber pot into a communal channel every day), and other indignities. In the aftermath of the riot, things did change: Lord Woolf conducted an inquiry, suggesting a number of positive developments, and recognising in public the need to countenance improving the quality of life of prisoners. But the basic issue remained: politicians, of all stripes, believed that high prison numbers were evidence of authority and rigour. This was Home Secretary Michael Howard in 1993: 'Let us be clear.* Prison works. It ensures that we are protected from murderers, muggers and rapists – and it makes many who are tempted to commit crime think twice.'

Tony Blair at this time gave us his mantra 'tough on crime, and tough on the causes of crime'; Prime Minister John Major responded

---

* As we know, this is in my top three of hated political clichés: politicians always say this as if it somehow bestows clarity and honesty on the obscurantist or unimaginative blather that follows. It would be better if they were clear, rather than talking about being clear. Theresa May is the High Priestess of the self-regarding exhortation to clarity.

with the recognition that 'society needs to condemn a little more and understand a little less'. It is no coincidence that 1993 was the year for such tough talk. The murder of James Bulger, a two-year-old beaten to death by two ten-year-olds, sparked an understandable moral panic. The result was an establishment consensus on the need to be more punitive in response to crime. The perpetrators, Robert Thompson and Jon Venables, were sentenced to eight years in prison, increased to fifteen after public outrage. At a similar time, in Norway, Silje Redergard, a five-year-old girl, was beaten by three six-year-olds and forced to strip in the snow; she died of hypothermia. There was no public soul-searching, no policy change, no questions about law and order. That month, the boys responsible returned to school. Other civilised states are, perhaps, less prone to panic than us.

In 2018 there were more than 85,000 people in prison, each one costing around £40,000 a year to house and feed. Prison numbers have more than doubled in the last twenty-five years; they are the highest (140 for every 100,000 people) in Western Europe. The vast majority of prisoners are men (more than 80,000): it has been calculated that men are responsible for 85 per cent of all indictable crimes in England and Wales, and 98 per cent of all sexual offences. The scientific explanation for this is not as clear-cut as you might think. Testosterone may have a part to play, but so too will societal norms around how genders should behave (the view that men need to be more aggressively, and therefore transgressively, dominant). The women in our prisons are predominantly non-violent (81 per cent), and likely to have experienced violence themselves (more than two out of three have suffered sexual abuse in their lifetimes). Ethnic people in Britain are also disproportionately likely to find themselves banged up, accounting for 25 per cent of the prison population, and just 13 per cent of the actual population. When Dostoevsky said that 'the degree of civilisation in a society can be judged by entering its prisons', he was right.

The British prison service, like the NHS, has spent the last seventy years (and more) in a state of functional crisis. Prison officer numbers have fallen, thanks to austerity measures in the last few years: there were 25,000 in 2010, and just 18,000 in 2016. Officers can earn as little as £9 per hour,[31] and are expected to control and support a prison system that is – to all practical purposes – at full operational stretch. In the last few years, one solution (typically) has been to outsource the service, seeking to use our old friend the free market to drive down cost: Britain has the most privatised prison service in Europe.[32] One consequence for prisoners of the penny-pinching, whether private or public, is the impoverishment of conditions inside prison. We can measure it: there were 19,000 acts of self-harm in our prison system in 2016; assaults were up more than 30 per cent, as were deaths.

So does, as Michael Howard suggested, prison work? The purpose of prison seems to be threefold: to punish; to deter; and to re-habilitate offenders so they do not reoffend. It singularly fails in the latter task: 50 per cent of all prisoners reoffend in the first year; 70 per cent of all those under eighteen years old. Prisoners on shorter sentences are more likely to reoffend than those on community or suspended sentences. The cost to the state of the recidivism is esti-mated at £15 billion every year.

The Norwegian system is often heralded as a counterpoint, and example, to our own. In Norway, the incarceration rate is half of Britain's and its rate of recidivism is just 20 per cent. There are no life sentences: the maximum tariff for any crime is twenty-one years in prison.[33] And Norwegian prisons are not punitive (indeed to outsiders they appear somewhat luxurious), but focused on restora-tive justice (paying back for one's offence) and rehabilitation. If you were to visit Bastoy prison island, for example, everybody you meet on the journey, including the ferryman, would be a serving prisoner; when you got there, you would find prisoners accommodated in houses with their own cooking facilities. There appears to be no culture of angst towards the imprisoned; no desire to cause them harm and discomfort. In our country, that desire is ingrained. This was Walter Scott in 1828 (it could be a *Daily Mail* editorial of today): 'I do not see the propriety of making them dandy places of deten-tion. They should be places of punishment, and that can hardly be if men are lodged better, and fed better than when they were at large.'

Our 'dandy places of detention' are not dandy, and are now danger-ously over-subscribed. In Britain, some people should not be in prison because their crime is insufficiently serious or damaging to the public. One might argue that drugs offences fit this description: the simple enactment of a human desire to get high – which seems embedded in many of our collective psyches – has no place in the criminal justice system. When Portugal decriminalised all drugs in the early 2000s, it saw no increase in addiction, and decreases in petty crimes and experimentation. Making criminals of drug-takers produces a chain of criminality: supply is in the hands of unscrupulous gangsters who care little for their consumer. All the arguments you will hear about why drugs should be illegal (they are dangerous; they are bad for you; they are connected to criminality) are the same as those why they should be made legal: they can be made safe; people can be educated about taking them; they can be removed from the hands of criminals. I spoke to a former prison governor who told me that more than half of the people in prison did not really need to be there (and certainly more than half were there as a result of non-violent crime).

Some people – like Michael Hickey – should not be in prison, because they did not commit the crime in the first place. Miscarriages of justice (which especially rose to public attention in the 1980s and 1990s) are inevitable features of a fallible, human and partial system. In 2012 there were 5,711 appeals on sentences and 1,731 on convictions; on average 11 per cent of conviction appeals, and 25 per cent of sentence appeals, are successful. In 1995 the Criminal Cases Review Commission was formed to examine alleged miscarriages of justice: it refers cases back to the Appeals Court on 3 per cent of occasions (the majority of which are allowed).

This fallibility – however uncommon – is, of course, the telling argument against the death penalty, which was abolished in 1965 in the UK.

A short history of capital punishment

The death penalty has existed in Britain for almost all of its history; so too for the history of humanity more generally.[34] In Tudor times, you could be hanged, burned, quartered, beheaded or boiled alive. In the eighteenth century virtually anything was a capital offence (under the aptly named Bloody Code): forgery, poaching, damaging Westminster Bridge, associating with gypsies, being out at night with a blackened face, cutting down a tree, robbing a rabbit warren, and the like.[35] By 1861, effectively these had been reduced simply to murder charges; and seven years later, the (much rarer) executions were transferred inside prisons, away from public view. Had you been alive, though, for the sixty years around the turn of the eighteenth century in London, you could have watched the spectacle of public execution more than 1,200 times.

In the First World War 306 British soldiers received the death penalty for cowardice and desertion, creating a sense of revulsion that lingers until this day.* Indeed, the first half of the twentieth century revealed a growing moral squeamishness at the prospect of state-sanctioned death: 45 per cent of all sentences were commuted on appeal, and some notable cases demonstrated the risk of error in the system. In 1950 Timothy Evans was hanged for murdering his pregnant wife and their baby. The couple had sought to obtain an abortion from their landlord, John Christie, who had managed to convince them that he was a medical expert. He was, in fact, a necrophiliac serial killer, with two women already buried in his garden. He raped and murdered Beryl Evans and killed the baby; he then proceeded to act as a prosecution witness against Timothy. There were already suspicions about Christie: police could have spotted, for example, the human thigh bone propping up an awning in his garden. Evans's mother accused Christie of murder outside court; his wife Ethel leapt to his defence, calling him a good man. Sadly, she was strangled by him two years later. He was eventually executed in 1953; three years too late for Evans.

By 1957, the government was forced to introduce a Homicide Act to cling to the principle of the death penalty, having to restrict its application even further. It did still maintain that 'long-drop

---

* The Blair government initially refused a request to pardon all those executed, on the grounds it could not establish the facts of each case properly. The family of Private Harry Farr, executed for cowardice in October 1916, brought a judicial review of the decision, and managed to establish that he had been mistreated even by the standards of the day. In 2006 the Armed Forces Act gave pardons to all. The death penalty for cowardice was abolished between the wars.

hanging' was the most humane method, although this is now disputed.* By 1965, a new Labour government under Harold Wilson was in power, determined to end what it saw as barbarism, which it managed to do in the teeth of contrary popular opinion and the views of many in the Conservative Party.

Indeed, it is notable – and borderline terrifying – that public views of the death penalty are oddly tolerant. According to the British Social Attitudes Survey, support for the death penalty only dropped below 50 per cent for the first time ever in 2014 (it was 75 per cent in 1983). A recent BBC survey put the figure at 59 per cent, with the young only slightly less bloodthirsty than the old.[†] UKIP had restoration of the death penalty for terrorists[‡] and child killers in its 2017 election manifesto, its then leader, Paul Nuttall, confirming that he was willing to act as executioner himself.

Needless to say, there is no evidence that the death penalty serves any greater moral or public good. In America, murder rates are lower in non-death-penalty states than death-penalty states; the death penalty is disproportionately enforced on black people and those with mental illness. But our collective view on law and order is not always reflective of what is good or right: emotional ideas of retribution and painful sanction will always intervene.

Blue and black

Our ambivalent stance towards justice is perhaps most apparent in our response to the police: at once the tyrannical, porcine perpetuators of prejudice; and the brave boys in blue,[36] keeping our streets

---

* Famous executioner Albert Pierrepoint was proud of a method (which involved computing the weight of the victim to ensure the correct depth of drop) he believed ensured immediate death by a clean 'hangman's fracture'. Recent autopsies have shown that this was a myth – covered up deliberately by the establishment – and hanging led to a varied speed of death.

[†] More than half of those who voted Leave in the EU referendum support the death penalty, which may or may not be indicative of something.

[‡] One wonders whether it would prove an especial deterrent to a suicide bomber, of course.

safe. The police grew out of a more or less informal system of constables and watchmen, whose roles were formalised in the thirteenth century, and are most memorably recognisable in the Shakespearean characters Dogberry, from *Much Ado About Nothing*, and Elbow, from *Measure for Measure*.

The modern police force's origins are in the magistrate's court of the novelist Henry Fielding[37] in the first half of the eighteenth century. He was an unlikely magistrate, in some respects, having once tried to abduct his cousin when she was on her way to church. But he was, by the standards of the day, incorruptible, regarding the income gained as a magistrate (from soaking those brought before him) as 'the dirtiest money on earth'. Henry was succeeded as Chief Magistrate by his brother John, who had been blinded in a navy accident at the age of nineteen, and was known in court as the Blind Beak. Together they formed the Bow Street Runners, the first truly professional police force in 1749; and by 1792 there were seven Police Offices in London.

In 1829 the Metropolitan Police were formed by Sir Robert Peel,[38] with the aim of enforcing the law, largely by crime prevention. Soon, though, a detective branch was set up for the purpose of crime solving, and the idea of the ruggedly brilliant copper began to form in the popular imagination. This is largely due to the indefatigable Charles Dickens, who wrote a lot about the police in his magazine *Household Words*, reserving especially purple prose for a certain Inspector Field.[39] This comes from 1851:

> Saint Giles's church strikes half-past ten. We stoop low, and creep down a precipitous flight of steps into a dark close cellar. There is a fire. There is a long deal table. There are benches. The cellar is full of company, chiefly very young men in various conditions of dirt and raggedness. Some are eating supper. There are no girls or women present. Welcome to Rats' Castle, gentlemen, and to this company of noted thieves!
>
> 'Well, my lads! How are you, my lads? What have you been doing to-day? Here's some company come to see you, my lads! – THERE'S a plate of beefsteak, sir, for the supper of a fine young man! And there's a mouth for a steak, sir! Why, I should be too proud of such a mouth as that, if I had it myself! Stand up and show it, sir! Take

off your cap. There's a fine young man for a nice little party, sir! An't he?'

Inspector Field is the bustling speaker. Inspector Field's eye is the roving eye that searches every corner of the cellar as he talks. Inspector Field's hand is the well-known hand that has collared half the people here, and motioned their brothers, sisters, fathers, mothers, male and female friends, inexorably to New South Wales. Yet Inspector Field stands in this den, the Sultan of the place. Every thief here cowers before him, like a schoolboy before his schoolmaster. All watch him, all answer when addressed, all laugh at his jokes, all seek to propitiate him. This cellar company alone – to say nothing of the crowd surrounding the entrance from the street above, and making the steps shine with eyes – is strong enough to murder us all, and willing enough to do it; but, let Inspector Field have a mind to pick out one thief here, and take him; let him produce that ghostly truncheon from his pocket, and say, with his business-air, 'My lad, I want you!' and all Rats' Castle shall be stricken with paralysis, and not a finger move against him, as he fits the handcuffs on!

Dickens displays gleeful arousal at the power of authority here: the truncheon that is likely to be more ghastly than 'ghostly'; the power to catch those rats around him. Field, via Dickens's own Inspector Bucket in *Bleak House*, helped to inspire Sergeant Cuff in *The Moonstone* (1868) by Wilkie Collins, which T. S. Eliot called 'the first, the longest, and the best of modern English detective novels in a genre invented by Collins'. The genre, and the imagery around detectives, has proven to be a long-lasting one.

The reputation of the police force, which by 1857 had expanded out of London across the country, has ebbed and flowed over the years. By the end of the twentieth century, it had suffered a number of scandals and accusations of brutality and racism. The first black constable in London was as late as 1966, a man called Norwell Roberts, who was told on his first day by a sergeant: 'Nigger, I'll see to it that you never pass your probation.' By 1983, there were just 200 black policemen in London. In 1999 the epochal Macpherson Report ruled that the Met Police was 'institutionally racist'.

The report was commissioned following the murder of a young black man called Stephen Lawrence in 1993, who had been killed in a racist attack. Macpherson found that the police had not sought to investigate the case properly, and then had covered up their failures and even tried to smear the family in their pursuit of justice. The central suspects, including the killers Gary Dobson and David Norris – in a myriad of botched police decisions and failed procedures – were eventually either not prosecuted or acquitted.

The *Daily Mail* had led the way in supporting the family,[40] publishing in 1997 its most famous ever splash headline and sub-deck, naming those it believed to be responsible: 'Murderers (The *Mail* accuses these men of killing. If we are wrong, let them sue us)'. At that point, the prospect of justice seemed slim. However, one of the Macpherson recommendations had been to remove the famous 'double jeopardy' rule,[41] which prevented people – in this case Dobson – from being prosecuted twice for the same offence. In 2005 the law was changed to allow for a second prosecution; and in 2012 (nearly ten years after the murder), justice was finally done. Gary Dobson and David Norris were both given life sentences, with minimum tariffs of fifteen and fourteen years respectively.

How much racism remains in the force is a disputable point. In 2015 just 5.5 per cent of all police officers were from ethnic backgrounds; in 2016, London's Met Police conceded that ethnic people represented just 17 per cent of appointments, despite making up 28 per cent of applications. When police conduct stops and searches of suspects, they are twice as likely to do so to people from ethnic minorities, and six times as likely to black people. This was four times as likely in 2015, so the situation is worsening, even as the number of stops is decreasing. The scale of this discrepancy is likely to be at least partially down to racial prejudice, something that seems to pervade the criminal justice system.* As violent crime increases,

---

* Twenty-five per cent of adult, and a shocking 41 per cent of youth, prisoners are from ethnic minorities (compared to just 13 per cent of the overall population). David Lammy, the black Labour politician from London, produced a report into racism in the justice system in 2017, and noted that arrest rates are higher for BAME people, as are not guilty pleas, as are prison sentences. He has recommended serious changes to our processes: more transparency in decision-making, more diversity among decision-makers. One argument, though, is that crime tends to be committed by the socially disadvantaged, and people of colour are more likely to fall into that category.

calls for more stops are inevitable, even though there is no real statistical support for the argument that increased stops lead to reduced crime.

Speaking of diversity in the police: women have been allowed to be police officers since the First World War (although there were still fewer than 500 of them by the end of the Second). In 2015, 28 per cent of police officers were women. Reports exist of sexism within the institution, such as the testimony of Sue Sim, the former chief constable of Northumbria Police, who said, in 2016, that she faced a 'sexist, money-grabbing boys club': 'I have a significant fear for female victims of crime, for female officers within the force, for female staff members within the force. If people will be sexist towards a chief constable, then what are they going to do to these people?' Northumbria Police, it must be said, did not admit to these failings.

The question around female victims of crime is an important one, especially in regard to sexual assaults. There does appear to be a greater willingness to report sex crimes now: the number of rape claims recorded by police doubled between 2012 and 2016. However, just 7.5 per cent of allegations led to a conviction, a rate that has halved in the same period. So either more dubious claims are being made, or the system is failing to prosecute genuine claims with proper rigour. The CPS argues that more cases are being prosecuted (with around a 60 per cent success rate once they get to court), and that is true, but 80 per cent of all claims never get past the initial investigation stage at all. Worse still, the number of actual rapes may be six times greater than those ever reported, giving an eventual conviction rate that is utterly minuscule. The question must be asked whether the system gives sufficient support to women at the moment of their greatest need.[42]

There is a flipside to this picture, though. We are also suffering a crisis of improperly prosecuted rape cases. In 2017, several trials collapsed because police had not examined properly the huge bank of digital information connected to both the complainant and the accused (in the form of emails, social media and messaging), and vital information had not been disclosed. In 2018, the CPS undertook to review every rape case on the book to check for flaws. We are living in the worst of possible worlds here: a system unhelpful to genuine victims, but also unfair to the accused.

The purpose of this chapter is not to malign the police force, though. As we saw in 2017, police officers were the very epitome of bravery when it came to terrorist attacks on Westminster and London Bridge. In the latter case, just eight minutes after the alarm was raised that three terrorists were attacking people indiscriminately with knives, the terrorists lay dead in the streets, riddled with bullets. It was tough, exemplary policing.

Should all police be armed?

This question has arisen in the spate of recent terrorism, especially given that the policeman murdered at Westminster in 2017, PC Keith Palmer, was unarmed at the time. It is not a new question, by any means. In 1883 the *Evening Standard* responded to yet another moral panic with this editorial: 'It is not only foolish but absolutely cruel to send policemen out to combat men possessed with revolvers, without any other arm than a short club.'

That year, regulations were amended to allow police to be armed if they were on a dangerous beat; the practice lasted until 1936. The current position is that police have a number of firearms units, which can be deployed at need: 6,500 police are trained in the use of firearms, with 2,500 of them in London.

Largely, the British police have a fine record in not discharging their weapons negligently or unnecessarily. In 2016, police fired seven times; in the last twenty years fewer than forty people have been shot.* That is not to say there have not been controversies or mistakes. In 2005, in the febrile aftermath of the 7/7 bombings, Jean Charles de Menezes was shot for the imaginary crime of being

---

* America is an obvious point of comparison here, but interestingly – perhaps out of justified shame – the country does not collate the number of times police discharge their weapons, fatally or otherwise. The *Guardian* calculated that 1,146 people were killed by US police in 2015 and 1,092 people in 2016.

sweating, dark-skinned and carrying a backpack. Mark Duggan, an alleged gangster, was killed in 2011 by a marksman who held an 'honest belief' that Duggan was about to open fire himself. This behaviour by police prompted riotous protests across the country.

In essence, the test for firearms police is the extent to which they have a reasonable belief that there is a threat to life that can be forestalled by armed intervention. In April 2005 Anthony Long[43] fired six times into the head and body of Azelle Rodney, having acted on intelligence that he and others, armed with automatic weapons, were going to rob a drug deal. Long said this: 'All I had was seconds to make the decision whether I was going to let my colleagues be shot by someone with a submachine gun or whether I was going to take a life. I chose to take his life. That was the decision I made and I stand by it.'

No machine guns were found at the scene, although other weapons were. In 2013 an inquiry found that Long had no lawful reason to fire on Rodney. He was subsequently prosecuted for murder and acquitted. No police firearms officer has ever been convicted of murder in British legal history.

Tasers were introduced to the police force following a trial in 2003. They are electroshock weapons, firing electrodes into the skin of the target, creating pain and sensory overload, often resulting in muscle spasms, occasionally in death. The former Aston Villa football player, for example, Dalian Atkinson died in August 2016 having been Tasered three times outside his father's home. The employment of Tasers is becoming more frequent: they were used over 11,000 times in England and Wales in 2016, an increase of 9 per cent on the prior year. Most often, police officers 'red dot' suspects: which means activate the Taser as a threat, without then firing it.

Atkinson's family have since called for officers to wear body cameras, something that is being trialled in certain forces (although the overall numbers are, strangely, not released). A 2016 study by Cambridge University showed that complaints by members of the public fell by 93 per cent over twelve months against officers wearing cameras. This is the conclusion of Dr Barak Ariel, who led the study and gives food for thought: 'I cannot think of any other single invention in the history of policing that dramatically changed the way that officers behave, the way that suspects behave, and the way they interact with each other.'

However much body cameras are used in future, it is clear that the actions of police have never been more scrutinised. This is inevitable and salutary, especially given the standard of policing in the 1970s and 1980s, where scrutiny was virtually non-existent and abuses sadly common. We had the Battle of Orgreave in 1984, in which violence was perpetrated by armed police against striking workers of the British Steel Corporation in Yorkshire. The historian (and erstwhile Labour MP) Tristram Hunt called it 'almost medieval in its choreography . . . at various stages a siege, a battle, a chase, a rout, and finally, a brutal example of legalised state violence'. More prosaically, the Independent Police Complaints Commission[44] found, as the *Guardian* summarised it, 'evidence of excessive violence by police officers, a false narrative from police exaggerating violence by miners, perjury by officers giving evidence to prosecute the arrested men, and an apparent cover-up of that perjury by senior officers'.

Not only were police often violent and out of control in the past, their actions were covered up by the establishment. When the West Midlands Serious Crime Squad was rampaging through Birmingham in the period, beating and semi-asphyxiating (often black) suspects, it was investigated by the Met Police, but the report into the events was never published. People were never held to account. And then there was Hillsborough, where a coroner has now found that police negligence undoubtedly led to the deaths of ninety-six people. Thanks first to the police, blame was shifted on to the fans themselves, denouncing (invented) public intoxication and antisocial behaviour[45] as causes of the tragedy. It has taken a courageous – and almost unprecedentedly sustained – campaign by families finally to get to the truth, and to preserve the reputation not only of the dead but the living who attended the game with them.

This has left scars on the reputation of the police itself, as have the other scandals discussed here. In the nineteenth century the arrival of the force was treated with suspicion, as an example of the 'Frenchified' pseudo-military intervention of the state against the civil liberties of the people. Such a suspicion can never entirely be dismissed. And yet there is a recognition of the bravery of the officers who place themselves in harm's way to protect the rights of citizens, including the right to live in safety. Police work is onerous, dangerous and sometimes unloved. It is probably getting harder. We have around 125,000 officers in this country, and – as in every public service – numbers have gone down in the last decade. In 2017 we had the lowest number of police since 1985.

Officers down, most crime down, prison numbers up. The calculus of law and order in the UK is a strange and illogical one. Like every public policy area, its framework is an odd mix of politics, precedent and emotion. We must accept that the current mix is not truly sustainable, for reasons both of economics and ethics. We cannot afford – in any sense of the word – to have more than 85,000 people in prison year after year. It is not clear, though, how this will change any time soon.

7

Old and New Media

As far as I'm concerned, it's a damned shame that a field as potentially dynamic and vital as journalism should be overrun with
dullards, bums, and hacks, hag-ridden with myopia, apathy, and
complacence, and generally stuck in a bog of stagnant mediocrity
                                    Hunter S. Thompson (1937–2005)

A mini (misery) memoir

As I came to the end of my time at university, studying English, I
had the opportunity to go to Harvard, and try to forge a career as
an academic. Puffed up with the arrogance of youth, and a concomitant disdain for the ivory towers of intellectual seclusion, I decided
to make my own way in the world. That meant, in the first instance,
getting out of Loughborough, that small town in the centre of
England and the very margins of existence. Searching for jobs in
the *Guardian* (such advertisements once being a source of revenue
to papers; alas, no longer), I fixed upon the role of 'complaints
officer' for the Press Complaints Commission, a body I'd never heard
of. It paid £18,000 a year and would get me to London. I applied,
was interviewed, and off I went.

The PCC was the self-regulatory body for the entire British
newspaper and magazine industry. It was paid for by the industry (and
kept semi-deliberately starved of funds), but was functionally independent: the staff were not former journalists; the majority of the
decision-makers on the commission were public members. Its powers
were limited, but in their own way modestly effective: the negotiation
of published apologies and other remedies for breaches of the industry's

Code of Practice; the threat of public censure against any newspaper or magazine that defaulted. Despite the scale of its supposed reach and range, though, it was tiny: fourteen people based in a small Georgian house set back from Fleet Street. It stood, I see now, as a fitting metaphor for the newspaper world: slightly shabby, sometimes shambolic, and tenuously linked to the days of greater glory for the industry.

On my first day, I was given a desk with a computer that didn't work, and taken out to lunch at eleven fifteen in the morning. This was 2001, the tail-end of the vinous, expense-driven, addled era of daytime drinking for journalists. As we sat down, the director ordered a bottle of wine for every member of staff. Six hours later, we weaved back to the office; I was given one more glass of wine at my desk, and despatched on to a Tube full of more combobulated commuters. Welcome to the world of work.

Booze played a large part in the early days of the PCC, as it still did for many in the industry. One test for new members of staff was to survive a lunch at the *News of the World*: triple gin and tonics followed by interminable carafes of wine, being entertained by an unchanging rota of inky sots, all happily recalling their personal triumphs and failures from a happier era. Staff events began and ended in the gay bars of Soho,★ filled with lethal vodka tonics and occasional social awkwardness.

At work, my role was to investigate complaints from members of the public, negotiate corrections and apologies and write decisions to be approved by the seventeen-strong commission. I was joined by four other complaints officers, all in their early twenties, mostly from Oxbridge. In 2004 my wife-to-be joined the PCC. By 2005, we were living together in what we fondly (and inaccurately) imagined was secrecy.

In the intervals of work, though, every member of staff would be engaged in the tremendously unequal task of representing members of the public against newspapers that had wronged them. I do not wish to underplay the gravity of that. In my third year, we developed a system of twenty-four-hour help for people feeling harassed by

★ Fun fact: I became the only straight director in the history of the PCC; a triumph of diversity over discrimination.

journalists. They could call in, and we would send an email to every member of the newspaper industry to warn them off. This developed into a pre-publication warning system too (which still exists), where people could make representations about the accuracy or intrusiveness of a prospective story. This meant that I was on call every day and night for more than five years. On Friday nights in the mid-2000s, I would get calls from the press team of the Blair government, angry at something set to appear in the *Mail on Sunday* or *Sunday Times*, and have to act as a mediator (standing on a chair in my basement flat – the only place I had phone reception – pacifying harassed civil servants or irascible managing editors). In the summer, the new wave of *X-Factor* contestants would bring their own woes about press interest into their often dubious backgrounds. Football agents would call, theatrical agents, lobby groups, politicians. Almost every day, though, there would be the chance to speak to a grieving family member caught up in some legitimate story through no fault of their own, and genuinely provide help to stop the media being an additional burden to them.★

The system of self-regulation meant that we at the PCC simultaneously had to both hold in check, and jolly along, newspaper editors. They had to co-operate with us or the system failed. So we kept two channels of communication: one formal and quasi-legal; the other more informal, based on whatever personal relationships we could maintain, over lunches or drinks.[1] There was nothing corrupt ever; there was no trading of favours that I ever saw. Once a year, we would be invited to the *Daily Mail* offices in Kensington for drinks. They would be served, by a liveried butler, on a mezzanine balcony overlooking the central atrium. Executives would attend and make perfunctory small talk until the arrival of the editor – and most feared man in British journalism – Paul Dacre. He has

---

★ This leads to the question of the 'death knock', which revolts many non-journalists. Why should people be bothered after a tragedy; why not just leave them alone? The answer is this: some people value the chance to tell their story, either to protest an injustice or celebrate a life. The rules mean that a journalist is not allowed to break the news of a death to a family member (which is the function of police), or persist in their attentions after they are requested to leave. In the new world of citizen journalism, where contact is made by DM on Twitter, all physical contact by journalists is regarded suspiciously.

a reputation for violent outbursts of appalling language (known as 'double-cuntings' in the newsroom argot), but in formal situations is polite, almost awkward; he rocks on his heels, and speaks in a voice like Tommy Cooper. He sat on the commission for some of my time there, and his remarks – almost ceremonially formal – were always prefaced by him clutching the table to stop his hands from shaking. It only takes thirty seconds of a conversation with Dacre to realise that the views of the *Mail* are his, and genuinely held, held indeed with an almost religious fervour that brooks no heresy.

After two years, I became deputy director of the PCC, in charge of its complaints-handling function and that pre-publication system. By the end of 2009, I became director: I was twenty-nine years old. Too young for such a job; but the job itself felt a strange combination of being important and central (almost any news story has an ethical implication; and the PCC was dragged into almost every major controversy), and thankless and marginal (the powers involved were minimal; I am not sure how much we ever managed to achieve).

The job put me in regular touch with the various newspaper organisations, and gave me a sense of their tone and style. The *Daily Mail* and *Mail on Sunday*: fired with a self-righteous passion; terrified of the power of their editor-in-chief; keen to be respectable and part of the industry establishment. The *Sun* and *News of the World*: fiercely defensive about their popular success; proud of their connection to ordinary working people; petrified of missing a story. The *Daily Mirror*, *Sunday Mirror* and the *People*: not that different to their other red-top colleagues, but slightly less defensive, more secure in the positioning of their politics. *The Times* and *Sunday Times*: amused at the thought that their journalism could be called into question; authoritative to the point of arrogance; occasionally a little stuffy. The *Daily* and *Sunday Express*: shambolic and inept; terrified of their then-owner, and Napoleon of rubbish journalism, Richard Desmond.★

★ I met him once at a party. When I was introduced, he glared at me with his porcine eyes set deep within the recesses of his flushed face:

'Are you fucking queer?'

'Er, no, as it happens.'

'Well, you've got a beard.'

And the conversation ended. Not that there was a great deal more to say.

The *Financial Times*: stuffier even than *The Times*, and utterly dismissive of any notion that their work could be flawed. The *Daily* and *Sunday Telegraph*: formal and old-fashioned; blithely unaware, sometimes, of reality. The *Guardian* and *Observer*: pious and clever; caring and sneering. The *Independent* and *Independent on Sunday*: pious like the *Guardian*, but probably more charming with it; absolutely certain of the value of its morality; glibly conscious of the need for its place in the world, right up until the point it was closed because nobody bought it any more.

A very short history of print journalism

The first recognised newspaper in Britain was the *Oxford Gazette*, founded in 1665 as a mouthpiece for the Crown. It was born out of the aggressive pamphleteering of the Civil War period, where debates about the role of free speech began to rise alongside the calls for more representative democracy. The first daily paper came in 1702: the *Daily Courant*, published by a woman called Elizabeth Mallet, who thus had more journalistic power than many women in the centuries that followed. Soon, recognisable titles by recognisable journalists flourished: Daniel Defoe began the *Review* in 1704; Richard Steele produced the *Tatler* in 1709; Steele and Joseph Addison the *Spectator* in 1711. Addison noted soon after: 'There is no Humour in my Countrymen, which I am more inclined to wonder at than their general Thirst after News.' By the end of the century, this thirst was gratified on seven days of the week: the *Observer* appeared in 1791, as the first Sunday newspaper in Britain.

In the eighteenth century, newspapers gloried in the title of the Fourth Estate:* a central pillar of society. This was perhaps best

---

* This is based on the notion of three estates of the nation: the clergy, the nobility and the common people. Thomas Carlyle credited Burke with the coinage in 1840: 'Burke said there were Three Estates in Parliament; but, in the Reporters' Gallery yonder, there sat a Fourth Estate more important than them all.' He almost certainly had misread a passage by the historian Thomas Macaulay, who said in 1827: 'The gallery in which the reporters sit has become a Fourth Estate of the realm.'

typified in the person of John Wilkes, who was both an MP and a journalist, and published the *North Briton* newspaper in 1761, trumpeting loudly:

> The liberty of the press is the birthright of a Briton, and is justly esteemed the firmest bulwark of this country. It has been the terror of all bad ministers; for their dark and dangerous designs, or their weakness, inability and duplicity, have thus been detected and shewn to the public, generally in too strong and just colours for them long to bear up against the odium of mankind.

Journalists, ever since, have liked to see themselves as the firebrand heirs of Wilkes; the extent to which this is true has, ever since, been something of an open question. The next century saw an explosion of titles, including more than fifty in London alone. Newspapers were heavily taxed, though, which restricted their growth to an extent. The tax was repealed in 1855 (and newsprint is untaxed in terms of VAT★ to this day), and circulation rose to astonishing heights. As the twentieth century began, adult literacy hit 97 per cent (still unsurpassed), and almost every adult read a newspaper: the *Daily Mail* became the first paper to sell a million copies on its own, and the first to be aimed at women readers. It remains the only paper today with a female-dominated readership, which is why it is so filled with content written by women for women who hate women. The *Daily Mirror* was launched in 1903 as the first picture-dominated tabloid (it reached a circulation high of 5 million in 1964). It went on to spawn, as a competitor, the *Sun*, which was relaunched in 1969, having been purchased by Rupert Murdoch.

It is striking that newspapers – even at their peak – were constantly regarded as immoral and too fond of the salacious or scabrous story. Walter Scott, in 1829, called journalism 'a disgrace and a degradation'; he said he 'would rather sell gin to poor people and poison them that way'. In 1938 a government report bemoaned the slide towards celebrity tittle-tattle:

★ The idea is that the beneficial effects of reading should be encouraged, and so a tax break exists for the written word. It does not extend to digital journalism, interestingly.

A dangerous tendency has recently been manifesting itself by which entertainment ceases to be ancillary to news and either supersedes it or absorbs it; many people welcome a newspaper that under the guise of presenting news, enables them to escape from the grimness of actual events and the effort of thought by opening the backdoor of triviality and sex appeal. Such readers are left ill-informed and unable to participate intelligently in political debate.

The spectre of snobbery when discussing popular journalism is neither a new nor unfamiliar one. And concerns have always subsisted that the influence of newspapers has been malign or immoral, especially when it comes to a national participation in 'political debate'. It was Stanley Baldwin who famously thundered in 1931: 'What the proprietorship of these papers is aiming at is power, and power without responsibility – the prerogative of the harlot through the ages.'

Newspaper proprietors and editors play up to this, of course: before every election there are always pompous editorials in which a title declares for a particular side. It is impossible to prove how influential they actually are, of course. The *Sun* – which has supported the winning side in every election since 1979 – famously published a headline in 1992, claiming that 'It was the *Sun* wot won it'. It is striking how this claim, self-evidently one of unserious bravado by a swaggering editor, Kelvin Mackenzie, is taken seriously by the commentariat who are sceptical of the paper's veracity in every other respect. In fact, the *Sun* has always been as much interested in following its readership as leading it: it supported Brexit for that reason in 2016; it supported the Conservatives in 2017 along with almost 60 per cent of its readers.

I was in the *Sun* newsroom on the election night of 2015, where all the talk had been of a rise in Milibandism and the probability of a hung Parliament. The 10 p.m. exit poll suggested a narrow Tory win and cheers erupted. Not because of party loyalty (many journalists I know on the paper are not Tory voters), but because the *Sun's* line had been endorsed: there was a fleeting feeling that it remained relevant to its readers. In the 2017 election, though, it has been calculated that the readership of the right-leaning press accounted for only 4 million actual voters, a significant but not exactly dominant portion of the overall electorate. And almost a third of *Sun* readers voted Labour anyway.

While the broader influence of newspapers is overstated, their role in the political life of our country is not. Some of it is unquestionably healthy and legitimate: the 2009 scandal of the MPs expenses broken by the *Telegraph* was perhaps the exemplum of public-interest journalism on behalf of the public (also, of course an example of chequebook journalism, costing as it did £350,000, which the *Telegraph* probably would not have paid now).

Newspapers – even tabloids – devote plenty of space and resource to political coverage, and act as something of a conscience-pricker to those in power. They also help to set the agenda followed by broadcasters, and their influence on story selection for radio and TV news is a real silent power. Political journalists have an unusual relationship with their subjects, part friendly, part hostile, an assault that ever threatens to become an embrace. Both sides need each other: MPs to push out their message and to feel important; lobby journalists to have stories to bring back to the news desk. The term 'lobby journalist', by the way, dates back to 1885, when – in the wake of security concerns over Irish nationalist terrorism – the lobby of the House of Commons was restricted to all but a privileged number of named reporters. These became 'the lobby'. They are still a privileged bunch: they share stories and some contacts, and are given access to power that they guard jealously and furtively. This is from a guide to the lobby from the 1940s, which makes it sound a bit like *Fight Club*: 'Don't talk about lobby meetings . . . if outsiders appear to know that a lobby meeting is to be, or has been, held, do not confirm their conjectures.'

Objective observers might argue that political journalists are too close to their subjects, that the lobby system is too cosy and mutually beneficial. It was not the lobby who broke the expenses scandal, for example. But proximity to the source of information is largely necessary, and we live now in a time – thanks to live blogging, tweeting and twenty-four-hour news – in which we are probably better informed about the workings of Parliament, and the behaviour of elected officials, than at any point in its history.

Newspapers are very comfortable at exploring the scandals of others; they are woeful at considering their own internal problems. The best example of this is perhaps phone-hacking at the *News of the World*.

My bird's-eye view of the hacking scandal

The story is relatively well-known now. Phone-hacking – the interception of voice messages on mobile phones by either guessing or blagging their passwords – probably arose, or at least got widespread traction at Mirror Group Newspapers (the *Daily Mirror*, the *Sunday Mirror* and the *People*) in the mid-1990s. It was then brought across to the *News of the World*. To showbiz journalists it was revolutionary: the chance to eavesdrop on personal messages and – far more importantly – to stand up gossipy stories. If star X is seeing star Y, a voice message between them would confirm the existence of the relationship in a way that would withstand the stoutest denial.

At the *News of the World*, much of the phone-hacking was outsourced to a private investigator called Glenn Mulcaire, who was instructed to grub up facts by many on the paper, including the royal correspondent Clive Goodman. In 2006 Goodman published stories containing information that the royal family believed could only have come from private messages. It was a fatal mistake: any crime against them was bound to galvanise the police. It did, and Goodman and Mulcaire were subsequently convicted under the Regulation of Investigatory Powers Act, ironically the piece of legislation designed to control how the state accessed private material in pursuit of terrorist prevention. The editor of the paper, Andy Coulson, while disclaiming responsibility, resigned.

The position of News International (which owned the *News of the World*) was that this had been an example of a 'rogue reporter'. This was based primarily on wishful thinking and a reluctance to examine the evidence. The problem was that such evidence of widespread phone-hacking existed in the form of Mulcaire's notebooks, seized by police, shared with claimant solicitors, and revealing a list of thousands of targets far outside the scope of a royal correspondent. The 'rogue' defence could not hold for long.

However, the Press Complaints Commission – lacking any powers of investigation, and perhaps reluctant to concede even to themselves that such flagrant disregard for ethics and individuals' privacy had happened on its watch – had swallowed the company position. It recognised (rightly) that it could not go further than any police investigation, and so confined itself in 2007 to requiring that all publishers take steps to prevent the recurrence of phone-hacking in future. The police, having secured the conviction of the people who had so disquieted the royal family, was content to let the investigation drop, despite having firm knowledge that phone-hacking had been pursued by Mulcaire to a pretty substantial extent.

The matter rested for a while, but the *Guardian* newspaper continued to prod and probe. Its vigour was based not only on its legitimate interest in exposing bad behaviour, but also on twin antipathies: an almost pathological dislike of Rupert Murdoch, the owner of News International, and tabloid journalism; a political animus against what it perceived to be the damaging philosophy of right-wing populism. This latter fire was given further oxygen by the decision by David Cameron (then in opposition) to bring in Coulson as Director of Communications, a seemingly public signal that he did not care about the rumours swirling over hacking.

In 2009 the *Guardian* (which by then would have seen the Mulcaire notebooks and have known unequivocally that hacking had been widespread in the *News of the World*), revealed some of the extent of the malpractice, including the fact that the company had settled legal cases on the premise that hacking had taken place involving people other than Goodman (which was at odds with its public position). The police, even then, remained resolute in its position that no further action was needed.

It was here that the PCC made what was to be a fatal error. It decided – still lacking any power to determine anything properly – to re-examine the bland conclusions of its 2007 report, in light of the *Guardian*'s new allegations. By this point, the PCC's relationship with the *Guardian* was almost non-existent. Throughout the

2000s the *Guardian*★ had been critical of what it felt was the PCC's ineffectual attempts to corral the tabloid press, the cosiness of the self-regulatory model and the poverty of ethics in mainstream journalism. The personal relationship between the heads of the PCC and the editor of the *Guardian*, Alan Rusbridger, was extremely frosty, and remained so until I took over some years later. In 2009 the *Guardian* was sure of its position, but not able to disclose much of its evidence. On the other side, the *News of the World* was staunch in its denials, supported by the apparent decision of the police not to pursue the matter further.

Nettled by years of *Guardian* angst, and wounded by its criticism, the commission agreed to a report that reaffirmed the stance that phone-hacking had not been widespread, expressing surprise that the *Guardian* had not provided more evidence. What should have been anger and outrage at the *News of the World* (or, better still, silence in acknowledgement of a failure of its own powers) was transmuted into snide remarks about *Guardian* journalism. It could have been worse: I was shown a draft of the report that was personally critical of the editor Alan Rusbridger, and begged for it to be removed. It was, but to little avail. The PCC was on the wrong side of history, and was therefore soon to be consigned to it.

Throughout the next couple of years, the *Guardian* continually revealed information relating to the scale of the hacking. When Andy Coulson was brought into Downing Street as a civil servant (following the Conservative-led Coalition of 2010), its wrath and disbelief at the collusion between Tories and a corrupt newspaper man knew no bounds. In January 2011 the police finally yielded and began Operation Weeting into phone-hacking at the *News of the World*. The critical moment came in July 2011, when the *Guardian* revealed that the *News of the World* had hacked the phone messages

---

★ There was – and is – a schism in the industry between tabloid and broadsheet newspapers. The former (primarily the *Sun*, *Mirror* and *Mail*) supported the PCC for fear of something worse; the latter despised it from the lofty position of believing their journalism was faultless. Much personal animosity was involved on all sides, with the result that the PCC was, and was perceived to be, too close to the tabloids.

of the missing child Milly Dowler. What is more, the report said it had then deleted the messages, which gave 'false hope' to the family who believed that she must therefore have been alive. This latter claim turned out to be untrue, but was arguably one of the most powerful reasons for the revulsion against the paper. A further irony is that – while most examples of phone-hacking had been in pursuit of the low-rent stories about showbiz and sex – the attempt to find a missing girl was, on the face of it, in the public interest. However, the *News of the World* has no complaint: it was guilty of deliberate and unconscionable intrusion; it had disregarded its ethical standards in a breathtaking way. The edifice came crashing down: Coulson was arrested;[2] David Cameron called for a full public inquiry into the sins of the press, intended – *inter alia* – to replace the PCC with something stronger; the *News of the World* lost advertisers at a commercially crippling rate, and was closed on 10 July. In the prosecutions that followed, Coulson was found guilty of being involved in phone-hacking, as were several of his editorial team.

Phone-hacking was a perfect storm of politics, media rivalry and not a little incompetence and immorality. It was politicised because the Labour Party had a stake in tackling Murdoch: not least because the *Sun* had declared war on Labour by shifting its support to the Tories, on the very day of Gordon Brown's party conference speech in 2009.* Other titles wanted to damage News International too: Murdoch was seeking to obtain ownership of the broadcaster Sky, and media competitors – the *Guardian*, the *Telegraph*, the *Mail*, even the BBC – were desperate to stop him. The incompetence was internal to News International, failing to deal with the initial claims properly, failing to root out the problem back in 2006. The PCC was incompetent. The police were incompetent. The damage was incalculable.

My little part in the story continues. Cameron was keen to limit the damage he had brought – in the person of Coulson – to the very door of Downing Street. That was the reason he called the

---

* Labour mandarin Peter Mandelson, it was said, was so incensed at the manner of this betrayal he called up News International boss Rebekah Brooks and argued that 'you have made total cunts of yourselves'. He maintains he said 'chumps'.

Leveson Inquiry and gave it wide terms of remit: to investigate the 'culture, practices and ethics of the British press'. And I was by then running the damaged body that was at least partially responsible for all that. Public inquiries are serious matters: not only must you give evidence under oath, but you must swear that you have disclosed all relevant material. In the case of the PCC, almost all material was relevant.

What I decided to do was this: make a submission that revealed all the benefits of the PCC and all the flaws in the system. It turned out to be 140,000 words, even longer than this book, and the longest submission in the whole inquiry. If you talk to newspaper people about Leveson, many of them will still grumble and curse. With some justification: it was a kangaroo court in public, in which anybody with a gripe against the press over the previous twenty or thirty years had the chance to make allegations. Imagine a similar inquiry into the practice of lawyers or even doctors.

But Leveson was also salutary and necessary: after all, British newspapers had spent the previous 300 years making allegations often without consequence; and some of the criticisms this time were justified and needed to be heard. Editors are extraordinary characters, in my experience. They are a strange blend of iron ego and fragile flower. They are responsible for everything in their paper, but often practically *do* very little: if a national newspaper editor was arrested at 2 p.m., the next day's paper would be produced without a murmur.* They wield ultimate power over the content of their title, but are seldom held to account for that content. This is Anthony Trollope writing about the fictional journalist Tom Towers in *The Warden* (1855):

> He loved to sit silent in the corner of his club and listen to the loud chattering of politicians, and to think how they were all in his power – how he could smite the loudest of them, were it worth his while to raise his pen for such a purpose . . . Each of them was responsible to his country, each of them must answer if inquired into, each of

---

* The great *Guardian* editor C. P. Scott, author of the phrase 'comment is free, facts are sacred', didn't even get into the office until 7 p.m. He was a serving MP at the time.

them must endure abuse with good humour, and insolence without anger. But to whom was he, Tom Towers, responsible? No one could insult him; no one could inquire into him.

Well, Justice Leveson could indeed inquire into him and his ilk, some 150 years later. Such bashful figures despised the harshly unforgiving lights of a courtroom, of course, but the Leveson process was perhaps a rightful nemesis to their combined hubris.

I appeared one February morning, and spent three hours in court, being questioned by the leading counsel and by Leveson himself (a man metonymically associated for ever in my mind with a pair of glowering eyebrows). It was clear that Leveson wanted a straightforward answer to an impossible problem: how do you regulate a free press, how do you shackle something that society needs to be both restrained and free? An especially pressing problem when most information is being consumed online via social media and unregulated websites (as we shall see). His eventual report, over a million words long, had scarcely a few thousand about the internet. It was doomed to irrelevancy almost immediately. It did lead to the replacement by the newspaper industry of the PCC with IPSO, a body with slightly more powers. It also led to an absurd constitutional hodgepodge: papers needed to sign up to a recognised regulatory body (not IPSO) endorsed by the government in order to avoid being punished in the courts.* Five years after the inquiry, the regulation of the print media is in the same sorry state as it ever was.

When I see the photos of me at the inquiry, I scarcely recognise the strained, shabby and flabby face of someone operating under a pressure I failed to recognise at the time. I remember my wife booking me an appointment with a psychiatrist, which I missed because I had lost my wallet. I was coming apart at the seams: working, going home to two young children, punching holes in doors with mute frustration. I left the PCC soon after, and worked

---

* This is scarcely credible but true: newspapers who are not signed up to a recognised regulator may be forced by legislation to pay the costs of the other side in a dispute even if they win, and face exemplary damages if they lose. Such a position is unlikely to be permissible under Human Rights law (the right to a fair trial), but remains on our statute books in 2018.

for two years in crisis communications, helping companies at the centre of media and regulatory storms. After all, I had been buffeted by such ill winds myself.

One day, I was called by the new editor of the *Sun*, David Dinsmore, who asked me to be his managing editor. The *Sun* was still reeling from the aftermath of the phone-hacking scandal: the company had disclosed thousands of its journalists' emails to police, and its journalists had been arrested not for phone-hacking, but for paying public officials. My role was to help restore stability to the newsroom.

Having taken the job, I visited the paper late one summer afternoon. It was the time of the evening conference, a gathering of (largely male) executives, in suits and ties, to finalise the content of the next day's paper. I sat in the corner watching. An argument arose about the proposed splash: a senior public official (and crony of Boris Johnson) had been caught with a prostitute. The lawyer, a wonderful man,★ was expressing doubt about the privacy aspect, and asked for my view. All eyes turned to me. 'Well, the fact of a relationship undertaken while on public duty can't be private, can it?' I said. The room exhaled collectively; the haggard, whip-thin news editor looked up at me: 'Welcome to the *Sun*,' he said. 'Boris Bonking Bus Boss Bedded Broke Brass', said the splash the next day, alliteratively, bemusingly.

How newspapers actually work today

Though newspapers have been around for 300 years their operation is not entirely well-known to outsiders. Like all trades it comes with its own mysteries and idiolects: splashes and sub-decks; the back

---

★ The *Sun* lawyer is, interestingly, an evangelical Christian and Liberal Democrat with (appropriately enough) the patience of a saint. We would spend hours considering what was publishable and what was not, before spending many more debating the existence of God. My radio show on LBC – often focusing on problems with organised religion – used to send him into fits of apoplexy too, but he remained charming throughout.

bench; wobs and gutters;* and so on. There is also the reasonable question as to how, each day, a readable (generally speaking) product is created from scratch, containing tens of thousands of words to set alongside pictures and adverts.

It's a reasonable question to ask because, even when you are in the middle of it, the process can feel unlikely. Newspaper production is a scarcely controlled shambles from beginning to end. Newspapers start with a flat plan: a sheet of paper with the outline of each page on it, with the spaces for adverts marked on already. This is the first point: advertising dictates the shape of a newspaper; the stories are designed to fit around them (not the other way round). A newspaper without advertising is dead. It's easy to forget but the first several pages of newspapers used *only* to be advertising. The first time that *The Times* ran a front page that was not filled with ads was to announce the death of Winston Churchill in January 1965. Today, newspapers will do almost anything for the money, so we have returned to front pages with adverts across the top or bottom; or 'wraps' concealing the front page entirely.

A collapse in commercial (rather than circulation) revenue is the main reason why the newspaper industry is in terminal decline: advertising spend that used to go into print now goes directly to Facebook and Google, with nothing to replace it. In the 1980s and 1990s (and before), editors could simply chuck out adverts that interrupted the flow, or spoiled the look of a page. They would do it without consulting the team who had sold the advert, without telling the client who had bought the advert. A full-page ad (then perhaps worth £30,000) would be in the bin. Now it would be accepted on bended knee.

Newspapers are organised by desks: news; features; pictures; sport; (in tabloids) showbiz and TV; (in broadsheets) foreign and business; and so on. The editors of each desk's job every morning is to collate all the possible stories from all the reporters (staff or freelance) who work for them, so they can create a list to present to the editor at morning conference. The key to this meeting is the news list, which

---

* Wobs are 'white on black' headlines; the gutter is a notional line at the centre of a spread that cannot carry any text or images.

will contain a mixture of exclusive stories from specialist reporters, all-round stories (often taken from the central news agency, the Press Association, or other agencies around the country) and events planned for the day that will inevitably create news (a parliamentary debate, for example, or a company announcement).

Conference is different at each paper. At the *Guardian*, there was – until recently – a small meeting to review the previous day's efforts, followed by a group discussion involving potentially the entire staff, who trooped into a large room filled with cheerfully yellow sofas. They even invited guests to speak at it (including me, once). It felt like a very civilised salon, quite suiting the paper's elevated view of itself, quite unlike what I have seen elsewhere. The *Daily Mail*'s conference takes place in its editor's plush, walnut-lined office: Paul Dacre glowering from behind his enormous desk (which has no computer on it), sofas pushed back to the walls, and the centre occupied by the news editor, sitting on a chair like a victim of an interrogation.

The news editor's job is the hardest in journalism. He (it is almost always he)★ is tasked with producing a list that not only covers what he believes to be the main stories of the day, but also stories that are exclusive to the title. It is a thankless task, generally. The pressure, bad now, used to be unbearable. At the *Sun*, several years ago, an editor was so appalled by a list at conference that it was screwed up and thrown at the news editor. Conference was cancelled, and fifteen minutes later an email was sent to every member of staff in the building asking for stories 'because the news editor apparently doesn't have any'. Competition between newspapers now is almost non-existent, as hardly any news editors have the budget to aggressively chase stories; it used to be the dynamic that powered the whole industry. At night, hacks would be sent to train stations where the first editions were delivered, so they could phone back in what

---

★ There is an undoubted skew in senior journalism towards men. When the BBC was forced in July 2017 to declare its highest paid employees (all those earning more than the Prime Minister), two-thirds were male. Other prejudices abound: almost half of senior journalists across the national media went to private school and Oxbridge. City University conducted a survey (admittedly of only 700 people) and concluded that the journalism industry was 94 per cent white.

was in rival publications. Stories would be stolen, bollockings would be given. Unsurprisingly, in such an atmosphere of mistrust and controlled panic, ethical standards were liable to slip.

War stories among journalists are common, of course. The news editor who was so apoplectic at the loss of a story that he suffered an asthma attack. The journalist who feigned a heart attack to escape a confrontation with his boss, which continued anyway over his fraudulently twitching body. This is Christopher Hitchens in recollection mode:

> Was it true that the standby slogan of the *Express* foreign desk, for any hack stumbling onto a scene of carnage and misery, was 'anybody here raped and speaks English?'. I regret to say it was. Is it true that an *Express* scribe in some hellhole, his copy surpassed by a *Daily Mail* man who had received an honourable flesh-wound, received a cable: 'Mail Man shot. Why you unshot?'

Morning conference involves the editor listening to the proposed stories of the day. At the *Sun*, there was also a separate features conference to consider ideas for non-news-related material. By lunchtime, an editor would have sheaves of lists in his hand, and sit down with senior staff to plan the order of the content. That would mean literally drawing on a flat plan which stories go where. And there was always a rubric to follow: page 2 politics; page 3 something celebrity-focused; pages 4–5 the main story of the day, linked to the front page; pages 7, 9 and 15 the three next best stories;* page 13 a columnist; pages 16–17 the first feature; and so on. Other bits of 'furniture' also help structure the paper: the letters page; the TV listings; the agony column. The sport section is built the same way from the back page forwards. Clearly, the rubric will change dependent on the paper, but it will exist:[3] it is the key to imposing order on the chaos; it is why papers feel familiar to their regular readers.

The afternoon is then spent in the preparation of copy by journalists, which will then be channelled into their respective desks and

---

* Right-hand pages are felt to have primacy, because the reader's eye is drawn to them first.

then passed before a lawyer. Meanwhile, the whole other side of the operation kicks in: the production journalism. This is run by the back bench: the group of editors, led by the night editor, whose job it is to see that the physical product is created to the highest standard. These are the most senior figures in the operation of the paper, the people who can carry an inexperienced editor, whatever their merits.

Once stories are ready, they will be 'subbed': checked for sense and cut to the size required.★ Pages will be 'drawn': the tessellating shape will be constructed that has the requisite number of stories on it. Gaps will be filled with short items taken from a central file. Headlines will be written and re-written. In the early evening, the same conference process will happen again, to ensure that the day's news has been gathered, and the material projected in the morning has worked out. Pages will be scrapped; stories will be changed. At the *Mail* it is a source of pride that 7 p.m. marks the time at which everything significant is started again: the editor on the prowl with his green pen and his foul mouth.

By early evening, the decision is finalised as to what the front page ('the splash') will look like. At the *Sun*, this was one of the most important jobs of the editor. Before, say, 2010, the newspaper could shift an extra 100,000 copies on the strength of having a good story on its front; that is a rarity now indeed. The craftsmanship of headlines, though, is one of the great joys of tabloid journalism. *Sun* meeting rooms are named after famous headlines of its past: How Do You Solve a Problem Like Korea (on the threat of Kim Jong-Il); Super Caley Go Ballistic Celtic Are Atrocious (on a Scottish football match); and so on. Headline-writing is a competitive sport: people sit at their desk, brows furrowed, trying to come up with the funniest line. At the *Sun* there is a headline of the month competition too. About a couple of months into my time at the paper, there was a debate over how to headline a front-page story about the rise of

---

★ Writers never like their prose being cut, of course (as the heft of this book testifies). The great Henry James used occasionally to write for the *TLS*. Once, the editor was so bold as to remove a sentence and a half of the master's prose. James returned the proofs with a curt note: 'Here is the bleeding corpse. Yours is a butcher's trade.'

TB in dogs, of all things; I came up with 'Tuberculosis Rex', and felt a flicker of genuine pride when I saw it in the shops the next day.[4]

The problem for all papers, especially tabloid ones, is that a front page must be clear and decisive and unequivocal, while reality seldom is any of those things. That is why headlines are apt for criticism, scorn and parody as soon as they appear. As any editor will tell you, a decision taken at 9 p.m. one night can feel very different in the morning.

Newspapers' first editions go 'off stone' between 9 and 10.30 p.m., when they are sent to the printers[5] (in different locations in the country). Those first editions will then be packaged and delivered to the further reaches of the UK. A second edition follows sometime after midnight; sometimes a third in the very early hours of the morning. As a feat of logistics, this is an exceptional daily perform-ance, involving an entire micro-economy of people: printers, drivers, newsagents and the like. When you see people demanding for papers to be shut down – a common blurt of the social media militant – it is worth considering the employment of thousands of people who rely on newspapers' existence.

Reading through the process now, it is easy to see why the predicament of newspapers is so perilous. All that form and structure, when news is happening constantly and can now be transmitted instantly. That structure also prevents communication between the person writing the story and the person then responsible for its production. Often a tabloid reporter will file 1,500 words to the desk, which will then be subbed down to 600 words by one person, given a headline by another, under the direction of several other people. None of the production people will have spoken to the journalist once. In that way, newspaper production is a factory of Chinese whispers. It is not surprising that so many stories have errors; it is surprising how few.

Only correct

Almost all newspapers now run corrections columns, an idea pioneered in Britain by the *Guardian*. Although accuracy is a serious business, much joy can be found in the mistakes that are made. I remember the poor woman who complained to the PCC about a misprint in a local newspaper story that told of her heroic struggle against debilitating back pain during a working day in which 'she was not able to have time for a sit'. A stray 'h' entered the last word, to her total mortification. While we are on the subject, here are my three favourite newspaper corrections of recent times:

> Because of an editing error, an article on Monday about a theological battle being fought by Muslim imams and scholars in the West against the Islamic State misstated the Snapchat handle used by Suhaib Webb, one of the Muslim leaders speaking out. It is imamsuhaiwebb, not Pimpin4Paradise786. (*New York Times*)

> In our interview with Sir Jack Hayward, the chairman of Wolverhampton Wanderers, page 20, Sport, yesterday, we mistakenly attributed to him the following comment: 'Our team was the worst in the First Division and I'm sure it'll be the worst in the Premier League.' Sir Jack had just declined the offer of a hot drink. What he actually said was 'Our tea was the worst in the First Division and I'm sure it'll be the worst in the Premier League.' Profuse apologies. (*Guardian*)

> In an article on Saturday headlined 'Flying saucers over British Scientology HQ', we stated 'two flat silver discs' were seen 'above the Church of Scientology HQ'. Following a letter from lawyers for the Church, we apologise to any alien life-forms for linking them to Scientologists. (*Sun*)

The rise of online journalism

Online journalism is, of course, as prone (if not more so) to error.★ Let's compare the overall process of digital newspaper journalism,

★ This is the best correction to a news tweet I have seen: 'ISIS fighters are shaving bears and hiding in civilian homes to avoid airstrikes.' 'Correction: it was beards, not bears.' (NBC News Twitter)

which will generally be running on the same floor as the print operation in most media companies. In a title like the *Guardian*, the emphasis will be on the digital journalism, and a small team will re-purpose online stories for print at the end of each day. In titles seeking maximum reach (like the *Mail*), online teams are generally separate, and stories are written by young, under-paid people, chiselling out material by writing captions to pictures, grabbing items from social media and stealing stories from every other site (which is simultaneously stealing stories from them).[6] There is an entire ecology of crapness at the heart of this journalism. And it creates an almost entirely homogenous product. The websites of, say, the *Independent* – once a proud source of liberal journalism; now too often an archive of thinly sourced dross – and the *Express* are not dissimilar: they are both in search of the crack cocaine of a click.

Indeed, it is an apt coincidence that the term 'hit' works for both drug-taking and online consumption: they both reflect a need for a short-term, unsatisfying delivery of excitement. Stories are packaged by a 'social' team: clever young folk who will try to use Facebook and – to far less extent – Twitter[7] to get people interested. Again, this has become a homogenous trade in itself, with its own new-birthed clichés: 'this woman's response to a sext will amaze you'; 'J. K. Rowling just destroyed Donald Trump'; 'the Pope's view on the refugee crisis might shock you'; and so on. You will have been bombarded by some today, I bet. Other stories are written solely to satisfy the search engine of Google: journalists are told to write pieces that answer headline questions like 'Who is Piers Morgan, and why is he not presenting *GMB* today?', or 'What time is Chelsea vs Manchester United on?', or 'How do I cook a turkey?'.

The economics of online journalism are scarcely better than off-line. To get more clicks, you need more stories; to get more stories, you need more people churning out things quickly. There is an unbreakable link between overhead and scale. Meanwhile, display advertising is collapsing in the digital world. The unlimited supply of stories means there can be no rise in demand for space:

so advertising yields are declining online, just as they are in print. Most digital spend goes to two places: Facebook (which acts as a portal to the whole internet) and Google[8] (which controls what you see when you search). In 2016 Google took £4.6 billion of ad revenue, Facebook took £1.6 billion, while every British news organisation combined took £420 million. They were the ones paying for the journalism, of course.

It is striking to reflect that the Mail Online (either the first or second largest news website in the world) does not make huge profits. A site like Buzzfeed has, until recently, no display advertising: it seeks its revenue by 'native advertising', which is to say sponsored content, often videos. The idea is that a brand, say Heinz, will – openly – pay for a series of videos about, say, sandwiches, which will then be shared. This can bring back a substantial return; although, again, it is not clear that Buzzfeed is actually profitable as a result. Indeed in 2017 it announced its own wave of redundancies: the familiar pattern of print journalism reproduced inexorably in the new media.

My life at a tabloid

In my time at the *Sun*, I was responsible for helping enforce a pay-wall for digital content, and then for tearing it down to allow the subsequent creation of a *Mail*-like website. A pay-wall did not work for the simple reason that, if a story was good enough to charge for, it was immediately stolen by all the free sites; if a story was not good enough to charge for, you couldn't charge for it. The internet is not an opportunity for mass media because it already has the same characteristics of mass media: a desire for gossip, sex, humour and conversation. Facebook performs all the social functions of a media entity with none of the overheads.

My main job, though, as managing editor was to run the business of the paper: internal ethical processes; HR and employee welfare; legal and IPSO complaints; the budget; and so on. On Twitter even now, I get people abusing me for having worked at the *Sun*, when they see my liberal opinions on immigration or sexual rights or whatever. 'You edited the *Sun*,' the argument goes, 'how can you be supportive of immigration?'* Here is my response. I was never in a position to control the politics of a newspaper and the attendant story selection: that is decided by a combination of the proprietor, the editor and the bulk of the readership. My role was to try to make sure the journalism was working as well as it could, and the employees were as supported and healthy as they could be.

So I spent my time discussing the ethics of some individual stories and news-gathering, not deciding whether or not the politics of the story was – in my view – correct, but whether it could be legally and ethically published, and whether the manner of its investigation had been safe[9] and appropriate. Clearly, we did not get every decision like that right. And many stories were published without my prior knowledge.[10] But processes, especially around payments, were extremely rigorous. Most people do not realise this, but the biggest impact on tabloid journalism over the last decade was not Leveson or phone-hacking, but the Bribery Act (2010). This made it illegal to pay anybody (whether a public official or not) for private material relating to their job. All of a sudden, giving a barman £100 for a story about a celebrity in a pub could – theoretically – be judged to be illegal. Tabloids, and to a lesser extent other papers, have always been run by what is known disparagingly as 'chequebook journalism'; that now was under threat. My ethical stance on this is that the issue of payment should be a secondary one. If a piece of information is intrusive (with no public interest), it should not be published, irrespective of whether it has been paid for or not. So paying someone for something innocuous does not provide a particular moral dilemma. The law must be followed though, of course.

At the *Sun*, we kept a QC on permanent standby:[11] any proposed payment that might raise a bribery issue had to be sent to him. If he thought that there was a risk, a full analysis had to be done involving

---

* I am making this sound more polite than it is. Since working at the *Sun*, I have received death threats, my eight-year-old daughter has been named in rape threats, as well as the now-standard litany of messages calling me a 'fucking cunt' or wishing I 'died of the bad AIDS'.

the public interest, and the eventual decision had to be signed off by the senior lawyer of News Corp, the newspaper's ultimate owner, in New York. The days of carelessly chucking cash about were over.[12]

Amid all the grief, I witnessed the *Sun* running some strong campaigns: fighting for more money for women's refuges; raising hundreds of thousands of pounds for victims of a typhoon in the Philippines;[13] providing financial support (and sandbags) for people who had lost their homes in unseasonable floods in England. We also published some memorable stories,[14] my favourite of which related to a video from 1933 showing the Prince of Wales (later Edward VIII) teaching a Nazi salute to our infant Queen and her mother.

After a couple of years, things changed at the *Sun*. A new editor – Tony Gallagher – came in from the *Mail*, with manifestly the instruction to toughen the paper's stance on political issues like immigration. Just as I was set to leave, I was asked about my interest in the *Times Literary Supplement* for which I had written since I left university. And so my newspaper journey has ended on a weekly literary title, first published in 1902. Oddly enough, it is part of the journalistic world that has – in my view – a clearly defined future. Its main revenue is subscription, not advertising. It has a clear niche that cannot be readily reproduced many places elsewhere: long-form, expert articles on a broad range of cultural topics. Just as the fast-food explosion of the 1980s led to the development of slow-food and farmers' markets, so the recent arrival of click-bait, narcotic jolts of online journalism have created a market for journalistic slow culture, for detail and careful writing. We shall see.

But enough (you might reasonably cry) about the print journalism, what about the other, generally better behaved, aspect of the business? The world of broadcasting.

The British Behemoth Corporation

The story of British broadcasting largely begins and ends with the BBC,[15] which is one of the most visible, important and often wonderful aspects of our national identity. It is also a ubiquitous presence, funded by a compulsory tax, that represents a commercial threat to the free media market, employing more than 20,000 people on guaranteed revenues of more than £3.5 billion every year. (That is the reason it gets such a hard time in the press.)[16]

Its origins stem from the invention of radio, and its development by Guglielmo Marconi[17] at the turn of the twentieth century. It was from his British company that the first entertainment transmission was broadcast in 1920 (a performance by Dame Nellie Melba, sponsored by the *Daily Mail*), at which the scale and potential of radio broadcasting became abundantly clear. The technology had to involve the state, though. Radio broadcasts made use of a limited spectrum (of electromagnetic wave frequencies)* that was also required by civil and military communication. The government needed to control its use, and so by 1922 the idea of licensing was developed to manage access.

At the same time, it was decided that control over broadcast activity should not be delegated to commercial institutions, which might exploit it in a shameless and populist manner, but there was disquiet over it being entirely in the hands of government. So a classic British fudge was created: five years after the institution began broadcasting, in 1927, the BBC was formed as a corporation, guaranteed by Royal Charter, funded by a compulsory levy on wirelesses. Its early output was worthy and intellectually impressive, both in terms of news (getting going by 1928) and artistic efforts. Virginia Woolf produced three pieces for the radio beginning with 'Are too many books being published?' in 1927 and ending with her thoughts on 'Craftsmanship' in 1937. A recording of the latter exists, and Woolf speaks in a strangled pastiche of bourgeois Received Pronunciation that must have been startling even then. The Director of Talks was a bluestocking figure called Hilda Matheson, who did much to shape the credibility of the organisation.†

---

* No, I am not going to explain this further.

† She was also, rather wonderfully, conducting an affair with Woolf's lover Vita Sackville-West. Her letters, often on BBC headed paper, survive: 'All day – ever since that blessed and ever to be remembered indisposition – I have been thinking of you – bursting with you – and wanting you – oh my God wanting you.'

Matheson invented the radio programme *Week in Westminster*, which was designed to enable female MPs to speak directly to the newly enfranchised female voters.

Indeed, from the beginning, the pomp of the BBC was established and reinforced: its purpose characterised as 'to inform, educate and entertain', to place – in the words of its foremost presiding spirit, John Reith – 'the best of everything into the greatest number of homes'.[18] The arrival of television, a medium less refined than radio, has placed often unbearable strain on these principles.[19] The Second World War had delayed TV's arrival, and by 1947 only 20,000 households were in range of its broadcast base in London's Alexandra Palace. But the pace of development swiftly improved: by 1954 commercial television was allowed as a rival to the BBC, which itself drove change, especially in news broadcasting. Here, the challenge had always been to find a way to tell stories that might resist easy images (which is why golf was actually successfully televised before a news programme was). Independent Television News arrived in 1955 to help formulate the answer, satellites were launched in 1962 that could broadcast images from around the world, and in 1967 ITN's *News at Ten* created the modern news broadcast (still recognisable today).

In radio – thanks to the ubiquity of the wireless, what Dennis Potter called 'a whorled, fluted and beknobbed oblong which could allow anyone to feel like Joan of Arc' – the BBC kept a virtual monopoly for years. By the 1960s, there were pirate radio stations,[20] such as Radio Caroline, transmitted from offshore ships and forts to avoid the requirement of a licence. They were significant broadcasters, with healthy advertising (including ads from the government) and a combined audience of around 15 million. In 1967 the law was changed to make marine broadcasting illegal; and the BBC saw the opportunity to expand, creating Radios 1, 2, 3 and 4 and individual local stations.[21] At the same time, licences were granted to commercial radio stations, and the first one to arrive in 1973 was the London Broadcasting Company, or LBC.

Its remit was to produce news 'presented without the slightest editorialising. . . but not without opinion or comment'; it undertook that each comment would be 'prefaced by the statement that a personal viewpoint or prejudice is about to be expressed'. That disclaimer goes unstated now, but LBC still seeks to fill the niche of broadcasting partisan opinion that the BBC declines to fill itself.★

The BBC had used its access to the wireless licence fee to develop the technology for television (a process it was able, as Andrew Marr[22] has noted, to duplicate with online technology seventy years later),† and in 1946 the TV licence was formally introduced. It was originally £2 per year (£75 in today's money), increasing to £10 (£157 today) in 1967. Few things are more controversial in the BBC than the licence fee. You must pay the £145.50 (far better value, it must be said, than in 1967) if you own a TV, or use the BBC's iPlayer or if you use any technology to watch programmes designed to appear on television. In 2013 about 1.9 million households said they had no need of a licence, and about 5 per cent of all consumers annually evade the fee despite using the services. Enforcement officers working for the BBC (sub-contracted to the firm Capita) make around 4 million visits a year to seek out evaders; in 2014 there were 200,000 prosecutions.

Criticism of this system is obvious. The tax is flat and so regressive: it takes a greater percentage of a poor person's income than a

---

★ I hosted an LBC phone-in show for more than three years. It is an invigorating, low-fi experience. The idea is that you pick a subject for each hour, then develop a pointed angle on it. At the beginning of the hour you have to 'churn' for calls: talking until people feel moved to phone in. In front of you is an empty switchboard with twelve slots, each of which lights up when a caller comes in. The ideal, as you are speaking, is to see a flashing beat of colours; the horror is when it remains resolutely black. Then you have to keep on talking until something clicks. This is a pure sort of broadcasting, which places you in touch with the shifting sentiments of the public. I knew, for example, that Jeremy Corbyn would do well in the 2017 election because I had spent hours on the phone to supporters from all parts of the country calling in to talk him up. On another note, I once did an entire show with a stomach bug, and spent every ad break throwing up in a nearby bathroom.

† In 1999, under John Birt, the BBC led the way in producing online journalism. By the turn of the century, it was publishing more than 300 stories a day. The *Sun* in 2018 only did 500. In 2007 the BBC launched the iPlayer, its on-demand service that has led the way in British online television. The rumour is that it was only conceived because the BBC Three website had published inappropriate pictures of model Katie Price and a redemptive idea was hurriedly needed as a distraction. I am sure this is not true. Probably.

rich person's. It is enforced via the mechanisms of the state: around one in nine of all magistrates' cases are about TV licensing. Weirdly, it seems to fall more heavily on women than men: 70 per cent of all evaders are female; and licensing prosecutions constitute a third of all court cases against women. The guaranteed income of the BBC compromises the otherwise free market for news: its financial heft means it can dominate the market in local areas, driving newspapers effectively out of business. And it is unquestionably anachronistic: the licence dates from a time of spectrum scarcity, when the technology for watching television was a monopoly devolved from government. The internet means that anybody can make a 'television' programme; anybody can watch one. If the BBC is worth the money, the argument goes, it will make it as a subscription service on the open market.

And yet. As we shall see further, the internet has destroyed the market, the financial basis, for much journalism. The existence of the licence fee acts as a guaranteed funding mechanism for the professional production of news and features. Facebook might take all the advertising earnings from journalism, but it does not fund any of the actual content. The BBC funds high-quality news-gathering, and high-quality programme-making, and can continue to do so thanks to the licence fee.

The 1954 Television Act that allowed the advent of commercial television also formulated the requirement of broadcast impartiality (itself now under threat, as an idea, from the internet). As broadcast journalism was beamed directly into our homes on stations that require a licence from government, it was felt that it could not be partisan or polemical (in the same way as a newspaper, actively purchased or picked up, could). The only problem – and this is seldom acknowledged – is that no person or institution is or can be impartial. Humans are hardwired to be partial, to have opinions, to take sides. And yet broadcast impartiality is a regulatory fact, enforced by the broadcast regulator OFCOM. This is how the BBC teaches its staff about the subject: 'Impartiality is not the same as objectivity or balance or neutrality, although it contains elements of all three. Nor is it the same as simply being fair – although it is unlikely you will be impartial without being fair-minded. At its simplest it means not taking sides. Impartiality is about providing a breadth of view.'

How is such a wishy-washy notion enforceable? It simply is not in any credible way. Broadcasters in Britain are far more cautious and fair-minded than newspapers, but they can never be impartial (and journalists on *Channel 4 News*, for example, scarcely trouble to pretend to be; they are punchy and spiky and partisan). The BBC is – to my mind – exemplary in its attempts to be balanced, often to a fault. It is, perhaps, too willing to run a minority countervailing view in the aim of balance, although characteristically is self-conscious about doing so. This is the Director General of the BBC in 1965: 'There are some respects in which it is not neutral, unbiased or impartial. That is where there are clashes for and against basic moral values – truthfulness, justice, freedom, compassion, tolerance, for example. Nor do I believe that we should be impartial about certain things like racialism or extreme forms of political belief.'

This is well said, but hard again to enforce. Is climate change denial an 'extreme form of political belief'? Is the rise of a far-right party extreme or an example of 'racialism'? How balanced can one be in a world constantly tipping out of joint? The BBC retains trust (something we will return to) largely because of its admittedly well-funded professionalism and celebration of reason. But it still gets itself into some fearful messes sometimes.

A very brief look at BBC scandals

The shape of a BBC scandal is actually rather fixed, and tends to occur every couple of years: error of judgement, under-reaction, over-reaction, self-flagellation; repeat. As a news organisation it has a far prouder record than almost every other journalistic institution, but because it is funded compulsorily by the public, it rightly is held to account in a different way. That can be taken too far, though. When Andrew Gilligan in May 2003 broadcast on the *Today* programme the claim that the government had 'sexed up' the dossier claiming that Saddam Hussein had chemical weapons, the resultant scandal led to the suicide of his source, the scientist David Kelly, and a judicial inquiry under Lord Hutton. He eventually produced a report blithely uncritical of government, but swingeing in its remarks about BBC standards. The chairman of the BBC, Gavin Davies, resigned, as did its Director General, Greg Dyke, as did Gilligan himself, saying (not without justification): 'This report casts a chill over all journalism, not just the BBC's. It seeks to hold reporters, with all the difficulties they face, to a standard that it does not appear to demand of, for instance, government dossiers.'

The problem was that the BBC was too unwieldy to deal with what was a straightforward claim of inaccuracy, which was only partially justified. It had no mechanism to correct the individual details[23] (while standing by the inarguable point that political self-interest had interfered at some level with the intelligence process ahead of the Iraq War), and so became enveloped by antagonism.

The same thing happened in 2008, when the TV presenter Jonathan Ross appeared on comedian Russell Brand's radio show and left a prank call on the phone of actor Andrew Sachs, in which Ross shouted 'he fucked your granddaughter' (a young woman called Georgina Baillie). The whole enterprise from start to finish was laughable, and laughably British: two overpaid presenters behaving yobbishly; a man whose central television role was a crypto-racist portrayal of a hapless Spaniard in *Fawlty Towers*; a woman who not only had the misfortune to have sex with a sesquipedalian comedian, but also then be found to have been involved in mild spanking pornography and burlesque.

The show aired on 18 October, and more or less nobody noticed. On 25 October the *Mail on Sunday* was having problems with its splash. You can often tell when Sunday newspapers lose their main story on a Friday or Saturday: they have to grope around for something to put on the front page, and often over-hype something that should have remained tucked inside instead. A shortish media piece, having a go at Russell Brand and appearing in the middle of the paper, was continually edged forward throughout the day. Finally, lacking any other option, the editor gave it some welly on the front page. The BBC received a massive number of complaints, had nowhere to put them, had no immediate decision in response, then over-reacted: the controller of Radio 2 resigned, Brand resigned,

279

Ross was suspended. Georgina Baillie's Satanic Sluts probably did some good business for a spell, though.

In October 2012 the flagship news programme *Newsnight* was debating whether to run a story about BBC legend (and – it was becoming evident – notorious serial paedophile) Jimmy Savile. It decided not to, and claims were raised that it had compromised its journalistic integrity. The BBC under-reacted, then over-reacted with the announcement of an independent inquiry by a former Sky News journalist, Nick Pollard. Meanwhile, its other flagship news programme *Panorama* investigated its own newsgathering colleagues, and was given a no-comment response from then Director General George Entwistle. Pollard's report was scathing, and the BBC had to pay for legal representation[24] for all the senior figures involved, who were treated mercilessly.

Alas, in the interim, *Newsnight* had got into trouble again: this time it had decided to cover (rather than conceal) a paedophile story, involving a man allegedly senior in the Conservative Party. In advance of broadcast, it had tweeted about 'the senior Conservative' involved, whom many on social media★ correctly identified as Lord McAlpine. The problem was *Newsnight* could not prove he was a paedophile, had not gone to him in advance to check the facts, and subsequently was forced to concede he was not. The internal mismanagement machine of the BBC swung into action, and George Entwistle was monstered so badly on another flagship news programme, *Today*, that he had to resign.

Meanwhile, yet another report by the BBC had been commissioned, this time from Dame Janet Smith into the culture of the BBC during the Savile period. It finally appeared in February 2016, and made clear that Savile had abused seventy-two people, including children, at 'virtually every one of the BBC premises at which he worked' and that a 'culture of not complaining' and an 'atmosphere

---

★ This helped to establish the surely obvious principle that comments on Twitter could be caught by the standard publishing laws of libel and privacy. Sally Bercow, the wife of the Speaker in Parliament, had tweeted: 'Why is Lord McAlpine trending? ★innocent face★.' McAlpine sued her, and twenty other significant figures on Twitter, either obtaining settlements or enforced compensation. He died, a broken man, in January 2014.

of not complaining' had persisted at the corporation. On the face of it, this has been a genuine scandal, and one somewhat underplayed. If phone-hacking was sufficient for a judicial inquiry into the entire newspaper industry, why was institutionalised rape at a public body not examined in the same way? In the case of sexual abuse on its premises, the BBC for once had not been guilty of over-reacting.

The rise of fake news

Amid all this talk of scandal, we should not forget that the BBC is still more trusted than most institutions. But trust everywhere is falling, and not just in the world of the print media. This seems to me to be an inevitable consequence of the postmodern world. Postmodernism is a movement – not only in the arts but in our collective consciousness – that examines the structures behind the structures, looks questioningly at authorities and demands that the workings be shown. This is not a bad thing, intrinsically: blind obedience to those in power has historically allowed despotism, religious warfare and untold misery. But if you disbelieve all authorities, you lose sight of any means to judge between the real and the fake, the honest and the malign.

And that disbelief is now the spirit of the age. In 2003, according to YouGov: 81 per cent of people trusted the BBC, 65 per cent trusted broadsheet papers, 36 per cent trusted midmarket papers, and 14 per cent trusted tabloids. In 2015 those figures were: 58 per cent, 36 per cent, 17 per cent and 10 per cent. Leaving aside the fact that tabloids have never been much trusted, this is a collapse in any faith in the media as a whole. As Andrew Marr has said, 'Somehow, somewhere along the road, journalists stopped being shabby heroes, confronting arrogant power, and became sleazy, pig-snouted villains.' This is sadly true. But it is – and this is my point about an entire culture of mistrust that has arisen – no longer simply a media issue: in the last decade, trust in police has fallen by 23 per cent, doctors by 11 per cent, teachers by 18 per cent.

We are intoxicated by our new-found ability to question anything

and therefore everything; we are – without realising it – prisoners of our own cynicism. If we are led to believe we cannot believe anything, then the emphatic blurts of Donald Trump have the same status as a peer-reviewed medical journal; the howling shriek of a conspiracy theorist gets the same respect as the political editor of the BBC. Furthermore, to protect ourselves from the increased rage and angst that our suspicions have caused, we retreat into circles that only echo our own opinion. This is the so-called 'filter bubble' effect: we read and share material that already accords with our beliefs, in an attempt to fit in with peers who share those beliefs.*
Reality no longer matters; bullshit has triumphed. Indeed, if you go on social media, you will regularly find a quote attributed to Winston Churchill or sometimes Mark Twain: 'A lie can get halfway around the world before the truth has a chance to get its pants on.' Fittingly, neither of them said it, but the sentiment is correct nonetheless.

Our world of fake news and post-truth content creation is not opposed to reality, it is heedless of it. This is from the journalist Evan Davis[25] on the definition of 'post-truth':

> Rather than simply referring to the time after a specified situation or event – as in post-war, post-match – the prefix in post-truth has a meaning more like 'belonging to a time in which the specified concept has become unimportant to irrelevant'. This nuance seems to have originated in the mid-twentieth century, in formations such as post-national (1945) and post-racial (1971).

Harry Frankfurt wrote a famous essay in 2005 called 'On Bullshit', and made the same point: 'It is just this lack of connection to a concern with truth – this indifference to how things really are – that I regard as of the essence of bullshit.' It is at the heart of the phenomenon of fake news: stories produced solely for economic benefit, which have no interest in covering reality. The journalist Craig Silverman analysed the top fifty fake news[26] stories on Facebook in

---

* Online culture, said cultural theorist Mark Fisher, comes from a 'priest's desire to excommunicate, an academic-pedant's desire to be the first to be seen to spot a mistake and a hipster's desire to be one of the in-crowd'. None of that seems healthy.

2016, and six came from a site called ABCNews.com.co with head-lines like: 'Obama signs executive order banning the pledge of allegiance in schools nationwide' or 'Pope Francis shocks the world, endorses Donald Trump for President, releases statement'. None even tried to be genuine.

Interestingly, the pure fake news phenomenon is mostly an American one. British people are less vulnerable to outright invented news, because we have already admitted hyper-partisan, click-bait nonsense into the mainstream. Websites like the Canary★ and Skwawkbox have also risen up, purely designed to feed a market for left-wing conspiracy theories, heedless of their factual basis. The latter ran a long piece, for example, supportive of the entirely invented notion that there was a D-Notice[27] in place to prevent the number of fatalities in Grenfell Tower being known. The former ran a piece about the *Sun* ignoring the Manchester terrorist attack of 2017 on its front page, despite knowing that the front page appeared before the attack had even happened. Both outlets have been featured on the BBC; both are now accepted into our journalistic culture; both are avowedly political, committed to the service of Corbynism. And the old media, in any event, is often guilty of the same approach to news: partisanship driven to excess; clicks at all cost; that ecosystem of crapness once more.

The future of real news

The business model for journalism is shattered unequivocally and beyond reasonable repair. When newspapers made serious money, there was no pressure for them to be well managed (so they were not); when their industry was disrupted, there were not enough talented people in positions of authority to respond with speed and intelligence. In 2005 the revenue of British newspapers (in print and

---

★ The entire business model of the *Canary* is based upon generating clicks what-ever the basis for the story. For each piece, 50 per cent of ad revenue after costs goes to the writer, 10 per cent to the article editor, 20 per cent to management, 20 per cent to the company. This, manifestly, incentivises misleading bullshit.

online) was £4.9 billion; in 2016, it was £2.2 billion. Its cost base has gone up in that time. Newspapers have really two means of obtaining income: advertising; and cover price or subscription. The former is now disappearing with no chance of recovery. Each month more is taken by Facebook and Google, which will always have access to far more of an audience than any given journalistic outlet. Indeed, Mail Online has 15 million users a day; Facebook has *1.2 billion*.[28]

People who wish to make mass-market online content are locked into the same overhead problem as old-fashioned print publishers: a website, like a printing press, remains a tangible, unshiftable burden on resources. A room full of journalists churning out articles in a fevered flurry is still too expensive an investment, given the dwindling economic returns. Facebook – under charming indy kid, multi-billionaire and crypto-presidential candidate Mark Zuckerberg – simply waits for others to spend the money producing the content, then nicks it and takes the revenue attendant upon it. Adrienne LaFrance, a journalist at the *Atlantic*, made this inarguable point: 'Zuckerberg doesn't want Facebook to kill journalism as we know it. He really doesn't. But that doesn't mean that he won't.'

Media companies' relationship with Facebook is best summarised by that metaphor of narcotics again: they are steadily being destroyed by their addiction. And Facebook can make or break the economy of the sites from which it takes its news. How easy it is for stories to be discovered and shared is entirely in the hands of its algorithm: what type of stories its technology is promoting. In 2018 Facebook announced that it would deprioritise news items in favour of personal posts from friends. This is because it wants to duck responsibility for stories that are racist or fake or representative of the wincing toxicity of political debate. It wants to emphasise its 'platform' rather than 'publisher' status (the latter being more liable for regulation); it is showing that the business it is killing is not that important to it.

And not only is journalism as we know it dying, the corpse is starting to reek a little. When publications fold, their recent online history will not be proud authority-defying scoops in the manner of Wilkes; it will be from-hunger for click fodder scraped out of the bottom of the internet. Our collective thirst for information is unconnected to any quality supply of it. We endlessly scroll down our phones in search of news that will never satisfy us: technology has turned us all into Tantalus; there will always now be a story of some sort to read. In 1720 the *Gloucester News* apologised for the 'present scarcity of news', and ran fewer stories. On 18 April 1930 the BBC's news announcer had a script for the 8.45 a.m. bulletin that said: 'There is no news.' So they played piano music instead. Today, there would always be a reaction to a tweet from a politician or celebrity, a response to a polemic on Brexit or immigration, a confected controversy about climate change. We will never return to quietness again.

In America more than 20,000 journalism jobs have been shed in the last ten years. In Britain the number of journalists working in local newspapers[29] has almost halved in the same period. There are now more PRs in London, massaging messages in stories, than there are journalists writing them. The bestselling newspaper in Britain, the *Sun*, and the bestselling broadsheet, the *Daily Telegraph*, both sell less than half the amount they did in 2000. Anybody now running a newspaper spends more time contemplating cost-cutting and mass redundancies than doing anything else. Rupert Murdoch is said to have once predicted that – in the end – only three newspapers in Britain would be left standing: the *Sun*, the *Times* and the *Daily Mail*. That prediction is looking optimistic.

Andrew Marr said back in 2004 that the solution to the problems in journalism 'is in the brains and the hands and the soul of the British journalist'. He was being charming; he was wrong. Some newspaper journalists (especially in tabloids, especially online) have hastened the decline of the industry, of course. Those who have experienced the sometimes shoddy coverage of their own lives will not mourn its passing. But print newspapers are now locked into a cycle of decline: if advertising has gone, they must increase the cover price, while still cutting costs. So newspapers lose pages, writers, sub-editors, picture editors, foreign coverage and so on, but are forced to become more expensive at the same time. This puts them in an unrecoverable spin, as readers slowly realise that not only are they getting less for more, but that they get most of it for free on

Facebook anyway. Meanwhile, online versions are subject to rising costs and shrinking returns, so mass journalism on any platform is swiftly becoming uneconomical.

So what will guarantee the future of journalism? Well, there is the 'football club' model: a very rich person, for either selfish or selfless reasons (and, let's be honest, it will be the former) under-writing the losses of the business for the love of it. Or media businesses will have to diversify, in order to support the dwindling returns from journalism with other income streams. News Corp, where I work, is not only in the newspaper business, it is in the real-estate website business, the digital video-sourcing business, the radio business, the programmatic advertising business and so on. Written journalism will have to be a labour of love, a cost to be borne elsewhere, a drag on performance, a subsidised entity. That is not an especially secure place to be.

The world of broadcast is in better shape, but is in turmoil. The BBC still has its guaranteed income, which – in light of the above – should be celebrated rather than denigrated. But it is losing the battle to attract young people. BBC 1 reaches less than 60 per cent of those under twenty-four, compared to more than 80 per cent of older people. The average age of the BBC's total audience has gone up from fifty-four to fifty-nine in the last few years. Sky may now be four times the size of the BBC – with revenue of £12 billion in 2016; and now may be joined to the vaster resources of a company like Disney – but it faces competition from Netflix and Amazon, the latter of which certainly has the purchasing power to eclipse it. That is not necessarily a bad thing, but it is unclear whether such big companies will want to bear the expense of broadcast news, for example. YouTube,[30] the video streaming site launched in 2005 and purchased by Google for $1.65 billion in 2006, is watched now by 80 per cent of people between eighteen and forty-nine. More than 1 billion hours of video on it are viewed daily, and more than 1.5 billion people come every month, with the average session an extraordinary forty minutes. It is not likely to become a forum for genuine news either. The behemoths of broadcasting are being shrunk by contrast before our eyes.

There is a small amount of hope in places. Amid the surrounding culture of cheapness and facility, a counterculture has grown for serious journalism that people are willing to pay for. Pay-walls[31] – charging subscriptions for content – do seem to work in that context. *The Times* is growing again; my paper, the *TLS*, is increasing sales; the *Spectator*, *Private Eye*, the *New Statesmen*, the *Financial Times* are all in growth. None of them makes vast profits. And that is the rub: there is a business of serious journalism, but it is a small (as these things go) and niche one.

You may feel unconcerned: a triumph of quality, you think, over crapness. But think of this also: there is currently no feasible business model to support widespread court reporting, or local council reporting, or unremarkable but vital stories about daily existence; the unflashy basics of journalism. If the digital marketplace becomes the arbiter of story selection, then there will be fewer stories about planning permission or hospital closures and more about Kim Kardashian's knees. That is an ineluctable fact of life. Mass-market journalism has always been sensationalist and tawdry, but it has also always used its scale to tell serious or important-but-uninteresting stories too. In 2018, as its viability and scale diminish, it becomes less able and inclined to do both. We all lose from that.

8

Identity

> In our country for all her greatness there is one thing she
> cannot do and that is translate a person wholly out of one class
> into another. Perfect translation from one language into another
> is impossible. Class is the British language
>
> William Golding (1911–93)

To be British is to carry, always, a sense of the past. We are a small island, a tiny stage on which many acts – tragic, comic, heroic, shocking, splendid – have been played out before us. Stand almost anywhere in this country, and you can contemplate the generations who have passed before you, with lives both of interminable difference but also an inevitable sameness to yours. That shudder of atavism: to experience it is to be British. This was perhaps best expressed by the historian G. M. Trevelyan in 1949:

> The poetry of history lies in the quasi miraculous fact that once, on this earth, once on this familiar spot of ground, walked other men and women, as actual as we are today, thinking their own thoughts, swayed by their own passions, but now all gone, one generation vanishing into another, gone as utterly as we ourselves shall shortly be gone, like ghosts at cockcrow.

This is beautifully put (the ghost of Shakespeare in the last phrase, too)*, and particularly relevant for our sense of Britain: our crowded

---

* See the beginning of *Hamlet*, when Horatio says this:

> I have heard,
> The cock, that is the trumpet to the morn,
> Doth with his lofty and shrill-sounding throat
> Awake the god of day; and, at his warning,

country is inevitably crammed with ghosts, with legacies of the past. George Orwell thought that our national identity is 'continuous, it stretches into the future and the past, there is something in it that persists, as in a living creature'. So to understand Britishness, we need to have a sense of where we have come from. We shall try to draw that creature in this final chapter.

But what, after all, is Britishness in the first place? A loaded question that both energises and perplexes politicians. Because, if we know what it is, we can teach it to our children, we can demand it of our immigrants, and we can retain coherence as a nation in an ever fractured, ever connected world. It may encompass – at its best – ideas of tolerance (to a point), humour,[1] humility, stoicism, fondness for animals,* and diversity. At its worst: chippiness, hierarchy, inequality, booziness[2] and nationalism. It is likely to be a contradiction, a collision, a bugger's muddle (which, in its parochial mundanity, is a phrase itself rather representative of Britain).

Indeed, we can simply *feel* things are instinctively British, whether it be – as Jeremy Paxman put it – our 'phenomenal capacity for quiet moaning', or our harping on about how hot or wet or how mild it is,[†] or our love of heroic failure. The anthropologist Kate Fox wrote a fine book called *Watching the English* (2004), in which she wrestled with the complexity of our identity:

> This is not just an island, but a relatively small, or at least overcrowded island, and it is not too hard to see how such conditions might produce

---

> Whether in sea or fire, in earth or air,
> The extravagant and erring spirit hies
> To his confine.

* More than half of British households have pets, and the RSPCA was established more than half a century before the NSPCC. I offer this one story in contradiction, though. In 1939 there was a great pet massacre in London: 25 per cent of all cats and dogs (around 500,000) were killed by people frightened of the consequences of the forthcoming war. Hardly an animal-loving nation's finest hour.

† As Samuel Johnson said: 'It is commonly observed, that when two Englishmen meet, their first talk is of the weather; they are in haste to tell each other, what each must already know, that it is hot or cold, bright or cloudy, windy or calm.'

an inhibited, privacy-obsessed, socially wary, uneasy passive-aggressive and sometimes obnoxiously anti-social people; a negative politeness culture, whose courtesy is primarily concerned with the avoidance of intrusion and suspicion; an acutely class-conscious culture, preoccupied with status and boundaries and demarcations; a society characterised by awkwardness, embarrassment, obliqueness, fear of intimacy/ emotion/fuss – veering between buttoned-up over-politeness and aggressive belligerence.

It brings a prideful tear to the eye, doesn't it? But even as we recognise some of these eternal verities, we must also be sensitive to what is shifting in this country. In fact, we will always most keenly feel not what has been ever present, but what is moving and changing: like the mix of races and ethnicities; like the evolving status of women and the recent erosion of gender binaries; like the divisions between young and old, rich and poor, London and the provinces. Each one of these shifts, each tectonic in their way, has remodelled the outlines of our identity.

In this chapter we will look at the British archipelago as a whole, not just England, but many of the ideas of Englishness that previous authors have described stand for the other home nations too. The dry wit of Yorkshire, say, is not foreign to that of Perthshire. It is striking, though, that we live in a country without one uniform name: Great Britain (England, Scotland and Wales) vs the United Kingdom (England, Scotland, Wales and Northern Island, but not the Channel Islands or the Isle of Man) vs the British Isles (everywhere, including the Republic of Ireland). Britain and the UK are different entities, although I blur them like everybody else.

How multicultural is Britain?

Just over 13 per cent of our resident population (around 8 million people) are not white British. That figure was around 4 per cent (1.9 million people) in 1951. The country's total population increased by 28 per cent in the intervening sixty-odd years; the ethnic minority population quadrupled. That means that migration has created almost half of the total population growth in those decades.* The process has accelerated markedly in recent times, and it is visible between the censuses of 2001 and 2011: half of all non-UK-born residents arrived in that period.[3] Indeed, it is a striking and indicative fact that the census did not even have a question on race at all until 1991. The three top countries of origin by 2011 were India, Poland and Pakistan,[4] all three of which have forged close migration links to the UK for more than fifty years. And as more people have come in, people of different backgrounds have intermingled (some more than others):† the fastest growing ethnic group in 2011 was mixed race. Integration and self-segregation are two dominant and opposing trends of the twenty-first century.

So when people look back upon Britain of the 1950s (and the process of Brexit has been dominated by this sort of nostalgia), they are indeed looking at a different country. They did do things differently there. The Second World War, as we shall see, marks the key pivot point in the history of Britain's changing ethnic identity. But before we reflect on that, we should consider too what came before.

A short history of British race relations

Black people have been living in Britain for almost 2,000 years, if not considerably longer.‡ Thanks to the Roman Empire, a vast

---

* In 2016 Professor David Coleman revealed, to much expostulation in the *Daily Mail*, and the headline 'RIP Britain', that at current rates 'the white British population would cease to be the majority in the UK by the late 2060s'.

† Forty-eight per cent of Caribbean men and 34 per cent of Caribbean women are in mixed-race relationships. According to *The Economist*, 'A child under 10 who has a Caribbean parent is more than twice as likely as not to have a white parent.' You might need to read that sentence twice, as I did, to work out the maths there. In contrast, fewer than one in ten Muslims of Pakistani or Bangladeshi origin are in inter-ethnic relationships; just 3 per cent of children in those communities live in mixed households.

‡ In 2018, DNA analysis by University College London and the Natural History Museum showed that very early Britons (embodied by the remains of what is known as Cheddar Man, who lived around 10,000 years ago) had 'dark to black skin'. The lightening of British skin took place over subsequent years, as paler tones were more receptive to absorbing the limited sunlight.

multicultural conglomerate of nations, people from Africa have visited and stayed in this country from soon after it was colonised. Precise numbers are unreliable, but it is clear that the Roman military contained people of colour (the unit of 'Aurelian Moors' in the third century, for example) who would have been stationed here.[5] What is striking is that, for most of the next two millennia, the black population did not grow by very much: a dodgy (and probably inflated) estimate during the Somersett case in 1772 (see Chapter 6) put the number at 15,000; by 1918, the number was only around 20,000.

As global trade began around the time of the first Elizabeth, so Britain's connections to other cultures grew. And as that trade slid into economic and military domination (the creation of an empire), so our relationships with other nations became fixed predominantly into one of subjugation. It is hard to consider racial politics without recognising this one basic fact: our past activities have led to our present ethnic composition. The cultural theorist Stuart Hall put it best: immigrants 'are here because you were there'.

The historical enslavement of black Africans for profit is, in the modern world, considered mainly as a moral stain on the United States. It is somehow distant from Britain (as the writer Reni Eddo-Lodge★ noted, 'most British people saw the money without the blood'). But half of all slaves, up to 3.5 million, were transported in the eighteenth century in British ships. The wealth of British ports like Liverpool and Bristol was established thanks to the triangular trade involving slaves; the British control over the West Indies was a brutal and merciless exploitation of people and resources in pursuit of profit for a tiny few.

Of course, it is with some pride that we can say that Britain was prominent in ending widespread slavery, although it took its time

---

★ Her book is called *Why I'm No Longer Talking to White People About Race* (2017), an idea that stemmed from a blog she wrote when she explained that the 'gulf of an emotional disconnect' between her and white people made communication too wearisome. It's a very good book. She does seem still to speak to white people about race, though, so it does have a misleading title. You would never catch me using an all-encompassing, over-ambitious title just to sell a book, thankfully.

about it.* Anthony Trollope wrote that it was 'the sin from which we have cleansed ourselves' as a nation. Certainly, the British public had set themselves formidably against the institution: between 1787 and 1792, 1.5 million people (from a population of 12 million) signed a petition against slavery. In 1807 the trade itself was banned, thanks to the work of men such as William Wilberforce, Granville Sharp[6] and Thomas Clarkson[7] (the latter two less well-known than they should be), but slavery within the empire was not abolished until 1833.† And, when it was, the only reparation was made not to the freed slaves, but to the impoverished slave-owners.‡

It is easy to imagine that those early Victorians who fought against injustice were well along the journey towards tolerance and equality. However, that does not seem to be entirely the case. A prevailing attitude of disdain towards what were perceived as inferior races sat alongside a grudging willingness to allow them their liberty.[8] Charles Dickens, a virulent opponent of slavery, once sent his friend William Macready a copy of Frederick Douglass's[9] autobiography, making sure first that he removed the 'hideous and abominable portrait of him'. Ethnographical 'science' of the period provided specious cover for the ideas of racial superiority, which were accepted and promulgated without pangs of conscience. Everywhere you look in Victorian Britain, you see respected figures with reprehensible racial opinions.[10] Perhaps the worst at this was Thomas Carlyle, who wrote an essay in 1849 called 'Occasional Discourse on the Negro Question', reprinted a few years later as 'Occasional Discourse on the Nigger Question'. In it, he referred to black people as 'two-legged cattle . . . with little labor except to the teeth, which surely, in those excellent horse-jaws of theirs, will not fail'.

---

* The first bill to abolish the slave trade was introduced in 1791, and was defeated by 163 votes to 88. It failed continually to pass through Parliament for several years. In 1796 the margin was just four votes; it is said that some pro-abolition MPs, whose presence would have swung the vote, had forgotten about it and gone to the opera instead.

† A headstone was created in Jamaica: 'Colonial Slavery, died 31 July 1838, Aged 276 Years'.

‡ The government spent £20 million on this (around £17 billion in today's money), which constituted around 40 per cent of its total spend that year. Giving almost half of all expenditure to slave-owners was something that could happen in the nineteenth century without much of an outcry.

His opinions were not widely repudiated, nor was he much condemned.[11]

People of colour were, even by the First World War, generally distant figures, second-class citizens whose existence was far removed from the white masses, part of a colossal empire that was lucky to have Britain presiding over it. The global conflict, when it came, was held to be a 'white man's war', in which West Indians and Africans were not permitted to fight white people, instead allowed only battle in Africa or manual labour behind the Western Front. The same did not hold true for Indians, whose vast volunteer armies were deployed throughout Europe, presumably on the basis that the wars of empire throughout the nineteenth century had acculturated the British authorities to the idea of white people fighting alongside those of light brown skin. They did not extend this understanding to those of darker brown hue, though.

The Second World War changed everything in Britain for ever, including its racial politics. By 1943, the black population of Britain had swelled to 150,000 thanks to the arrival of black GIs, who found in this country a place more tolerant than their homeland.* General Eisenhower noted that 'To most English people, including the village girls – even those of a perfectly fine character – the negro soldier is just another man.' Meanwhile, the scientific racism of the Victorians was reaching its evil apotheosis in the eugenics of the Nazis: establishment arguments about racial superiority could never be so overt again.

For all that, Britain of 1945 was still very white, indigenous, traditional. And broke. Immigration as we know it today was born of a colossal job shortage, caused by the need to rebuild an economy shattered by prolonged warfare. An influx of foreign bodies was necessary for the country to survive: Poles, Latvians, Estonians, Italians, Maltese, Pakistanis, Indians and West Indians. There was some sense of moral responsibility when it came to Eastern Europeans, homeless and desperate thanks to the ravages of Nazi Germany on one side and the Stalinist Soviet Union on the other.[12]

---

* We might observe that the British love of the underdog placed a nation in instinctive sympathy with an oppressed race, provided that such an attitude could also be set aside at the end of the war. One pub in Bristol had a sign saying 'Only blacks served here'. It didn't last beyond the days of the conflict.

But self-interest was the dominant motive: 'asylum seekers were turned into economic migrants', in the words of historian Clair Wills.[13] That elision – between those who need help and those who merely want it – remains a vexed one in our current refugee crisis. In any event, Britain preferred to receive those from Baltic nations[14] to Jews, white people to black people.

The resultant mix was a culture shock, which is perfectly recognisable today. This is the *Daily Mirror* from 1948, in an article headlined 'Let Them Be Displaced':

> In taking Displaced Persons wholesale we have had a bad deal. Too many are living or working in some dubious way. Some, no doubt are in the Black Market. They live on our rations – and live very well. They add to our discomfort and swell the crime wave. This cannot be tolerated. They must now be rounded up and sent back.

Criminal, entitled foreigners making use of public services (daring to 'live well'): an image that is seared, it would seem, into British national consciousness. It was created, though, not by the EU and its expansion in 2004, but can be seen already fixed into the palimpsest of our cultural memory fifty years before.

You will have probably heard of the 'Windrush generation' in the context of post-war immigration. It was the name of a ship, the *Empire Windrush*, which brought a few hundred West Indians to Britain in search of work, landing at Tilbury Docks on 22 June 1948. 'Welcome home,' sang the *Evening Standard*. But black people were not really welcome. Despite the acute job shortage, the government had tried to discourage migration from the Caribbean, and accepted it only with reluctance. In 1947 the Ministry of Labour had commissioned a report saying that black people would be 'unsuitable for outdoor work in winter owing to their susceptibility to colds'.

Throughout the 1950s the spectre of racism rose in Britain, as addled and frightened notions of what people of colour might do to the balance of the country took hold. By 1953, the Home Office was already examining 'the possibilities of preventing any further increase in coloured people seeking employment in the United Kingdom'. In

1955, the Transport and General Workers Union* of the West Midlands went on strike because a man of Indian origins had been employed as a bus conductor. 'Race riots' took place in 1958 in Notting Hill, which were in fact organised attacks on black people by white Teddy Boys,† observed with amused tolerance by many in the country. One police report noted that 'by far the greater majority of the people were assembled to watch what they called nigger baiting'. Racial discrimination was rife, as it became more acceptable to judge difference rather than sameness between people of alternate backgrounds. This is a quote, discovered by Clair Wills, from a manager in the 1960s:

> Whenever I have to put off staff, I sack the coloured ones first. I must. There would be a riot if I did anything else. The trouble is that whenever you dismiss West Indians they make such a fuss. They say you have done it because of colour prejudice, and that makes you feel like such a rotter.

Britain was – and is – a nation containing its fair share of rotters. Legislation at the time was working in two directions on the issue of race. In 1948 the British Nationality Act had explicitly allowed any subject of the British Empire to live and work in the UK, an astonishing act of openness towards up to a quarter of the global population (although it is unlikely that anybody thought that mass migration would follow). The government, though, was explicit about its anti-racist approach. This was the Home Secretary, James Chuter Ede: 'Some people feel it would be a bad thing to give the coloured races of the Empire the idea that, in some way or other, they are equals of the people of this country. The government do not subscribe to that view.'

By 1962, however, a different government had pushed through the Commonwealth Immigration Act, which restricted people without work vouchers from entry into the country. The Labour opposition leader Hugh Gaitskell called it 'cruel and brutal anti-colour legislation', which Labour itself then promptly reinforced and extended in 1968 when it was in power. The die had been cast: as

---

* Incidentally, the racism and protectionism of unions is a deep stain on their history, and one of which they might profitably be reminded on occasion.
† Cute name for dandyish men of the 1950s who aped the fashions of the Edwardian period (hence 'Teddy'); but their conduct often veered towards thuggishness.

Reni Eddo-Lodge points out, in 1948 people were called 'citizens', in 1962 they were 'immigrants'; an epochal shift. Although there was still a demand for unskilled jobs in factories, which people from India or Pakistan, say, were eager to fill, the government ceded to the demands of politics rather than economics. Without wishing to overstate the parallel, it is precisely the mentality that still governs much of our own immigration debate.

One spokesman for the disaffected Briton was Enoch Powell, whom we have met earlier as Health Secretary. He was angered by the 1965 Race Relations Act (updated in 1968; the first attempts by the government to legislate for equality), and argued that British people should have 'the right to discriminate'. He also spoke in that wistful voice of nostalgia that we still hear in anti-immigrant rhetoric:

> Our generation is one which comes home again from years of distant wandering. We discover affinities with earlier generations of English who felt no country but this to be our own . . . back through the brash adventurous days of the first Elizabeth and the hard materialism of the Tudors and there at last we find them.

That fear, that nagging itch, that once Britain was coherent and homogenous, and now is being enfeebled by the influx of foreign elements, remains all too familiar. Powell, of course, went further: his infamous Rivers of Blood speech★ made him politically distasteful, but popularly successful. 'In this country,' he intoned, 'in fifteen or twenty years' time, the black man will have the whip hand over the white man.' This astonishing inversion of the slavery metaphor (and the concomitant negligence of the historical record it must reveal) remains startling in its clumsy hatefulness. But Powell was saying what many were thinking. In 1964 a Tory candidate, Peter Griffiths,

★ This was made in April 1968, against Commonwealth immigration and the recent Race Relations Act: 'As I look ahead, I am filled with foreboding. Like the Roman, I seem to see the River Tiber foaming with much blood.' Powell was dangerous not only because his speech was so apt to incite anger and violence, but because it was so popular. Seventy-four per cent of people, according to one contemporaneous poll, agreed with him. Today, he would have quit the Tories, joined UKIP, and made a living as a talk radio host. In 1991 Margaret Thatcher conceded that he had 'made a valid argument, if in sometimes regrettable terms'. The 'Tiber' quote comes from Virgil's *Aeneid*, by the way.

was elected to the Midlands constituency of Smethwick with the slogan 'If you want a nigger for a neighbour, vote Labour'. Malcolm X, the American dissident with a fair knowledge of discrimination, visited Smethwick, saying: 'I have heard that the blacks are being treated in the same way as the Negroes were treated in Alabama – like Hitler treated the Jews.'

This was an understandable over-statement. Griffiths was called a 'parliamentary leper' by Harold Wilson and soon booted out of office. Laws enforcing racial equality were reinforced over the next thirty years. The first black MPs entered Parliament in 1987, the pioneers being Diane Abbott, Paul Boateng and Bernie Grant. Things slowly, wearyingly, got better.* But the question remains: how fair, really, is Britain today?

British racial (in)equality

In 1976 a man called Robert Relf put up a sign on his house saying 'For sale to an English family only' and refused to take it down; he was imprisoned on the grounds of contempt of court for breaching the Race Relations Act. In 2017 a property tycoon called Fergus Wilson was censured for banning non-white tenants because of the 'cost of removing the smell of curry at the end of their tenancy'. He could not see what the fuss was about. While there can be no doubt that Britain is a less racist place than it was thirty years ago, it is still a racist place.

There are statistics that begin to help paint a picture of it: that black people are twice as likely to be charged with drugs possession; that 30 per cent of British black men are on the DNA database, compared to 10 per cent of white men;† that black people are

---

* In 2017 there were fifty-two non-white MPs in Parliament: 8 per cent of the total. Still not representative of the 13 per cent of ethnic citizens.
† A counter-argument, of course, is that this reflects a higher proportion of criminal acts committed by black people. But – and I think this is key – unless we wish happily to argue that black people somehow have a greater genetic propensity towards crime, we still must conclude that the systemic treatment of black people is likely to place them in situations (higher risk of poverty, primarily) where crime is more likely.

proportionally more likely to be sectioned (and regarded as dangerous), but less likely to obtain a diagnosis of dementia (and receive care). Black people are far more likely to be unemployed, especially young, black men. On average, black graduates earn 23 per cent less than their white peers and are less likely to rise to the top of their professions. Indeed, when we consider the power-brokers of British society, we confront an obvious colour bar. The *Guardian* in 2017 drew up a list of 1,000 of the UK's top political, financial, judicial, cultural and security figures and just thirty-six were from ethnic backgrounds. Only seven of those were women (we'll get to that in a bit).

Things are getting better, of course: ethnic representation in the Civil Service has doubled to nearly 12 per cent in the last decade (nearly directly proportionate to the ethnic population); there is widespread, greater representation in most public areas of life. But not yet fair representation. It begs a reasonable question: are we slowly getting it right (and so do not need to worry any more)? Yes (but no).

In 2017 a mixed-race, transgender model called Munroe Bergdorf was fired from L'Oréal for saying this: 'Honestly I don't have energy to talk about the racial violence of white people any more. Yes ALL white people. Most of ya'll don't even realise or refuse to acknowledge that your existence, privilege and success as a race is built on the backs, blood and death of people of colour. Your entire existence is drenched in racism.'

It seems to me that she was guilty of overstatement (and unforgivably using the word 'ya'll'), but makes a legitimate point about structural racism. There is less open discrimination now, but equality of opportunity has not magically – as we see above – occurred as a result. Perhaps it is too early to tell: people in senior positions in the 2010s were graduating in the 1970s and 1980s, a time of not only fewer immigrants, but also more open discrimination. An optimist might well argue that time is the undefeatable harbinger of progress, a pessimist that certain underlying inequalities are too stubborn to shift. The latter argument is that of many left-leaning theorists, following the thinking of people like Marx (who considered that bloody revolt was the only solution) and the French intellectual Michel Foucault. In their terms, society (inevitably in a white European country) has been constructed by, and around, its most powerful figures: white men. Any changes that are made would have to address the submerged structure, not simply the outward manifestations.

Of course, and this needs stating, the power structure does not simply favour all white men, it just prioritises some of them. Attention should always be paid to white people who under-perform, who are left behind. The mistake in our polarised world is to consider race (or gender, or any category) as a zero-sum equation: if ethnic people are discriminated against, all white people must be privileged; if some white people are disadvantaged, there is no discrimination against ethnic people. As we have seen, it is a fact that the worst-performing group in British schools is white, impoverished boys. This is from a 2014 Parliamentary Committee: 'Poor white British children now come out of our schools with worse qualifications than equally poor children in any other major ethnic group . . . We don't know how much of the under-performance is due to poor attitudes to school, a lack of work ethic or weak parenting.'

An argument can be made that immigrants to this country (of whatever generation) are self-selecting self-improvers. Their existence in this country is based, at some level, upon a willingness to seek a better life. Such families are – and this feels uncontentious – less likely to accept stasis or decline in their prospects. When I did an LBC show on the subject, I spoke to many people from immigrant families who were told by their parents that they needed to fight for every chance, because those chances would be restricted. Poor white children may be 'out-parented' by their ethnic counterparts.

Gender, inevitably, is another area where our polarising discourse creates false oppositions: if the country is patriarchal, then men must always benefit. That is not true. There are – as we see above – challenges facing boys and men in Britain. Suicide is something of a gendered phenomenon, for example. It is the leading cause of death for British men under fifty years of age; over a quarter of men who die between the ages of twenty and thirty-four take their own lives.[15] The reasons for this are not clear: a tendency for men to suppress emotions rather than talking about them; the likelihood of men taking bolder steps to end their life (so suicide attempts are more successful); an emerging sense of confusion about traditional masculine roles in society. Paul Beresford MP once said this, and it still slightly boggles my mind: 'Men tend to find themselves at the very top or the very bottom of the ladder . . . I think of the male suicide rate every time I hold the door open for a lady.'

So if you see a perplexed and sorrowful old man in Parliament ruefully clutching a door, now you know why. He is right, of course, to consider the problem of male suicide; he is right to consider the notion of men who do not benefit from the patriarchal skew of society. But we all must recognise that such a skew persists.

British gender (in)equality

Virginia Woolf[6] invented, in *A Room of One's Own*, the conceit of Shakespeare's sister,* Judith, an imaginary figure whom she uses as a symbol of the frustrated potential of women. Judith, inheriting the same genius as William, could never have prospered, could never have been heard. Woolf imagines her end: 'She found herself with child by that gentleman and so – who shall measure the heat and violence of the poet's heart when caught and tangled in a woman's body? – killed herself one winter's night and lies buried at some cross-roads where the omnibuses now stop outside the Elephant and Castle.'

Silent and silenced: a fitting enough monument to female oppression over the course of the country's history. Much of the British feminist struggle over that time is perhaps now familiar. We might start with Mary Wollstonecraft's *Vindication of the Rights of Woman* in 1792, which clearly articulated the structural disadvantages faced by women: 'taught from their infancy that beauty is a woman's sceptre, the mind shapes itself to the body and roaming around its gilt cage, only seeks to adore its prison'. This was not just an eighteenth-century concept, of course: the perceived inferiority of women was fixed when the story of Eve beguiling poor Adam was first set down; women as the second sex, the insidious and pretty sex, the subordinate sex.

---

* This idea led to a song of the same name by the Smiths in 1985, which in turn inspired the naming of the band Shakespear's Sister (yes, misspelled), who had a number one hit in 1992 with the song 'Stay'. Anybody under the age of thirty should probably have skipped this footnote, to be honest.

During the nineteenth century notions of equality, of politicisation, of militancy became more urgently widespread in Britain, and the question of fair representation for women was consequently higher on the agenda. In 1870 only a third of men could vote; in 1884 it was closer to 70 per cent: the idea of universal suffrage was finding its time. The philosopher John Stuart Mill called the subjection of women 'one of the chief hindrances to human improvement' in a century where progress was essentially a new religion. Indeed, it was the union of female matchmakers, and their protests about appalling treatment, that launched the modern union movement we know today.*

Of course, there were naysayers, some of them surprisingly women. Florence Nightingale did much to advance the cause for female competence in the workplace, but was no campaigner for female advancement: 'I am brutally indifferent,' she said, 'to the wrongs or rights of my sex.' George Eliot, who will live through posterity as one of its most profound female voices, thought that 'woman does not yet deserve a better lot than man gives her'. Her fellow novelist Elizabeth Gaskell also was no friend of the sisterhood: 'I would not trust a mouse to a woman's judgement if a man's judgement was to be had. Women have no judgement.' It would be wrong, too, to neglect the grating voice of that shit of the nineteenth century, our friend Thomas Carlyle: 'The true destiny of a woman . . . is to wed a man she can love and esteem and to lead noiselessly, under his protection, with all the wisdom, grace, and heroism that is in her, the life presented in consequence.'

This opinion, alas, is not entirely unknown today. As the twentieth century arrived, though, so the movement for the female vote

---

* This is a fascinating story, by the way. In 1882 Bryant & May, a company of matchmakers (now there is an industry disrupted by technology, by the way), unveiled a statue to Prime Minister William Gladstone. The cost of the statue had been taken from the (risibly low) wages of the matchwomen who worked in the factory, who were also compelled to take an unpaid half day off to watch the unveiling. Unsurprisingly, they were unhappy, throwing bricks at the statue and cutting their fingers to stain it red, crying 'our blood paid for this'. In later years, these same women went on an all-out strike, which brought the business to the table to improve conditions. Charmingly, if you see the Gladstone statue now, which stands in Bow Churchyard in London's East End, it still has red paint on its hands, touched up by unseen figures as time goes by, guardians of the matchwomen's flame.

became inexorable.[17] Emmeline Pankhurst led the Women's Social
and Political Union, with a passion and drive that led some to liken
her later to Lenin and Hitler. Protests became violent, imprisonable
and unignorable:[18] Emily Davison was killed running under the
King's horse in the Derby of 1913; a woman called Mary Richardson
slashed the *Rokeby Venus* by Velázquez in 1914.[19] War, as so often in
our story of Britain, was the true catalyst for change. In 1918 women
over thirty got the vote; in 1928 women had the same voting rights
as men. The first female MPs (who succeeded to their husband's
seats, naturally) in Parliament came along after 1919: Lady Astor and
Margaret Wintringham.* In 2017 there were 208 female MPs in
Parliament, though this is just 32 per cent of the total. In a comparison of parliaments around the world, Britain comes thirty-ninth.†
Labour's policy of having all-women shortlists has meant that it has
had between two and three times the number of female MPs as the
Tories over the last twenty years – though it still hasn't had a female
leader, and has shown notably little appetite to select one.

So gender equality has triumphed? Well, up to a point, Lady
Copper. Women now retain the same formal legal rights as men;
and it is illegal to pay them differently. And yet women earn around
80p for every pound earned by men. Why is that? Women are more
likely to do part-time work, for a start, because society still recog-
nises‡ them as carers and family managers, home cooks and cleaners,
which means they are more likely to juggle paid with unpaid roles.
Women are more likely to be in lower-skilled jobs, probably for the
same reason. Women do not progress to senior positions as readily:
there are more men called John or David running Britain's major
companies than there are women. Childbirth and childcare are
critical factors here: the gender pay gap for full-time workers under

---

* Technically the first woman elected as an MP, in 1918, was Constance Markievicz,
who represented Sinn Fein, and so refused to take a seat in the House of Commons.
† The leader: Rwanda with over 60 per cent women. It doesn't make it a beacon
of equality, of course.
‡ Some believe, of course, that – from a biological and evolutionary perspective
– men and women are fundamentally so different that, inevitably, their societal
roles have differed. This argument can only work in a pre-technological society,
though, where division of labour is based on things like muscle strength.

forty is just 2.3 per cent; including both part- and full-time jobs, women actually get paid more than men when they are younger. But the intrusion of children then puts a brake on senior job prospects. A female journalist friend of mine talked to me once of 'the fraud peddled to women (who are brought up being told in school they should be ambitious and work hard and can achieve whatever they want in life) which they only realise is untrue when they come to have children'. She went on: 'We're encouraged to aspire to a life our society is not able to support because it ultimately relies on us to bring up the kids.'

And employment is not the only metric of societal fairness. Some 85,000 women are raped in England and Wales every year (as we have seen, many offences go unprosecuted), and one in five women will have experienced sexual violence in their adult lifetime. These figures are shocking enough, but they relate only to criminal activity. The number of women who are subject to unwanted sexual advances that fall short of assault is probably unmeasurable to a precise extent. A survey in 2016 put the figure at more than 50 per cent for women in the workplace suffering unwarranted behaviour based on their sex; another in 2017 said that up to two-thirds of young women had been subject to sexual harassment while drinking.

Both feel sadly plausible. I ran some phone-ins on LBC about sexual harassment, and was amazed both at the scale of responses and the grimly stoical tone of the callers.[20] Any woman reading this is, of course, unlikely to be surprised at all: as a man I think about the problem all too infrequently and so have the luxury of being astonished; women live it for their entire lives. During the show, my wife texted to say that she had had somebody follow her just that week in a car, hanging out of the window, trying to get her attention, before calling her a 'fucking bitch' and departing. She hadn't mentioned it to me before, because it was so unexceptional. There was the woman who talked about running across a central London bridge at six o'clock in the evening, physically stopped by a man trying to touch her bottom. There were tales of groping and leering and propositioning. It turned my stomach.

At least, I suppose, we were talking about things that so often go unmentioned. Indeed, the twenty-first century in Britain may come to be classed as the gendered century, such is our collective pre-occupation with issues relating to sex and identity. Stories around transgender people, their struggles and their desires, are now commonplace, and regarded as somehow representative of an age that is losing a sense of eternal verities. The traditional position is that men and women should be seen as different, are binary opposites; and that it is simply faddishness to suggest otherwise.

This to me is foolish. Of course, the vast majority of people are born into a certain sex and think no more about it. For a small minority, though, this is simply not the case. One way to think about it is to distinguish between sex (based on your reproductive organs) and gender (what your inner feeling, whatever that is, describes you to be). For most people, the two are the same; the condition of gender dysphoria exists when the two differ. Figures are disputed about its prevalence, but it seems that around 1 per cent of the population would consider itself to be 'gender nonconforming'. So it is not a big deal, societally speaking.

But the very existence of transgender people seems to be unsettling, especially to the religious, elderly and the poorly educated.* While the vast majority (82 per cent), according to the British Social Attitudes Survey of 2016, describe themselves as 'not prejudiced at all' in this area, less than half of respondents feel that trans people should be definitely employed as police officers or primary school teachers (43 per cent and 41 per cent respectively). The lesson, as ever, is that we are always more prejudiced than we think.

Tabloid papers went through a period (largely coming to an end) of an especially prurient, slightly sniggery obsession about the subject. When I was at the *Sun*, I arranged a meeting between sub-editors and a group called All About Trans. It was fascinating: a room of nervous, largely male journalists together with men and women about whom they had published stories without much thought. One woman there had been a helicopter pilot with Prince William before

---

* The British Social Attitudes Survey shows clearly that people without formal educational qualifications are more likely to be socially conservative. Religious influence is also clear: 59 per cent of atheists think transgender prejudice is always wrong; 46 per cent of religious people.

transitioning. I introduced her to the person who had, years before, written a story headlined something like 'Will's pal loses his chopper'. She was patient and understanding; he recognised the trauma of her life and the unhelpful impact of the headline. Collective attitudes shifted at the paper as a result. If you spend time with any or many trans folk, you soon see the psychic scars of their existence: altering their bodies and outward lives is not faddish or somehow glib, but based on a deep-seated search for self.

Of course, concerns can remain about children and gender, and what seems to be a brand-new pathologisation of ordinary confusions about growing up, the turning of life's natural ambiguities into a life-changing condition. It is okay to discuss this, even to disagree about it. As it stands, while gender dysphoria is real, there is no accepted neurological basis for its existence; it happens but we do not entirely know why.

In 1989 when the Gender Identity Development Service (GIDS) opened at the Tavistock Clinic in London, it received two referrals in the first year. In 2016, 1,400 under-eighteens were referred, nearly 300 of whom were under twelve. This is the sole place to which transgender children are referred, so these amount to national statistics. My friend, the journalist Jenny Kleeman, has also uncovered a startling figure: four times as many teens assigned female at birth use the Tavistock compared to those assigned male. This is fascinating, if you pause to consider it: the ratio of female–male trans children outnumbers male–female by four to one. Here is a legitimate question: why is it not an even split? Other questions follow. Is it because female puberty in British society is so fraught with challenge and unhappiness that transitioning becomes more attractive? Does this imply a greater psychological basis for some people's dysphoria than many would wish to concede? It is an issue worth examining.

Children who may be considered to have issues around their gender are not placed on irrevocable reassignment programmes: cross-sex hormone treatment is not given until sixteen;[21] and surgery is not allowed until eighteen (and is a comparative rarity then). But support and treatment are now routinely offered.

Is that bad or dangerous? Surely not. Even if the prevalence of dysphoria is less than 1 per cent, it is sufficiently recognisable now to warrant proper processes. And the consequences of intolerance are appalling: almost half of trans teens attempt suicide at some point; 80 per cent have self-harmed. Compassion and understanding are vital.

Political correctness gone . . .

Attendant on this issue, though, are concerns about a gradual loosening of gender boundaries everywhere, in a way that falls short of actual gender transitioning. In 2017 the superstore John Lewis caused minor outrage by saying all clothing (including dresses) would be for both 'boys and girls'. A campaign group exists in this area called Let Clothes Be Clothes,[22] whose heart may be in the right place, but whose prose leaves a little to be desired: 'Science,' notes its website, 'tells us there is very little difference between girls and boys, and you would need to survey a huge amount of people in order to find that difference.' Take a bow, science!

The idea, surely uncontroversial, is that children should not be overly conditioned by their gender in terms of what they wear or how they play. The brand Mothercare was rightly criticised for having a range of beglittered clothes for girls with slogans like 'sparkle', and more sober garments with a science theme for boys with slogans like 'genius'. We can persist in the notion that there are differences between boys and girls, that most people are comfortable in their sex, while still allowing that it is never healthy for certain roles to be more readily assigned to one sex over another. The world will not end if girls get to play with swords, or boys with dolls.

Here, I fear, we are entering into the realm of disputes around 'political correctness', even 'political correctness gone mad', which I have been trying to postpone. It is, however, a very British concept, encompassing as it does the triumvirate of moaning, self-consciousness and a suspicion that forces somewhere might be trying to sneak something past us. We might start more neutrally: the comedian Stewart Lee has called political correctness 'an often clumsy negotiation towards a formally inclusive language' that was 'better than we had before', which seems sensible. It can, though, create a cultural backlash. The journalist Archie Bland in the summer of 2017 wrote a long *Guardian* piece on the rise of the new laddish world of 'banter', which astutely described a cultural response at work: 'Political correctness asserts that a racist joke is primarily racist, whereas banter asserts that a racist joke is primarily a joke.'

The former seems to me to be a healthier judgement. It is, largely, a good thing that we try to aim our discourse away from belittling or mocking people on account of their backgrounds. Before political correctness, we allowed in our mainstream culture: minstrel shows and black willy jokes, 'Paki' and 'gayboy' as insults, bottom pinching, 'she was asking for it', 'slitty eyes', and so on. I think of political correctness as a tax we pay for reducing prejudice; and it can be indeed a hefty price when it is joylessly enforced, and limits free expression, and precludes honest debate. But worth paying for all that.

We are in danger of focusing on comparatively trivial manifestations, perhaps. Larger claims about political correctness are now often made, which we should also explore. For example, was it to blame for a national refusal to recognise the rise in sexual crime by Muslim gangs?

Integration, integration, integration

Earlier in this chapter, we considered the overall scale of immigration. Despite endless promises by successive Tory governments (and especially their Home Secretary, turned robotic Prime Minister, Theresa May), net migration has not by 2018 come down to the 'tens of thousands' but has fluctuated between 200,000 and 300,000, dipping further only since the EU referendum.

As we have seen, the economic impact of such people flow is nothing especial to worry about on a broad level. Indeed, much of our daily life is entirely buttressed by immigrant labour. If you go into an office, or walk the streets, either very early or very late, you will see the tired faces of immigrants, many with dark skins, performing menial tasks for your benefit. We should be grateful, humbled, perhaps even shamed by the phenomenon of the night workers, most of whom were not born in this country. And – despite

Brexit – there is evidence that more Britons recognise the economic benefits of immigration than ever before: according to the British Social Attitudes Survey, in 2002 the majority felt that immigration was damaging our economy, in 2014 there had been a 20-point swing and the majority inclined the other way. This suggests, contrary to received wisdom, that we are now *more* optimistic about migrants than before. There is, however, still a huge split: Britain is the most divided country in Europe on this question between the opinions of the educated young and the under-educated old.★

Economics is one thing, politics is quite another. UK citizens are less positive about the cultural impact of immigration than almost any country in Europe. And we get a sense of the worries when we look at the difference in attitudes between 2002 and 2014: more people now feel the ability to speak English (87 per cent, up from 77 per cent), a commitment to the British 'way of life' (84 per cent, up from 78 per cent) and possessing needed skills (81 per cent, up from 71 per cent) are important criteria for selecting migrants. The concern here, and it is a valid one, is that some immigrants to this country are not fitting in, or not being allowed to fit in.

Communities of migrants have always gathered together in any country, but the lack of integration does appear to be worse in the case of people from South Asia (and often Muslims from Pakistan, India and Bangladesh; two of the three most common countries of origin when it comes to migration to Britain). In January 2015 more than 500 schools across 43 local authorities had 50 per cent or more pupils from Pakistan or Bangladesh. In some wards of Blackburn, Birmingham, Burnley and Bradford, 70–85 per cent of the population are Muslim. Muslim people from these countries live together in higher residential concentrations than people from other religions, often on lower than average incomes.

A brief digression on the numbers in minority religions, as they often swell in the popular imagination. According to census data from 2011, around 5 per cent of the population in Britain is Muslim

---

★ So the percentage of young graduates who are positive about immigration is 46 per cent higher than that of school leavers from an earlier generation. In Germany the difference is 30 per cent; in Ireland it is 26 per cent.

(about 2.7 million; up nearly 70 per cent since the last census of 2001), which is the most common non-Christian religion in Britain. Here are the others: Sikh (400,000 people; up by 100,000); Jewish (300,000; down from a 400,000 high in the 1950s); Hindu (817,000; up almost 50 per cent); and Buddhist (248,000; up by almost a third). So, we are unquestionably seeing an increase in people with values – insofar as religion prescribes them – taken from a different frame-work to traditional British ones.

How much of a problem is this? Well, the ghettoisation of people marked by skin colour or religious beliefs will always be a cause of social unrest and concern. And the ideology of Islam – especially in its Saudi-inspired Wahhabist interpretation – unquestionably carries with it the potential for barbarism: for misogyny and male oppression, for violent submission, for intolerance. But intolerance works both ways; and so does integration. It is worth considering how welcoming our indigenous communities have been, and are being, to people from the subcontinent. I suspect the answer is less even than in previous generations.* In 2017 one in five Muslims had never entered a non-Muslim home. How many have been invited is also a question worth pondering.

I went to school in Leicestershire, one of the most diverse areas in Britain. I grew up friends with people whose families came from India, Pakistan and Bangladesh, boys called Shafiq, Ajay, Mohammed. Their culture was vibrantly different in some ways, but fiercely familiar in others: we all played football and cricket, we all watched violent action films. I honestly did not know anything about my friends' religion, any more than they did mine. Of course, the terrorist attack of 9/11 (which took place after I had left school) changed everything. The connotations of the word 'Muslim' changed the instant the rubble and bodies started to fall. A person was not a Bangladeshi, but a Muslim. Race relations altered for ever.

So we now live in a country where Muslim communities are

* White British and Irish ethnic groups are least likely to have ethnically mixed networks; Pakistani and Bangladeshi people are least likely to have friends from outside their neighbourhood. The two are connected.

more isolated, more suspected than ever before. To that crucible of angst we now add the sexual abuse scandals that involve predominantly Muslim men. When it was finally discovered that, between 1997 and 2013, at least 1,400 children of the northern town of Rotherham, most of them white girls, had been sexually abused* mostly by British-Pakistanis (and this had been condoned or covered up for a decade), there was legitimate outcry.[23] One reasonable conclusion was that the ethnicity of the perpetrators had affected the willingness of the police and council to investigate the abuse. The town's former MP Denis MacShane said that the authority was 'not wanting to rock the multicultural boat'. Dame Louise Casey, a senior welfare specialist, was tasked with inspecting the council, and found that 'staff perceived that there was only a small step between mentioning the ethnicity of perpetrators and being labelled a racist'.

So misguided racial politics played a role, and cultural attitudes towards white girls played a role. But we should not discount other factors here. First, many of the perpetrators were in that night-time economy, primarily minicab drivers, giving them opportunity to commit offences like this; more importantly, they were all men (and the council had a problem with its sexual politics too).[24] Sexual abuse is, predominantly, a male problem. And it is a problem that crosses race and religion. It would be wrong, and glib, to say that crimes such as these are solely connected to race or religion. It would be wrong also, though, to fear to say that race and religion played a part here. Just because racists want to talk up problems in some Muslim communities, doesn't mean that it is racist to note that they exist.

Louise Casey went on in December 2016 to examine problems of integration in the whole country, and did conclude that misplaced concerns about racism had affected the governance of the nation: 'Too many public institutions, national and local, state and non-state, have gone so far to accommodate diversity and freedom of expression that they have ignored or even condoned regressive, divisive

---

* The abuse was of an appalling sort: gang rape, forcing children to watch rape, dousing them with petrol before threatening to immolate them.

and harmful cultural and religious practices, for fear of being branded racist or Islamophobic.'

We are seeing two sides of the problem of segregation: a separation of cultures, exacerbated by the fear of examining the consequences of that separation. And the victims here are inevitably not just indigenous people. Hate crime (the very definition of violence spawned by suspicion and ignorance) rose by almost 20 per cent between 2015 and 2016: there were more than 60,000 reported attacks (and the unreported number is likely to be four times as many).

Against this background, it is common to argue that multiculturalism – the act of various groups living together in harmony, without losing their individual identity – has not lived up to its promises. Angela Merkel said it in 2010: 'The multicultural concept is a failure, an absolute failure.' David Cameron followed suit a few months later: 'State multiculturalism has failed . . . We have failed to provide a vision of society to which they feel they want to belong. We have even tolerated these segregated communities behaving in ways that run counter to our values.'

This has now, of course, become orthodoxy, but without any orthodox solution, other than a reduction in immigration. But our immigration laws already allow us to control movement from the Asian subcontinent, and have done for decades. They have not changed attitudes. One answer is to suggest that concepts of British values need to be enforced on migrants. But integration cannot happen at the point of compulsion: 'enforced tolerance' is an oxymoron. Perhaps language skills should be a condition of residency; perhaps government could intervene to ensure that housing was allocated to people of differing ethnicity. We can acknowledge we live in dangerous, divisive times; we may not yet have all the solutions to healing the division.

Two nations

It would be obtuse to argue, though, that ethnic or gender tension is the central divide in British society. It is not, and never will be.

They are both an expression of the larger schism:* between the haves and have-nots, the rich and the poor. There are others (which we will now get to): class, age, geography. But everything boils down to economics and opportunity. This line from Disraeli's novel *Sybil* remains our set text, alas: 'Two nations between whom there is no intercourse and no sympathy; who are as ignorant of each other's habits, thoughts, and feelings, as if they were dwellers in different zones, or inhabitants of different planets. The rich and the poor.'

When we consider British identity, we must consider British inequality. As we saw in the economics chapter, this is visible not only in income, but in assets: the richest 10 per cent of households hold 45 per cent of the wealth; the poorest 50 per cent, by contrast, own merely 8.7 per cent. That's the economics. When we look at opportunity, we see that success breeds success: 74 per cent of judges went to private school, for example, as did 61 per cent of doctors (even though the nation itself sent just 7 per cent of children to such schools). There is also something that might be called the 'class salary gap': people from more affluent backgrounds earn up to 25 per cent more than their peers doing the same jobs. That's the opportunity bit.

But isn't class a relic of the past?

It is trite, but incorrect, to say that the upper classes no longer wield power in Britain. About a third of Britain's total land is owned by aristocratic families. And posh people have always been in charge: according to the journalist Michael Crick, 22 per cent of all ministers in Britain between 1900 and 1979 went to Eton. As a nation, we instinctively crook the knee before privilege. Witness the popularity of Boris Johnson and Jacob Rees-Mogg.

Evelyn Waugh once said that 'there are subjects too intimate to print. Surely class is one?' The more likely feeling today (especially

* Reni Eddo-Lodge puts it brilliantly when she says: 'Feminism will have won when we have ended poverty.'

if you are not an arriviste literary grumbler like Waugh) is that class is an irrelevant subject: more than two-thirds of people say that they do not belong to one. But that is not the case.

Class-consciousness rose, really, in the nineteenth century, with the growth of the industrial working population. Suddenly, the workers had a visible mass, a collective scale, and could be regarded as a group. At the same time, improvements in education led to the rise of a managerial class of men (naturally), who lacked wealth or family background, but were placed in charge of running things. From 1832 onwards, voting rights became more contested, and the privilege of wealth in connection to democracy was gradually removed. All these steps heightened an awareness of place in the social structure; and tension grew between those who were willing to accept it and those who wished to change it.*

From the beginning, class has been associated with a sense of morality. Charles Booth, a nineteenth-century shipping magnate, had a map constructed of London that showed areas from the 'wealthy' to the 'lowest class. Vicious, semi-criminal'.[25] Virginia Woolf, a perfect example of a snob, showed how you can elide poverty with a lack of hygiene, physical and moral:

> The London poor, half drunk and very sentimental or completely stolid with their hideous voices and clothes and bad teeth, make one doubt whether any decent life will ever be possible, or whether it matters if we're at war or at peace. But I suppose the poor wretches have not much notion of how to express their feelings.

What could, after all, be more British than such snobbery? In 1955 Nancy Mitford wrote an essay (which actually sparked Waugh's remark about class quoted above) that tried to define the difference

---

* 'All Things Bright and Beautiful', a Victorian hymn you may have sung at school, has this stanza:

> The rich man in his castle,
> The poor man at his gate,
> God made them high and lowly,
> And ordered their estate.

Hi, children: God wanted you to be hungry, for inexplicable reasons! A strange concept to allow the young to swallow.

between 'U' and 'non-U', upper and non-upper. She found a series of linguistic signs that surprisingly remain indicators today:

> Toilet vs lavatory*
> Serviette vs napkin
> Settee vs sofa
> Lounge vs living room
> Tea vs supper
> Sweet vs pudding

I come from what would be held to be a 'working-class' family, and grew up using the first word in all those pairings. That idiom marks me out as someone from a certain background and location. If you use the second word, you are definably privileged by birth. And yet I was inculcated with the notion that, whatever your background, you should strive never to be 'common'. My parents were determined to rise from poverty to respectability, something that was inevitably both financial and moral. It was 'common' to smoke, to watch too much TV, to be idle, to drink at airports, to be too evidently British on holidays abroad, to have a tattoo. This was never said with a sneer, but with a sense that life was always about aspiring to be better, to avoid sinking in to what was worse.

This benign snobbery has been complicated by changing economic circumstances: self-advancement is no longer so straightforward; easy categorisation of what was once regarded as the lower classes is no longer possible in modern Britain. Woolf's 'London poor' could now encompass a host of social types: a young immigrant, learning the language; a retired mechanic, struggling on a pension; a professional graduate, laden with debt and with no prospect of home-ownership; a single mother, struggling on insufficient benefit; a disabled person judged fit to work, but with no prospect of getting a proper job; a driver stuck in the gig economy, waiting for the next fare. Reni Eddo-Lodge raised a vital point when she said that 'We should be rethinking the image we conjure up when we think of a working-class person. Instead of a white man in a flat cap, it's

---

* When I started writing for the *TLS* as a young graduate in 2001, I once submitted a review that had the word 'toilet' in it. It was silently, icily changed to 'lavatory' and nobody said anything to me about it.

a black woman pushing a pram.' She is almost right: a better argument, though, would be to replace the 'instead of' with 'as well as'.

As we have seen: race is class; gender is class. So too is age: a thirty-year-old now is worth 21 per cent less than in 1983; a sixty-year-old is worth twice as much. Young people grow up facing immediate debt if they go to university, and little prospect of owning a property unless they enter the elite. The current generation reaching adulthood may plausibly be poorer than their parents, in terms of purchasing power and prospects.

Geography is class. This is almost impossible to overstate: there is a widening gap of wealth and prospects between London and the south-east and the rest of the nation. We discussed this briefly in the health chapter, and we can see it in mortality rates, shockingly: if you are a man living in Blackpool you will die, on average, nine years earlier than a man in Kensington. Overall, people in the north of England are 20 per cent more likely to die before seventy-five than those in the south. Or look at smoking rates in pregnancy (a sign of education levels, or desperation levels, or self-preservation levels): in London it is 2 per cent, in Blackpool it is 27 per cent.

In recent years, London has drawn wealth from around the country, inexorable as a magnet. Its economic value is now the same as the country's seventeen other urban areas combined. Since 2008 the gap has increased. According to *The Economist*: 'economically, socially and politically, the North is becoming another country'. It noted that a sixty-mile radius of London has 'all the major banks, most of the major theatres, the media and arts worlds, the five best universities . . . the hubs of all the country's major industries, 70% of the FTSE 100, most of Britain's airport capacity'.

Its solution is interesting: move the capital of the UK up north. At the moment, we have a repair bill for the Palace of Westminster of up to £4 billion. We could seize the opportunity to move Parliament to, say, Manchester or Birmingham. At the moment, elites in Britain are concentrated pretty much solely in one place; that could change. It happens in broadly fairer countries: Germany has Berlin, Frankfurt and Bonn; Australia has Sydney, Melbourne and Canberra; Spain has (albeit controversially) Madrid and Barcelona. We should try this.

Of course, the blackened husk of Grenfell Tower is a stark reminder, a mass *memento mori*, that inequality exists within London as elsewhere, that poverty huddles close to wealth in Britain. Many of the victims of Grenfell showed other indicators of unfairness: they were young or immigrant, disenfranchised too.

Is it time to abandon hope?

Britain remains a divided country, a country of economic apartheid, a country of polarisation and anger. But it also – as Bill Bryson reminded us at the beginning of this book – remains a comparative beacon of common sense, of tolerance, of orderliness in a generally even more messy and disorderly world. And our tolerance, believe it or not, is increasing. I have referred to the British Social Attitudes Survey in this chapter, and it remains revealing about our collective sense of self: it shows how Britain has become more liberal over time. Consider same-sex marriage: 17 per cent accepted it in 1983; 64 per cent in 2016. Or the right for a woman to choose to have an abortion:[26] 29 per cent accepted it in 1983; in 2016 it was 70 per cent. Mixed-race marriage is largely accepted; homosexuality is largely accepted.

Coincidentally (or probably not), Britain has become a less religious place. For the first time perhaps ever, more than half of adults in this country say they have no religion. And this is likely to grow: nearly three-quarters of eighteen- to twenty-five-year-olds have no faith at all. This rejection of organised religion is – to an atheist like me – a good thing. It is indeed not a coincidence that church attendance has fallen since the 1960s, a time when university attendance started to rise. Rationality and tolerance are, at least in my view, more likely to be found outside the walls of a church or mosque than inside them.

This is not to say that Britain is spiritually barren. A 2013 survey found that '77% of people believe there are things in life that we simply cannot explain through science or any other means.' Most people (in my phone-in experience) have some desire to seek spiritually some essence of goodness or morality.★ In Grace Davie's *Religion in Britain* (2014), there is an exchange with someone surveyed in Islington, who gets to the heart of it:

'Do you believe in a God who can change the course of events on earth?'

'No; just the ordinary one.'

This is, of course, typically British: muddled and compromised; but workably so. And that is this country at its best: a hodgepodge of ideas and races and backgrounds that often succeeds despite itself. Winston Churchill once objected to the rise in Commonwealth immigration, worried that we would have a 'magpie society'. 'That would never do,' he harrumphed. He was wrong. A magpie society is something to aspire to: not only black merging with white; but also one that skips around, taking what is appealing from the widest number of sources, restless and mobile. Britain is at its worst when it is stationary: when poverty is unshiftable; when communities sit, in stasis and opposition, unintegrated; when the exchange of people, customs and ideas is feared and restricted; when ideas around gender or race are immured by historic prejudices. We shouldn't romanticise the Britain that is divided and fragmented and unfair. Nor should we ignore its best qualities either.

★ My view, if you are interested: I believe entirely in the randomness of existence. The earth exists in its form thanks to a chance combination of chemicals; evolution happened thanks to endless mutations of genes, which only has the certainty of fatefulness in retrospect. Everything is luck and happenstance. And that is invigorating: nothing is pre-ordained, nothing should be accepted as inevitable. God will not fix things; there is nothing waiting for you after your body rots away. I bet you are glad you asked now.

Epilogue

Thus far with rough and all-unable★ pen
Our bending author hath pursued the story,
In little room confining mighty men,
Mangling by starts the full course of their glory.
Small time, but in that small most greatly lived.
This star of England.
         William Shakespeare, *Henry V*, epilogue

It is very late one night, in the early winter of 2017, as I am finishing this book. Parts of my every day spent thinking about the muddle, the contingent sprawl of the nation, occasionally pausing to consider what the future might reasonably hold. And then the very notion of future is crystallised for me once more. My wife leans over, sleepy yet preoccupied (as she has been, to my discomfort, all evening), to tell me that she is pregnant again.

The wonderful, surprising prospect of a third child — a second girl, as it will turn out — who will be eighteen in 2036. Phoebe. Who will grow up as an infant in the 2020s, become a teenager in the 2030s. For whom Britain will have to be a place of care and consideration, opportunity and viability. Of course, as Andrea Leadsom discovered when she used Theresa May's childlessness against her in the abortive Conservative leadership contest of 2017, procreation gives nobody the monopoly on concern for what lies ahead of us. But the new life, for which I am responsible, inevitably makes me think about the strength and weakness, the sheer sustainability, of our current state.

★ Pun very much intended, by me (not by Shakespeare, obviously).

As Phoebe celebrates her eighteenth birthday in summer 2036, what will have become of the ideas and institutions of Great Britain? She is lucky already. She will live around London, on the right side of the nation's geographical chasm; she will live longer as a result, she will get better healthcare, more chances; she will be, thanks to her social class and gender, unlikely to get drawn into the justice system, and be harmed by it; she will be less likely than ever in history to be a citizen of a nation at war; she will be blessed with the beauty of being mixed-race (being a quarter Caribbean), with none of the trauma of structural racism, thanks to the pale colour of her skin. But she may still face many of the other challenges of our troubling times: a persistent intrusion of technology into her emotional well-being; a crippling shortage of housing, and a statistical unlikelihood of owning a home; a jobs market radicalised by innovation, but still stubbornly unrewarding to a woman; sexism and threatening behaviour by men in power.

It all makes me, as this book has made me, question what changes would be necessary to improve her – your, our – collective lot in the next two decades. There is much to ponder, or demand. We will need to rethink the concept of work, and its function; we will need to take drastic steps as to how the economy is structured and how the state may be allowed benevolently to intervene in it. Universal Basic Income will have to be trialled properly and tested. Technology firms will have to fund the retraining of those whom their innovation has deprived of a livelihood. Expensive assets (like bonds and securities; or second homes and investment properties) will have to be properly taxed so that wealth is not fixed into place, but can flow more readily. We could call that 'trickle-down economics'.

The supply side of housing will need actually to be fixed: houses built at the levels demanded by our growing population, built by government infrastructure projects if necessary (not shoddily outsourced through PFI) on land that is no longer allowed to be hoarded by the wealthy. A managed housing crash will be necessary to ensure that inflated property prices do not simply benefit the lucky old, but can be kept at a sustainably low level for the aspirational young, hoping for a place to raise a family. The capital city, and the caravan of investment that follows it, should be shifted – with Parliament – to a northern city. The aim should not be the mere statistical success of managed numbers (low unemployment figures, or GDP buoyed by the fantasies of the financial sector), but a genuine spread of wealth.

The National Health Service must be depoliticised. It should be taken out of the hands of politicians and their vote-grubbing dependence on a five-year cycle of misinformation and manipulation. As a nation, we have conceded that monetary policy should not be the property of elected officials (that is why interest rates are the responsibility of the Bank of England). We need to stop the political weaponisation of healthcare. Place the future of the health system into the hands of an independent commission (comprising health professionals and cross-party politicians), capable of massive structural change, which can plan not simply to survive next winter, or next election, but the next decades of our national destiny. It will need to look at what – in the twenty-first century – a free health service can achieve, and what it cannot; and how it might be supplemented by other mechanisms. It will ensure that social care – that desperately vital aspect of ensuring that the dwindling years of a person's life are supported with diligence and dignity – is recognised as part of the overall health system, and funded. At the same time, we must find a way to demand that personal responsibility for our own well-being is rendered truly part of the social contract.

Our education system should be simplified: no faith schools, no tax breaks for private schools, no GCSEs, no grammar schools. Just comprehensive education that prioritises universality until fourteen, and then gives parity of esteem to two routes towards the job market and a sense of valued occupation: vocational training; and academic inclination. Maintenance grants should be restored to help support the poorest members of society get to university, the children of immigrants and the white working class. Indeed, we must demand equality within all the institutions of our lives: equal pay between genders; proportionate representation of those of ethnic origins in positions of power. We should embrace mingling and merging: of race, of gender, of cultural and social background. And accept that polarisation of positions is seldom a good thing.

Our attitude to justice should change: no longer must we demand incarceration to feed our desire for revenge and retribution. A shift should be made towards restorative justice: criminals paying for what they have done in money or time, rather than the state paying to cage them in a self-evidently futile fashion. There should be a planned decriminalisation of certain drugs (starting with cannabis), which will allow a shift of emphasis and resource towards mental healthcare rather than prosecution.

Indeed, the primacy of our collective mental health will need to become a national preoccupation: in a world of bleeps and blurts, sensory overload and the insidious removal of privacy, we will need collectively to establish how we protect our most valuable resource: the sanctity of sanity.

Do I believe that such changes are possible? Yes. Plausible? Alas, no. We will muddle along, of course, perhaps improving here or there. Real national shifts, sadly, only tend to come on the heels of calamity, massive events that change the shape of a society.* And Britain has never been much keen on seismic revolutions. But I don't want to end this book on a dystopian vision of wastelands, empty cities scoured by a nuclear wind, as wild bands of survivors push shopping trolleys of dog food and smartphone chargers through former symbols of our civilisation. 'This is the way the world ends. This is the way the world ends. This is the way the world ends. Not with a bang but a whimper,' as T. S. Eliot put it. Britain is resilient, malleable, and – above all – persistent. There remains much to love, to be proud of, in this great mess of our country. We must go on, we can't go on, we'll go on. But that doesn't mean we have to accept everything along the way.

---

* This is the compelling thesis of American academic Walter Scheidel in his book *The Great Leveler* (2017): 'Four different kinds of violent ruptures have flattened inequality: mass mobilization warfare, transformative revolution, state failure and lethal pandemics. I call these the Four Horsemen of Leveling.' And, yes, the use of one 'l' in 'Leveler' and 'Leveling' is oddly annoying.

Further Reading

I declare after all there is no enjoyment like reading!
Caroline Bingley, in *Pride and Prejudice* by Jane Austen

Chapter 1: Economics

Capital (2012) by John Lanchester

This is the best fictional treatment of the banking crisis, telling the capacious tale of its trickle-down effect on a group of Londoners. Comparisons to Dickens are not without value here, but a little trite (so don't effortfully make one at a dinner party). It is a big thoughtful book by someone who understands finance and literature, and you do not get many of those.

Psmith in the City (1910), by P. G. Wodehouse

I love this book's gentle description of the tedium of life in a London bank, filled with toiling clerks and public schoolboys dreaming of a fortune in the East. The plot hinges on a county cricket match, so do not read this expecting anything too startling. Wodehouse's character of Psmith ('the "p" is silent as in phthisis, psychic and ptarmigan'), a gently amusing, bemonocled figure of charm and wit, is one of the finest comic creations in British literature.

Vanity Fair (1848) by William Makepeace Thackeray

This has the subtitle 'A Novel Without a Hero', and represents – through the eyes of a distinctly unreliable narrator – a review of the lives of rich and upper-class characters in London. Its focus, its beating heart, is Becky Sharp, a beautiful and brilliant young woman who has to make her way in the world without possessing a fortune. She marries above her station, but remains in thrall to poverty. She is forced to use her magnetism as a means of surviving, and the novel is deeply ambiguous about the effect of that, containing a real Victorian sense of fascinated revulsion at the prospect of female sexuality. As with Austen, though, the driver of the plot is money, and how to keep it (often without earning it).

Money (1984) by Martin Amis

Amis is – in my view – a better literary critic than literary author, but this is probably his best book, where his satirical cleverness does not hold his storytelling hostage. It is actually about the unreal world of celebrity, but brilliantly conveys the consumerist culture of 1980s Britain and America. A line in the book, 'You gotta run on heavy fuel,' inspired a single by Dire Straits.

Making Money (2007) by Terry Pratchett

A latish addition to the Discworld series from Britain's best comic writer since P. G. Wodehouse. This tells the story of what happens when the reformed conman Moist von Lipwig takes over the Royal Bank of the city of Ankh-Morpork. The central joke is that, as we have seen, the concept of money is effectively a fantasy, so a fantasy novel featuring golems and vampires is the most appropriate place to discuss it. If you haven't read Pratchett before, don't start here, but go back to the first one, *The Colour of Magic* (1983).

Pride and Prejudice (1813) by Jane Austen

Jane Austen is always on the money, in every sense. Her prose is especially sharp and sensitive to the tension between those who have it and those who do not; measuring precisely the pressures of household economy, and how they can squeeze and shape relationships. She is literally now on the money, too: appearing on the £10 note since 2017. The quote on the note comes from *Pride and Prejudice*, surely her greatest and most charming novel: 'I declare after all there is no enjoyment like reading.' There is an irony here Austen would have appreciated: the line is spoken by Caroline Bingley, who is no reader at all, desperately pretending to like books in order to impress the smouldering Darcy. Austen aficionados will tell you *Persuasion* (1817) is the better novel; ignore them.

Sybil, or The Two Nations (1845) by Benjamin Disraeli

This novel has given us a symbol for this entire book: how a nation has been ever divided between 'THE RICH AND THE POOR' (capitalisation his). Disraeli is now far better known as a politician (including as the only Jewish Prime Minister in our history) than an author, but he had some self-confidence in his literary ability ('When I want to read a book, I write one'). This novel is important, without being especially entertaining, but still worth a read.

Great Expectations (1861) by Charles Dickens

One of the most memorable novels by Dickens: it tells the story of the development of a young orphan called Pip, who has to come to terms with his poverty and dubious inheritance. The idea of tainted money is particularly crucial to the plot, as Pip's increased 'expectations' come from an initially mysterious, eventually disreputable source. Dickens first wrote an ending that was rather daringly, mournfully inconclusive, and was pressed to change it into something more conventionally happy. It is not entirely clear that he managed. Read the book for the great beginning (a scary convict fleeing the monstrous hulks in the marshes of Kent), the eerie Miss Havisham, and the fact that Thomas Carlyle disparaged it.

Chapter 2: Politics

A Clockwork Orange (1962) by Anthony Burgess

Burgess wrote this novel quickly, and hated how popular it became (eclipsing everything else he ever wrote). It is written in a startlingly vivid dialect, influenced by Russian, and has lingered because of its lurid presentation of 'ultra-violence' by the narrator, Alex. As with many 'classic' novels, its ongoing significance has been aided by an iconic film, in this case by Stanley Kubrick. The film, unlike the original version of the book, has no happy ending.

Brave New World (1932) by Aldous Huxley

The title comes from Shakespeare's *The Tempest*, and the story – written at a time of huge flux and economic depression – animates the issue of how dangerous state control of the individual is. It also predicts major issues of the present, among them genetic engineering and social conditioning. In the book, Henry Ford is seen as a God-like figure ('Our Ford') and Shakespeare a banned author with dangerous ideas about liberty of thought. It began as a parody of fictional utopias, and became an outstanding critique of industrialised society.

1984 (1949) by George Orwell

This still sells more than a quarter of a million copies every year, gave the world the metaphors of 'Big Brother' and 'Room 101', the phrases 'double-think' and 'thoughtcrime', and helps us all understand how authoritarianism can rise even amid civilisation. While it also conveyed a sense of British post-war misery, it has become especially relevant in response to the idea of Trump's America, dramatising, as it does, the state's ability to weaponise disinformation. Trump is capable, as was the Party in *1984*, of asserting that 'two and two made five', although in his case you might be forgiven for thinking he was just unable to do the maths.

The Prime Minister (1876) by Anthony Trollope

I have picked this one, the fifth in the series of Trollope's parliamentary novels, but the whole series represents the greatest Victorian investigation into the Westminster world, covering all types of political wrangling from coalitions to the Irish question. Trollope is probably the major Victorian writer you have read the least, but – as a failed politician – is rather good at the failing world of politics.

Atlas Shrugged (1957) by Ayn Rand

This is, by no definition, a good book. Rand's philosophy of 'Objectivism' (basically the social-Darwinian view that people prosper by being selfish) is dramatised in vast and scarcely credible fashion, telling the story of the mysterious demagogue John Galt. Ayn Rand is read by the horrible, rich son in the film *Dirty Dancing* (he recommends her other book *The Fountainhead*), which is a guide to how sophisticated her thought was. You need to have read Rand, as she is part of the discussion of the development of the right, even if you might not enjoy reading her.

Much Obliged, Jeeves (1971) by P. G. Wodehouse

A very late Jeeves and Wooster novel, this is good at conveying the essential silliness of British politics in its account of the Market Snodsbury by-election. Bertie's chum Ginger Winship is standing for Parliament, egged on by his ambitious fiancée Florence Craye, and unwillingly assisted by former fascist and underwear designer Roderick Spode. It all ends with everyone recognising that being a politician is not worth the bother, which is unquestionably true and always worth saying.

The Ragged-Trousered Philanthropists (1914) by Robert Tressell

This indictment of capitalism was rejected by three publishers, and only published three years after the death of the author (an impoverished painter whose real name was Robert Noonan). It provides a sobering context for the rise of the Labour Party at the beginning of the twentieth century, and animates Marx's critique of capitalism. Adrian Mole nearly read it ('I haven't looked through it yet but I'm quite interested in stamp collecting'), and should have done. The 'philanthropists' are the workers who donate their effort for insufficient reward.

What Might Have Been (1907) by Ernest Bramah

Let's end this section on another dystopia, this one avowedly anti-socialist. Bramah is an interesting character: he wrote detective stories, was once the private secretary to Jerome K. Jerome, and then became such a recluse nobody could discover anything about him. A debate raged as to whether he actually existed. *What Might Have Been* shows what might happen if the dreaded socialists were to take power, an England – according to a contemporary review – 'sans army, sans navy, sans colonies, sans everything except rates and taxes, which the upper and middle classes pay, and the rest live on'. The result is a civil war, which only ends when benevolent capitalism reasserts itself. Make your own jokes here.

Chapter 3: Health

Middlemarch (1871–2) by George Eliot

You might think this is a stretch to include this sprawling Victorian novel, subtitled 'A Study of Provincial Life' (and actually a work of historical fiction, set in the 1830s), in the medical section. And you would be right. It does have a notable character who is a doctor, Tertius Lydgate, who seeks to adopt modern ideas of disease prevention, and to challenge orthodoxies. He is a scientist who 'wanted to pierce the obscurity of those minute processes which prepare human misery and joy', and so misses out on what it means to be human. His awkward relationship with Rosamond Vincy, desperate for money and elevation, is tellingly told: Henry James did not think there were any scenes 'more powerfully real . . . in all English fiction'.

The English Patient (1992) by Michael Ondaatje

This correctly won the Booker Prize, and is a beautiful treatment of the impact of war and loss on a small group of people. It might better be placed in our section on the military, as it dramatises the tensions between survivors trapped near Florence at the tail end of the Second World War. Or the chapter on identity, as it considers the interwoven connection between races, and the impact of colonialism. But it is also a testament to the lingering power of the body to survive, and its relationship with the power of the mind to remember. On the first page, we are told that Hana, the nurse, 'knows the body well', and the book goes on to prove it. It also says a 'penis is like a sea-horse', but we'll move on from that. A more tender, thoughtful version of Hemingway's *A Farewell to Arms*.

A Country Doctor's Notebook (1920s) by Mikhail Bulgakov

Bulgakov (like Chekhov) was originally a doctor, and wrote a series of short stories about his experience, including his own addiction to the morphine he was prescribing. They are macabre, but funny, in the way doctors' memoirs often are, swerving between the vibrant messiness of life and the cold outcome of death. By the way, if you have not read Bulgakov's triumphant *The Master and Margarita* (written before 1940, but not published until the late 1960s), about – among other things – the arrival of the Devil into Moscow society and a revisionist story of Jesus, then put this book down and read it now. It is the strangest, most unsettling novel of the twentieth century.

The Golden Notebook (1962) by Doris Lessing

One of five works by a Nobel Laureate I have recommended, Lessing's book is not strictly about medical matters, but does touch upon issues of fragmented mental health. It is experimental in structure: a conventional narrative by a writer character, Anna Wulf, interspersed with different notebooks. Anna says early on that 'everything is cracking up', and the whole novel is a response to concerns that modernity is leading to fragmentation. Those concerns have only accelerated in the intervening age.

The Bell Jar (1963) by Sylvia Plath

Originally published under the pseudonym Victoria Lucas, this novel has wrongly been filed under a sort of 'books addressing teenage angst' categorisation, but is in fact a beautiful meditation upon the creeping power of depression. The title's 'bell jar' symbolises the oppressive, airless feeling of being depressed. As with *The Golden Notebook*, it is striking how the issues of female suppression (especially sexual) and mental illness have needed to be treated together in fiction. Both these novels are now regarded as feminist classics.

Wide Sargasso Sea (1966) by Jean Rhys

Continuing in the same vein is this prequel to Brontë's *Jane Eyre* (1847), about the first wife of Mr Rochester, a creole woman called Antoinette Cosway. She is removed from home and family in Jamaica, renamed 'Bertha', and condemned to a confined life in England. As a result, she becomes the archetypal 'madwoman in the attic' (the title of a seminal book by Sandra Gilbert and Susan Gubar on Victorian fiction). Again, mental health and societal health are elided in the story.

The Magic Mountain (1924) by Thomas Mann

This tells the story of Hans Castorp, a young man who heads off to Davos, not then synonymous with annual jollies for plutocratic narcissists, but the location of a tuberculosis sanatorium where his cousin is being treated. There, he becomes enmeshed in a miniature society, utterly removed from the real world (which is heading towards the First World War). He is told that he himself has tuberculosis, and slowly becomes institutionalised. It is an eerie, airless novel, in which you feel yourself taken away from the normality of existence to the controlled and rigid environment of a hospital. This is all made more compelling, because we know that such order is set to be destroyed by the chaos of conflict.

The Portrait of a Lady (1881) by Henry James

The greatest of novels by James, who made a career of meditating at length upon the similarities and differences between America and Britain. It is included here because of the character of Ralph Touchett, the shambling, benign invalid, suffering from terminal pulmonary disease: 'tall, lean, loosely and feebly put together, he had an ugly, sickly, witty, charming face – furnished, but by no means decorated, with a straggling moustache and whisker. He looked clever and ill – a combination by no means felicitous.' Ralph enables the central character Isabel Archer to explore the fullest expanse of her fate by bequeathing her his fortune. Her failure to benefit from this, and to suffer the crippling indignity of marrying a man who strangles her vibrancy, is the central tragedy of the novel.

Chapter 4: Education

The Prime of Miss Jean Brodie (1961) by Muriel Spark

Muriel Spark attended James Gillespie's High School for Girls in Edinburgh and there, as an eleven-year-old girl, met a teacher called Christina Kay, 'a character in search of an author'. The latter was keen to impress upon her pupils a full breadth of knowledge, of things like the Renaissance or the gods of Ancient Greece. She also was something of a fascist, in especial thrall to Mussolini. In Spark's imagination, she was transmuted into Miss Jean Brodie, the charismatic figure who manipulates a 'set' of girls and seeks to improve them. In doing so, she created a character for the novelistic pantheon, the most charismatic and unknowable of teachers in Western fiction.

Decline and Fall (1928) by Evelyn Waugh

This is Waugh's funniest novel, as well as being his first one. It tells the story of a teacher, Paul Pennyfeather, compelled into the profession because he has been wrongly expelled from Oxford for public nudity. The school, Llanabba Castle in Wales, is heavily based on Waugh's own early brush with teaching, and is a place of beatings, pederasty and general weirdness. Put it this way: one child is accidentally shot during Sports Day, and doesn't survive.

The most memorable character is fellow teacher Grimes, who manages the rare feat of being an incorrigible paedophile (getting caught in which activity he calls being 'in the soup') and yet somehow warmly charming at the same time. Waugh based him on a real teacher he knew: 'he has left four schools precipitously, three in the middle of the term through his being taken in sodomy and one through his being drunk six nights in succession. And yet he goes on getting better and better jobs without difficulty.' Anyone cynical about Oxbridge or public schools will enjoy this book.

Tom Brown's School Days (1857) by Thomas Hughes

The archetypal tale of public school life, which has passed into popular culture, telling as it does of bullying and fagging. It is also designed to eulogise the Rugby headmaster Thomas Arnold (father of poet Matthew), who – as we saw – revolutionised the public school system. The tone is preachy, for which Hughes made no apology: 'When a man comes to my time of life and has his bread to make, and very little time to spare, is it likely that he will spend almost the whole of his yearly vacation in writing a story just to amuse people?' The best consequence of the novel is the creation of the Flashman character (see below) and – if you like that sort of thing – the fact that it clearly helped to inspire J. K. Rowling's Hogwarts.

Nicholas Nickleby (1839) by Charles Dickens

This was Dickens's third novel, and came at around the same time as his first son (he referred proudly to both as his 'infant phenomenon'). It gave the world the repulsive school Dotheboys Hall, a place of vile abuse under the auspices of one-eyed Wackford Squeers. That allusive name is indicative of Dickens's tone here: a sort of light comedy despite the dark subject of systematised cruelty it depicts. Dickens, the journalistic force that he was, had visited a number of schools, and was seeking to highlight some of the iniquities of the system. That he could do it through humour is testament to his brilliance, and perhaps the rather pitiless spirit of the age.

Villette (1853) by Charlotte Brontë

I could have picked *Jane Eyre* here, of course, whose heroine suffers the indignities and discomforts of the horrendous Lowood School for poor and orphaned girls. The first person narration of that book has placed generations of girls (and boys) at the centre of this institution, one of many Victorian cathedrals of abuse in the name of charity. Like Jane's friend Helen Burns, two of the Brontë sisters died of tuberculosis, perhaps abetted by poor conditions at their own school.

There is, however, a respectable argument that *Villette* is the greater of Charlotte Brontë's novels. George Eliot certainly preferred it, saying that there was something 'preternatural in its powers'. It is a re-write of Brontë's first (and initially unpublished) novel, *The Professor* (1857). Like that, it bears passing resemblance to part of Brontë's early life: she was a teacher at a Belgian school, and in the grip of unrequited love for a teacher there. There are gothic touches, feminist cruxes, to go alongside the determined realism throughout. Tell your friends you prefer it to *Jane Eyre*, and you will appear to be quite the sophisticate.

Mike and Psmith (1909) by P. G. Wodehouse

This book represents the first appearance of Psmith, my favourite Wodehouse character. It is a representative of a very English genre of 'school stories', which were popular in the early part of the twentieth century and told of scrapes and 'rags' in public schools. In this one, Psmith and his friend, the doughty cricketer Mike Jackson ('except on the cricket field, where he was a natural genius, he was just ordinary'), are sent under protest to a minor establishment called Sedleigh, where they make a place for themselves by virtue of Psmith's forceful, courteous charm. This is like the charming cousin to *Decline and Fall*, a gentle introduction to the world of Wodehouse.

Changing Places (1975) / *Small World* (1984) / *Nice Work* (1988) by David Lodge

This is a trilogy of sublime 'campus novels', set between the fictional cities of Rummidge in the UK (Birmingham) and Plotinus in the US (Berkeley). They are written by a literary professor himself, and are full of in-jokes. So *Changing Places* contains debates about different literary forms of the novel (like epistolary or confessional), and also uses those forms in its own text; *Small World* is full of academic experts on the subject of romance, and is itself a romantic quest-narrative; *Nice Work*'s heroine, the formidable Robyn Penrose, is an expert in the nineteenth-century industrial novel, and the narrative surrounding her is a pastiche of Dickens and Gaskell and so on. Read these books and you will want to study English at university, I promise you. Lodge is also the most Updikean of English novelists when it comes to sexual frankness.

Possession (1990) by A. S. Byatt

The central crux of the novel is the investigation by two English academics, Roland Michell and Maud Bailey, into the unlikely love life of two Victorian poets (invented by Byatt), Randolph Henry Ash and Christabel LaMotte. The latter rather recall the Brownings, Robert and Elizabeth, who themselves developed a romance excited by the written word. The book splits its attention between the two time periods, and is filled with letters, poems and diaries written in the Victorian style. The poetry can get a little hard-going (as is true, of course, in *The Lord of the Rings*), but *Possession* is a great achievement of the imagination, as well as a thoughtful investigation into the act, and the art, of biography.

Lucky Jim (1954) by Kingsley Amis

I do think this is one of the more over-rated novels in the English canon, but it was Amis's debut and made his immediate name. Christopher Hitchens called it 'the funniest book of the past half century', and you may trust him more than me. It tells of the near-farcical exploits of Jim Dixon, a lecturer at a provincial university, and is filled with the broad comedy of English embarrassment. Dixon ends up giving a drunken lecture on the subject of medieval England, which recalls Gussie Fink-Nottle's similarly soused address to a girls' school in Market Snodsbury. *Lucky Jim* is dedicated to Philip Larkin (who lived on Dixon Drive in Leicester), and there is a sense of the lugubrious ridiculousness in the book that might be described as Larkinesque.

Chapter 5: Military

Aubrey/Maturin series (1969–99) by Patrick O'Brian

This twenty-novel collection begins with *Master and Commander* (1969) and ends with *Blue at the Mizzen* (1999), and can be considered as one giant super-novel (indeed super-naval-novel). It gives us Captain Jack Aubrey, a flaxen-haired and blue-eyed hulk of a man, resolute, obstinate and often lucky in his leadership of a variety of ships during the Napoleonic Wars (between 1800 and 1815). His constant companion (and musical partner) is Stephen Maturin, a figure who is slight and dark (Irish-Spanish), self-medicates with opium and is an expert in practical surgery, languages, botany, zoology and spying. Together they form one of the most endearing and enduring duos in all fiction: think Holmes and Watson (but with intelligence levels reversed).

The Flashman Papers (1969–2005) by George MacDonald Fraser

It is hard for me to think of a series of novels that has given me more lasting pleasure in re-reading than these. Even writing this little section, I lost half a day in silent satisfaction, guiltily enjoying *Flashman in the Great Game* (1975) for the twentieth time. The framing device is simple and wonderful: Fraser pretends to have discovered the autobiographical pages of Harry Flashman, last seen as the caddish bully in *Tom Brown's Schooldays*. Flashman has grown into a self-confessed coward, bigot and philanderer (good at only three things: 'horses, languages and fornication'), whose unfair fortune makes him prosper in all the major engagements of the Victorian military.

The genius of Fraser was to play his hero fast and loose, and his history deadly straight. So each novel is filled with footnotes of historical facts.

The Great Game covers the period of the Indian Mutiny, a seminal event in British colonialism that was never mentioned once to me in sixteen years of education.

The Things They Carried (1990) by Tim O'Brien

This may be the greatest work of fiction about warfare ever written (a large claim, I know). It is also the greatest literary response to the Vietnam War, in which O'Brien himself served. It is an interlocking series of vignettes about the conflict, which (movingly, shatteringly) elide the physical reality of the experience with the mental and emotional.

The title story does this acutely, paragraph after paragraph cataloguing what soldiers have to carry with them at war:

> letters from a girl named Martha . . . whatever presented itself, or whatever seemed appropriate as a means of killing or staying alive . . . USO stationery and pencils and pens . . . the shared weight of memory. They took up what others could no longer bear. Often, they carried each other, the wounded and weak. They carried infections . . . They carried the land itself – Vietnam, the place, the soil – a powdery orange-red dust that covered their boots and fatigues and faces. They carried the sky.

Not all burdens are physical, but some are.

Catch-22 (1961) by Joseph Heller

The phrase – meaning a double bind – is now more famous than the novel, which is a brilliantly absurdist account of life in the American air force during the Second World War (which Heller himself experienced). The catch is this: any airman who is insane should not be allowed to fly; anybody who refuses to fly is rational and thus cannot be insane. The 256th squadron is filled with airmen who do not want to die in futile battle, and their often tragic fate is told in comic, mordant style. They are led by Yossarian, the man with an 'odious, alien, distasteful name', determined not to follow the 'American way' of dying gloriously. 'Kafka meets Blackadder' is perhaps the most affectionate endorsement of the novel I can give.

All Quiet on the Western Front (1929) by Erich Maria Remarque

So much of our cultural experience of warfare comes, inevitably, from the British perspective. This book is German (its original title was *Im Westen nichts Neues*, 'nothing new in the West'), but it has given a phrase permanently to the English language. This itself most eloquently epitomises the universality of its message. The author wished to convey the senselessness, the boredom of war (this novel was 'least of all an adventure, for death is not an adventure to those who stand face to face with it') and does so through the clarity of its storytelling. This is an account of what Gertrude Stein called the 'lost generation', but from the German side. The Nazis banned the novel as degenerate, on the grounds that it was insufficiently patriotic in its description of the German war effort.

Regeneration (1991) by **Pat Barker**
A wonderful novel that dramatises life in Craiglockhart War Hospital, where Siegfried Sassoon and Wilfred Owen (whom we have met) were patients. The title comes from the concept of 'nerve regeneration' pioneered by the real-life psychiatrist W. H. R. Rivers, a man placed in the morally ambivalent position of having to treat patients for shell shock simply to enable them to return to the front to be killed. Barker has said this: 'One of the things that impresses me is that two things happen to soldiers in war: a) they get killed or b) they come back more or less alright. It's really focusing on the people who do come back but don't come back alright, they are either physically disabled or mentally traumatised.' *Regeneration* is the first in a trilogy, the last of which won the Booker Prize.

Slaughterhouse-Five (1969) by **Kurt Vonnegut**
The title comes from the name of the building in which the novel's central character Billy Pilgrim, a chaplain's assistant in the US army, is imprisoned during the Allied bombing of Dresden in 1945. As we have seen, this prolonged firestorm broke the Geneva Convention. The narrator of the novel says this: 'That was I. That was me. That was the author of this book.' And it is true that Vonnegut was captured during the Battle of the Bulge, transported to Dresden, and imprisoned in a building called Schlachthof Funf. His letters home tell of the atrocities he experienced, in understated prose: 'I told the guards just what I was going to do to them when the Russians came. They beat me up a little. I was fired as group leader.' But the novel is not understated: it is vertiginous in its time and perspective shifts; it includes Billy's capture by aliens. It is an extraordinary thing.

Richard Hannay series (1915–36) by John Buchan

You may have heard more about the most famous of the five novels in the series, *The Thirty-Nine Steps*, but the next two are the greatest, and set during the First World War: *Greenmantle* and *Mr Standfast*. The former examines the rise of an Islamic cult as a potential ally for the Germans; the latter is a spy story that culminates in the final German push on Amiens in 1918.

Buchan was a huge sentimentalist (and conservative, and – in the manner of the times – something of a racist), desperately impressed by the valour of fighting men. The books are full of bluff references to the 'big shows' of battles, which might more critically be termed 'mass slaughters'. Richard Hannay, the general-turned-spy, is a spokesperson for an unreconstructed view of masculinity and bravery. Buchan termed his spy thrillers 'shockers' in the sense of fast-paced pot-boilers, and he was right. Read these books if you have a cold, wrapped in a blanket, oblivious to the glints and beeps of the technology around you.

The Yellow Birds (2012) by Kevin Powers

A debut novel from a *rara avis* indeed: a modern-day soldier who is also a poet. His book is about the insatiable ability of warfare to consume those who – despite being its active agents – are in fact its powerless victims: 'While we slept the war rubbed its thousand ribs against the ground in prayer . . . while we ate, the war fasted, fed by its own deprivation . . . it tried to kill us every day.' Its central character, John Bartle (whose name is one letter away from 'battle') struggles to keep his sense of identity amid the uniformity and the barrage of propaganda. It quotes Vonnegut's maxim from *Slaughterhouse-Five*: 'so it goes', the inexorable course of conflict.

Chapter 6: Law and Order

Little Dorrit (1857) by Charles Dickens

A bit more Dickens, you'll be pleased to see. This is set in and around Marshalsea, the great London debtors' prison (which housed Dickens's impecunious father, after he could not pay a debt of £40 to a baker). Dickens wrote how his 'whole nature was so penetrated with grief and humiliation' by the experience of the consequences of debt; and it never left him. Amy (the eponymous heroine) was born in the prison, 'an oblong pile of barrack building, partitioned into squalid houses standing back to back, so that there were no back rooms; environed by a narrow paved yard, hemmed in by high walls duly spiked at the top'. The novel also features the 'Circumlocution Office', a brilliant satire of an ineffectual government department: 'Whatever was required to be done, the Circumlocution Office was beforehand with all the public departments in the art of perceiving – HOW NOT TO DO IT.'

The Complete Sherlock Holmes (1887–1927) by Arthur Conan Doyle

Featuring the greatest of detectives, this is the collection of stories that gives me more pleasure than any other. When I was young and impoverished, I spent £100 I couldn't afford on a hardback version of the canon, which was filled with footnotes examining the stories as if they were real accounts by Watson, merely transcribed by Conan Doyle.* There is Holmes: gaunt, brilliant, egotistical, capable of existing without food or sleep (but not tobacco). Watson: brave, devoted, occasionally hot-headed. Their friendship, scarcely acknowledged even to themselves, is one of the greatest in the pantheon.

Papillon (1969) by Henri Charrière

When I was a teenager, I was given this book for Christmas as part of a collection of interesting foreign fiction. I started reading it in the morning, was a begrudging and distant presence at dinner, and finished it by lunchtime on Boxing Day.

It tells the remarkable story of the convict Henri Charrière, a tough and street-smart villain from the streets of Paris (with a butterfly tattoo on his chest), who is sentenced to life imprisonment in French Guiana (transportation known as the 'dry Guillotine', because it was liable to leave you equally dead). We learn of his numerous escapes from numerous prisons, his sojourns in Trinidad and Guajira (where he becomes the effective headman of a village, impregnating two sisters and generally living it up), his survival of two years in solitary confinement, his brawls and scraps, his heroic rescue of the governor's daughter from shark-infested waters. Ask anybody who has read the book, they will immediately wince and recall the charger: the metal cylinder lodged deep within the rectum, which acts as a portable storage for money in prison.

---

* Who could possibly find such a plethora of footnotes entertaining? You might reasonably ask.

The Count of Monte Cristo (1844) by Alexandre Dumas

Dumas was a font, an overflowing torrent, of writing. He made use of the ideas and inspirations of others to create something approaching a factory of storytelling. *The Count of Monte Cristo* is one of the great prison escape stories (it is in the library of Stephen King's Shawshank Prison, for example, as an inspiration), as Edmond Dantès gets out of the real-life Chateau d'If and wreaks terrible revenge on the rotters who wrongfully banged him up there. While in prison, Dantès is schooled by a fellow inmate to be the perfect gentleman (in terms of knowledge and fighting skills), and then subsequently given treasure by him. So this is both a fantasy of revenge and riches. Massive, flawed and well worth your time.

Gould's Book of Fish (2002) by Richard Flanagan

Subtitled 'A Novel in Twelve Fish', this is that rare achievement: a readable postmodern novel. Postmodern fiction tends to be achingly effortful: writing about writing about writing. Here Richard Flanagan, an Aussie, speaks through the historical figure of a convict, William Buelow Gould, who was sentenced to forty-nine years' imprisonment in the penal colony of Sarah Island in 1825. There, he painted a series of fish in watercolours (for 'scientifick' purposes), which still survive and can be seen in the Tasmanian State Library.

There is a touch of Pynchon here, some musing about the nature of artistic creation, and lots of arch nods to major writers like Borges, Joyce and Dante. But the strength of the novel lies in the generous, unforgettable evocation of the man and his prison surroundings. At one point, Gould is forced to pleasure the Pastor's wife with a perfumed bust of Voltaire, and that is enough to convince me that this is literary self-awareness finally put to good use. While this is a beautiful book, it is also a horrifying one: 'scarified backs sloughing into maggot-ridden putrescence'; 'the insidious damp . . . seeping out of sphincters rotting from repeated rapes'. Worth reading, even if postmodernism brings you out in a rash.

The Rumpole series (1978–2007) by John Mortimer

Just as reading the James Herriot books (starting with *If Only They Could Talk*, 1970) made me want to become a vet, these stories – about a fat, bibulous, freedom-loving, Wordsworth-quoting barrister for the defence – made me want to become a lawyer. Thankfully the fit passed. Rumpole is a great comic creation, consistent over decades in his lovable presentation. It is hard to imagine him now without picturing the British actor Leo

McKern who absolutely inhabited the character when he played him on the BBC. Mortimer was a barrister himself, and conveys – amid the laughs and quirks – the grim process of British justice.

One Day in the Life of Ivan Denisovich (1963) by Aleksandr Solzhenitsyn
I was given this book as a prize at school, and read it in one sitting, open-mouthed and squirming. Ivan Denisovich is wrongly sentenced to ten years in a forced labour camp in Stalin's Russia; the novel tells, in minute detail, just one day of his brutal world of the gangs of the gulags, where icy terror is occasionally warmed by moments of humanity. Solzhenitsyn had been in the gulags himself, for disparaging Stalin, and only got the book published because Stalin's successor Khrushchev personally allowed it. The tiny moments of victory – apparently so crucial in any prison life – are what linger still in my mind (the extra morsel of food, the scrap of iron concealed from the authorities, the fixing of a window to keep out the chill): Denisovich says they make him 'almost happy', which is the saddest line in the whole thing.

Crime and Punishment (1866) by Fyodor Dostoevsky
I read this novel one winter in London, absorbed by it on chilly Tube journeys and snatched half-hours in gloomy afternoons. I found myself frequently unwell, my nerves peeled, my body aching and racked with coughs. When I read some Victorian criticism of the book, I discovered that this was not uncommon: Dostoevsky's fiction is so remorseless, so vividly bleak, it can actually make you ill. Don't let that put you off, though: *Crime and Punishment* is the greatest meditation on justice there is, written by a man who had himself been spared the firing squad and bundled off to Siberia. Its central character, Raskolnikov, is a murderer (motivated by a sort of intellectual curiosity) with whom we sympathise, from whom we shrink, an ambivalence that is key to the book's power.

Chapter 7: Old and New Media

Psmith, Journalist (1915) by P. G. Wodehouse
Unquestionably the greatest novel on the subject of journalism, it transports Psmith to New York where, seeking distraction, he takes over a gentle, boring magazine called *Cosy Moments*. Together with a cowboy journalist (literally; he is from Wyoming), an office boy, a befuddled boxer and a

New York gangster, he turns the title into a campaigning force against the powerful vested interests of local slum landlords. '*Cosy Moments* cannot be muzzled', is the motto that any newspaper should profitably copy. Unlike in real life, a move towards a serious political agenda leads to a huge uptick in sales, and Psmith triumphs once more. There is a modest amount of social realism along the way (the horrific slum conditions, the corrupting atmosphere of a boxing match), especially for a Wodehouse novel.

Scoop (1938) by Evelyn Waugh

Called by everybody else the greatest novel on the subject of journalism, it also focuses on an unlikely central figure in the form of William Boot, a contributor of nature notes ('feather-footed through the plashy fen passes the questing vole' is one of his immortal efforts) to Lord Copper's *Daily Beast*, who is mistakenly sent to cover 'a very promising little war' in Africa. Much comic confusion results, and the insane world of British journalism (from megalomaniac owners to untrustworthy hacks) is witheringly portrayed. The great Christopher Hitchens praised it for its 'mirror of satire held up to catch the Caliban of the press corps', and almost any red-nosed addled bore from journalism's pre-internet age will also refer to it fondly. Ordinary, decent people like it too, of course.

Amsterdam (1998) by Ian McEwan

This wrongly won the Booker Prize, mainly – one suspects – out of a sense of regret for him not having won before. It is a very slight (yet very well-crafted) thing, and has a major character who is a newspaper editor, beginning to come to terms with the declining sales of his title. Of course, considered in the current world of financial cataclysm for the industry, his situation seems positively arcadian: 'It's time we ran more regular columns. They're cheap, and everyone else is doing them. You know, we hire someone of low to medium intelligence, possibly female, to write about, well, nothing much.' That's investment in journalism at a level quite unimaginable today.

New Grub Street (1891) by George Gissing

Gissing is deeply unfashionable now, but at one point was highly regarded, including by Orwell, who claimed he was 'ready to maintain that England has produced very few better novelists' and that *New Grub Street* was his 'most impressive book'. Although its subject is really the literary life, one of its central characters is Jasper Milvain, a journalist who recognises the eternal truth that commerciality is the key to success. He ends up as an editor of a periodical, propped up by his new wife's money. Gissing's journals reveal a man in thrall to the despairing desire to be a writer, and misery at how hard it was. Joyce once said Gissing's style was like 'Triestine noodle and bean soup', all stodge.

Towards the End of the Morning (1967) by Michael Frayn

Now this novel is indeed about journalism, and the still-vibrant world of Fleet Street in the 1960s. It features journalists, though, who deal with a paper's more mundane furniture: the nature column, the crossword and the like. This is clever indeed, as such parts of a paper are always unloved and ignored, right up until they are changed (to a storm of angry complaint). Elsewhere in the book are all the expected descriptions of journalistic life, the newsrooms reeking of angst and failure, the lost world of booze and expense fiddling: 'Various members of the staff emerged from Hand and Ball Passage during the last dark hour of the morning, walked with an air of sober responsibility towards the main entrance, greeted the commissionaire and vanished upstairs in the lift to telephone their friends and draw their expenses before going out again to have lunch.'

Books Do Furnish A Room (1971) by Anthony Powell

This is the tenth in the sequence of the novel series *A Dance to the Music of Time*, wrongly seen as England's answer to Proust's *A la Recherche du Temps Perdu*. Powell (pronounced 'Pole', if you ever need to say it) is not read very much now, but his fans are fiercely loyal (and often American, in my experience). He provides a lucid account of life in England among the literate upper-middle classes, just merely buggering along. Books Bagshaw is typical of the British journalist, able to hack out stories without the burden of real expertise: 'He possessed that opportune facility for turning out several thousand words on any subject whatever at the shortest possible notice: politics: sport: books: finance: science: art: fashion – as he himself said, "War, Famine, Pestilence or Death on a Pale Horse". All were equal when it came to Bagshaw's typewriter.'

The Quiet American (1955) by Graham Greene

This is rightly seen as a percipient account of American intervention in Vietnam ahead of the destructive war, and is based upon Greene's own journalism at the beginning of the decade. A central character is a British man, Thomas Fowler, who is the very type of cynical, jaded journalist, compromised by his own facility of invention. He does not lack courage, but has been stripped of all idealism: 'Was any news good enough to risk expulsion?' he asks. 'I doubted it.' He also represents an interesting study in practical ethics: how much should a journalist become part of the story? To Fowler, he is no more than an impartial witness: 'The human condition being what it was, let them fight, let them love, let them murder, I would not be involved. My fellow journalists called themselves correspondents; I preferred the title of reporter. I wrote what I saw. I took no action – even an opinion is a kind of action.' He is kidding himself, of course.

The Shipping News (1993) by Annie Proulx

Proulx is one of the most original and pleasurable American novelists now working, a brilliantly inventive chronicler of the hard-bitten lives of hard-scrabble towns. She is typically unsentimental about local journalism. Here, we follow the life of Quoyle, an ugly New York journalist ('features as bunched as kissed fingertips') who relocates to his ancestral home of Newfoundland in order to escape the misery of modern urban life. He soon becomes a reporter for the local rag, the *Gammy Bird*, where he faithfully writes up traffic accidents and shipping arrivals (items of secondary interest for a title whose main coverage is of sexual abuse stories). This is an absurdist book, and the newspaper is deliciously, realistically eccentric, populated by characters like Nutbeem, who steals news from the radio when he is not reporting sex cases, or the angry editor Jack Buggit. Here is Buggit on journalism: 'We run a front-page photo of a car wreck every week, whether we have a wreck or not. That's our golden rule. No exceptions.'

Bridget Jones's Diary (1996) by Helen Fielding

Another figure who has passed into popular culture, Bridget is an over-weight, emotionally needy smoker, so inevitably her job is that of a journalist. She also began life (as novels used to do) in the pages of a newspaper, in this case the *Independent*. This is secondary to the main thrust of the story, which is about female friendship and the comically brittle nature of urban life. Fielding is sometimes credited for the establishment of the chick lit genre, which flowered in the late nineties, making a few women authors (and several publishers) very rich. Really, she was pioneering the notion of writing relatable stories about the sort of embarrassing things that can happen in life, which pointed ahead to much of the confessional, novelised memoirs we have today. *Bridget Jones's Diary* is also a vigorous nod to *Pride and Prejudice*: a couple, one of whom is called Darcy, despise each other for their arrogance right up to falling in love. Elizabeth Bennet smokes a bit less, though.

The Circle (2013) by Dave Eggers

One of the first of the major novelists really to take on the monstrous beast that is modern technology as a subject, Dave Eggers satirises the world of big tech companies like Google and Facebook, all shiny and squeaky on the surface ('This is the ultimate transparency. No filter. See everything. Always.'), all malign social engineering beneath. At one level, as a character says, this could be dismissed as just poking fun at the new world that 'has dorkified itself', at another it testifies to a real threat to our collective sanities and identities.

Chapter 8: Identity

White Teeth (2000) by Zadie Smith

I arrived at university to study English a few years after Zadie Smith had left, and bemusedly watched the reaction to her committing the unpardonable sin of being clever, beautiful and successful. *White Teeth* was disparaged through gritted teeth in bedrooms and halls across Cambridge. It is, however, a very good debut novel, bursting with ideas and self-consciously playing with the form itself. It provides a fine discussion of immigration and integration within the capital, seen from endlessly shifting perspectives. Indeed Smith is a real laureate of London, often fixing her stories in its north-western environs (see *NW* especially). The critic James Wood invented the term 'hysterical realism' in an essay about *White Teeth*, to describe the sort of big blockbuster novel that 'knows a thousand things but does not know a single human being'. It is a truer account of American fiction, really; although Smith did acknowledge it, at least partially, as 'painfully accurate'.

The Remains of the Day (1989) by Kazuo Ishiguro

Our fifth Nobel Laureate on this list, and another book blessed with an iconic film to press its credentials in perpetuity (this one a Merchant Ivory concoction of period porn, starring Anthony Hopkins and Emma Thompson). One might disagree with Ishiguro winning the Nobel Prize (this, his best novel, doesn't necessarily feel like it has the heft of greatness about it), but his work is undeniably much beloved. It is also written with great assurance, in this case telling the story of Stevens, the butler to an English aristocrat, who denies his love for his former colleague, the house-keeper Miss Kenton. There is much to ponder about the relationship between the powerful and their adherents, the social changes of the inter-war period, and the tragedy of feelings that can be experienced more than expressed.

Mary Barton (1848) by Elizabeth Gaskell

One of the most prominent state-of-the-nation novels, a genre created in the Victorian period, this was subtitled 'A Tale of Manchester Life'. It is Gaskell's debut, written following the death of her son, but also in conster-nation about the misery of working existence that surrounded her: 'I had always felt a deep sympathy with the care-worn men, who looked as if doomed to struggle through their lives in strange alternations between work and want.' Gaskell researched the condition of northern workers with care, made use of dialect, and thus produced a significant piece of jour-nalistic fiction. The first half is far more political than the second (when plot demands take over), and a contemporary review asked the question whether 'it may be kind or wise or right to make fiction the vehicle for a plain, matter of fact exposition of social evils'. To which the answer is yes, yes and yes.

Orlando (1928) by Virginia Woolf

This might be the strangest book on the list: a story of an Elizabethan poet who changes sex after a nap in Constantinople and lives for hundreds of years, thus getting the chance to meet plenty of notable literary figures along the way. It has excited those interested in writing about gender issues ever since, but it is also a fantastic story with plenty of beautiful writing. The character is based on Woolf's friend and lover Vita Sackville-West (her diary said of it: 'Vita; only with a change about from one sex to another'). The *New York Times* called the novel an example of the 'fourth dimension of writing', or 'an application to writing of the Einstein theory of relativity', so you can see why you should read it.

The Diary of a Nobody (1892) by George and Weedon Grossmith

This book has given us the phrase 'Pooterish', after its central character, the clerk Charles Pooter. It describes anything that is workaday but takes itself too seriously. It is an exceptionally British idea; indeed Britain's posturing in the post-Brexit world is distinctly Pooterish, a collective joke that many are unwilling to see. Charles Pooter is deeply class-conscious, sensitive to slights, caught between the mundane world of the lower middle class and the endless hope that his life will rise above it. The *Daily Mail* is Pooterish, ready to take offence, tensely protective of its place in the world, terrified of a fast new future.

The Secret Diary of Adrian Mole Aged 13¾ (1982) by Sue Townsend

A slightly pretentious, awkward young man coming from Leicestershire, you say? I have no idea why *Adrian Mole* resonated with me so much. An almost perfect comic creation, Adrian's authentic voice of angst leaps from his diary entries: 'I have realised I have never seen a dead body or a real female nipple. That is what comes of living in a cul-de-sac'. (He tries to remedy this by approaching Sharon Botts, who will 'show everything for 50p and a pound of grapes'.) Mole's story covers the rise and fall of Thatcherism, and the later (lesser) books that of Blairism, and are hugely representative of the period. He is an heir to Pooter, without question.

Brick Lane (2003) by Monica Ali

This novel conveys the sights and sensations of life in a Bangladeshi community in modern Britain. The manuscript got Ali a two-book deal, and industry hype well before *Brick Lane* ever reached the public. It centres on Nazneen, who comes – via an arranged marriage to a lovable auto-didact called Chanu – from rural Bangladesh to Tower Hamlets, and sets about understanding this new, rather bleak environment. There is something of the Dickensian approach to sprawling London life, but also a thoughtful consideration of how cultures in Britain can (often profitably) collide.

Saturday Night and Sunday Morning (1958) by Alan Sillitoe

Another debut novel, this is set in the Midlands and is one of the best examples of traditional British 'working-class' fiction. It covers, in realist fashion, the life of Arthur Seaton, who 'sweats his guts out' in a bicycle factory by day, but seeks release on Saturday nights ('the best and bingiest glad time of the week') in the local pubs, pursuing women, including – in distinctly unsentimental fashion – married ones. The frustrations of young men, the agentless plight of women (there is a home-made abortion scene that graphically makes this point), in the Britain of the period are ruggedly, but lyrically, shown.

The Well of Loneliness (1928) by Radclyffe Hall

This was published in the same year as *Orlando*, and was more specific in its discussion of lesbianism, telling the story of a woman called Stephen Gordon and her ultimately unsuccessful relationship with Mary Llewellyn. The *Sunday Express* ran a campaign to have the book banned ('it is a seductive and insidious piece of special pleading designed to display perverted decadence as a martyrdom'), and there was an obscenity trial by the end of the year. In it, the publisher first tried to pretend there was no lesbianism in the book, then reluctantly argued that there was, but it was described in a literary fashion. The magistrate thought this only made it worse, and ordered the novel destroyed. The decision was upheld by a twelve magistrates, who had not been allowed to read the book at all. In 1949 *The Well of Loneliness* was republished, and nobody seemed to mind that much.

The Buddha of Suburbia (1990) by Hanif Kureishi

Ultimately a novel about the angst of the marginalised and their continued search for identity, its hero is a mixed-race teenager, who wants to get out of the tedium of suburban life and into the exciting world of theatrical London ('bottomless in its temptations'). There, he seeks to come to terms with issues of race, sexuality, class and politics. It is a very busy novel, full of brash episodes, and great fun to read. But it is also important as one of the first to deal so explicitly with life as a plural person in Britain.

Notes

Introduction

1. Benjamin Disraeli (1804–81): a man who managed to be a writer and Prime Minister (a bit like Boris Johnson is in his own head). He was a leading figure in the development of the Tory Party, and came up with the concept of 'one nation' politics, used by Labour's Ed Miliband in the 2015 election, as well as the idea of clambering up the 'greasy pole' (which Ed didn't entirely manage). He was also Jewish, though not especially religious or proudly so, and suffered from anti-Semitic remarks throughout his life.

2. Charles Darwin (1809–82) has a justifiable claim to be the most significant figure mentioned in this book: an insatiably curious man who developed the theories of evolution and sexual selection that more or less govern how we regard ourselves as a species. He was the sort of amateur only the Victorian age could produce, always getting his hands dirty, whether it be drying out frogspawn on the edge of his bathtub or peering under stones to establish the behaviour of worms. He also apparently broke wind a lot, but you cannot have everything.

Chapter 1: Economics

1. Frédéric Bastiat (1801–50) came up with the Parable of the Broken Window, which refuted the idea that destruction was necessary for the economy (the idea that glaziers need someone to break a window in order to have any business). His point was about opportunity cost or the thing 'not seen': the window's owner may spend six francs with the glazier to fix the window, but that means he is not spending it elsewhere. No new wealth is created. It also ignores morality: if

347

destruction was seen as an economic good, then we should be demanding war and arson the whole time. Which would be bad for us, and the economy. Probably file this one under: economists over-thinking.

2. The world, in essence, functions by the endless movement of debt. We borrow from banks, banks borrow from each other, and the government borrows from investors. The rate at which banks borrow from other is called LIBOR (London Interbank Offered Rate). So, you do not say 'LIBOR rate' in the same way that you shouldn't say ATM machine (automated teller machine machine) or PIN number (personal identification number number). LIBOR became famous because of the scandal by which banks were manipulating the interest rates to make more money for themselves.

3. In September 2016, UK public sector employment was 5.4 million, with employment in central government at 2.95 million (the most since records began in 1999). Two-thirds of public sector employees are women (due to the main expenditure coming in education and healthcare).

4. In 1880 government expenditure constituted only 10 per cent of the UK's GDP (wealth was concentrated in private hands); in 2014 it was 43 per cent. Under Tony Blair and Gordon Brown, the state expanded to 50 per cent of GDP: half of everything produced of value came from the state.

5. I commend the book *Money: An Unauthorised Biography* (2013), by Felix Martin, to you. He discusses the island of Yap, in which the currency comprises stones from a foot to twelve feet wide. The point is that they are tokens of exchange and wealth without intrinsic value (indeed some are too large to be moved and their ownership is just asserted).

6. John Locke (1632–1704) is probably best known as an empiricist (a believer in the test of experience); he was the main British voice behind the *tabula rasa* argument: our minds are a blank slate or 'white paper' on which sensory experience is written. This is heartening: it argues for our own autonomy, our own right to develop how we want to.

7. As real currencies are no longer connected to precious metals at all, the quantity of them can be increased easily. Ironically, the 'crypto-currency' Bitcoins are limited in number, thanks to being recorded on a public ledger called a blockchain, so theoretically have a solid value. They are mostly used for buying drugs on the internet, though (I've,

er, heard). Andrew O'Hagan once wrote seventeen pages explaining Bitcoins in the LRB; Google that if you are interested.

8. See Martin Amis's grubbily brilliant novel, *Money* (1984):

> His job has nothing to do with anything except for money, the stuff itself. No fucking around with stocks, shares, commodities, futures. Just money. Sitting in his spectral towers on Sixth Avenue and Cheapside, blond Ossie uses money to buy and sell money. Equipped with only a telephone, he buys money with money, sells money with money. He works in the cracks and vents of currencies, buying and selling on the margin, riding the daily tides of exchange. For these services he is rewarded with money. Lots of it.

9. Alongside Adam Smith, probably the major figure in any articulation of the story of capitalism. If you think of Smith as thesis, Marx as antithesis, dialectically you get to the heart of it. Karl Marx (1818–83) was a fiercely angry atheist Jewish man, who believed that capitalism would fall due to a revolution of the working classes. In 1848 he wrote: 'There is only one means by which the murderous death agonies of the old society can be shortened, simplified and concentrated and that is by revolutionary terror.' Such cuddliness lent itself well to the communism and Stalinism that made much of his intellectual capital. But later Marx was also rather fond of England, where he lived for more than thirty years. He had digs in Dean Street, Soho, a place that is now a restaurant where a side order of chips costs the same as his weekly rent. That's capitalism for you.

10. Both positive stats here come from Deirdre McCloskey, a modern economist who is something of a fervent fan of capitalism, which she credits for 'alleviating poverty worldwide and enlarging the scope of human life'.

11. One recalls, regarding the penchant for giving inventions female names, the anarchist in *Blackadder the Third* who bursts on the Prince Regent shouting: 'Smash the spinning Jenny! Burn the Rolling Rosalind! Destroy the going-up-and-down-a-bit-and-then-moving-along Gertrude!'

12. James Watt (1736–1819) didn't invent the steam engine; his patented condenser improved an existing concept. He didn't get the idea from his ma's kettle, either, but he did use a kettle in the lab (for tea-making). Watt did invent the concept of horsepower, though.

13. Richard Arkwright (1732–92) was driven to an entrepreneurial life

because people in Derbyshire stopped buying his wigs. He leaned heavily on the work of others, had his methods persistently questioned and his patents often overturned: in that sense, he is a fairly representative figure for modern capitalism.

14. Adam Smith (1723–90) is perhaps the most quoted economist ever, and the *Wealth of Nations* the first economics book. He was Scottish, helping to establish the proud tradition that almost all the intellectual capital in the growth of the modern world came from either the north of England or Scotland. In 2007 a minor planet was named after Smith: a stony asteroid from the inhospitable outer reaches of an asteroid belt, which presumably reminded someone of Scotland.

15. Charles Babbage (1791–1871) is most famous for developing the Difference Engine and the Analytical Engine, a precursor to the computer. The former was never built, nor was its imaginatively titled sequel Difference Engine No. 2, but both were intended to make mechanical calculations. The Analytical Engine used punched cards to input data, and also to store it. It was, therefore, basically a Steampunk computer. Babbage never finished this either, and its final development was driven by Ada Lovelace, the first ever computer programmer and most notable woman of science you may never have heard of.

16. George Stephenson (1781–1848), another northerner. Known as the Father of the Railways, he was the first to build track between cities for steam engines.

17. Until recently Hamilton's claim to fame was being assassinated by Vice-President Aaron Burr over a political argument (as described in the wonderful 1973 novel by Gore Vidal called *Burr*). He was also the man most responsible for developing the American federal financial system, including a national bank. Today he is most famous for inspiring Lin-Manuel Miranda to write the brilliant hip-hop-inflected musical *Hamilton*, where he is mythologised as an immigrant, hard-working hero.

18. An extraordinary conference held in June 1944 in the United States to plan how the world's economy was to function once the war had ended. Representatives of forty-four countries attended (with the UK being represented by John Maynard Keynes), including the Soviet Union, which was a communist dictatorship.

19. Something of a rare combination, if truth be told: an intellectual who can both count and write. His book *How to Speak Money* (2014) helped me a lot in the understanding of basic concepts, which I am trying

to communicate to you. 'Why not just read his book then?' is a question to which there is no really satisfactory answer.

20. William III and Mary II, who came over in 1688 to accept the throne. They were Protestants and thus considered preferable to James II, the birth of whose son presaged a Catholic dynasty to come, which was unacceptable to most English people. This exchange of power is sometimes called the Bloodless Revolution, which isn't strictly accurate, although compared to most revolutions it was handled with typically British understatement.

21. Taken from the beginning of Richard III by Shakespeare: 'Now is the winter of our discontent / Made glorious summer by this sun of York'. The fact that the winter of 1979 was cruelly cold helped the label stick even more.

22. The Prime Minister James Callaghan returned from a summit in Guadeloupe on 10 January 1979 slap bang into the middle of the mess. He made the mistake of denying its existence: 'I don't think other people in the world would share the view that there is mounting chaos.' The *Sun* leapt on it to produce a headline that would stick to Callaghan: 'Crisis? What crisis?'. He didn't say that, of course, but that did not matter.

23. Too famous to require much of a footnote. Martin Amis once said 'the only interesting thing about Mrs Thatcher is that she isn't a man.' Christopher Hitchens said that 'she stinks of sex'. Trying to assess her legacy without the commonplaces of gender consciousness or misogyny has proved difficult. Thatcher was an enemy to the industrial working class whose livelihoods she destroyed; and a heroine to those she inspired. My grandad (whom we will meet later) worked in a Derbyshire power station, and managed – under Thatcher – to own his own house. To my gran, there were three people you could never criticise in her presence: Thatcher; the Queen Mother; and Brian Clough.

24. Until Donald Trump, Ronald Reagan (1911–2004) was the oldest President of the US, just short of seventy when he took office. The next oldest was William Henry Harrison (1773–1841), who was sixty-eight at his inauguration, at which event he caught a cold which killed him one month later.

25. The following figures are for the US, but the UK will be similar: in 1800, 68 per cent of people worked the land, 18 per cent worked in manufacturing, and 2 per cent in services; in 1950, 14 per cent worked the land, 53 per cent in manufacturing, and 28 per cent in services;

in 2012, 2 per cent worked the land, 18 per cent in manufacturing, 80 per cent in services

26. An awful lot of classical thought was preserved – especially the work of Aristotle – because it was copied by Islamic scribes, and rediscovered during the Renaissance by the Europeans. The decline of Islam from an enlightened, advanced culture of tolerance and education to its modern narrowness and often belligerence is truly one of the most precipitous falls in history.

27. Largely by Scots and northerners, but it still counts.

28. Worked out by dividing the gross fixed capital formation (GFCF) by the GDP. GFCF was devised by Simon Kuznets, whom we have met before, and basically shows how much new stuff the economy is acquiring.

29. Hard to keep track, what with thinking about one thing and another, but some notable crises before the big one include: 1995, the Mexican financial crisis; 1997, the Asian financial crisis; 2000, the end of the dot.com bubble. Essentially, these crises occur when everybody thinks assets are worth more than they are; and everybody realises at about the same time that they are not.

30. Some terminology you will have heard of here: if a trader is 'short' on a position, he is betting that it will decline in value; if he is 'long' he believes it will grow. So 'a short' is when an investor sells an asset that they have borrowed in the expectation that the price of the asset will go down (to enable them to buy it back later at a profit). Michael Lewis called his book *The Big Short* (2010), because he was telling the story of how some clever people bet that the sub-prime market was going to collapse. They were 'short the sub-prime market'.

31. John Lanchester has coined the term 'reversification' for the way in which, in the financial industry, 'words come, through a process of evolution and innovation, to have a meaning opposite to, or at least very different from, their initial sense'. A 'security' should be something solid; in fact it is something that can be traded at risk. I told you you should read his book!

32. Economics is truly the home of the awful euphemism. 'Sub-prime' means dodgy. The best banking term I discovered, though, was NINJA: a potential subject of a loan with no income, no job or assets. Banks should beware of ninjas. They weren't, of course.

33. A figure of importance comparable to Smith and Marx. John Maynard Keynes (1883–1946) believed that the market, left to its own devices,

would fail, and governmental interference was necessary to stop 'boom-and-bust' cycles, and to ensure that spending was maintained during recessions. His advice was followed during the Golden Age of Capitalism after the war, but fell victim to the new model of neo-liberal economics. It is largely down to the philosophy of Keynes that the banking crisis did not devastate more than it did. Even he was not immune from the lacerating criticism perpetually doled out against economists; one joke in the 1930s ran: 'Where five economists are gathered together there will be six opinions and two of them will be held by Keynes.'

34. Take, for example, the new phenomenon of light-speed trading. Traders using algorithms pick up on the minuscule variations in prices, and trade them, not in seconds but in micro-seconds. If you do this at enough scale (millions of times a day), you can generate profit. But nobody is regulating this; nobody truly understands its impact.

35. The last surplus was in 2002 and was of £243 million. The debt currently stands at more than £1.5 trillion, so that surplus would have dented it to the tune of less than 0.02 per cent.

36. One sign of this is the yields on sovereign bonds. If you watch the news, these are words that you will have heard but perhaps – like me – not understood. Essentially, the government (the sovereign in this instance) issues bonds in return for its borrowing, and promises to pay interest (or 'yield'). UK bonds currently have low yields (just over 1 per cent; lower than the US) because investors are willing to accept that due to their confidence in the UK's ability to pay over the long run. Government bonds are also known as 'gilts' because they used to have golden edges.

37. The famous words of Dickens's Micawber apply to household economics, but not at all to macroeconomics. National debt does not equal misery. This is what Micawber said: 'Annual income twenty pounds, annual expenditure nineteen nineteen and six, result happiness. Annual income twenty pounds, annual expenditure twenty pounds ought and six, result misery. The blossom is blighted, the leaf is withered, the god of day goes down upon the dreary scene, and in short you are forever floored. As I am!'

Dickens modelled Micawber on his father, with some apparent affection. He was no Keynesian though.

38. A great example of how political slogan-making can alter perception. NOBODY calls the bedroom tax the 'under-occupancy penalty' or the Tory choice of 'spare bedroom subsidy'.

39. According to the click-bait website for millennial liberals, the *Independent*, nineteen out of twenty families affected by the charge have no smaller properties available in their local area.

40. Another IFS quote: 'We have not seen a period remotely like it in the last 70 years and quite possibly the last 100 years.' Attentive readers will note that such a historical era included both the Great Depression and the Second World War.

41. You may remember this from third-year maths (where I used to sit reading *Lady Chatterley's Lover*, as it happens), but: mean is the average obtained by adding all the numbers in the set and dividing it by their number; the median is taking the middle point in the set

42. These figures come from the Equality Trust.

43. The ONS released figures showing that income inequality increased throughout the 1980s (thanks to trickle-down economics not trickling down) and has now declined back to the mid-1980s level. Wealth inequality has increased, because rich people's assets are worth more, and poor people don't have many assets to speak of.

44. The financial sector employed 1.2 million people in 2012, and contributed £63 billion in tax receipts (11.6 per cent of the total). We earn more and export more in this sector than any other country in Europe.

45. The Office of Budget Responsibility, which sounds like something invented by Dickens, but isn't. It was established by the Coalition government in 2010 to offer independent oversight of the UK's finances, largely by economic forecasting and measuring government performance against its targets.

46. This is a startling stat from the OBR: looking ahead fifty years, it sees that high net migration will delay public sector debt, due to the youth of the migrants. With high migration, the debt will be 73 per cent of GDP by 2062; with no migration, it will be 145 per cent. 'Higher migration could be seen as delaying some of the fiscal challenges of an ageing population . . . rather than a way of resolving them permanently', natch.

47. According to the Centre for Entrepreneurs in 2014, migrants produce nearly double the entrepreneurial activity of UK-born people: 500,000 migrants have launched businesses in recent years.

48. And even if those people are themselves Bulgarian, they will pay tax into British coffers.

49. Data here comes from the Centre for Economic Performance, a research

centre within the LSE, and the *National Institute Economic Review*, which puts the figure at 1p per hour lost in the unskilled sector.

50. £7.20 per hour x 30 hours per week x 48 weeks per year = salary of £10,368.

51. The review, published in July 2017, was titled 'Good Work', which was – ironically – a response by not that many of the commentators towards it. It crystallised the issues around the gig economy, but fell short of making concrete recommendations (such as increased national regulations upon companies like Uber). Instead, it suggested that gig workers should be renamed 'dependent contractors', and be entitled to holiday pay and sick pay. They should only effectively be paid the minimum wage, though, *on average*: meaning they could be allowed to accept lower rates if they chose to work at periods of lower demand. In some ways, Taylor's approach no more than recognised a necessary fact: modernity cannot be fought. An increase in technological intervention – that brings, say, a customer in direct contact with a private driver – will necessarily bring with it certain freedoms and certain penalties.

52. By which I mean: when the Bank of England did, as reported by journalist Aditya Chakrabortty.

53. If it still can be so called; one effect of Brexit is to reignite the debate about independence for Scotland, and a united Ireland.

54. One question that recurs is how much does the EU need us as a trading partner. In 2015 we exported £220 billion of goods and services to the EU; the EU exported £290 billion to us. However, that £220 billion represents 44 per cent of all our exports; the £290 billion only around 8–17 per cent of the EU's. Advantage EU.

55. Steven Pinker wrote a book about this, *The Better Angels of Our Nature* (2011), charting the 'multiple declines of violence in human history', which feels intuitively accurate. He has written a follow-up called *Enlightenment Now* (2018), which seems to make the same point again.

56. The Trussell Trust charity distributed more than 1.1 million three-day emergency supplies to people in 2015.

57. An argument, incidentally, that justifies the rich not paying more tax. In 2017 the IMF judged that 'empirical judgements do not support' the argument that higher taxes for the rich would affect growth.

58. Interestingly, Franklin D. Roosevelt had a similar idea during the Second World War: a maximum income of $25,000 (about $300,000 in today's money). It never took off.

59. If you ignore the fact that 2 million more people voted for Hillary Clinton than for him.

60. Stephen Crabb and Sajid Javid of the Tories were committed to a £100 billion Growing Britain Fund, to spend on things like school buildings, social housing and flood defences. Jeremy Corbyn proposed £500 billion of public spending around the same time.

61. See *The Road to Serfdom* (1944) by Friedrich von Hayek and *Free to Choose* (1980) by Milton Friedman.

62. Bankers themselves will feel the bite, as trading decisions will be taken by algorithms, not people. Up to 1.7 million banking jobs will go in the next decade due to digitisation.

63. The organisation Social Justice Ireland in 2012 costed the scheme at 39 billion euros, per year, which it believed could be funded by welfare efficiencies and an income tax (on all supplementary earnings) of 45 per cent. There are currently trials for UBI in Finland, and – closer to home – Fife in Scotland.

Chapter 2: Politics

1. Not the 'Mother of Parliaments', by the way. England as a whole, according to John Bright in 1868, is that maternal figure.

2. During the French Revolution, a febrile time also in British politics, both the Prime Minister, Pitt, and the Leader of the Opposition, Charles Fox, could both be described as Whigs.

3. The only British Prime Minister to be assassinated, Spencer Perceval, was shot in 1812 by John Bellingham, who felt that the government owned him compensation, and that his petitions had been ignored. He was swiftly hanged, needless to say.

4. One of the least attractive men in the history of British politics, and that is quite the accolade. It was Castlereagh who was behind the Six Acts, the government's repressive response to Peterloo. Shelley excoriated him in verse:

> I met Murder on the way –
> He had a mask like Castlereagh –
> Very smooth he looked, yet grim;
> Seven bloodhounds followed him.

Castlereagh ended his life by cutting his own throat amid mysterious claims of blackmail by a transvestite prostitute. His body displayed the conspicuous marks of syphilis.

5. Thomas Carlyle (1795–1881), a Scot like so many of the thinkers of the age, is probably best known now as a historian of the French Revolution. Carlyle had a famously difficult relationship with his wife Jane, alternately cast as a shrew or a victim, prompting Samuel Butler once to quip: 'It was very good of God to let Carlyle and Mrs Carlyle marry one another, and so make only two people miserable and not four.'

6. It was this latter policy that lured a young Winston Churchill away from the Conservatives, which has meant – in the minds of many – he never could truly be classed as a Tory.

7. Jingoism comes from the Victorian period, and a music-hall number about fighting the pesky Russians in support of Turkey:

> We don't want to fight but by Jingo if we do
> We've got the ships, we've got the men, we've got the money too.
> We've fought the Bear before, and while we're Britons true,
> The Russians shall not have Constantinople.

8. 'The unknown Prime Minister', according to Liberal leader Asquith. Admit it, you had not heard of him.

9. The campaign focused on him rather than his party, but he performed poorly. He claimed at one point that socialism would always 'fall back on some sort of Gestapo'; a piece of scare-mongering that was too much for the country to tolerate.

10. Later Tory leader Harold Macmillan commented that 'It was not Churchill who lost the 1945 election, it was the ghost of Neville Chamberlain.'

11. This was the Profumo affair in which war minister John Profumo was caught with a showgirl called Christine Keeler, who also had a client named Captain Yevgeny Ivanov, an 'attaché' at the Soviet Embassy. Macmillan did not deal with the problem quickly or decisively enough. It turns out he was lucky the scandal was not bigger. MI5 files show that Profumo had also had a long-running relationship with a glamorous Nazi spy called Gisela Winegard, from before the war through to the 1950s.

12. Hugh Gaitskell, who had blundered in opposition, giving way to the next great Labour figure, Harold Wilson.

13. This was designed to reduce exchange rate variability between European

countries, ahead of the introduction of the euro. Britain eventually decided to join in 1990, and thus undertook that the pound would never fall by more than 6 per cent against other currencies. This was disastrous because the pound was very weak, and so the government was merely agreeing to intervene when it did fall. The result two years later (under John Major) was that the government had to buy the pound in foreign markets and jack up interest rates to stop inflation, costing us billions. On 'Black Wednesday', 16 September 1992, it admitted defeat: we crashed out of the ERM. George Soros, the financier, had been shorting the pound throughout, predicting this chaos: as its value fell, he made £1 billion profit instantly.

14. The most toxic policy of my lifetime: a plan to replace the rates system, which taxed properties locally, with a community charge, which taxed people individually. There was no upside to it, and it meant that millions of people were asked to pay more. It became a nightmare to collect, was fiercely resisted, and ultimately cost Margaret Thatcher her job. One side effect was that many people came off the electoral register to dodge the poll tax, so they couldn't vote in the 1992 election, which may help account for the surprise Tory win.

15. This took place at an infamous dinner in the Granita restaurant in Islington back in May 1994, following the death of Labour leader John Smith. Allegedly, Brown agreed not to stand against Blair in return for wide powers in government, and an undertaking that Blair would step down in his favour after two terms. Both sides have issued varying denials, but the thrust now appears to be accepted. The relationship between Blair and Brown became poisonous in power, the two factions briefing against one another as if they were mortal foes.

16. In 1983 Margaret Thatcher used it to goad the Labour front benches about their concerns over an election: 'The right hon. Gentleman is afraid of an election, is he? . . . Afraid? Frightened? Frit?'

17. The Gentleman Usher of the Black Rod is responsible for the upkeep of Parliament. Happily, in 2018 it will become the Lady Usher of the Black Rod for the first time in history. The first one was called Walter Whitehorse in the later fourteenth century. It is actually a significant managerial and security role, but generally best known because the person uses a big rod to knock on the door of Parliament on the day of the Queen's Speech.

18. This dates back to the time of Henry IV, and the role originally involved the oversight of matters heraldic, like coats of arms.

19. Until the time of Victoria, the death of a monarch precipitated an election, as the government was seen very much as the representative of the Crown. Victoria's views were hugely influential: she promoted the career of Disraeli with great eagerness. It was George V who helped legitimise Labour, by his recognition of Ramsay MacDonald as Prime Minister material.

20. A bill is not supposed to take more than a year to pass, but some are allowed to be carried over to the next year. The arrival of an election kills all legislation dead, though, and everything has to start again afterwards.

21. Yep, the Queen pops up again. Although the last monarch to refuse assent was Queen Anne in 1707.

22. Parliament used to have the power to imprison and fine people (last done in 1880 and 1957 respectively) for contempt towards its activities. In 1880 Charles Edmond Grissom was imprisoned for the pardonable sin of failing to attend the Tower Hill Level Bridge Committee. In 1957, the Commons considered imprisoning the editor of the *Sunday Express*, John Junor, who had published an article claiming that members had evaded petrol rationing and was insufficiently apologetic about it.

23. These examples come from the indispensable book *How Parliament Works* (2015) by Robert Rogers and Rhodri Walters, which is full of important facts. While I am here, I should nudge you in the direction of two other books that were useful to me: *The Conservatives: A History* (2011) by Robin Harris; and *Speak for Britain: A New History of the Labour Party* (2010) by Martin Pugh.

24. As of 2017, there are 822 members. The largest assembly is in China.

25. MPs first received payment for their services in 1911, when they got £400 a year.

26. This is not popular with MPs, needless to say. This is Paul Flynn MP on the subject: 'A malign beast invaded and occupied MPs' territory. It has little sight or hearing and communicates in incomprehensible jargon and hieroglyphics. It must be kept docile and not aroused too often from its lair. Its irrationality must be learned, imitated and practised.'

27. There is agitation for a system of recall that could shorten this. The idea is that, if enough constituents sign a petition, a by-election should be called; in this way, unpopular behaviour could be challenged instantly. MPs, generally speaking, are oddly not in favour of this.

28. The phrase is Disraeli's, who was never short of a well-written line. And, yes, it is also the name of an episode of *Yes Minister.*

29. The amount of public money allocated to Scotland, Northern Ireland and Wales is worked out by something called the Barnett formula, devised by a civil servant ahead of the first devolution referendum in 1979. It was introduced on the fly to solve the question of how to deal with devolved spending, and Barnett himself has called it a 'terrible mistake'. Reassuring that it has now lasted for as long as my lifetime.

30. Here's a bone of contention: the money from tuition fees is shared across the UK, and therefore Scottish universities benefit from it, without having to charge their students. It is a total mess, really.

31. Indeed, John Major had campaigned in 1997 with a slogan suggesting that there were '72 hours to save the Union'. By that point, nobody was listening to him anyway.

32. The UK government indicated that there was no guarantee that Scotland could retain the use of the pound. As soon as the SNP had to start thinking of other currencies on the hoof ('groats' were even mentioned at one point), the argument was lost.

33. An almost literal holocaust in the original sense of burned sacrifice: 71 people dead (largely the poor, often immigrants) following failed fire regulations, political neglect and ignored complaint. A public inquiry may establish responsibility for these failings, although we must hope that – like with Hillsborough – it doesn't take thirty years.

34. It took the murder of eight-year-old Victoria Climbié, a young girl burned by cigarettes, tied up, beaten with bike chains, all within the sight of police, social services, doctors and the Church, to prioritise this function properly in local government. The Children Act of 2004 meant that councils, under their Children's Services departments, are required and enabled to co-ordinate responses to potential issues of abuse.

35. Switzerland, following a squeaker of a referendum in 1992, voted by 50.3 per cent to come out of the EEA. It now does bilateral deals with the EU, which are complicated and more or less equivalent to what it would get had it stayed in.

36. It employs more than 6,000 people in support, is split in its base between Brussels and Strasbourg and has a budget of £1.5 billion.

37. The book to read if you want the grim facts and quotes and blow-by-blow account is *All Out War* (2016) by Tim Shipman. It is so close to the action you can almost smell Michael Gove's mouthwash in it.

38. Sixty-four per cent of 18–24s voted; 90 per cent of over-65s. Ian McEwan, the novelist and thus one of the liberal elite, took comfort

from this: 'By 2019 the country could be in a receptive mood: 2.5 million over-18-year-olds freshly franchised and mostly remainers; 1.5 million oldsters, mostly Brexiters, freshly in their graves.'

39. The government's own internal briefing notes in 2018 predicted that a free trade agreement with the EU would lead to a reduction in UK economic growth (compared to the status quo) of 5 per cent, a 'no deal' separation would lead to a reduction of 8 per cent, and an EEA membership to a reduction of 2 per cent. Of course, as we have seen, Brexit is about politics, not economics.

40. John Stuart Mill (1806–73): a notable philosopher probably best remembered for his development of utilitarianism (the idea that what gives the greatest good to the greatest number is the right ethics basis for decision-making). His father had aimed to create a genius, and so gave him an astonishingly intensive academic upbringing: learning Greek by three, Latin by eight, scholastic logic by twelve.

41. For there to be a vote of confidence in a Tory leader, just so that you know, forty-eight Tory MPs need to signal their dissatisfaction to the Chairman of the 1922 Committee (its internal party body). For a Labour leader to face a formal challenge, 20 per cent of its MPs and MEPs must support one candidate, who then needs to declare their intention to run.

Chapter 3: Health

1. Worth noting that Beatrice Webb in 1909 called for a 'public medical service'; and a Royal Commission of 1926 for a 'service to be supported from the general funds'. William Beveridge worked for Beatrice Webb on her 1909 report.

2. William, Baron Beveridge (1879–1963) was an economist and, briefly, a Liberal MP. Ironically, he lost his seat in 1945, the very time his report was to be put into action. He was also a eugenicist in that he believed in controlling reproduction among the unsuitable. You get a sense of that from the tone of his report, even though its eventual consequence was an attack on inequality.

3. Like a Harry Potter book, it was published to queues of demanding readers: 100,000 copies were sold in a month, and 600,000 overall.

4. Arguably one of the most significant prose works in the English language, written in prison by John Bunyan sometime in the 1660s.

It tells the allegorical tale of Christian, an everyman figure in search of salvation. He gave the world the concept of Vanity Fair, which provided a title to the great novel by Thackeray. My favourite literary response to *Pilgrim's Progress* is *Mr Standfast*, one of the sequels to *Thirty-Nine Steps* by John Buchan, in which the wonderful grizzly Peter Pienaar gets his moral guidance from Bunyan. If you have never read the Hannay books by Buchan, you simply must.

5. Perhaps only Britain would vote in a landslide against the government of its greatest wartime leader, Winston Churchill. However, as we have seen, Churchill's Conservatives were battling political fatigue (the party had been in power, in one form or another thanks to coalitions, for fifteen years) and the sense that only a socialist party would rebuild the devastated country on principles of fairness.

6. Aneurin Bevan (1897–1960) was known as Nye since childhood, and will always be a hero to Labour folk. The son of a miner, himself a trade unionist, he represents a certain type of benevolent socialism. Having established the NHS, he resigned from government in 1951 in protest against the proposed introduction of prescription charges for spectacles.

7. These examples, plus the wobbly uterus one that follows, are quoted in the brilliant book *The Five Giants: A Biography of the Welfare State* (1995) by the journalist Nicholas Timmins. I found no great NHS book in my research, but this broader one (taking in other policy areas) is well worth a read.

8. Another Tory 'character', he went on to become a key member of Margaret Thatcher's early Cabinets. He appears in the wonderful 'Dear Bill' letters by *Private Eye* (in which Denis Thatcher writes to his golfing chum) as the 'Mad Monk'. I used to read *Dear Bill* books religiously as a child, although they did affect my youthful prose a little. Relatives were always bemused to receive thank-you letters from me, ending with phrases like 'yours, in the drink' or 'yours, from the snug'. They never said anything, though.

9. Bodkin Adams was having a homosexual (frowned upon in those days) affair with the mayor of Eastbourne (awkwardly the magistrate in charge of hearing the case, before recusing himself) and also the Deputy Chief Constable of the local force. The Lord Chief Justice was seen dining with the mayor during proceedings. Shockingly, he was acquitted, with lots of suspicious shenanigans occurring with things like admissible evidence.

10. Just under 700 doctors were struck off in the last five years, a majority of whom – interestingly – were trained abroad.

11. Mortality figures due to negligence rather than natural causes are extremely hard to establish in retrospect. Numbers between 400 and 1,200 have been mentioned, although the official inquiry has been clear that no definitive position can be established.

12. The first in 2010 was an NHS inquiry; he returned with the powers of a full public inquiry, which was published in February 2013.

13. Prescription charges were introduced in England in 1952, abolished in 1965 and restored in 1968. Worth remembering that charges like this (and dental care) only amount to 5 per cent of the NHS budget. The vast majority is – across the board – based on general taxation.

14. This was introduced in 1911, and expanded with the creation of the welfare state in 1948. Employers used to buy special stamps and fix them to contribution cards given to employees, which acted as proof they were entitled to benefits and were retained while they were in employment. Hence the phrase 'handing someone their cards' to mean firing them.

15. All these numbers are taken from the latest available data for each country.

16. The Organisation for Economic Development and Cooperation (OECD) began as the Organisation for European Economic Cooperation (OEEC), established in the aftermath of the Second World War to administer the Marshall Plan of US aid to Europe. It became the OECD in 1961 and is now a forum for thirty-five countries, primarily well-developed in the Western world, to advance policies of mutual economic benefit.

17. Overweight means having a Body Mass Index of 25–29.9; obese means having a BMI of 30 and more. Now BMI is not a perfect calculation, as it does not distinguish between fat and muscle: it simply is weight divided by the square of height (kg/m2). I am sixteen stone and six foot five and am classed as borderline overweight, despite going to the gym four times a week and carb-dodging in a thoroughly emasculating fashion. But, as a rule of thumb, it is a legitimate indicator.

18. Six out of ten adults spend more than four hours a day sitting or lying down. I know I do. We are burning, probably, around 800 fewer calories a day than fifty years ago.

19. Here's a counterfactual on smoking: the tax revenue from smoking is around £12 billion a year, and smokers die – on average – earlier than

their non-chuffing counterparts, thus saving the NHS the burden often of long-term care. The great cynic Sir Humphrey Appleby lauded as 'national benefactors' those 'smokers who voluntarily lay down their lives for their friends'. He noted that 'financially speaking it's unquestionably better that they continue to die at their present rate'.

20. There are 3,000 alcohol-related admissions to A&E every day. I'd judge but when I was nineteen, I got drunk after finishing my exams at university, was running around and broke my collarbone. I can still recall the shame of looking the medical staff in the eye.

21. And we should be clear that 'Diet' drinks are not good for you. Donald Trump, when he was just a funny, gauche, semi-forgettable, cat-bottom-mouthed figure on reality TV, once tweeted: 'I have never seen a thin person drinking Diet Coke.' Which, unlike most things he has said as President, is funny and true. Do you know the best diet drink? Water.

22. Born Eric Blair (1903–50), the journalist and author who is most likely to be quoted by virtue-signalling journalists and authors like me. His satirical novel *Animal Farm* (critiquing Russian communism) was rejected for publication by T. S. Eliot (on behalf of his publishing company Faber) as it did not have 'the right point of view from which to criticise the political situation'. This was 1945 and Britain was still an ally of Stalin's Russia, which Eliot did not wish to antagonise. Eliot also thought, hilariously, that 'what was needed (some might argue) was not more communism but more public-spirited pigs'.

23. This report was commissioned by a Labour government, but was published reluctantly by the Conservative government who arrived in 1979. They tried to bury it, both by releasing it on an August Bank Holiday with only 260 copies published, and by pouring cold sick over it in the very introduction written by the minister:

> I must make it clear that additional expenditure on the scale which could result from the report's recommendations – the amount involved could be upwards of £2 billion a year – is quite unrealistic in present or any foreseeable economic circumstances, quite apart from any judgement that may be formed of the effectiveness of such expenditure in dealing with the problems identified. I cannot, therefore, endorse the Group's recommendations.

24. The French philosopher René Descartes (1596–1650) argued that the soul existed in the pineal gland, the bit of the brain at its base that

looks like a pine cone. This seems unlikely, but nobody since has authoritatively suggested how precisely the mind and the brain inter-relate.

25. Work-related stress accounts for 45 per cent of all working days lost to ill-health.

26. That's 32,467 new doctors, 18,432 new nurses and 5,729 GPs according to the NHS's own figures.

27. This one from the Nuffield Trust, a healthcare think-tank.

28. Having a baby is the most common reason for hospital admission in England. Births are at the highest in forty years, up by almost a quarter in the last decade.

29. According to the Scottish Accounts Commission in 2016, the current system there is 'unsustainable', and an extra £667 million will be needed to fund the shortfall by 2020. In Scotland, as in England, budget cuts have bitten at the local level.

30. According to the Nuffield Trust, in winter 2016 there were times in which a third of all hospital trusts had 100 per cent occupancy rates: no free beds at all. The NHS had to open on average 3,500 escalation or emergency beds to meet demand, the equivalent of more than five new hospitals every day.

31. An example of the law of unintended consequences here: the laudable decision to raise the minimum wage has added a cost burden to care homes who pay it to many of their employees.

32. The government in 2016 authorised local councils to increase council takes by a small percentage in order to make up some of the shortfall.

33. This means they are adjusted for inflation, based on the value of the consumer price index. That is a measurement of how much an average basket of goods and services has increased in price over the year. In January 2017 it rose by 1.8 per cent; if it continues to rise it will cause economic problems, especially if income levels continue to stagnate. The CPI is also a useful tool to show the things a society currently values and so places into its 'average' basket: in 2016 computer games and soft-ware, coffee pods and microwave rice were added; CD-ROMs, nightclub entry charges and rewritable DVDs were removed. The retail price index (RPI) is similar, but also takes in costs of things like housing. It is always higher than the CPI. That is why the government likes to link the payments it receives to the RPI, but the payments it makes to the CPI.

34. There were 1.3 million on NHS waiting lists in 1998; by 2008, that was under 600,000.

35. This is something of a moot point, in that there is evidence that people who report to hospitals at the weekend are sicker and more desperate, and therefore that increased allocation of staff will not affect mortality rates that much. There is little empirical evidence either way on this.

36. This has got better in recent years. In the 1970s junior doctors worked an average 102-hour week (a little more than five twenty-hour days).

37. The basic salary of a first-year doctor is £27,000 for a purported forty-hour week, although they get more for working unsociable hours (hence this dispute). The average for a junior doctor all-in is around £37,000, which goes up to £70,000 as they become specialists. Consultants earn between £76,000 and £102,000 from the NHS, but can supplement their earnings privately.

38. Lord Carter published a review in 2015 on efficiency in the NHS and found mass variance in spending on the same items like hip replacements available from £788 to £1,590. Running costs for a hospital (in £ per square metre) vary from £105 at best to £970 at worst.

39. Cosmetic surgery is available in rare cases where people can establish either a physical or mental reason for it (although it is extremely likely that people lie to benefit from it). One set of figures suggests that, in 2013, the NHS spent around £50 million on cosmetic treatments, although many of them will be based on medical need. IVF (In Vitro Fertilisation) costs the NHS between £100 and £400 million every year.

Chapter 4: Education

1. Anthony Eden, the Prime Minister in 1956, echoed the same point when he said: 'The prizes will not go to the countries with the largest population. Those with the best systems of education will win.' This principle, as we shall see, has motivated a country like Singapore. It has not done so with Britain.

2. In the same time, the proportion in secondary schools has gone from 16 to 28 per cent. There has been a detectable population explosion in migrant children to account for this: the number of children born to non-UK-born women more than doubled between 1999 and 2010 (the years in which most children now at school were born).

3. It was 5.7 per cent of our GDP in 1974; it is around that level now.

4. In 2017, following the bruising election for the Conservatives, the

government undertook to move £1.3 billion back into schools, but take it from the overall pot destined for education as a whole (probably the bits paying for new buildings). This sort of economic sleight of hand would be subversive if it were done with any guile, but looks merely hapless as it is not.

5. The initial proposals meant that 9,000 urban schools would lose out on some funding and 11,000 would gain. With an election to fight in 2017, the government promised that nobody would lose out.

6. He stopped using the term in public after 2013, and it never really took off. The principle is that the role of the state can be reduced by the benevolent, voluntary activity of individuals.

7. This accounts for 29 per cent of all schools, and 62 per cent of all secondaries. Two per cent of all schools are free schools.

8. These can be 'voluntary-aided', where the religious organisation contributes building costs; or 'voluntary-controlled' where the organisation has a more influential governance role.

9. Faith schools have an exemption from the Equality Act of 2010 to enable them to do this. Free schools have to offer at least 50 per cent of all places on a non-faith basis, whether oversubscribed or not.

10. Lots get talked about Muslim faith schools, but there are just twenty-seven of them funded by the state. As of January 2017, there were forty-eight Jewish, eleven Sikh and five Hindu schools; all others were Christian.

11. Samuel Johnson (1709–84): the fantastic, and fantastically grotesque, scholar, author, literary critic and all-round symbol of the eighteenth century. His *A Dictionary of the English Language* published in 1755 was a landmark piece of scholarship and stubborn brilliance. A couple of my favourite definitions:

> DULL: not exhilaterating (sic); not delightful; as, to make dictionaries is dull work.
> SOCK: something put between the foot and the shoe.
> TO WORM: to deprive a dog of something, nobody knows what, under his tongue, which is said to prevent him, nobody knows why, from running mad.

12. Shakespeare, Milton, Newton were all grammar school boys, so this system must have done something right. One of the (snobbish) arguments against Shakespeare writing his plays is that a grammar school boy could never have gained sufficient knowledge to do so. But this

seems misplaced: at school, he would have read the classics and some histories to augment his knowledge of rural life that provided much of his imagery. Plus, he was a genius. How much he enjoyed school is a different matter: he skewers a teacher in the character of Holofernes in *Love's Labour's Lost*; and has Romeo say: 'Love goes toward love as schoolboys from their books; But love from love, toward school with heavy looks.'

13. This nugget, and much of the history of our education system, comes from that fine book that helped us with the NHS: *The Five Giants* by Nicholas Timmins.

14. The Education Minister W. F. Forster asked a question that has occurred to the occasional Tory mind ever since: 'Why should we relieve the parent from all payments for the education of his child . . . the enormous majority of them are able, and will continue to be able, to pay these fees.'

15. Thomas Arnold (1795–1842): his success as headmaster of Rugby School (where the eponymous game was invented) was copied elsewhere. He was robustly of the view that school should be about development of the soul and the morals, rather than the intellect. He was anti-science ('rather than have physical science on my son's mind, I would gladly have him think the sun went round the earth and that the stars were so many spangles set in the bright blue firmament'), anti-language ('boys at a public school never will learn to speak or pronounce French well, under any circumstance') and led to a pronounced view that education was not about practical skills or scientific knowledge that has influenced our entire system to the university level. Thomas Hughes set *Tom Brown's School Days* at Rugby under Arnold, which also gave the world the far more stirring character of Flashman.

16. He could have said 'required' but, as this is Britain, he did not. The effect was the same.

17. Facing budget problems, she famously ended the provision of free milk for primary school children, thus earning the soubriquet 'Thatcher the Milk Snatcher'. Actually, Harold Wilson had already snatched free milk from secondary school children in the 1960s, but nobody remembers that. The saving, by the way, was a relatively paltry £8 million; probably not worth it in the end.

18. As early as 1952, research showed that coaching could improve eleven-plus performance by more than fourteen points.

19. In 2008 the Sutton Trust educational think-tank concluded that grammar schools were enrolling 'half as many academically able children from disadvantaged backgrounds as they could'.

20. Even a cross-party Education Select Committee in 2017 conceded this point: there was a consensus of experts that little evidence supported either the idea of advanced attainment or social mobility in grammar schools. Neil Carmichael MP, the chair of the committee, said that 'The focus on opening new grammar schools is, in my view, an unnecessary distraction from the need to ensure all our young people are equipped with the skills to compete in the modern workplace.'

21. Exam results are obviously key factors in league tables, so the future of schools, the careers of teachers, are very much at stake here.

22. The OFSTED equivalent in Wales is called Estyn, in Northern Ireland it is the Education and Training Inspectorate (ETI). In Scotland the whole system is governed by Education Scotland, and so school inspection appears less independent; cynics would say it is in everyone's interests for schools to be seen to be doing well.

23. In 2003 Wales launched the Welsh Baccalaureate as an alternative to A-level with some bits and bobs (about society and well-being) added on. It hasn't really taken off as an option.

24. Indeed, Cambridge was founded by refugees from Oxford, concerned at the violence between townies and students. Here is a fascinating fact for you: early Oxford had a murder rate of 120 per 100,000, which was (according to my *TLS* colleague, and history guru, David Horspool) 'higher than Caracas or San Pedro Sula, Honduras, currently the two most violent cities in the world not at war'. When you watch the pimpled, Oxonian weeds on *University Challenge*, do think of their bloodied forebears.

25. Some £3.5 billion over ten years, at a time when all public expenditure amounted to £11 billion a year.

26. The country's second most august university, Oxford, objected so strenuously to the government's cuts that it refused to give Margaret Thatcher an honorary doctorate, citing her 'deep and systematic damage to the whole public education system in Britain'.

27. It was the top third of *parental* earners whose children would pay the full thousand, the amount tapering off as earnings decreased. The concept of the graduate tax was avoided.

28. Reaching a peak of 49 per cent in 2011 (approaching the target set by Tony Blair of 50 per cent of all possible people of student age).

29. In Northern Ireland, they are capped at £3,805.

30. Here is the apology:

> We made a pledge, we did not stick to it, and for that I am sorry. It was a pledge made with the best of intentions – but we should not have made a promise we are not absolutely sure we could deliver. I shouldn't have committed to a policy that was so expensive when there was no money around. Not least when the most likely way we would end up in government was in coalition with Labour or the Conservatives who were both committed to put the fees up.

Most of this statement could have been said by any politician of any stripe about any policy. Google 'Nick Clegg sorry' and enjoy how Clegg's video message was turned, via autotune, into a song.

31. Indeed, it is likely that some 77 per cent of all loans will not be paid back in full. The government writes off the rest of the debt after thirty years.

32. One calculation, by the financial adviser Martin Lewis, is that a person who has taken out the full tuition fee and maintenance grant would need to get a graduate job paying £45,000 per year, increasing by 2 per cent above inflation every year, in order to pay off the loan in full in the thirty-year period.

33. Scottish students who are disadvantaged receive around £560 less a year in financial support than their other British counterparts.

34. This did not stop the policy appearing in the 2017 Labour manifesto, and was held to be one of the reasons for the 'Corbyn surge' among younger voters.

35. There is a fascinating article on this by Ian Cobain in the *Guardian*. Give it a Google.

36. When our friend Benson was writing in 1903, he could title his book *The Schoolmaster*, and have no problem with gendered pronouns. The world is markedly different now: barely over a fifth of all teachers are men.

37. Pupils who spent more than six hours online a day had an average PISA science test score of 483, compared to 540 for those who spent less than two hours online.

38. PISA released a happiness index for pupils for the first time in 2017: Britain performed badly. Around one in six fifteen-year-olds said they were unhappy with their life (ranking the UK thirty-eighth out of forty-eight countries). In 2018, PISA will launch a new test intended

to measure pupils' tolerance for other cultures and their ability to spot fake news. Scotland, Australia and Canada will take these tests, but countries like England, Finland, and the US will not (on the grounds that they are still untried in terms of value).

Chapter 5: Military

1. British military history is full of the brilliantly eccentric heroes of the upper classes, for so long the staple of the *Telegraph* obituary pages. Take Adrian Paul Ghislain Carton de Wiart (1880–1963), who survived three wars (Boer, First and Second) having been shot in the face, head, stomach, ankle, leg, hip and ear. He tore his own fingers off at one point when a doctor refused to amputate them. At the age of sixty-one, during the Second World War, he was sent as leader of the mission to Yugoslavia when his plane crashed in the sea. He swam to shore and was captured by the Italians. He then made five escape attempts, one involving seven months of tunnelling. At another point, he was free in Italy disguised as a peasant for eight days: he spoke no Italian, had an eye patch, one arm, and multiple visible scars.

   Or Major Allison Digby Tatham-Warter (1917–93), who carried an umbrella as a means of identifying himself because he was so bad at remembering passwords. During the battle, he led a charge against the Germans in a bowler hat, waving his umbrella, which he then used to maim the driver of an armoured car by shoving it through the observational slit. He also escorted a priest away from enemy fire, telling him, 'Don't worry about the bullets, I've got an umbrella.' Having been captured, he – of course – escaped, disguised himself as a 'deaf-mute son of a lawyer' and led the guerrilla army operating in Holland until he could rejoin the regular forces.

2. See *Henry IV Part 2*, in which Falstaff goes recruiting alongside Justice Shallow, and accepts 'three pounds' to let off the reluctant Mouldy and Bullcalf from their duty. Shallow is the former crony of Falstaff who wants to re-live their old scurrilous glories as drunken, horny students. 'We have heard the chimes at midnight,' acknowledges Falstaff, which gave Orson Welles the name of his version of the *Henry* plays with the fat knight at its centre.

3. Samuel Pepys (1633–1703) was Chief Secretary of the Admiralty, and helped drive the professionalisation of the navy. He is more famous as

the diarist who wrote more than a million words (in a cryptic shorthand) about his life and the city around him. Thanks to it, we know he buried his favourite parmesan cheese to shield it from the Great Fire of London, that he had an operation to remove bladder stones, and that he cheated on his wife, including with a 'monstrous fat' woman.

4. Francis Drake (c.1540–96) is notable for circumnavigating the globe and annoying the Spanish, who put a bounty on him thanks to his piratic attacks. This included the time he 'singed the King of Spain's beard', by raiding Cadiz harbour with fireships. The story of Drake refusing to interrupt his game of bowls due to the announcement of the Spanish Armada is probably apocryphal, alas.

5. Take America, which has been a dominant economic power since the nineteenth century, and did not seek to create a formal empire for itself. Two concepts are worth remembering. The Monroe Doctrine (1823) was an idea promulgated by President James Monroe that America would not interfere in European affairs and would expect Europeans to cease empire-building in the New World. 'Manifest destiny' was a term probably coined by a newspaper man in 1845, and meant the ideal of expansion westwards within the American continent.

6. Cursed often by the military today, this was the first recognition that the public should be informed by external observers of what happens in warfare. It was largely suppressed for much of the next century, but has gradually become the norm. When you see a broadcaster in a flak jacket surrounded by falling artillery, think of a Victorian scribbler on a donkey in the Crimea.

7. Russell wrote this (rhetorical) question: 'Are there no devoted women among us able and willing to go forth to minister to the sick and suffering soldiers . . . Are none of the daughters of England, at this extreme hour of need, ready for such a work of mercy?' One person who was ready and able was Florence Nightingale (1820–1910), a nurse who sailed out to the Crimea to help. She became known as the 'Lady with the Lamp', tirelessly pacing the filthy and unhealthy corridors of the hospitals that she gradually battled to improve. Her long-term legacy was a recognition of the value of sanitary conditions – including via hand-washing – as a means of limiting the spread of infections.

8. In the town of Cawnpore, Sir Hugh Wheeler led one of the great defences in the history of warfare when he held an entrenchment against overwhelming force for three weeks. When he eventually surrendered (for the sake of civilian women and children), he was

double-crossed, and his ragtag group of survivors murdered. Women and children were butchered and thrown, some dead, some still clinging to life, into a well.

9. A needless conflict perpetuated by the criminal opinion that the Zulu tribe needed to be exterminated rather than befriended. It led to the humiliating Battle of Isandlwana (1879), in which 1,300 soldiers were killed and then the heroic defence of Rorke's Drift in which 139 soldiers (39 of whom were wounded) held off a force of 4,500 Zulus.

10. The phrase is Richard Vinen's, whose 2014 book *National Service: A Generation in Uniform 1945–1963* is the source for much of this information in this section.

11. There is a story of a man being reported as absent without leave, only for it to be discovered that he had been living for six months, confused, in the Catterick Camp toilets and stealing food at night.

12. Peter Burns, quoted in *All Bull: The National Servicemen* (1973) edited by the experimental novelist B. S. Johnson.

13. The *Daily Herald* ran a headline 'Is your son a murderer?' about the widespread nature of abuse. One Mau Mau suspect was bayoneted through the ear, so he could be led on a wire.

14. Allegations were made about the rape by soldiers of a thirteen-year-old girl and the strangulation of a ten-year-old boy. We do know that there was bloody retribution to the murder by EOKA of two British army wives: one storeman recalled how batons were issued to any soldier who wanted one, and one sergeant returned to barracks with the butt of his gun bent and 'covered in bits of skin, and hair and blood'.

15. Part of the conflict was known as 'the Dirty War', in which intelligence services infiltrated the IRA. Questions are now asked as to what level of violence was then permitted to be perpetrated by agents of the state in the name of spying. It is likely that people were murdered by those working for British intelligence anxious to maintain their cover.

16. The former invaded because of spurious intelligence – since disproven – that Saddam Hussein had weapons of mass destruction; the latter because of its use as a base for terrorists. It is notable that 9/11 in itself provides little specific justification for either incursion. Fourteen out of the nineteen terrorists, including Osama Bin Laden, were from Saudi Arabia, a military ally and wealthy customer of both Britain and America. Bin Laden, when he was killed extra-judicially (but morally acceptably), was found in Pakistan.

17. Bayonets were invented at the siege of Bayonne in 1640, when French musketeers stuck their pikes in the muzzles of their guns. It is extraordinary that this primitive, ad-hoc weapon has lasted for 500 years.

18. His book began as an article in the *Literary Review*, and contains a photograph in its early pages of a soldier reading the *London Review of Books*. Despite the vicious internecine rivalry of the literary journal world, I am still being nice about it.

19. They used as their starting text the Lieber Code, which had been signed by Abraham Lincoln in 1863 and forbade the killing or torturing of prisoners in the American Civil War.

20. The US long argued that these rules could not relate to the treatment of terrorists, as they were themselves 'unlawful enemy combatants'. This meant, in its view, CIA operatives could use torture with impunity. The Supreme Court ruled in 2006 that this was not the case, and terror suspects had convention rights.

21. The US did not agree that protection should be afforded to irregular forces who did not seem to 'distinguish themselves from the civilian population'. It was concerned that terrorists, posing as civilians, would receive all the benefits of combatant status.

22. And, no, the US does not accept its jurisdiction either. Spot a pattern here?

23. Herbert Kitchener (1850–1916) became Secretary of State for War in 1914, and is most famous for the iconic 'Your country needs you' poster, his hugely moustachioed face staring sternly, while he wags his finger in dire warning against any shirkers out there. He died in 1916 aboard the HMS *Hampshire*, which was sunk by a German mine.

24. The fact that it was the British, not the Germans, who invented concentration camps is, then, broadly true.

25. The despicable Phil Shiner, who filed 2,740 complaints against troops has now been struck off for his corrupt behaviour.

26. This was the first major armed forces charity, formed in 1921. It runs the annual Poppy Appeal on Remembrance Day, which raises £35 million a year, or about a third of its income. The charity acts as an advocate on all military issues affecting personnel, and provide both funds and care to those in need.

27. The RAF in the Second World War had 1.1 million personnel, so the reduction in seventy years is rather striking.

28. France in the 1960s objected to any integrated military command structure, i.e. one multinational set of leading officers, and kicked out

NATO headquarters from its territory. It was still allowed to remain a member.

29. In 2015 it stopped even counting the dead in the conflict; a neat symbol of its futility in the arena.

30. The UN's commitment to freedom is sometimes questioned for this reason. For example, in 2011 its General Assembly held a minute's silence for North Korean dictator Kim Jong-il. Although maybe they foresaw how much worse his chubby bully of a successor would be.

31. These members are supposed to be democratically elected, but the Asia region only puts up four countries for the four positions on the council (China, Iraq, Japan and Saudi Arabia) and all are elected unopposed. China is scarcely a beacon of human rights either.

32. Whether or not this was the right answer, the debate was an appalling example of British politicking instead of focusing on the real issue at hand. Ed Miliband, then the Labour leader, used the issue – unforgivably in my view – as a proxy means of undermining the authority of the Conservative government. He won that particular squabble, but not in any edifying way.

Chapter 6: Law and Order

1. This is a movement, run within parts of the Christian Church, to increase understanding of the faith through discussion. Almost 30 million people worldwide have taken part in its courses. It operates in over 70 per cent of the UK's prisons, involving 60,000 prisoners since 1997.

2. That year, Abraham Thornton, a bricklayer, was accused of murder by William Ashford, the victim's brother. The former, rather dashingly, demanded the right of battle. When he was refused, he escaped to America and went unprosecuted. The law was repealed soon after.

3. Gavin Millar QC was quoted as saying that 'the offence has always been in the head of the Crown Prosecution Service, not actually in law'. The charges related to aiding and abetting someone to commit misconduct in public office, using Edwardian legislation that had never before related to journalists.

4. The principle goes back to Aristotle, at least, who said that 'it is better for the law to rule than one of the citizens.'

5. The then Prime Minister David Cameron went on the *Late Show with*

David Letterman around the anniversary of the Magna Carta, and couldn't translate it. Considering he went to Oxford and Eton (and the translation is, effectively, just an anglicisation of the Latin words), Cameron was either pretending to be unschooled or is just rather dim.

6. This is true today: between 1940 and 1990 the Supreme Court of America approvingly cited Magna Carta more than sixty times.

7. Never used that often in practice: forty-eight times in the century before its abolition. That is no comfort to the poor bastards who had their arms and legs nearly wrenched off, I acknowledge.

8. The so-called Star Chamber (named due to a painting on the ceiling), which has become a term now used for any improper, arbitrary court of justice.

9. Court records were kept in Latin until 1731, and linguistic fossils of that system are continually unearthed in court today. The language of courts in the seventeenth century was a curious mix of Latin, French and English. This is my favourite legal sentence ever, taken from 1667: 'Pur avoider le stuffing del rolls ove multiplicity del matter.'

10. Including the devolution of powers to make laws to the assemblies of Scotland, Wales and Northern Ireland.

11. A former Chief Justice, who wrote a beautifully clear book called *The Rule of Law* (2010), which was very useful in the writing of this chapter.

12. The Scottish legal system, for example, contains an odd hodgepodge of English and European influences, and also is more influenced by the precedent of Roman law (which it heavily copied in the fifteenth century). In practice, there are some differences with England: in criminal trials (which have fifteen members of the jury, not twelve) there is the third verdict of 'not proven', for example, to denote a case where there is suspicion of guilt but insufficient evidence to convict; there are sheriffs' courts instead of magistrates' courts; prosecutions are undertaken by the Procurator Fiscal Service, a department of the Scottish government.

13. In the endless world of austerity and cuts, this is down from around 30,000 in the 1990s. Increasingly, paid professionals called stipendiary magistrates are used in the more serious cases.

14. They are the modern version of the assizes (an old English term meaning court session), which date back to the early medieval period. Then, judges representing the Crown would tour the country to hear cases awaiting them. They would follow pre-arranged paths, known as circuits, around specific areas. We still have those jurisdictional

regions today, and the regional judges are known as circuit judges.

15. So called because they were good at cajoling or soliciting the court to do things.

16. John Mortimer's Horace Rumpole – perhaps the greatest legal character ever written – called them Queer Customers, as they were far too silky smooth for his liking.

17. Judges used to be appointed directly by government, so this was a welcome assertion of greater independence. I am oddly fond of this body, for personal reasons. My wife and I worked together at the Press Complaints Commission, which was not ideal as I was her boss. She decided reluctantly to leave, and had to find another job. She was offered one by the JAC, which she didn't really want and did not take up because she found out she was pregnant on the day she got the offer. So to me (and I realise this is not a relatable link) I associate the independent appointment of judges in England and Wales with my beautiful wife Nadine and my daughter Nelly.

18. The Supreme Court is the highest court of appeal for civil cases in Scotland and Northern Ireland, but the final appeal on criminal matters is devolved.

19. This replaced the House of Lords as the highest court in the land, starting work in 2009. Before that, Law Lords used to sit in panels of five to seven and issue their view (with the decision going with the majority). Until 1876 even non-lawyer members of the Lords could get involved, ridiculously. The Supreme Court is broadly similar in structure, but sits outside the Palace of Westminster.

20. There is a famous newspaper case that illustrated this. The *Daily Mirror* published photographs of the irascible model Naomi Campbell leaving a rehabilitation clinic, following her public denials that she was a drug addict. She sued on the basis of invasion of privacy and won: the High Court found the images (but not the fact of her addiction) intrusive. Mirror Group Newspapers (MGN) appealed and won: the Court of Appeal ruled that the images were 'peripheral' and used at the editor's discretion. Campbell appealed to the House of Lords, which ruled three to two that the pictures added something of 'real significance'. A mess of contradiction.

21. If someone is sentenced to less than four years in prison, they will serve only half that time. A prisoner with longer than four years will only serve half the time if he receives permission to that effect from the Parole Board. In any event, he will serve no longer than two-thirds

of his sentence. For life sentences, judges will be expected to set a period after which the convict will be eligible for parole (this used to be the preserve of the Home Secretary until 2000). Judges can impose 'whole life orders', and are expected to do so in the case of multiple murderers engaged in sexual abuse, terrorists, child-killers and police killers. Other murderers could get a thirty-year minimum tariff.

22. In effect, this has created a 'super statute', which requires the courts to interpret all other laws in such a way that they are compatible with it. If a law is not HRA-compatible, then it must be sent back to Parliament for reconsideration.

23. Eleanor Roosevelt (1884–1962) was a diplomat and activist, indisputably one of the most important women of the twentieth century, and married to Franklin Delano Roosevelt (America's only four-term President). While Franklin was engaged in a long-running affair with his secretary, Eleanor probably pursued her own same-sex inclinations elsewhere, under the observation of J. Edgar Hoover's FBI.

24. One of the proposed solutions to the Grenfell Tower crisis was the requisition of expensive, empty second homes in west London. This was popular according to polling (59 per cent approved in one survey), but would be a clear breach of the owners' human rights.

25. Stories like this abound. As I happen to write this, I see that the *Daily Mail* is objecting to judges halting the extradition of Romanian criminals on the grounds that they will be imprisoned in a space just two metres squared. Such practice would breach Article 3 of the ECHR, which prohibits torture and unusual punishment. On the one hand, the British taxpayer is being put to the cost of denying extradition; on the other, it is responsible for preventing human beings from incarceration in inhuman conditions. It depends how much one values human life in its entirety, set against the demands of the national economy.

26. The former Assistant Commissioner at Scotland Yard during 7/7, Tarique Ghaffur, called in 2017 for internment as a means of dealing with the terror threat, for example.

27. The system of blood money persisted until early medieval times: the idea that each offence could be converted into a financial award. This, for example, is from one of the earliest laws in the name of Aethelbert, King of Kent: 'If a person . . . receives a blow from a raised hand, let him who struck the blow pay a shilling. If the bruise that arises from the blow should be black outside the clothing, let him pay 30

sceattas in addition, if it should be inside the clothing, let him pay 20 sceattas in addition, of each bruise.' Don't ask me what a sceatta is worth; I have no idea.

28. Jeremy Bentham (1748–1832) was the founder of utilitarianism, formulating the notion that 'it is the greatest happiness of the greatest number that is the measure of right and wrong'. He got the idea of the Panopticon from his brother Samuel, who was working in Russia. The idea was that it would be cheap to run, as it needed fewer wardens and the prisoners would be constantly gripped by 'the sentiment of a sort of omnipresence'. Bentham was keen on codification and rationalisation: he even developed a whipping machine to ensure a fair and uniform means of punishment. He was so keen for his body to be preserved after his death that he kept two glass eyes with him at all times, so embalmers would have something to use. Bentham's body is still kept in a case in UCL, although his head – having been stolen by pranksters in 1975 and ransomed for £10 – is now kept separately.

29. Wilde had to turn a crank, a lever with no machinery attached, and to pick oakum (separate the strands of thick rope). Other forms of physical punishment were the treadmill and the moving of cannon balls from one side of a room to another. The purpose was degrading, exhausting mistreatment.

30. Mountbatten established the categorisation of prisoners by their security risk from A (threat to the public or national security) to D (to be trusted with an open prison).

31. In the 1980s prison officers were encouraged to work massive amounts of overtime, as a means of boosting their earnings. Many earned more than the prison governors, their bosses. The practice was stopped in the 1990s.

32. In 2012, 11,000 prisoners in England and Wales were being held in fourteen private jails; in Scotland 1,400 were in two private jails.

33. This includes far-right mass killer Anders Breivik, who murdered seventy-seven people in 2011. A Norwegian court ruled that his isolation was in breach of his human rights. Breivik did a Nazi salute at the beginning of his human rights appeal, suggesting we should add a lack of irony to his other evident flaws. Breivik can be kept in prison for more than twenty-one years only if he remains a dangerous threat to society (which is likely in his case).

34. The Mesopotamian King Ur-Nammu (around 2000 BC) had a legal

code requiring death as punishment for murder, rape, robbery and adultery. The code under the tough-talking Athenian magistrate Draco, in the seventh century BC, made death the sole punishment for all crimes. Yes, that is where the term 'draconian' comes from.

35. Much of the information in this section comes from *The Abolition of the Death Penalty in the United Kingdom* by Sir Julian Knowles: a very clear pamphlet on the subject that I hope will become a longer book one day.

36. The original policemen were given blue uniforms to distinguish them from the military red (as one fear throughout the early years was of a militarised police). The colour has stuck.

37. Most famous for the picaresque *The History of Tom Jones, a Foundling* (1749), one of the first proper novels in the English language. Fielding himself says (in the book) he is 'the founder of a new province of writing'. Samuel Johnson called it a 'vicious' and 'corrupt' work, mainly because it was rather free in its description – and lack of condemnation – of extramarital sex.

38. Robert Peel (1788–1850) was twice Prime Minister, and twice Home Secretary. It is thanks to him that police officers became known as 'bobbies' or 'peelers', the former still a term used (at least in the Midlands, where I grew up) to this day.

39. He became the basis for Inspector Bucket in *Bleak House* (1853), one of the first detectives in British literature.

40. By an odd coincidence, the father of Stephen Lawrence had worked as a decorator for *Mail* editor Paul Dacre. Stephen had been in his house. This pricked the conscience of the editor, who made it a personal crusade to go after the killers irrespective of the legal status of the investigation. He recalled, the night of that front page, waking up 'drenched in sweat, convinced my career was over'. He was never sued.

41. The basis for this principle goes back to the post-Conquest period, and the Norman law of *autrefois convict* and *autrefois acquit*. A crime can be re-prosecuted now only if the Court of Appeal quashes the conviction due to 'new and compelling evidence' and the Director of Public Prosecutions approves.

42. In 2017 Harriet Harman (herself a lawyer) proposed that the process of trying rape cases should be made easier by automatically banning any reference to the victim's previous sexual history. As it happens, such references already require the specific approval of a judge and are

relatively rare. If Harman's proposal were to be accepted, a defendant in a rape case could deliberately lie about her own sexual past, and no rebuttal would be allowed. This is likely to mean an unfair trial, in breach of Article 6 of the HRA. This is a good example of a politician (in charge of our laws) apparently not understanding how the law works. Which is one of the reasons we have so many badly written laws.

43. According to newspaper reports, he was known as 'The Eliminator', having shot three criminals in the past. Long had received £5,000 compensation from police after senior officer Sue Akers had been heard jokingly saying, 'I've always wanted to meet the Met's very own serial killer.'

44. The IPCC was formed in 2004 to deal with complaints against the police, or to initiate investigations itself. It is partially staffed by former police officers, but the commissioners who run it have to be independent. Its reputation is not spotless, as is inevitable with any self-regulatory mechanism. The Home Affairs Select Committee in 2013 judged it to be 'woefully under-equipped and hamstrung in achieving its original objectives. It has neither the power nor resources that it needs to get to the truth when the integrity of the police is in doubt.' As of 8 January 2018, it has been renamed the Independent Office for Police Conduct. In Scotland, the police complaints system is run by the Police Investigations and Review Commissioner; in Northern Ireland by the Police Ombudsman for Northern Ireland.

45. The *Sun*, to its everlasting shame, swallowed this version of events without challenge. The notorious Kelvin MacKenzie splashed the claims under the headline 'The Truth'. His subsequent failure to apologise sufficiently for the error has haunted him and the paper ever since. Virtually no copies of the *Sun* have been sold in Liverpool in the decades that have followed. The taint of inaccuracy – and, worse, sticking up for the establishment at the expense of ordinary football fans – has forever lingered.

Chapter 7: Old and New Media

1. This included the *Daily Sport* and *Sunday Sport* newspapers. Despite their names, they had almost nothing to do with sport: they contained pornographic pictures, salacious court reports and silly stories. They

did not contribute to the funding of the PCC, but did occasionally commit very obvious ethical infractions that ran the danger of bringing the industry into disrepute. So we had, informally, to ensure their co-operation. One night, we went to Manchester (where they are based) and took their senior journalists out to dinner: they promptly ordered all the most expensive food and drink on the menu. By the end of the night, we were all firmly agreed about the need to maintain press self-regulation. A week later, I received a package in the office: a gift of twenty different pornographic DVDs, catering to all tastes and leanings, and a fourteen-inch rubber dildo. It was their way of saying thank you for the dinner, I like to think.

2. There was reportedly a conga around the *Guardian* newsroom when this was announced.

3. The *TLS*, for example: page 2 contents; 3–5 the lead; 6 the letters page; 7 the next main story; 20–21 a feature commentary; 22 a first-person column.

4. I enjoyed this splash, during my time at the paper, about an investigation into cocaine use over Christmas in cathedral toilets (don't ask): 'Ding Dong Merrily We're High'.

5. These have inevitably reduced in number; indeed many newspapers are printed by the same company. News UK, which owns the *Sun* and *The Times*, also prints the *Telegraph*, the *FT* and the *Metro*.

6. In July 2017 the trade magazine (now online only) *Press Gazette* ran a story in which it showed how the *Independent* had refused to pay for material (in effect an entire court report) it had lifted direct from *Wales Online*. 'There's no copyright in news,' it said, a quote that resounds like 'there's no honour among thieves.'

7. Twitter looms large in many people's lives, but it is nothing like as important as Facebook (300 million users vs more than 1 billion). It is also a bully pulpit, designed to reward famous people who can amass hundreds of thousands of followers and feel self-important as a result.

8. In 2016, of all the new digital advertising growth, a staggering 94 per cent (around £1 billion) went to Google and Facebook. More than half of the overall digital market goes to the same two companies.

9. Journalists are axiomatically gung-ho, and I was asked things like whether people could go undercover to run a half-marathon in North Korea, or be smuggled into Syria to meet ISIS fighters.

10. My biggest regret at the *Sun* was that I did not read in advance a

column by schlock pseudo-figure of hate Katie Hopkins, which described refugees metaphorically as 'cockroaches'. This column had not been sent to me (as it normally would), and I learned about it the following evening when – thanks to a Twitter storm – the complaints came flooding in. Hopkins should not have written those things; and they should have been edited out.

11. Julian Knowles, as it happens, who we met in the last chapter as the author of the pamphlet on the death penalty. He has now become a High Court judge.

12. The *Sun* used to have a safe on the premises with up to £50,000 in cash inside it; other tabloid newspapers were also floating in cash. In every paper, fraudulent expense claims were apparently the norm, with the stock phrase 'entertaining a confidential source' obscuring straightforward embezzlement. One journalist, I was once told, had 'built his conservatory out of expense claims'. By my time, quite correctly, expenses for unnamed sources could no longer be claimed.

13. The *Sun* itself became the fifth largest 'country' to donate money in the aftermath, its readers donating more than, for example, France.

14. On the four hundredth anniversary of Shakespeare's birthday, we published a spread containing descriptions of every one of his plays, some converted into *Sun* splash headlines. So: *Henry IV* became 'Fatman and Robbin'; *Romeo and Juliet*, 'Sleeping with the Enemy'; *Hamlet*, 'Massacre at the Palace', with a blurb offering 'free cigar for every reader'; and so on. I wrote summaries of each play; a subbing genius left blank the space below *Much Ado About Nothing*.

15. Charlotte Higgins has written a lovely, succinct history of the corporation called *This New Noise* (2015), which was tremendously useful to me in this chapter.

16. John Reith, the Presbyterian autocrat who shaped the organisation from its inception, once said: 'Some prophets are foretelling a colossal struggle between the powerful press interests and ourselves. I do not believe there need be any such thing.' The prophets were 100 per cent correct, of course.

17. Marconi (1874–1937) was also a proud fascist and his tomb carries a quote from Mussolini: 'with his discovery he set his mark upon an era of human history'.

18. Old Broadcasting House even has a dedication written in Latin from 1931, calling it '*templum hoc atrium et musarum*', 'this temple of arts and muses', filled with people inclining their ears '*quaecunque pulchra sunt*

et sincera quaecunque bonae famae', 'to whatever is beautiful and decent and worthy of good report'.

19. Reith's views on the *Hole in the Wall* game show (minor celebrities in latex leaping through, erm, holes in a wall) would be fascinating, for example.

20. Pirate stations still exist, but have moved from the sea to the city. There are about 150 urban pirate stations in the UK, listened to by an often ethnic audience keen to hear authentic voices from their own community. About a quarter of Londoners listen to pirate radio, apparently.

21. Beginning, I am pleased to say, with Radio Leicester. A proud achievement for the Midlands, I think you will agree.

22. Marr, he of the notably nobbly physiognomy, wrote a book called *My Trade* in 2004 about British journalism, which remains a bracing read. But it is also bracing for its now quaint faith in journalism, its understandable ignorance over the storm that was to come.

23. Regulation of the BBC has long been a total muddle (and I say that having presided over the muddle that was the PCC). From 1927 to 2007, the BBC was overseen by a Board of Governors, whose job it was to regulate (and receive complaints), and to represent both the interests of the public and the corporation itself. It was a collection of the great and the good, hopelessly incapable of handling a crisis. In the wake of Hutton, the governors were replaced by the BBC Trust, which was promptly given the same structural flaw: the task of being both regulator and cheerleader. In 2017, in the aftermath of the Savile scandals, the system of regulation was handed to the national broadcast regulator OFCOM.

24. And for help in managing the scandal: your very own author was roped in to help one of the executives deal with the media fallout.

25. Interestingly, three decent books on the subject of post-truth were all published within weeks of each other in 2017, by the journalists Evan Davis, Matthew d'Ancona, and James Ball. All are worth reading, although I found Ball's most useful in writing this part of the chapter.

26. Weirdly, much of the early pro-Trump fake news material originated in one town in Macedonia: Veles (population 45,000). This is not a hotbed of radical republicanism. It is simply a town with young people who have realised that they can confect stories with a political angle, and earn up to £5,000 a month from advertising.

27. I am glad you asked about D-Notices, because they are so often the

subject of loony piffle from conspiracy theorists. At the PCC I actually worked with the committee responsible for what are now called Defence and Security Media Advisory Notices. In the event that newspapers wish to publish information that might touch on national security or military operations, they are sometimes in touch with a representative of this committee. He has the power to recommend non-publication of specific details. Here is the crucial bit: there is no power of enforcement at all connected to this. A newspaper can ignore a DSMA-Notice, and there can be no official sanction. Of course, the system largely works because no newspaper wishes genuinely to compromise national security, and will often listen in good faith. No conspiracy, though.

28. The figure over the course of a month is 2 billion. Which means that 66 per cent are using it every day. The *New York Times* in 2014 calculated that people were spending, collectively, 39,757 hours on the site every day. Facebook is now valued at more than half a trillion dollars.

29. Local papers were, of course, the place in which most journalists learned their trade. They have been hollowed out to an extreme extent over the last two decades. They were once the voice of communities, respected as such, given credibility because they were written by people who lived in their communities (unlike the distant figures of national journalists). This is J. B. Priestley on the distinction: 'I have never been able to understand how London editors contrive to know what their readers want, because they never meet any of their readers, never exchange a word with them. They are no more in touch with the actual public than are Grand Lamas.'

30. Founded by three programmers, Chad, Steve and Jawed, it uploaded its first video on 23 April 2005. It was entitled 'Me at the zoo' and showed eighteen seconds of Jawed standing in front of an elephant. The biggest YouTube star is someone known as PewDiePie (real name: Feliz Kjellberg): he has 55 million subscribers to his channel showing him talking about computer games, who have watched his videos more than 15 billion times. He made $15 million in 2016, which is not that much given the audience.

31. The *Guardian* is ideologically resistant to pay-walls, although could have profited from one. It now seeks funding by begging letters on its website, and has done quite well: 230,000 people make voluntary payments. It lost £45 million in 2016, something of a success in comparison to the £60 million in 2015. Its aim is to break even.

Chapter 8: Identity

1. A character in Alan Bennett's *The Old Country* (1977) said that the English 'are conceived in irony. We float in it from the womb. It's the amniotic fluid, joking but not joking. Caring but not caring. Serious but not serious.'

2. This is Iago in *Othello*: 'I learned drinking in England, where indeed they are most potent in potting. Your Dane, your German, and your swag-bellied Hollander are nothing to your English.'

   In fact, Britain is thirteenth of 196 countries in terms of scale of binge-drinking (Belarus holds the crown). About 1 million hospital admissions happen as a result of drinking every year. Things are improving slightly: we drink less than we did in 2004, largely thanks to a decrease in young people boozing.

3. This is mainly due to the expansion of the EU in 2004. Britain, under Tony Blair, elected not to place any restrictions (which would have been permissible under EU rules) on inward migration. As a result, large numbers of Eastern Europeans have come to Britain: the Polish population, to take the most dramatic example, increasing from 58,000 to 580,000 in ten years.

4. In 1951 it had been Ireland, Poland and India. Irish migration is seldom discussed as a social issue, but has played a large role in shaping post-war Britain. By 1961, nearly a sixth of all Irish people of working age were living in the UK.

5. Mary Beard, my colleague at the *TLS*, and Classics professor at Cambridge, got into an online scrap with an American professor called Nassim Nicholas Taleb on this unlikely subject. She maintained that there was likely to be ethnic diversity in Roman Britain; he felt that the limited genetic data did not support it. It turned ugly – in the way of the world now – with Taleb calling Mary a 'bullshitter' and questioning her credentials. Would he have done the same with a man? We will never know.

6. Granville Sharp (1735–1813) was a renaissance man (a scholar, musician, classicist, self-taught lawyer). He spent his life defending escaped slaves through the courts, was known as 'the protector of the negro', and was sadly a misguided supporter of a scheme to repatriate many to Sierra Leone (which in essence led to the founding of that modern nation).

7. Thomas Clarkson (1760–1846) won a Latin essay competition at Cambridge University on the horrors of slavery and then devoted his life towards abolishing it. He toured the country advocating on the issue, surviving an assassination attempt by sailors in Liverpool paid to eliminate him. It is Clarkson seen speaking in the famous Haydon painting of the 1840 Anti-Slavery Convention in London, such was his centrality to the movement.

8. These examples, and much else in the chapter, come from the splendid *Black and British* (2016) by David Olusoga, which is a superb piece of general history writing. Well worth a read.

9. Frederick Douglass (1818–95) escaped from slavery and became a prominent black voice in the abolitionist movement and for equality more generally. His first autobiography, *Narrative of the Life of Frederick Douglass, an American Slave*, is a seminal text on the subject, and became an international bestseller. Douglass toured Britain in 1847, and spoke warmly about his treatment (perhaps keen to emphasise the contrasting situation in the US): 'I passed through them all; your colosseums, museums, galleries of painting, even your House of Commons . . . In none of these places did I receive one word of opposition against my entrance . . . the right hand of fellowship, of manly fellowship, was extended to a negro such as I am.'

10. Trollope called black people 'an inherently servile race'; Charles Darwin signed off his letters to his wife 'your old nigger CD'.

11. In 1865 there was something called the Morant Bay Rebellion: a dispute between Jamaicans who wished (justifiably) to farm the empty plantation land and the British authorities who thought they were getting uppity. It was suppressed by the governor Edward John Eyre using military force (in what would today be considered a war crime), leading to the killing and maiming of hundreds of people. The outcry among some in Britain was met by a committee of men in support of the governor. Look at the roll-call of that committee: Carlyle (naturally), Dickens, Tennyson, Charles Kingsley (author of *The Water Babies*, 1863) and John Ruskin. That is a large chunk of our canonical Victorians there.

12. In February 1945 Eastern Europe was carved up by the Allies at a conference in Yalta. Churchill allowed Stalin to claim eastern Poland as part of the USSR, in one fell swoop creating millions of refugees who could never return home. In Germany alone at the end of the war were 7 million displaced people.

13. Wills's *An Immigrant History of Post-War Britain* (2017) is an exceptional

distillation of stories about how Britain responded to immigration. It is both a pleasure to read, and also unhappy reading: 'It was a test of the values and organisation of British society, and society – in large part – failed the test.' Many of the individual examples of race relations in this chapter are taken from the book.

14. The 'Baltic cygnet' scheme was one in which young women were invited to work as nurses or cleaners in hospitals. The *Evening Standard* called them 'gentle swans', and their contribution to the post-war effort was largely welcomed. As women who often married British men, they were also quickly integrated too.

15. This aspect is only recently being recognised. A 2012 Department of Health Suicide Prevention Strategy for England was a fifty-seven-page document that made no reference to gender at all. It, creditably, referenced vulnerable groups like the young, LGBT people, refugees and so on. But it did not consider men as a distinct entity.

16. No great friend in the fight for societal equality in some ways, being an interminable snob. She also said of feminism that we must 'destroy an old word, a vicious and corrupt word that has done much harm in its day'.

17. It is worth noting that the term 'suffragette' was invented in 1906 as a term of derision by a columnist in the *Daily Mail*. Some of the quotes in this chapter are collected in *Feminism: A Very Short Introduction* (2005) by Margaret Walters.

18. A distinction must be drawn between suffragettes and suffragists, the latter committed to peaceful protest only. One of the least known major events in support of votes for women was the Great Suffrage Pilgrimage of 1913: thousands of women trekking across the country to campaign for change, a peaceful forerunner of all the women's marches ever since.

19. Her quote: 'I have tried to destroy the picture of the most beautiful woman in mythological history as a protest against the Government for destroying Mrs Pankhurst, who is the most beautiful character in modern history.'

20. Donald Trump, of course, was recorded saying this about women: 'When you're a star, they let you do it. You can do anything . . . Grab them by the pussy.' In response, a Canadian author, Kelly Oxford, asked women on Twitter to 'tweet me your first assaults'. She received two stories per second for fourteen straight hours, and 9.7 million comments overall.

21. Hormone blockers are used at the onset of puberty to delay the process, allowing time for full consideration of the options.

22. Not to be confused with *Let Toys Be Toys*, of which it is an offshoot. Over several years, this group has revealed how children's vision of themselves is shaped in a gendered way: boys in adverts playing with vehicles, action figures and guns in an aggressive fashion; girls, more passively, indulging in grooming and nurturing activities. The shaping is so embedded in the culture that it is hard even to recognise it as present: of course, boys like guns and girls like make-up. But, why is that exactly?

23. Similar scandals were revealed in Newcastle and elsewhere, suggesting a systemic problem.

24. The initial report into the scandal noted that 'the existence of such a [sexist] culture . . . is likely to have impeded the Council from providing an effective corporate response to such a highly sensitive social problem as child sexual exploitation.'

25. Fear of the collective mob and their power to commit crimes is there in Shakespeare. Look especially at the Roman plays, in which Elizabethan London was unconvincingly disguised: *Coriolanus* battling 'the mutable, rank-scented many'; or *Julius Caesar*, when 'the rabblement hooted and clapped their chapped hands and threw up their sweaty nightcaps and uttered such a deal of stinking breath.' Morality is recast as hygiene.

26. Abortions have been legal in Britain since 1967 for pregnancies below twenty-eight weeks. This was reduced to twenty-four weeks in 1990. Abortion rates are declining too. They are also happening to older women. Teenage pregnancies are becoming much rarer (they have halved since 1998), and so abortions for teenagers have reduced dramatically too.

Index